Tarascon Primary

Tarascon Primary Care Pocketbook, Second Edition

FOR TARASCON BOOKS/SOFTWARE, VISIT **WWW.TARASCON.COM**
See faxable order form on page 240

- Tarascon Primary Care Pocketbook
- Tarascon Pocket Pharmacopoeia® Classic Edition
- Tarascon Pocket Pharmacopoeia® Deluxe Edition
- Tarascon Pocket Pharmacopoeia® PDA software
- Tarascon Pocket Orthopaedica®
- Tarascon Adult Emergency Pocketbook
- Tarascon Pediatric Emergency Pocketbook
- Tarascon Internal Medicine & Critical Care Pocketbook
- How to be a Truly Excellent Junior Medical Student

"It's not how much you know, it's how fast you can find the answer."®

**Important Caution
Please Read This!** The information in the *Tarascon Primary Care Pocketbook* is compiled from sources believed to be reliable, and exhaustive efforts have been put forth to make this book as accurate as possible. *However the accuracy and completeness of this work cannot be guaranteed.* Despite our best efforts this book may contain typographical errors and omissions. The *Tarascon Primary Care Pocketbook* is intended as a quick and convenient reminder of information you have already learned elsewhere. The contents are to be used as a guide only, and health care professionals should use sound clinical judgment and individualize patient care. This book is not meant to be a replacement for training, experience, continuing medical education, or studying the latest literature and drug information. This book is sold without warranties of any kind, express or implied, and the publisher and editors disclaim any liability, loss, or damage caused by the contents. *If you do not wish to be bound by the foregoing cautions and conditions, you may return your undamaged and unexpired book to our office for a full refund.*

Tarascon Primary Care Pocketbook
Second Edition

ISBN 1-882742-44-3. Copyright ©2004, 2006 Joseph S. Esherick, MD. Published by Tarascon Publishing®, PO Box 517, Lompoc, California 93438. Printed in the USA. All rights reserved. No portion of this publication may be reproduced or stored in any form or by any means (including electronic, photocopying) without our prior written permission. Tarascon Publishing is a division of Tarascon Inc. *Tarascon Publishing* and *It's not how much you know, it's how fast you can find the answer* are registered trademarks of Tarascon Inc.   CY1

Tarascon Primary Care Pocketbook
Second Edition

Joseph S. Esherick, M.D., FAAFP
Departments of Family Medicine and Internal Medicine
Ventura County Medical Center, Ventura, California
Clinical Assistant Professor of Family Medicine, UCLA School of Medicine

Editorial Board*

Carl Constantine, M.D.
Department of Internal Medicine, Ventura County Medical Center, Ventura, California

Matt Farson, M.D.
Department of Family Medicine, Ventura County Medical Center, Ventura, California

Fred Kelley, M.D.
Associate Director of Obstetrics and Gynecology
Ventura County Medical Center, Ventura, California

Robert L. Deamer, PharmD, BCPS
Drug Education Coordinator, Kaiser Permanente, Ventura County, California

Todd Flosi, M.D.
Department of Pediatrics, Ventura County Medical Center, Ventura, California

*Affiliations are given for informational purposes only, and no affiliation sponsorship is claimed

Cover Artwork: Vaccinating the Baby, Ed Hamman, 1890. Courtesy of the National Library of Medicine, Images from the History of Medicine.

Note from the author: The *Tarascon Primary Care Pocketbook* is intended to be a quick reference guide for clinicians and students practicing primary care medicine. I have attempted to compile the core information in a concise fashion about most primary care topics. I have adapted the clinical practice guidelines from nationally recognized medical associations and have footnoted the primary references when possible. I would like to thank all of my mentors and colleagues who have passed on to me countless clinical pearls most of which I have incorporated into this book. I would also like to thank Janet Parker who has worked so hard to acquire virtually all of my reference articles. Although painstaking efforts have been made to find all errors and omissions, some errors may remain; if you find an error or wish to make a suggestion, please email us at editor@tarascon.com. This book is dedicated to my wife Gina and my daughter Sophia who constantly encouraged me and supported me through this entire project.

↑ : increased/elevated	GU: genitourinary
↑↑ : very high	hr: hour
↓ : decreased/depressed	hgb: hemoglobin
+ : positive or present	HIV: human immunodeficiency virus
- : negative or absent	HLA-B27: human leukocyte antigen-B27
+/- : and/or	HTN: hypertension
♂ : male	Hz: hertz
♀ : female	IU: international units
> : greater than	IUD: intrauterine device
≥ : greater than or equal to	IV: intravenous
< : less than	kcal: kilocalorie
≤ : less than or equal to	kg: kilogram
µL: microliter	L: liter
ACEI: angiotensin converting enzyme inhibitor	Lb: pound
ACTH: adrenocorticotropin hormone	lymph: lymphocytes
AIDS: acquired immunodeficiency syndrome	m: meter
ANA: antinuclear antibody	mcg: microgram
ARB: angiotensin receptor blocker	MEq: milliequivalents
BP: blood pressure	mg: milligram
CA: cancer	MI: myocardial infarction
CA 15-3, CA 19-9, CA 27.29 and CA-125: cancer tumor markers of that number	min.: minute
	mL: milliliter
CD_4: helper T cells with CD_4 receptors	mm: millimeter
CEA: carcinoembryonic antigen	mmol: millimole
CHF: congestive heart failure	mmHg: millimeters of mercury (torr)
cm: centimeter	mo: month
CNS: central nervous system	monos.: monocytes
COPD: chronic obstructive pulmonary disease	mOsm: milliosmoles
	MRI: magnetic resonance imaging
COX-2: cyclooxygenase-2	MRA: magnetic resonance angiogram
CrCl: creatinine clearance (mL/minute)	ng: nanogram
CT: computed tomography scan	NSAID: nonsteroidal anti-inflammatory drug
CXR: chest x-ray	pg: picogram
d: day	PMN: polymorphonuclear neutrophil
DC: direct current	PPD: purified protein derivative
dL: deciliter	RF: rheumatoid factor
DM: diabetes mellitus	RPR: rapid plasma reagin test
ECG: electrocardiogram	SQ: subcutaneous
fT_4: free levothyroxine (T_4) level	SSRI: selective serotonin reuptake inhibitor
FTA: fluorescent treponemal antibody	t or tsp: teaspoon
G6PD: glucose-6-phosphate dehydrogenase	TIA: transient ischemic attack
	URI: upper respiratory tract infection
GI: gastrointestinal	U: units
gm: gram	VDRL: venereal disease research laboratory
	WBC: white blood count
	yr: year

Adult Valvular Heart Diseases

Category	Mitral Stenosis	Mitral Regurgitation	Aortic Stenosis	Aortic Regurgitation	IHSS	Innocent Murmur
Etiology	• Rheumatic • Congenital	• Rheumatic disease • Endocarditis • Mitral valve prolapse • Papillary muscle dysfunction	• Rheumatic disease • Bicuspid aortic valve • Calcific stenosis	• Rheumatic • Bicuspid aortic valve • Endocarditis • Aortic dissection • Marfans/syphilis aortitis	• Congenital	• Normal valves
♂ or ♀	♀ > ♂	♂ > ♀	♂ > ♀	♂ > ♀	♂ > ♀	♂ = ♀
Age at diagnosis	14-28 years	30 – 50 years	40 – 50 years	40 – 50 years	15 – 50 years	1 – 15 years
Clinical Features	• CHF symptoms • Hemoptysis • Palpitations (atrial fibrillation)	• CHF symptoms • Palpitations (Atrial fibrillation) • Long latency	• Angina: 5 years survival • CHF: 2 years survival • Syncope: 3 years survival • Sudden death	• CHF symptoms • Angina • Long latency	• Angina • CHF symptoms • Syncope • Sudden death • Long latency	• None

Adapted from the 1998 American College of Cardiology guidelines for the the Management of Valvular Heart Disease (JACC, 1998; 32: 1486-1588) and NEJM, 1539; 351: 1539 and reproduced with permission from Daniel S. Clark, M.D., Director of Cardiology; Ventura County Medical Center, S₁ = first heart sound, S₂ = second heart sound, S₃ = third heart sound, S₄ = fourth heart sound, NYHA = New York Heart Association, ACEI = angiotensin converting enzyme inhibitor, IHSS = Idiopathic Hypertrophic Subaortic Stenosis

Adult Valvular Heart Diseases

Category	Mitral Stenosis	Mitral Regurgitation	Aortic Stenosis (AS)	Aortic Regurgitation	IHSS	Innocent Murmur
Exam Findings	• ↑ S₁ • Apical diastolic rumble • Presystolic accentuation • Opening snap (OS) of mitral valve	• ↓ S₁ • + S₃ gallop • Apical systolic blowing murmur→ axilla • No increase after premature ventricular contraction (PVC)	• ↓S₂ • Harsh systolic murmur 2nd right intercostal space (ICS)→ carotids • ↑ after PVC • Paradoxical split S₂ • Gallavardin sign	• + S₃ gallop • Diastolic murmur • Quincke's pulse • DeMusset sign • Duroziez sign • Corrigan (water hammer pulse) • Traube sign • Bisferiens carotid pulse	• Harsh systolic murmur 3rd left ICS • Supine ↓ and standing ↑ intensity • + S₄ gallop • Bisferiens carotid pulse	• Soft systolic ejection murmur 2nd left intercostal space
Indicators of Severity	• Short S₂- OS interval • Long murmur	• None	• Long murmur • + S₄ gallop • Sustained PMI	• Wide pulse pressure • Austin-Flint murmur • + S₃ gallop	• Bisferiens pulse	• None
Medical Therapy	• Furosemide • Digoxin • Warfarin	• Furosemide, digoxin & warfarin • ACEI (acute MR)	• Statins may have marginal effect on AS progression* • AVR if:	• ACEI or long-acting nifedipine • Add furosemide and digoxin for CHF	• β-blocker • Verapamil • Disopyramide	• None
Surgical Therapy When	• CHF NYHA class 3 on rx • MVA <1.5 cm² + symptoms	• CHF NYHA 3 on meds • ESD >55 mm • LVEF <60%	▲ mild symptoms ▲ AVA <1.0 cm² ▲ AV gradient >60 mmHg	• NYHA 3 on meds • LVEF <55% • ESD >55 mm	• When symptoms start	• None

PMI = point of maximal impulse, ESD = end-systolic diameter, AVR = aortic valve replacement, AVA = aortic valve area, LVEF = left ventricular ejection fraction, MVA = mitral valve area, rx = therapy, ACEI = angiotensin converting enzyme inhibitor. * - see Circulation, 2004; 110: 1291-5 and NEJM, 2005; 352: 2389-97.

Etiologies of Atrial Fibrillation (Afib mnemonic is CPR HEARTS)
- **C :** coronary artery disease, acute CHF or acute myocardial infarction
- **P :** pericarditis (or myocarditis)
- **R :** rheumatic heart disease (or valvular cardiomyopathy)
- **H :** hypertrophic or hypertensive cardiomyopathy or severe hypoxia
- **E :** embolus (pulmonary)
- **A :** alcohol
- **R :** ruled out other causes (lone Afib)
- **T :** theophylline toxicity, thyrotoxicosis or trauma (blunt chest)
- **S :** surgery (e.g., post-coronary artery bypass grafting), sick sinus syndrome or sympathomimetic toxicity

Classification of Atrial Fibrillation
- Paroxysmal
- Persistent (converts with electrical/chemical cardioversion)
- Permanent (resistant to electrical/chemical cardioversion)

CHADS₂* Score to Determine A Patient's Risk for Stroke

CHADS$_2$ Score	Adjusted Stroke Rate#	CHADS$_2$ Stroke Risk
0	1.9	Low level
1	2.8	Low level
2	4.0	Moderate level
3	5.9	Moderate level
4	8.5	High level
5	12.5	High level
6	18.2	High level

* CHADS$_2$ Score = 1 point each for CHF exacerbation in last 100 d, HTN, age > 75 and DM; 2 points for history of stroke/TIA.

= number of strokes per 100 patient-years from the National Registry of Atrial Fibrillation

Adapted from Annals Intern. Med. 2003; 139: 1009-17.

Antithrombotic Therapy to Minimize Cardioembolic Stroke Risk
- Therapy indicated for persistent, permanent or recurrent paroxysmal Afib
- Chronic anticoagulation with warfarin titrated to international normalized ratio = 2.5 (INR range 2-3) indicated for moderate-high CHADS$_2$ score or valvular afib
- Aspirin 325 mg PO daily if low CHADS$_2$ score & normal left ventricular function
- Warfarin contraindications: noncompliance, active substance abuse, unstable psychiatric conditions, hemorrhagic diathesis, blood dyscrasias, severe thrombocytopenia, recent neurosurgery, ophthalmologic or trauma surgery, active bleeding, pericarditis, endocarditis or history of intracranial hemorrhage

Atrial Fibrillation Rate versus Rhythm Control
- Based on AFFIRM, RACE and STAF trials, rate control with antithrombotic therapy is preferred in most patients
- Rhythm control is an option for intolerable symptoms or poor exercise capacity
- Unlikely to stay in sinus rhythm if afib > 6 months or left atrium > 5 cm
- DC Cardioversion if patient unstable: hypotension, angina or heart failure

Agents for Atrial Fibrillation Rate Control
- Diltiazem 120 – 360 mg PO daily in divided doses
- Metoprolol 50 – 200 mg PO daily in divided doses
- Verapamil 240 – 480 mg PO daily in divided doses
  - ➢ Use calcium channel blockers and ß-blockers very cautiously if left ventricular ejection fraction < 0.4 or decompensated CHF
- Digoxin load with 0.25 mg PO q6h until ventricular rate is controlled (4 doses usually sufficient) then 0.125–0.25 mg PO daily as maintenance.
  - ➢ Decrease dose in renal failure
  - ➢ Controls only resting ventricular rate
- Amiodarone if patients have hypotension, CHF, pre-excitation syndrome or rapid ventricular rate refractory to standard medications listed above.
  - ➢ **Recommend consultation with a cardiologist**
  - ➢ Multiple drug interactions
  - ➢ Watch for heart block, pulmonary toxicity and hypo- or hyperthyroidism

Need for Synchronized Electrical or Chemical Cardioversion?
- Timing of cardioversion
  - ➢ If the duration of atrial fibrillation is **definitely** less than 48 hours **or**
  - ➢ Negative transesophageal echocardiogram and heparin x 48 hours **or**
  - ➢ After 3 weeks of adequate anticoagulation
- Biphasic shock using anterior and posterior placement of pads has the highest rate of successful electrical cardioversion (nearly 100%)
- Continue warfarin for at least 4 weeks after successful cardioversion
- If chronic antiarrhythmics are used, the preferred agents are amiodarone, propafenone, sotalol and disopyramide.

Work-up of Atrial Fibrillation
- EKG
- Chest radiograph
- 2D-Echocardiogram
- Labs: complete blood count, basic metabolic panel, thyroid stimulating hormone +/- blood alcohol level and urine drug screen
- Noninvasive testing to rule out cardiac ischemia

Special Circumstances
- Ventricular rate > 220 or increased rate after atrioventricular nodal blocking agent given suggests an accessory pathway.
  - ➢ Transport to hospital for DC cardioversion, procainamide or amiodarone
  - ➢ Consider catheter ablation of accessory pathway
- Hyperthyroidism
  - ➢ β-blocker and anti-thyroid medications for rate control
  - ➢ Consider acute anticoagulation given very high risk of embolic events.
- Catheter ablation of atrial focus for refractory rate control on medications

References: J. Am. Coll. Cardiol., 2001; 38: 1266. JAMA, 2003; 290 (2): 2685-92, Ann. Intern. Med., 2003; 139: 1009-33, NEJM, 2001; 344: 1411-20 and NEJM, 2002; 347: 1825-40

Etiologies
- Ischemic Heart Disease (40% of all cases)
- Valvular Heart Disease (12% of all cases)
- Hypertensive Heart Disease (11% of all cases)
- Nonischemic dilated cardiomyopathy (32% of all cases)
- Pericardial disease
- Chronic pulmonary disease progressing to Cor pulmonale
- Myocarditis
- Hypertrophic cardiomyopathy
- Peripartum cardiomyopathy
- Toxin/medication-induced [e.g., alcohol, cocaine, methamphetamines or anthracyclines (especially in combination with trastuzumab use)]
- Infiltrative diseases (e.g., hemochromatosis, sarcoidosis or amyloidosis)
- High-output heart failure (e.g., thyrotoxicosis or beriberi)

Clinical Presentation of Heart Failure (CHF)

Left Heart Failure Symptoms	Left Heart Failure Signs	Right Heart Failure Symptoms	Right Heart Failure Signs
Exertional dyspnea	Pulmonary rales	Nocturia	Hepatomegaly
Orthopnea	S_3 gallop	Anorexia	Leg edema
PND	Displaced apical impulse	Right upper quadrant pain	Jugular venous distension
Weakness			Ascites
Nocturnal cough			Hepatojugular reflux
Exertional fatigue			
Exertional dizziness			

PND = paroxysmal nocturnal dyspnea and S_3 = 3rd heart sound
- Absence of exertional dyspnea makes heart failure very unlikely
- Displaced apical impulse, jugular venous distension and S_3 gallop are the most accurate signs of CHF

AHA/ACC Stages of Heart Failure (JACC, 2001; 38 (7): 2101-13)

Stage A	No structural heart disease. Has risk factors for CHF
Stage B	Has structural heart disease. No symptoms/signs of CHF
Stage C	Structural heart disease with mild-moderate CHF symptoms/signs
Stage D	Advanced heart disease with severe CHF symptoms/signs

New York Heart Association (NYHA) Classification of Heart Failure

Class 1	Asymptomatic except with very strenuous activity
Class 2	Symptoms with moderate exertion
Class 3	Symptoms with activities of daily living
Class 4	Symptoms at rest

General Measures for Heart Failure Management
- Lifestyle modification: ≤ 2 drinks alcohol daily, smoking cessation, aerobic exercise 2-3x/week and weight reduction in obese patients
- Diet: 2 gram sodium, low cholesterol diet
- **Avoid:** NSAIDS & most anti-arrhythmics (especially disopyramide & quinidine)
- Vaccinations: pneumococcal and influenza vaccines

Evaluation of Patients with Congestive Heart Failure
- **Blood tests**: complete blood count, electrolytes and creatinine, urinalysis, B-type natriuretic peptide (BNP) and thyroid stimulating hormone
- **BNP** > 500 pg/mL: 90% positive predictive value for CHF; < 100 pg/mL: 90% negative predictive value; and 100-500 pg/mL is equivocal for CHF. Other causes of BNP elevation include chronic renal failure (creatinine clearance

< 60 mL/minute), Cor pulmonale, pulmonary hypertension, pulmonary embolus, shock and acute respiratory distress syndrome.

- **Chest X-ray**: examine for cardiomegaly, cephalization of pulmonary vessels, Kerley B-lines and pleural effusions
- **Electrocardiogram**: evidence of ischemic heart disease, left ventricular hypertrophy, arrhythmias or low voltage
- **2-D Echocardiogram**: systolic dysfunction (ejection fraction< 0.4), diastolic compliance, segmental wall motion abnormalities and valvular abnormalities
- **Patients with angina**: need a coronary angiogram or noninvasive testing

Therapy for Heart Failure due to Left Ventricular Systolic Dysfunction

Preload reduction
- Furosemide PO/IV +/- PO metolazone or PO chlorthalidone (30 minutes prior)
  ➢ Aggressive diuresis until patient euvolemic then maintenance oral dose
- Nitrates (transdermal, oral or IV) can be added for CHF refractory to diuretics.
- Consider morphine sulfate 2-4 mg boluses IV in ER if blood pressure allows.
- If CHF is refractory to above therapy, can consider either noninvasive pressure support ventilation or nesiritide 2 mcg/kg IV bolus then 0.01 mcg/kg/minute IV.

Maximize afterload reduction
- ARBs are equivalent to ACEI for afterload reduction (but are more expensive).
- Angiotensin converting-enzyme inhibitor (ACEI) therapy with goal oral dosages: captopril 50 mg tid, enalapril 10 mg bid, ramipril 10 mg daily, lisinopril 20 mg daily, quinapril 20 mg bid, benazepril 20 mg bid or fosinopril 20 mg daily
- Angiotensin II Receptor Blocker (ARB) indicated **if ACEI-induced cough** Titrate to goal dosages: losartan 50 mg PO bid or valsartan 160 mg PO daily
  ➢ ARB added to ACEI + β-blocker ↓ cardiovascular death & CHF admissions.
- Hydralazine + nitrates: hydralazine 75-100 mg PO tid + isordil 40 mg PO tid

Aldosterone Receptor Antagonists
- Spironolactone 25 mg PO daily for NYHA Class 3-4 CHF
- Eplerenone 25-50 mg PO daily for NYHA Class 2-3 CHF when added to ACEI
- Follow closely for hyperkalemia that can occur with either agent.

Beta-blocker therapy
- Start low doses of carvedilol, metoprolol or bisoprolol when patient is euvolemic.
- Goal dose when resting heart rate 55-65: carvedilol 25-50 mg PO bid, metoprolol 75-100 mg PO bid and bisoprolol 5-10 mg PO daily

Digoxin therapy
- Titrate to improve symptoms but keep digoxin level < 1.1 ng/mL

Wean off loop diuretics (if possible)
- Long-term loop diuretic therapy decreases survival

Biventricular pacing/Cardiac resynchronization (see page 19 for details)
- Consider for medically refractory New York Heart Association Class III/IV CHF

Therapy for Heart Failure due to Diastolic Dysfunction
- Judicious diuretic therapy until patient euvolemic. Avoid chronic loop diuretics.
- If present, treat cardiac ischemia medically or via revascularization.
- Initiate a lusitropic agent (e.g., beta-1-selective blocker, verapamil or diltiazem)
- ACEI or ARB therapy is beneficial as an adjunct to a lusitropic agent.

References: JACC, 2001; 38 (7): 2101-13. NEJM, 2002; 347: 161. JAMA, 2003; 289 (20): 2685-94. NEJM, 2004; 351 (11): 1097-1105. Congestive Heart Failure, 2004; 10 (5): 1-27 and NEJM, 2001; 345: 1667-75

Classification of Hypertension (HTN) in Adults (>18 years old)

Normal	< 120/80 mmHg
Prehypertension	120-139/80-89 mmHg
Stage 1 hypertension	140-159/90-99 mmHg
Stage 2 hypertension	≥ 160/100 mmHg
Stage 3 hypertension	≥ 180/110 mmHg

Risk Stratification for Hypertensive Patients

Risk Factors	End-organ Damage
Cigarette smoking	Heart disease
Obesity (body mass index ≥ 30 kg/m²)	• Left ventricular hypertrophy
Family history of cardiovascular disease ♀ < 65 years or ♂ < 55 years	• Coronary artery disease • Congestive heart failure
Dyslipidemia	Stroke or transient ischemic attack
Diabetes mellitus	Nephropathy (microalbuminuria or
Very sedentary lifestyle	creatinine clearance < 60 mL/minute)
Age > 55 yrs (♂) or > 65 yrs (♀)	Peripheral vascular disease
Men or postmenopausal women	Retinopathy

Lifestyle Modifications
- Weight reduction (aiming for BMI < 25 kg/m²): decreases SBP 5-20 mmHg
- < 2 drinks of alcohol/day (♂) and ≤ 1 drink/day (♀): decreases SBP 2-4 mmHg
- Aerobic exercise (≥ 30 minutes/day ≥ 4 days/week): decreases SBP 4-9 mmHg
- < 2.4 grams sodium/day: decreases SBP 2-8 mmHg
- Dietary Approaches to Stop Hypertension or "DASH" diet: ↓ SBP 8-14 mmHg
- Adequate dietary potassium, magnesium and calcium intake
- Smoking cessation
- Low saturated fat, high fiber and low cholesterol diet

Drug therapy
- Indicated for hypertension refractory to lifestyle modifications x 2-3 months
  - ➢ For diabetes or chronic renal disease, aim for BP ≤ 130/80
  - ➢ For nephrotic syndrome aim for BP ≤ 120/70
- Initial therapy in patients with no compelling indications for specific drug classes
  - ➢ Thiazide diuretics (drug of choice for most patients if creatinine < 2 mg/dL)
  - ➢ Alternative options are: ß-blockers, angiotensin converting enzyme inhibitors, calcium channel blockers or angiotensin receptor blockers
- Add second agent for inadequate response at goal dose
  - ➢ Stage 2 hypertension usually requires at least 2 drugs
  - ➢ Consider thiazide diuretic if not already taking
  - ➢ Switch agents for unacceptable side effects to first agent
- Add third agent from a different class (see below) for inadequate response

Lab Evaluation
- Complete blood count, electrolytes, renal panel, calcium, lipid panel, urinalysis and electrocardiogram

SBP = systolic blood pressure, BP = blood pressure, BMI = body mass index

Features of Secondary Hypertension	Possible Etiologies
Sudden onset of severe hypertension or newly diagnosed in those < 30 or > 60 yr	Renal vascular disease **or** renal parenchymal disease
Abnormal urinalysis	Renal parenchymal/glomerular disease
Hypokalemia and ARR > 66.9 ng/dL#	Primary hyperaldosteronism
Hypercalcemia	Hyperparathyroidism
Paroxysmal severe hypertension	Pheochromocytoma
Abdominal mass	Polycystic kidney disease
Flank bruit	Renal artery stenosis
↑ glucose, striae, truncal obesity, etc.	Cushing's syndrome
Resistant hypertension on three meds	Renal vascular/parenchymal disease
Markedly decreased femoral pulses	Coarctation of aorta
Central obesity, loud snoring, daytime hypersomnolence, nonrestorative sleep	Obstructive sleep apnea

Specific Indications for Antihypertensive Drug Therapy

Indication	Drug class
Diabetes with proteinuria	ACEI* or ARB* or verapamil or diltiazem
Congestive heart failure	ACEI*, ARB*, ß-blockers or diuretics
Isolated systolic hypertension	Thiazide diuretics or dihydropyridine CCB
Post-myocardial infarction	ß-blocker or ACEI*
Angina	ß-blocker or calcium channel blocker
Atrial fibrillation	ß-blocker or verapamil or diltiazem
Dyslipidemia	Alpha₁-blockers (never as monotherapy for HTN)
Essential tremor	ß-blocker
Hyperthyroidism	ß-blocker
Migraine	ß-blocker or verapamil or diltiazem
Osteoporosis	Thiazide diuretics
Benign prostatic hyperplasia	Alpha₁-blockers (never as monotherapy for HTN)
Renal insufficiency	ACEI* or ARB*
Cerebrovascular disease	Thiazide diuretic, ACEI, ARB or amlodipine
African-american race	thiazide diuretics (1st line) or verapamil or diltiazem

ACEI = angiotensin converting enzyme inhibitor, CCB = calcium channel blocker, ARB = angiotensin receptor blocker and * -caution with ACEI or ARB use if creatinine > 3 mg/dL), # - ARR = aldosterone/renin ratio after 30 minutes sitting > 66.9 ng/dL confirms with 100% specificity and ARR < 23.6 ng/dL excludes 97% of cases of primary hyperaldosteronism

Mechanism of Action of Various Antihypertensive Medications

Diuretics	Negative Inotropic	Sympatho-lytics	Renin-angiotensin-aldosterone blockers	Vasodilators
• thiazide diuretics* (creatinine <2 mg/dL) • furosemide (creatinine >2mg/dL)	• Beta-blockers • verapamil • diltiazem	• Beta-blockers • clonidine • methyldopa	• Beta-blockers • angiotensin receptor blockers • angiotensin converting enzyme inhibitors	• hydralazine • alpha₁-blockers • minoxidil • dihydropyridine calcium channel blockers

References: Arch Int. Med, 2003: 289: 2560-72. NEJM, 2003; 348: 610-7 and JAMA, 2002; 288:2981-97
* - After the first couple of weeks, the mechanism of thiazide diuretics is vasodilation and not diuresis.

Cholesterol targets: primary target is LDL and secondary target is non-HDL
- Non-HDL cholesterol goal (mg/dl)= LDL cholesterol goal (mg/dl) + 30 mg/dl

Step 1: Obtain fasting lipid panel (9-12 hours fasting) every 5 years if > 20 yrs old

Step 2: Presence of coronary artery disease (CAD) or CAD risk equivalent?
- CAD risk equivalents: diabetes mellitus, carotid artery disease, peripheral arterial disease **or** abdominal aortic aneurysm

Step 3: Any major coronary artery disease (CAD) risk factors (other than LDL)?
- Cigarette smoking, HTN ≥ 140/90 or on meds, HDL< 40 mg/dl, first-degree relative with CAD (♂ < 55 yrs or ♀ < 65 yrs), Age (♂ ≥ 45 yrs or ♀ ≥ 55 yrs)
- HDL ≥ 60 mg/dl removes one risk factor from total count

Step 4: If ≥ 2 risk factors and no CAD or CAD risk equivalent, assess 10-yr CAD risk based on Framingham risk score (www.nhlbi.nih.gov/guidelines/cholesterol)

Step 5: Therapies in Different Risk Categories

Risk Category	LDL goal (mg/dl)	LDL level to start TLC	LDL level to start meds
CAD, CAD risk equivalent or 10-yr risk > 20%	<100 (optional<70)	≥ 100 mg/dl	≥ 100 mg/dl with TLC
≥ 2 risk factors or 10-yr risk ≤ 20%	<130 (optional<100)*	≥ 130 mg/dl	10 yr risk ≥10%: ≥ 130 10 yr risk <10%: ≥ 160
0-1 risk factor	<160	≥ 160 mg/dl	≥ 190 mg/dl

* - optional LDL goal for 10-year CAD risk 10-20%

Step 6: Initiate Therapeutic Lifestyle Changes (TLC) if LDL above goal
- American Heart Association Type II or DASH diet (low saturated fat, high fiber), weight loss, aerobic exercise (30 minutes at least 3 times a week)
- Treat any causes of secondary hyperlipidemia: diabetes, nephrotic syndrome, hypothyroidism, obstructive liver disease or meds (progestins or steroids)

Step 7: Identify and treat metabolic syndrome
- Metabolic syndrome if ≥ 3 risk factors: abdominal obesity (♂ > 40 inches and ♀ > 35 inches), TG ≥ 150 mg/dl, HDL < 40 mg/dl (♂) and < 50 mg/dl (♀), BP ≥ 130/85 mmHg or fasting glucose ≥ 110 mg/dl
- Treat with weight loss, exercise, blood pressure and lipid management
- Metformin 500 mg PO bid

The three muscle syndromes seen with lipid lowering medications
- Myalgias: (affects 1-5% of all patients on statins)
- Myositis: muscle aches + mild increased creatinine phosphokinase (CK)
- Rhabdomyolysis: severe muscle pain with elevated CK >10x normal

Risk Factors for Myositis
- High statin dosage, hypothyroidism, age > 65, chronic renal insufficiency, diabetes, crush injury, post-operative period, alcohol abuse and medications (fibrates, nicotinic acid, cyclosporine, colchicine, macrolides, azole antifungals, nefazodone, verapamil, amiodarone, diltiazem and cytochrome P-450 inhibitors)

Laboratory monitoring on lipid lowering medications
- Transaminases at baseline, 3 months, 6 months and then every 6-12 months
- CPK at baseline and then if any muscle symptoms occur

LDL = low-density lipoprotein, HDL = high-density lipoprotein, TG = triglycerides

Statin therapy to lower LDL 30-40%

Medications	Daily dose	LDL reduction	Side effects	Contraindications
atorvastatin	10 mg	39%	Myopathy or hepatitis	Significant liver disease. Use certain drugs with caution (see myositis drugs on page 14)
lovastatin	40 mg	31%		
pravastatin	40 mg	34%		
simvastatin	20 – 40 mg	35 – 41%		
fluvastatin	40 - 80 mg	25 – 35%		
rosuvastatin	5 – 10 mg	39 – 45%		

Bile acid sequestrants

cholestyramine	8 – 24 gm/d	LDL↓ 15-30%	GI upset and decreased absorption of other meds	Triglycerides > 300 mg/dL or obstipation
colestipol	2 – 16 gm/d	HDL↑ 3-5% TG – 0%		
colesevelam	3.8 gms/day	LDL ↓ 10%		

Cholesterol absorption inhibitors

ezetimibe	10 mg daily	LDL↓ 14%	GI upset and diarrhea	

Fibrates

gemfibrozil	600 mg bid	HDL ↑ 5-15%	Dyspepsia or myopathy	Gallstones Renal failure Cirrhosis
fenofibrate (Tricor)	48-145 mg/d	TG ↓ 25-50% LDL no change		

Other lipid lowering medications

nicotinic acid	1.5 - 4 gms/day	LDL↓ 5-25% HDL ↑ 15-35% TG ↓ 20-50%	Flushing* Gout Hepatitis	Liver disease Gout +/- Diabetes

* - incidence of flushing dramatically decreased by taking aspirin prior to nicotinic acid dose and starting at 100 mg/day then gradually advance to full dose over 2 weeks.
- In general, first choice is a statin unless severe hypertriglyceridemia >500 mg/dL when fibrates or nicotinic acid preferable to prevent pancreatitis

Combination therapy to meet lipid goals
Isolated high LDL
- Statin + nicotinic acid (best combination for cardiovascular risk reduction)#
- Statin + ezetimibe
- Statin + fibrate#
- Statin + bile acid sequestrants

Elevated LDL and triglycerides
- Statin + fibrate#
- Statin + nicotinic acid#

Elevated LDL and low HDL
- Statin + fibrate#
- Statin + nicotinic acid#

- These combination therapies increase the risk of myositis over monotherapy.

LDL = low-density lipoprotein, HDL = high-density lipoprotein, TG = triglycerides
References: JAMA 2001; 285: 2486-97, J. Amer. Coll. Cardiology, 2004; 44: 720-32, Cleveland Clinic J Med, 2003; 70: 991-7, NEJM, 2004; 350: 15. JAMA, 2004; 291: 1071-80 and JACC, 2002; 40: 567-72.

CORONARY ARTERY DISEASE 10-YEAR RISK

Framingham model for calculating 10-year risk for coronary artery disease (CAD) in patients without CAD or CAD risk equivalents: diabetes, peripheral arterial or carotid artery disease or abdominal aortic aneurysm. (*JAMA* 2001; 285:2497).

MEN					WOMEN			

Age	Points	Age	Points		Age	Points	Age	Points
20-34	-9	55-59	8		20-34	-7	55-59	8
35-39	-4	60-64	10		35-39	-3	60-64	10
40-44	0	65-69	11		40-44	0	65-69	12
45-49	3	70-74	12		45-49	3	70-74	14
50-54	6	75-79	13		50-54	6	75-79	16

Choles-terol*	Age (years)					Choles-terol*	Age (years)				
	20-39	40-49	50-59	60-69	70-79		20-39	40-49	50-59	60-69	70-79
<160	0	0	0	0	0	<160	0	0	0	0	0
160-199	4	3	2	1	0	160-199	4	3	2	1	1
200-239	7	5	3	1	0	200-239	8	6	4	2	1
240-279	9	6	4	2	1	240-279	11	8	5	3	2
280+	11	8	5	3	1	280+	13	10	7	4	2

*Total in mg/dL

Age (yrs)	20-39	40-49	50-59	60-69	70-79		Age (years)	20-39	40-49	50-59	60-69	70-79
Nonsmoker	0	0	0	0	0		Nonsmoker	0	0	0	0	0
Smoker	8	5	3	1	1		Smoker	9	7	4	2	1

HDL mg/dL	Points	HDL mg/dL	Points		HDL mg/dL	Points	HDL mg/dL	Points
60+	-1	40-49	1		60+	-1	40-49	1
50-59	0	<40	2		50-59	0	<40	2

Systolic BP	If Untreated	If Treated		Systolic BP	If Untreated	If Treated
<120 mmHg	0	0		<120 mmHg	0	0
120-129 mmHg	0	1		120-129 mmHg	1	3
130-139 mmHg	1	2		130-139 mmHg	2	4
140-159 mmHg	1	2		140-159 mmHg	3	5
160+ mmHg	2	3		160+ mmHg	4	6

Point Total	10-Year Risk	Point Total	10-Year Risk		Point Total	10-Year Risk	Point Total	10-Year Risk
0	1%	9	5%		< 9	< 1%	17	5%
1	1%	10	6%		9	1%	18	6%
2	1%	11	8%		10	1%	19	8%
3	1%	12	10%		11	1%	20	11%
4	1%	13	12%		12	1%	21	14%
5	2%	14	16%		13	2%	22	17%
6	2%	15	20%		14	2%	23	22%
7	3%	16	25%		15	3%	24	27%
8	4%	17+	30+%		16	4%	25+	30+%

- See hyperlipidemia section for goal LDL based on Framingham risk score.

Cardiac Risk Factors
- First-degree relative with coronary artery disease (♂ < 55 yrs or ♀ < 65 yrs), Age (♂ ≥ 45 yrs or ♀ ≥ 55 yrs), diabetes, hypertension, hyperlipidemia, peripheral arterial disease, carotid artery disease and cigarette smoking

Classification of Chest Pain
- Typical angina: substernal chest pressure, tightness, or heaviness exacerbated by exertion or emotional stress and relieved by rest or nitroglycerin.
- Atypical chest pain: Meets 2 of the above 3 criteria
- Noncardiac chest pain: Meets 0 or 1 of the above criteria
  > Chest pain replicated by twisting/bending movements, chest wall palpation or deep breathing is very unlikely to be from coronary artery disease (CAD).
- In patients with known CAD, the probability of significant coronary stenosis is shown in the table below based on the patient's sex, age & type of chest pain.

Pretest Probability of Significant CAD* Based on Chest Pain Classification

Age (yrs)	"Nonanginal Chest Pain"				Atypical Chest Pain			
	Men		Women		Men		Women	
	- RF	≥ 1 RF	- RF	≥ 1 RF	- RF	≥ 1 RF	- RF	≥ 1 RF
35	3%	35%	1%	19%	8%	59%	2%	39%
45	9%	47%	2%	22%	21%	70%	5%	43%
55	23%	59%	4%	25%	45%	79%	10%	47%
65	49%	69%	9%	29%	71%	86%	20%	51%

	Typical Angina			
Age (yrs)	Men	Men	Women	Women
	- RF	≥ 1 RF	- RF	≥ 1 RF
35	30%	88%	10%	78%
45	51%	92%	20%	79%
55	80%	95%	38%	82%
65	93%	97%	56%	84%

RF = cardiac risk factors: diabetes, cigarette smoking or hyperlipidemia
* - Significant CAD is > 50% narrowing of a coronary vessel by coronary angiography
Adapted from Annals of Internal Medicine, 2004; 141: 57-64.

Screening for Coronary Heart Disease
- Risk stratification indicated for intermediate to high pretest probability of significant CAD or for significant change in stable angina.
  > Exercise treadmill if able to exercise and no pre-excitation syndrome/paced rhythm/ > 1mm ST depression at rest or left bundle branch block.
  > Adenosine or dobutamine radionuclide testing if unable to exercise, prior revascularization, equivocal treadmill or abnormal ECG as above.
- No role for screening asymptomatic patients with electron-beam computed tomography or ambulatory ECG monitoring.
- C-reactive protein ≥ 2.0 mg/L has odds ratio 1.9 for significant CAD.

Guidelines for the Management of Chronic Stable Angina
- Aspirin 81 mg PO daily (also for asymptomatic pts with 10 yr CAD risk ≥ 10%)
- β-blocker unless contraindicated (decompensated CHF, hypotension, severe heart block or bradyarrhythmia, bronchospasm or refractory claudication)
  > Dihydropyridine calcium channel blocker can be used if patients have heart block, CHF, bradyarrhythmia, bronchospasm or refractory claudication.
  > Non-dihydropyridine calcium channel blocker if bronchospasm/claudication.
  > Long-acting nitrates can be used for any of the β-blocker contraindications.
  > Nitroglycerin 0.4 mg tablet sublingual or spray q5minutes x 3 prn angina
- Angiotensin converting enzyme inhibitor in patients with coronary artery disease and diabetes or left ventricular ejection fraction ≤ 0.40 (HOPE trial)
- Statin → low-density lipoprotein level < 100 mg/dL (and possibly < 70 mg/dL)
  > Therapy to lower non-high-density lipoprotein cholesterol < 130 mg/dL
  > Reduction in cardiovascular mortality even applies to patients ≥ 80 years.

- Smoking cessation
- Weight loss and increased exercise for obese or metabolic syndrome patients
- There is no proven cardioprotective effect of supplemental Vitamins A, C, E, β-carotene or of EDTA chelation therapy for patients with ischemic heart disease.
- Re-evaluate q4-6 months x 1 year and annually thereafter if symptoms stable.

Management of Refractory Stable Angina despite Optimal Medical Therapy

- May try enhanced external counterpulsation, transcutaneous electrical nerve stimulation or trans- or percutaneous myocardial revascularization.

Guidelines for the Management of Asymptomatic Patients with CAD

- Recommendations for aspirin, statins and ACEI same as for stable angina
- β-blocker indicated for patients post-myocardial infarction.
- Baseline echocardiogram for any evidence of a prior myocardial infarction

Indications for Coronary Angiography

- High-risk treadmill test (see below) at low workload
- Large reversible defect during radionuclide (thallium or technetium) testing
- Very high pretest probability (even without noninvasive testing)
- Refractory angina to optimal medical therapy

High-risk Treadmill Features

- Symptom-limited treadmill at < 5 Mets exercise by Bruce protocol
- ST segment elevation or depression > 2 mm with exercise
- Diffuse ST segment depression with exercise
- ST segment changes last longer than 5 minutes into the recovery period.
- Hypotension with exercise
- Typical angina associated with ventricular arrhythmias

ACC/AHA Recommendations for Percutaneous Coronary Intervention (PCI)

- 2-3 vessel coronary disease in non-diabetics
- Refractory angina to optimal medical therapy
- High risk features on treadmill, radionuclide testing or stress echocardiogram

ACC/AHA Recommendations for Coronary Artery Bypass Grafting (CABG)

- Significant left main disease > 50% occlusion
- 3 vessel coronary disease > 70% with left ventricular ejection fraction < 0.5
- 2 vessel coronary disease with significant proximal left anterior descending artery stenosis and left ventricular ejection fraction < 0.5
- 2-3 vessel coronary artery disease in diabetics with refractory angina
- Refractory angina not amenable to PCI

Follow-up Treadmill or Exercise Radionuclide Testing

- Annual treadmill test for stable angina (exercise prescription)
- Thallium treadmill 3-6 months after PCI/CABG (or earlier for symptoms)

Post-Myocardial Infarction (MI) Management

- Aspirin 81 mg PO daily and β-blockers (even with compensated CHF)
- Angiotensin converting enzyme inhibitor (ACEI) initiated within 36 hours
  > Angiotensin receptor blockers are alternatives if intolerant to ACEI.
- Statin initiated early to achieve low-density lipoprotein level < 70 -100 mg/dL
- No role for estrogen replacement therapy
- Follow-up symptom-limited treadmill test at 4-6 weeks post-MI
- Baseline 2D-Echocardiogram to assess left ventricular systolic function
- Lipid panel q3months to achieve lipid levels outlined in hyperlipidemia chapter

References: JACC, 2003; 41: 159-68. JACC, 2002; 40: 1777-85. Mayo Clin. Proc., 2004; 79 (1): 1284-92. Ann. Int. Med, 2004; 141: 57-64, 102-12, 562-7. Ann. Int. Med., 2004; 140: 569-72. Ann. Int Med, 2002; 136 (2) 157-72. Framingham risk table reproduced with permission from the Tarascon Pocket Pharmacopoeia, 2006, Tarascon publishing.

ACC/AHA Guidelines for Use of Pacemakers and Cardioverter-Defibrillators

Indications for Pacemaker Insertion
- **Symptomatic bradycardia:** any documented bradyarrhythmia that is directly responsible for the development of syncope, near syncope, lightheadedness or transient confusional states from cerebral hypoperfusion
- **Pacing for Acquired Atrioventricular (AV) Block**
  - ➤ **Reversible causes of AV block have been ruled out**
  - ➤ Type II second-degree AV block (especially if a wide QRS or symptoms)
  - ➤ Third-degree AV block (complete heart block) – asymptomatic
  - ➤ Can consider for first-degree AV block (PR > 0.30 seconds) or Type I second-degree AV block with symptomatic bradycardia
- **Pacing for Chronic Bifascicular or Trifascicular Block**
  - ➤ If ambulatory ECG monitoring reveals intermittent Type II second-degree AV block or third-degree AV block
- **Pacing in Sinus Node Dysfunction**
  - ➤ Symptomatic sinus pauses (≥ 3 seconds)
  - ➤ Symptomatic chronotropic incompetence
- **Pacing in Carotid Sinus Syndrome and Neurocardiogenic Syncope**
  - ➤ Documented asystole > 3 seconds with minimal carotid sinus pressure
  - ➤ Recurrent neurocardiogenic syncope associated with bradycardia
- **Pacing in Tachy-Brady syndrome**
  - ➤ Pacemaker inserted to prevent symptomatic bradycardia when AV nodal blocking agents used to rate control rapid atrial fibrillation
- **Atrial Overdrive Pacing to Terminate Tachyarrhythmias**
  - ➤ For patients unresponsive to antiarrhythmic therapy, atrial overdrive pacing may be used for symptomatic, recurrent supraventricular tachycardia shown to be terminated by pacing

Indications for Implantable Cardioverter-Defibrillator (ICD) Insertion
- History of sustained ventricular tachycardia (VT) or ventricular fibrillation
- Nonsustained VT with CAD and left ventricular systolic dysfunction
- Best implanted and managed by a trained electrophysiologist.

Indications for Biventricular Pacing/Cardiac Resynchronization Therapy
- Medically refractory New York Heart Association Class III/IV CHF with left ventricular ejection fraction ≤ 35%, QRS interval ≥ 120 milliseconds and PR interval > 150 milliseconds
- Placed by pacemaker specialist for timing adjustments for synchronization

Pacemaker Follow-up is Transtelephonic or Office Monitoring
- Check pacemaker every 2 weeks for 1 month then every 6 months until battery power starts to fall then every 3 months until battery power low then every month.

All pacemaker decisions should be made in consultation with a cardiologist

References: J Am Coll Cardiol, 2002; 40 (9): 1703-19 and J Am Coll Cardiol, 2004; 43 (2): 1145-8.

Etiologies
- 90% idiopathic or of viral etiology
- Other causes: neoplastic, tuberculous (Tb), bacterial, Dressler's syndrome (post-myocardial infarction), post-irradiation, chest trauma, uremia, post-cardiotomy, autoimmune diseases (systemic lupus erythematosus & rheumatoid arthritis) and medications (hydralazine, isoniazid, phenytoin and procainamide).

Clinical Presentation
- Sudden onset of constant, sharp or stabbing, retrosternal chest pain
- Worsened by deep inspiration, lying down and possibly with swallowing
- Improved with leaning forward
- Pain often radiates to the neck, jaw, arms and trapezius muscle ridges.
- No improvement with nitroglycerin

Physical Exam
- Pericardial rub heard at some time during their clinical course in 85% of patients: harsh, high frequency, scratchy sound best heard with the patient leaning forward using the stethoscope's diaphragm
  > Classic rub with 3 components: ventricular systole, ventricular diastole and atrial systole. 50% of rubs triphasic, 33% biphasic and rest monophasic
- Signs of cardiac tamponade: muffled heart sounds, hypotension, tachycardia, jugular venous distension and pulsus paradoxus (fall in systolic blood pressure > 10 mmHg with inspiration)
- Temperature > 38°C uncommon except in purulent pericarditis

Electrocardiographic Changes
- **Stage 1:** Diffuse, **concave** ST segment elevations and diffuse PR segment depressions in all leads except aVR where ST segment depression and PR segment elevation occurs.
- **Stage 2:** ST and PR segments normalize
- **Stage 3:** Diffuse T wave inversions
- **Stage 4:** Normalization of the T waves
- Electrical alternans may be seen if a large pericardial effusion exists.
- The ratio of ST segment elevation (in millimeters) to T wave amplitude (in millimeters) > 0.24 in lead V6 is highly specific for acute pericarditis.
- Diffuse T wave inversions + concave ST ↑ and PR ↓ suggests myopericarditis

Prognostic Factors Warranting Admission to Hospital
- Fever > 38°C, subacute onset over weeks, immunocompromised, history of trauma, anticoagulant therapy, myocarditis, elevated troponin I, evidence of cardiac tamponade or a large pericardial effusion (echo-free space > 2 cm).

Work-up of Acute Pericarditis
- Labs: complete blood count, renal panel, troponin I +/- ANA or RF or PPD
- If Tb or malignant effusion suspected, pericardial fluid should be sent for cytology and mycobacterium tuberculosis RNA by polymerase chain reaction assay and adenosine deaminase activity (>30 U/L suggests Tb) assay
- Chest radiograph
- Echocardiogram indicated in all patients with suspected pericarditis

Treatment of Acute Pericarditis
- Oral indomethacin 75-225 mg/day or ibuprofen 1600-3200 mg/day
  > Colchicine 0.6 mg PO bid can be added if symptoms persist > 2 weeks.
- Prednisone 1-1.5 mg/kg/day orally only for severe, recurrent pericarditis or connective tissue diseases
- Pericardiocentesis: therapeutic for clinical evidence of tamponade or diagnostic for possible tuberculous or neoplastic pericarditis

ANA = antinuclear antibody, RF = rheumatoid factor and PPD = positive purified derivative test
Reference: NEJM, 2004; 351; 21: 2195-2202 and Circulation, 2003; 108: 1146-62.

Lee's Revised Cardiac Risk Index for Non-Cardiac Surgery[1]
Risk Factors: high-risk surgery[2], ischemic heart disease[3], history of congestive heart failure[4] or cerebrovascular disease, insulin therapy and creatinine > 2 mg/dL.

Risk Class	# of risk factors	Rate of cardiac complications[5]
I	0	0.4%
II	1	0.9%
III	2	7%
IV	3 - 4	9.2 - 18%
V	5 - 6	32%

Guidelines for Perioperative Medical Management for Non-Cardiac Surgery

Labs	Indications for Preoperative Laboratory Testing
Hemoglobin	Anticipated large blood loss or symptoms/history of anemia
Electrolytes	Renal disease, CHF, endocrine disease and meds that can affect
Renal panel	> 50, HTN, heart disease, DM, major surgery & meds that affect
Liver panel	Chronically ill, malnourished, liver disease and meds that can affect
PT/PTT/PLT	Bleeding diathesis, liver disease, anticoagulant use & major surgery
ECG	> 50, cardiac disease, cardiac symptoms or risk factors, DM or HTN
Chest x-ray	> 50, cardiopulmonary disease, active symptoms or abnormal exam

PT = prothrombin time, PTT = partial thromboplastin time, PLT = platelets, ECG = electrocardiogram

- Emergency surgery goes directly to the OR
  - ➢ Consider perioperative ß-blockers if indicated and feasible
- Presence of any major clinical risk predictors: unstable coronary syndrome[6], decompensated CHF, significant arrhythmias[7] or severe stenotic valve disease?
  - ➢ Consider preop coronary angiogram or delaying/canceling surgery
- Indications for preop coronary artery bypass grafting or percutaneous coronary intervention are identical to the standard indications for these procedures (p. 18)
- Smoking cessation ≥ 8 weeks prior to major thoracic or abdominal surgery markedly reduces the risks of postoperative pulmonary complications.
- Indications for perioperative ß-blockers
  - ➢ Presence of any of Lee's revised cardiac risk index criteria
  - ➢ ≥ 2 minor criteria: ≥ 65, HTN, smoker, cholesterol > 240 mg/dL or diabetes
  - ➢ Ideally start ß-blockers 1 week prior to surgery and continue 1 week postop
  - ➢ Titrate ß-blockers to resting heart rate 55-65 (↓ periop CV events 80%).
- Contraindications to ß-blockers: decompensated CHF, atrioventricular block, hypotension, bronchospasm or severe bradycardia.
- Perioperative clonidine 0.2 mg/day x 4 days post-op if unable to use ß-blockers[8]
- Before elective non-cardiac surgery, wait 4-6 weeks post-MI, 1 week post-angioplasty, 4-6 weeks post-coronary stent placement and 8 weeks post-CVA.
- Initiation of statins on post-op day 1-2 may decrease perioperative CV events.
- Postop: High risk patients should be on cardiac monitor x 48 hours and have an ECG immediately postop and daily x 2 days + Troponin I daily x 2 days.

---

[1] Circulation, 1999; 100: 1043-9.
[2] Intrathoracic, intraperitoneal, suprainguinal vascular or major surgery with large fluid shifts
[3] History of MI or positive exercise test, current angina, nitrate use or ECG with pathologic Q waves
[4] History of CHF, pulmonary edema, paroxysmal nocturnal dyspnea, pulmonary rales, S3 gallop or chest radiograph with pulmonary vascular redistribution
[5] Combined MI, CHF, ventricular fibrillation, complete heart block or cardiac arrest
[6] Recent MI with ischemic risk, unstable or New York Heart Association class III/IV angina
[7] High-grade atrioventricular block, symptomatic ventricular arrhythmias with heart disease, supraventricular arrhythmias with rapid ventricular rate
[8] Anesthesiology, 2004; 101: 284-93.

Venous Thromboembolism (VTE) Prophylaxis in Surgical Patients

Surgery	Early walking	Elastic stockings	IPC	Low-dose UH	LMWH
Any low-risk surgery	X				
Mod. risk general surgery		X	X	X	X
High risk general surgery			X	X	X
Very high risk general surgery			X	X	X
Mod-high risk gynecologic surg.			X	X	X
Mod. risk urologic surgery		X	X	X	X
High risk urologic surgery			X	X	X
Hip fracture, THA or TKA				X	X
Neurosurgery			X		
Trauma					X

IPC = intermittent pneumatic compression, UH = unfractionated heparin, LMWH = low molecular weight heparin, THA = total hip arthroplasty, TKA = total knee arthroplasty, low-risk < 40 and no VTE risk factors, moderate risk = 40-60 yrs or major surgery, high risk = > 60 or VTE risk factors and very high risk = major surgery and VTE risk factors or surgery for malignancy

Preoperative Cardiovascular Assessment for Non-Cardiac Surgery

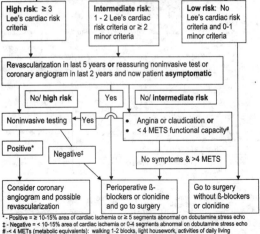

* - Positive = ≥ 10-15% area of cardiac ischemia or ≥ 5 segments abnormal on dobutamine stress echo
‡ - Negative = < 10-15% area of cardiac ischemia or 0-4 segments abnormal on dobutamine stress echo
# -< 4 METs (metabolic equivalents): walking 1-2 blocks, light housework, activities of daily living
   4 METs: climb flight of stairs, heavy house work, bowling, dancing, golf or doubles tennis
References: J Am Coll Cardiology, 2003; 42: 234-40. Med. Clin. N. America, 2003; 87: 77-136. Circulation, 2002; 105: 1257-67. Arch. Intern. Med., 2004; 164: 1729-36.

Acute Arterial Insufficiency
- Most common cause is a cardioembolic event
- Ischemic complication rate rises dramatically if time from onset of symptoms to embolectomy is > 6 hrs: 10% if time < 6 hrs, 20% at 8 hrs and 33% at 24 hours
- Clinical features of arterial insufficiency (6 P's)
  ➢ Pain, pallor, pulseless, paresthesias, paralysis and poikilothermia (cold)
  ➢ Sudden onset of symptoms favors an embolic event
- Treatment
  ➢ Immediate heparinization and consult a vascular surgeon for embolectomy

Chronic Arterial Insufficiency
- Clinical features of peripheral arteriosclerotic disease
  ➢ Intermittent claudication described as cramping discomfort of muscles with ambulation relieved by rest. Graded by blocks walked before symptoms.
  ➢ Aortoiliac disease: thigh/buttock claudication +/- impotence (Leriche syndrome)
  ➢ Femoropopliteal disease: calf claudication
  ➢ Signs: dystrophic nails, absent/weak peripheral pulses, loss of hair of distal extremity, cool distal extremity with shiny skin
- Risk Factors: smoking, positive family history, hyperlipidemia, diabetes, hypertension and vascular disease elsewhere

Evaluation of Claudication
- Ankle/Brachial index (ABI) 0.6 - 0.8 = mild arteriosclerotic disease, 0.4 - 0.6 = moderate disease and < 0.4 = severe disease (usually have rest pain).
  ➢ Measure first doppler sound as cuff is deflated at the brachial artery and either the posterior tibial or dorsalis pedis artery. The ankle/brachial index is determined by dividing the ankle by the brachial systolic blood pressure.
  ➢ Diabetic patients with calcified arteries can have falsely elevated ABI.
- Duplex ultrasound of arterial system and segmental limb pressures: good noninvasive studies to estimate degree of lower extremity arterial obstruction.
- Aortogram with peripheral run-off is the gold standard test.

Treatment
- Lifestyle modification: smoking cessation and graded exercise program
- Lipid control with a statin: low-density lipoprotein < 100 mg/dL (possibly < 70 mg/dL in very high-risk patient*) + high-density lipoprotein > 40 mg/dL
- Tight diabetic and blood pressure control (BP < 130/80)
- Aspirin 75-325 mg PO daily
- Cilostazol 100 mg PO bid can improve claudication symptoms, exercise capacity and appears to be superior to pentoxifylline.
- Beta-blockers have no proven adverse effect on claudication and they in combination with ACEI protect against cardiovascular events in these patients.
- Arterial bypass or percutaneous transluminal angioplasty indicated for disabling claudication, rest pain, gangrene, Leriche syn. or nonhealing, ischemic ulcers
- No benefit of warfarin to decrease reocclusion rates of arterial grafts.

* - Known coronary artery disease or coronary artery disease risk equivalent and additional risk factors
Reference: Chest, 1998; 114 (5): 666-82. NEJM, 2001; 344: 1608 and Lancet, 2001; 358: 1257.

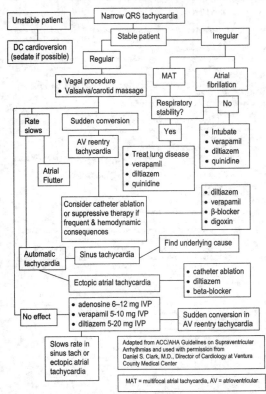

Adapted from ACC/AHA Guidelines on Supraventricular Arrhythmias and used with permission from Daniel S. Clark, M.D., Director of Cardiology at Ventura County Medical Center

MAT = multifocal atrial tachycardia, AV = atrioventricular

Notes: Supraventricular tachycardia in association with a pre-excitation syndrome should be evaluated for catheter ablation. Reference: J. Amer. College of Cardiology, 2003; 42: 1493-1531.

Etiologies of Syncope (mnemonic = SVNCOPE)
- **S**ituational – micturition, defecation, severe coughing, valsalva
- **V**ascular – subclavian steal, vertebrobasilar insufficiency or carotid sinus hypersensitivity
- **N**eurological – neurocardiogenic, brainstem transient ischemic attacks or basilar migraines
- **C**ardiac – cardiac ischemia, obstructive valvular, arrhythmias or tumor
- **O**rthostatic hypotension
- **P**sychiatric
- **E**mbolism (pulmonary embolism)/Everything else (e.g., drug overdoses)

History
- Sudden onset suggests arrhythmia, pulmonary embolus or carotid sinus hypersensitivity.
- Tonic-clonic movements, incontinence or tongue biting (seizure activity)
- Preceding events, precipitating factor (fear, pain, sight of blood), prodromal sensations (diaphoresis, nausea, dizziness, visual defects, weakness)?
  - ➢ These and gradual onset suggest neurocardiogenic syncope
- Exercise-induced or occurred at rest?
  - ➢ Exertion-related often cardiac ischemia or obstructive valvular lesion
- Associated chest discomfort, palpitations or dyspnea?
  - ➢ Cardiac disease or psychiatric disorder
- Related to positional changes?
  - ➢ Orthostasis, atrial myxoma or carotid sinus hypersensitivity
- Postevent condition: confusion, fatigue, injury, duration of recovery
- History of arrhythmias, coronary artery disease, congestive heart failure, psychiatric history, pulmonary embolus or prior syncopal episodes?
- Family history of sudden cardiac death (suggests arrhythmic syncope)
- Age < 55 yrs, ♀, diaphoresis, palpitations, post-event fatigue and recovery > 1 minute all suggest neurally-mediated syncope and not arrhythmic syncope

Exam
- Check for orthostasis (↓ ≥ 20 mmHg Systolic BP (SBP) supine to standing)
- Careful cardiac and neurologic examination
- Carotid massage (positive with ↓SBP ≥ 50 mmHg or asystole ≥ 3 seconds)

Diagnostic Evaluation
- ECG: evidence of structural heart disease or conduction disease?
- 2D-Echocardiogram if cardiac dysfunction or valvular anomalies suspected
- Ambulatory ECG if cardiac etiology suspected
  - ➢ Frequent symptoms (Holter monitor) & infrequent symptoms (Event monitor)
  - ➢ Positive if: symptoms and sinus pause ≥ 2 sec., sinus bradycardia ≤ 40, supraventricular tachycardia ≥ 180, Type II second-degree atrioventricular block, complete heart block or sustained ventricular tachycardia ≥ 30 sec.
- Tilt-table testing: recurrent unexplained syncope with negative cardiac work-up
- Electrophysiologic testing not indicated for unexplained syncope if ECG normal.
- Rule out pregnancy in a young woman (? ruptured ectopic pregnancy)

References: Ann Int Med, 1997; 126: 989-96. Ann Int Med, 1997; 127: 76-86.

Condition	Clinical Features	Treatment
Atopic Dermatitis (AD) (or eczema) British Medical J, 1999; 318: 1600 Lancet, 1996; 348: 769. Immunology and Allergy Clinics of N. America, 2004; 24: 631. FDA product alert March 2005	• Pruritus and family history of atopy • Symmetric rash + propensity for flexural areas • Common findings: generalized xerosis, infrahorbital darkening and skin folds (Dennie Morgan lines), hyperlinear palms • Infants: dry erythematous patches on cheeks and chin with fine scaling • Children: erythematous papules + plaques in flexural areas +/- lichenification; pityriasis alba • Adults: may present as childhood eczema • Nummular eczema: coin-shaped plaques • Dyshidrosis: hand erythema with scattered vesicles +/- peeling skin or lichenification ▲ ▲	• Avoid frequent bathing, hot water, abrasive towels, wool or itchy fabrics and scented cleaning and cosmetic agents. • Avoid scratching and consider antihistamines for pruritus • Moisturizing cream or ointment applied to damp skin bid-tid • Low-potency steroid cream to face, axilla or perineum bid • Medium-high potency steroid ointment bid for severe hand eczema, moderate body eczema or for nummular eczema • Very high potency steroid cream daily for lichenified plaques • Antistaphylococcal antibiotics for superimposed infections • 1% pimecrolimus cream bid for mild-mod AD if age >2 years • Tacrolimus cream 0.03% (children > 2 yrs) or 0.1% (adults) bid for moderate-severe atopic dermatitis ➤ Caution as pimecrolimus and tacrolimus use has been associated with the development of some cancers. • Consider cyclosporine 5 mg/kg/d for severe, refractory AD
Acne J. Am. Acad. Dermatology, 1995; 32: 56. British J. Dermatol, 1997; 137: 563. JAMA, 2004; 292: 726 NEJM, 2005; 352: 1463-72. Medical letter, 2005; 3(35): 49-56	• Comedonal: red papules with a central black orifice (open) or white vesicle (closed) • Pustular: red papules with central pustules • Nodulocystic: red cystic and nodular lesions • Acne conglobata: communicating cysts, abscesses and draining sinuses • Distribution: face, upper back and neck. • Risk factors: oral steroids, exposure to industrial solvents or occlusive body gear use	• **Comedonal acne:** topical retinoids are first-line therapy: ▲ Tretinoin, adapalene or tazarotene gels or creams qhs • **Papulopustular acne (mild-moderate):** topical antibiotics (benzoyl peroxide, azelaic acid, clindamycin or erythromycin) with topical retinoids daily or bid ▲ **Mod-severe:** PO tetracyclines or erythromycin x 2-6 mo. • Can add oral contraceptive pills with low androgenicity for ♀ • **Severe nodular or refractory acne:** isotretinoin 0.5-1 mg/kg/d x 15-20 weeks. Causes dry skin, alopecia, is teratogenic, hepatotoxic and can cause hypertriglyceridemia

Condition	Clinical Features	Treatment
Onychomycosis J. Amer. Academy Dermatology, 1999; 40: S21. Arch. Dermatology, 2002; 138: 811.	• Whitish, yellowish or brownish discoloration of the nail plate caused by dermatophyte infections. • Definitive diagnosis by identifying fungal hyphae on potassium hydroxide exam of nail bed scrapings.	• Terbinafine 250 mg PO daily x 6 weeks (fingernails) and x 12 weeks (toenails) • Itraconazole 200 mg PO daily x 8 weeks **or** 400 mg PO daily for 1 week each month for 2 months (fingernails) • Itraconazole 200 mg PO daily x 12 wks **or** 400 mg PO daily for 1 week each month for 3 months (toenails) • Monitor liver panel monthly and for drug interactions
Psoriasis J. Amer. Academy Dermatology, 2001; 45: 487 and 544. J. Amer. Academy Dermatology, 1998; 38: 705. British J. Dermatology, 2002; 146: 118. NEJM, 2001; 345: 248 JAMA, 2003; 290: 3073 NEJM, 2003; 349: 2014 Lancet, 2001; 357: 1842. J American Academy of Dermatology, 2005; 52: 671. NEJM, 2005; 352: 1899-912.	▲ 40% with positive family history • Plaque-type psoriasis ▲ Erythematous, sharply demarcated plaques with silvery scale • Scalp, extensor elbows/knees, back ▲ Guttate psoriasis • Multiple erythematous plaques < 1 cm with silvery scale on trunk • Frequently follows strep infection ▲ Pustular psoriasis • Erythroderma with scaling & pustules ▲ Erythrodermic psoriasis • Diffuse erythroderma with scaling ▲ Inverse psoriasis • Rash involves intertriginous areas • Nails frequently pitted	• **Mild plaque-type:** high-potency topical corticosteroids • **Moderate plaque-type or guttate psoriasis:** high-potency topical corticosteroids and vitamin D₃ analogues (calcipotriene cream* or tacalcitol ointment) +/- topical retinoids (tazarotene*) • **Severe plaque, pustular, erythrodermic psoriasis +/- arthritis** ▲ Psoralen-ultraviolet A (PUVA)* therapy + systemic retinoids (e.g., acitretin* 25-50 mg PO daily: teratogenic, hepatotoxic & ↑ lipids) ▲ Methotrexate* 7.5-20 mg PO qweek. Monitor liver panel. ▲ Cyclosporine 3-5 mg/kg/day. Monitor renal function and BP ▲ Efalizumab 0.3 mg/kg IV or 1 mg/kg SQ qweek x 8-12 weeks ▲ Alefacept 0.075 mg/kg IV or 15 mg IM qweek x 12 weeks ▲ Etanercept 25 mg SQ 2x/week x 24 weeks ▲ Infliximab 5 mg/kg IV at 0, 2 and 6 weeks • **Inverse psoriasis:** low-potency topical corticosteroids • **Scalp psoriasis:** tar shampoos or high-potency corticosteroids in an alcohol solution - These medications are all teratogenic

Condition	Clinical Features	Treatment

Rosacea
 	
J. Amer. Academy Dermatology; 2002; 46: 584.
 	
Arch Dermatology; 1998; 134: 679
 	
NEJM, 2005; 352: 793-803.
 	
Medical letter; 2005; 3 (35): 49-56.
	• Affects adults, onset between 30-50 yrs, ♀>♂
	• Facial erythema and telangiectasias involving the nose, cheek, chin, eyelids and forehead
	• Flushing may become enhanced by hot or spicy foods, alcohol, heat, sunlight or stress.
	• Red papules often with overlying pustules on background of erythema involving central face
	• Phymatous rosacea is thickened skin **and prominent pores of nose, chin, forehead or ears**
	• Ocular rosacea with erythema & telangiectasias of lids, blepharitis and conjunctival injection
		• Use mild, nonscented soaps and strong sunscreen
		• **Treatment of papulopustular rosacea:** 0.75% metronidazole cream bid **or** 15% azelaic acid gel bid **or** 10% sodium sulfacetamide + 5% sulfur cream bid
		  ▲ Oral doxycycline 100-200 mg/d **or** erythromycin 500-1000 mg/d **or** metronidazole 200-400 mg/d x 6-12 weeks then topicals for mod-severe cases.
		  ▲ Add tretinoin cream qhs for recalcitrant cases
		  ▲ Isotretinoin 0.1-0.5 mg/kg/d x 6-8 mo. for severe disease; **only treatment for telangiectasias.**
		• **Phymatous rosacea:** electrosurgery or laser rx.
		• **Ocular rosacea:** artificial tears & eyelid cleansing if mild & PO antibiotics as above x 12 wks if severe.

Seborrheic Dermatitis	• "Cradle cap" in infants: erythema of scalp with a whitish-yellow thick scale
	• Tinea amiantacea develops in young children: thick, plates of white scale occur in patches on the scalp.
	• Adults develop erythematous patches with overlying fine, dry white scale. The involvement is on the scalp, nose, nasolabial folds, eyebrows, external ear canals and behind ears.
	• Skin and scalp is often oily
	• Consider HIV infection if new onset and severe disease in an adult.
		• Cradle cap treated with baby oil on scalp and combing with a fine bristle comb or toothbrush
		• Tinea amiantacea treated with coal tar shampoos qhs and washed off in morning.
		• Adult seborrheic dermatitis treatment
		  ▲ 2% ketoconazole **or** 2.5% selenium sulfide shampoo daily or every other day for scalp involvement
		  ▲ Low-potency topical steroid **or** ketoconazole cream or 0.75% metronidazole cream applied daily effective for facial rash.
		  ▲ Consider ketoconazole 400 mg PO x 1 prior to topical therapy for severe cases

Basal Cell Carcinoma (BCC)
- **Clinical Presentation of BCC**
  - ➤ Nodular BCC: nodule with a pearly, translucent surface and telangiectasias
    - o Typical location is on the head and neck
  - ➤ Sclerosing BCC: whitish, hard plaque with indistinct margins
  - ➤ Superficial BCC: reddish plaque with overlying scale usually on the back
- **Diagnosis** best made by a punch biopsy
- **Treatment Options**
  - ➤ Surgical excision with 5 mm margins
  - ➤ Consider Moh's micrographic surgery for BCC on the nose, ears, lips, eyelids, genitals and for recurrent BCCs.
  - ➤ 5% imiquimod cream qhs 5x/week x 6-16 weeks for superficial BCCs
  - ➤ Curettage and electrodessication for nodular BCCs not on the head
  - ➤ Radiation therapy or intralesional interferon-alpha therapy are options for very elderly patients or those unable to tolerate surgical excision.

Cutaneous Squamous Cell Carcinoma (SCC)
- **Clinical Presentation**
  - ➤ Typically nontender papule or plaque with a dark, hyperkeratotic, adherent scale and/or overlying ulceration
  - ➤ 2/3 arise from a pre-existing actinic keratosis or cutaneous horn
  - ➤ Commonly on scalp, face, lips, forearms or dorsum of hands
- **Diagnosis** best made by a punch biopsy
- **High-risk Features for Metastasis**
  - ➤ Depth > 4 mm, poorly differentiated SCC, perineural or intravascular invasion, size > 2 cm, recurrent SCC or location on ear, lips or genitals
- **Treatment Options**
  - ➤ Surgical excision with 4-5 mm margins is the treatment of choice
  - ➤ Consider Moh's micrographic surgery for SCC on the nose, ears, lips, eyelids, genitals, fingers and for recurrent squamous cell carcinomas.
  - ➤ 5% imiquimod cream bid or 5% 5-fluorouracil cream bid x 4-8 weeks can be used for Bowen's disease (squamous cell carcinoma *in situ*)
  - ➤ Radiation therapy for well-delineated, primary SCCs < 2 cm

Melanoma
- **Clinical Presentation**
  - ➤ Superficial spreading melanoma: brown or black macules or patches usually with irregular borders and color variation
  - ➤ Nodular melanoma: nodules that may be black, brown, red or hypopigmented (amelanotic melanomas)
  - ➤ Acral lentiginous: hyperpigmented patch on the palms, soles or subungual
  - ➤ Lentigo maligna: arises from melanoma *in situ* usually on the head or neck
- **Diagnosis**: excisional biopsy if lesion small or incisional biopsy if large.
- **Staging**: sentinel lymph node biopsy for lesions >1 mm thick or Clark level ≥ IV or if ulcerated, chest x-ray, lactate dehydrogenase, albumin and hemoglobin
  - ➤ If lymph node biopsy + → chest/abdomen CT scan, head MRI & PET scan
- **Treatment Options**
  - ➤ Definitive treatment is surgical excision with the following surgical margins based on the microscopic depth of the melanoma found by biopsy

Melanoma depth	In situ melanoma	≤ 1 mm depth	1.01-2 mm depth	2-4 mm depth	> 4 mm depth
Margins	5 mm	1.0 cm	1-2 cm	2 cm	2-3 cm

References: NEJM, 2001; 344: 975, Cancer, 1995; 75: 699, NEJM, 2004; 351: 998 & Lancet, 1996; 347: 803

Etiologies of Adrenal Insufficiency

Primary Adrenal Insufficiency	Secondary Adrenal Insufficiency
• Metastatic carcinoma of lung, breast, stomach or colon or lymphoma • Miliary tuberculosis • AIDS-associated infections* • Waterhouse-Friedrichsen syndrome • Autoimmune adrenalitis • Adrenal hemorrhage/infarct • Antiphospholipid syndrome • Meds: ketoconazole, rifampin, phenytoin, barbiturates or megestrol acetate	• Systemic glucocorticoid therapy > 3 consecutive wks within the last year • Pituitary or hypothalamic tumors • Lymphocytic hypophisitis • Postpartum pituitary necrosis (Sheehan's syndrome) • Pituitary tuberculosis, sarcoidosis or histoplasmosis

*- most commonly HIV, cytomegalovirus infections or histoplasmosis infection

Symptoms of Adrenal Insufficiency
• Fatigue, malaise, weakness, poor memory, depression, psychosis, anorexia, postural dizziness, nausea/vomiting, abdominal pain, myalgias and arthralgias.
• Salt craving in primary adrenal insufficiency
• Decreased libido can occur with pituitary lesions

Signs and Typical Labs in Adrenal Insufficiency (AI)

Both Types of AI	Primary AI	Secondary AI
• Unexplained fever • Hypotension or orthostatic hypotension • Hyponatremia • Hypoglycemia • Mild hypercalcemia • Normocytic anemia • Eosinophilia	• Hyperpigmentation of palmar creases, extensor surfaces and buccal mucosa • Hyperkalemia • Non-anion gap acidosis • Possible vitiligo	Pituitary lesions may exhibit: ○ Amenorrhea ○ Secondary hypothyroidism ○ Diabetes insipidus ○ Sexual dysfunction

Diagnosis of Adrenal Insufficiency in Outpatient Setting
• Fasting AM serum cortisol level ≤ 3 mcg/dL essentially rules in AI.
• Cosyntropin stimulation test using 250 mcg cosyntropin (synthetic ACTH) IV/IM
  ➤ Measure serum cortisol levels at time 0 and 60 minutes post-cosyntropin
  ➤ Any cortisol level ≥ 18-21 mcg/dL essentially rules out primary AI or chronic, severe secondary AI (may miss cases of mild or recent-onset secondary AI)
  ➤ An insulin tolerance test can be useful for equivocal cases, but it should be performed under the guidance of an endocrinologist.
• If fasting AM or post-stimulation serum cortisol level is low, measure a plasma adrenocorticotropin hormone (ACTH) level between 6 – 8:00 AM.
  ➤ ACTH is increased in primary AI & is decreased or normal in secondary AI.

Diagnosis of Adrenal Insufficiency in Acutely Ill Patients
• AI likely if random cortisol < 15 mcg/dL and unlikely if cortisol > 34 mcg/dL
• If cortisol level 15 – 34 mcg/dL, check a 250 mcg cosyntropin stimulation test and a post-stimulation rise in cortisol < 9 mcg/dL signifies relative AI.

Treatment of Presumed Adrenal Crisis
• 5% dextrose in isotonic saline until normotensive
• Dexamethasone 4 mg IV bolus then 4 mg IV q6h until results of cosyntropin stimulation test known (dexamethasone will **not** interfere with cosyntropin test)

Maintenance Therapy of Adrenal Insufficiency
• Maintenance daily oral dose: prednisone 5 - 7.5 mg or hydrocortisone 25-35 mg
• Increase maintenance dose 2-3-fold during moderate illness or minor surgery
• Hydrocortisone 50 mg IV q6h during severe illness or for major surgery
• Dehydroepiandrosterone 50 mg PO daily improves libido & well-being in ♀
• **Patients should have a Medic Alert bracelet & medical identification card**

References: NEJM, 2003; 348 (8): 727-34. Ann. Int Med, 2003; 139 (3):194-204. NEJM, 1999; 341:1013-20.

Hypercalcemia Etiologies (80-90% from hyperparathyroidism or cancer)
- Hyperparathyroidism (~80% of cases from isolated parathyroid adenoma)
  - Most common cause of hypercalcemia Presentation is usually asymptomatic, metabolic alkalosis and calcium level usually < 11 mg/dL
  - Elevated or high normal serum intact parathyroid hormone (iPTH) level
- Malignancy (bony mets or humoral hypercalcemia of malignancy)
  - Breast, prostate, lung, kidney, bladder cancers or multiple myeloma
  - Serum chloride/bicarbonate ratio low and calcium level often ≥ 13 mg/dL
  - 95% cases identified by history, exam, routine chemistries, complete blood count, chest x-ray and serum protein electrophoresis
  - Increased PTH-related peptide in humoral hypercalcemia of malignancy
- Other causes include: milk-alkali syndrome, vitamin D intoxication, tuberculosis, sarcoidosis, thyrotoxicosis, familial hypocalciuric hypercalcemia (urine calcium/creatinine < 0.01), Paget's disease, adrenal insufficiency, pheochromocytoma, lymphoma, prolonged immobilization, meds (thiazide diuretics, tamoxifen, vitamin D and gonadotropin releasing hormone analogues, estrogens, androgens, caspofungin and teriparatide) & very high calcium intake.

Clinical Presentation ("bones, stones, psychic moans and abdominal groans")
- Bone pain • Diffuse abdominal pain, anorexia, nausea and constipation
- Renal stones • Lethargy, fatigue, depression, confusion & cognitive impairment
- Electrocardiogram changes: shortened QT and prolonged PR intervals

Work-up of Primary Hyperparathyroidism
- Evaluate for osteopenia/osteoporosis: DEXA-bone mineral densitometry scan
- Evaluate for renal stone risk: renal ultrasound and 24h urine for calcium/creatinine ratio to assess degree of hypercalciuria (usually > 0.02).
- Parathyroid Tc 99m sestamibi scan if surgery is being considered.

Treatment Options for Asymptomatic Primary Hyperparathyroidism
- Parathyroid surgery indicated for any of the following: serum calcium is > 1 mg/dL above the upper limit of normal, 24h urine calcium is > 400 mg, creatinine clearance ↓ by ≥ 30%, bone density scan reveals a T-score < -2.5 at any site, age < 50 **or** medical surveillance is not a realistic option.
  - Surgery indicated for all pts with symptomatic primary hyperparathyroidism
- Medical surveillance with biannual serum calcium and creatinine and annual DEXA-bone mineral densitometry scan & 24h urine for calcium and creatinine.
- PO intake of elemental calcium 1000 mg/day and Vitamin D 400 IU/day.

Hypocalcemia Etiologies

• Chronic renal failure	• Rhabdomyolysis	• ↑↑ hypomagnesemia
• Hypoparathyroidism	• Respiratory alkalosis	• Massive transfusion
• Tumor lysis	• Acute pancreatitis	• Vitamin D deficiency
• Post-thyroidectomy	• Post-parathyroidectomy from hungry bone syndrome	
• Furosemide, phenytoin, phenobarbital, steroids, aminoglycosides and cisplatin		

Corrected Calcium Calculation (gm/dL)
- Calcium(corrected) (gm/dL) = calcium + [0.8 x (4 – serum albumin in gm/dL)]
- Pseudohypocalcemia: hypoalbuminemia is most common cause of low calcium

Clinical Presentation
- Neuromuscular irritability (Chvostek's sign and Trousseau's sign), tetany, paresthesias, muscle cramps and seizures
- Psychiatric disorders: psychosis, depression and cognitive impairment
- Electrocardiogram changes: prolonged QT interval +/- heart block

Treatment of Hypocalcemia
- If etiology unclear, check intact PTH and 1,25-dihydroxyvitamin D levels
- 1 – 2 grams of elemental calcium orally with meals daily divided bid – tid
- Add calcitriol 0.25 mcg PO daily for hypoparathyroidism or vitamin D deficiency

Reference: NEJM, 2000; 343: 1863-75. Critical Care Clinics, 2001; 17(1): 139-53. J. Clin. Endo. Met, 2002; 87: 5353-61. NEJM, 2004; 1746-51 and AFP, 2004; 69: 333-40. DEXA = dual-energy x-ray absorptimetry

Clinical Features of Cushing's Syndrome
- Centripetal obesity involving the face, neck, trunk and abdomen
  - "Moon facies"
  - "Buffalo hump" or dorsocervical fat pad
- Skin changes: atrophy, easy bruisability and purple striae
  - Hyperpigmentation occurs with ↑↑ adrenocorticotropin (ACTH) secretion.
- Menstrual irregularities
- Adrenal tumors can cause precocious puberty in boys and hirsutism, virilization, acne and decreased libido in women.
- Proximal muscle wasting
- Osteoporosis
- Diabetes mellitus
- Hypertension and hypokalemia
- Mood disorders, emotional lability and sleep disturbances common
- Relative immunosuppression with increased infection rate

Diagnosing Cushing's Syndrome
- Exclude use of exogenous glucocorticoids or medroxyprogesterone acetate.
- Low-dose dexamethasone suppression test to screen patients
  - 1 mg IM dexamethasone at 11 P.M.-12 A.M. & check serum cortisol at 8 A.M.
  - Normal if serum cortisol < 1.8 mcg/dL (rules out Cushing's syndrome).
  - If AM serum cortisol is > 1.8 mcg/dL, perform a midnight plasma or salivary cortisol or a combined dexamethasone suppression-CRH stimulation test.
- Midnight cortisol levels diagnostic for Cushing's syndrome:
  - Plasma cortisol levels taken from IV of sleeping patients ≥ 7.5 mcg/dL.
  - Enzyme-linked immunosorbent assay for salivary cortisol > 0.25 mcg/dL.
- Dexamethasone suppression-CRH stimulation test
  - Dexamethasone 0.5 mg PO q6h x 48h starting at noon and ending at 6 AM.
  - CRH 1 mcg/kg IV at 8 AM and check serum cortisol 15 min. later (8:15 AM).
  - Serum cortisol > 1.4 mcg/dL diagnostic for Cushing's Syndrome
- Hypercortisolism (pseudo-Cushing's syndrome) can occur in people with polycystic ovary syndrome, severe depression or anxiety and chronic alcohol abuse, but levels do not increase as seen in Cushing's syndrome as above.

Determining the Cause of Cushing's syndrome
- 2-3 measurements of ACTH + serum cortisol 09:00 AM
  - Cortisol >15 mcg/dL and ACTH < 5 pg/mL = primary adrenal disease
  - ACTH > 20 pg/mL = definite ACTH-dependent disease
  - ACTH 5- 20 pg/mL = equivocal
- For ACTH-independent disease, proceed with a CT scan or MRI with thin cuts through the adrenal glands to rule out an adrenal tumor or adrenal hyperplasia.
- For ACTH-dependent disease, obtain an MRI of the pituitary
  - Pituitary tumor signifies Cushing's disease and warrants neurosurgery consultation.
  - Consult endocrinologist for equivocal cases that usually require bilateral inferior petrosal sinus ACTH sampling following IV CRH administration.

Treatment of Cushing's Syndrome
- Regardless of the cause, surgical excision is the treatment of choice.

ACTH = adrenocorticotropin hormone and CRH = corticotropin releasing hormone
References: J. Clin. Endocrinol. Metab., 2003; 88: 5593-5602 and Ann. Int. Med., 2003; 138 (12): 980-91.

Diagnosis of Diabetes Mellitus (DM) in Nonpregnant State
- Symptoms of DM **and** random plasma glucose ≥ 200 mg/dL
- Fasting plasma glucose (FPG) ≥ 126 mg/dL x 2 (confirmed on a separate day)
- 2-hour 75 gm oral glucose tolerance test (OGTT) ≥ 200 mg/dL
- Impaired glucose tolerance if fasting glucose 100 -125 mg/dL or 2 hr glucose 140-199 mg/dL after 75 gm anhydrous glucose load

Criteria for Screening Asymptomatic Patients
- All people ≥ 45 years of age at least q3 years
- Recommend screening adults at a younger age q1 -2 years if overweight [body mass index (BMI) ≥ 25 kg/m²] and any of the following additional risk factors:
  - Habitually sedentary lifestyle
  - First-degree relative with diabetes
  - High-risk ethnic population (e.g., African-American, Hispanic, Native American, Asian-American or Pacific Islander)
  - History of baby weighing > 9 pound or history of gestational diabetes
  - Adult patients with hypertension or vascular disease
  - HDL ≤ 35 mg/dL or triglyceride level ≥ 250 mg/dL
  - History of impaired glucose tolerance
  - History of acanthosis nigricans or polycystic ovary syndrome (PCOS)
- May screen with FPG or 2 hr glucose tolerance test (75 gm anhydrous glucose)
- Consider screening children q2 yrs for Type 2 DM if over 10 years **and** BMI > 85% for age and sex **and** two additional risk factors:
  - **Risk factors:** first- or second-degree relative with type 2 DM, high-risk ethnic group as above, acanthosis nigricans, HTN, dyslipidemia or PCOS

Glycemic Goals for Nonpregnant Patients with DM

	AC plasma	qhs plasma	AC CBG	qhs CBG	HgbA₁c (%)
Goal range	90-130	110-150	80-120	100-140	< 7.0*
Adjustment	<90 - >150	<110 ->180	<80 - >140	<100 ->160	>8.0

AC = preprandial plasma glucose, qhs = bedtime plasma glucose, CBG = capillary blood glucose (mg/dL) and HgbA₁c=hemoglobinA₁c. * - consider goal of ≤ 6.0% in highly-motivated Type I DM patients

Classification of DM

Characteristics	Type 1	Type 2	MODY
Age at onset	Usually < 20 years	Usually > 30 years	< 25 years
Family history	10-15%	Very common	Common
DKA	Common	Very rare	Rare
Symptom onset	Sudden	Insidious	Insidious
Body habitus	Thin-normal weight	Usually obese	Usually obese
C-peptide	Low	High	Low normal
Islet cell/insulin Ab	Present	Absent	Absent
Autoimmune dzs	Often present	Rare	Rare

MODY = maturity-onset diabetes of youth, DKA = diabetic ketoacidosis, Ab = antibodies, dzs = diseases

General Management Guidelines for DM patients
- **Every visit:** check blood pressure, DM diary, weight/BMI and review meds
  - Check feet each visit for all neuropathic patients
- **Every 3 months:** check Hemoglobin A₁c
- **Annual:** fasting lipid panel, creatinine, thyroid stimulating hormone (in Type I diabetics), electrocardiogram, comprehensive foot exam, dental exam, assess for nephropathy, monofilament testing for peripheral neuropathy, dilated eye

exam by an eye specialist, influenza vaccination if ≥ 6 months of age and adult
pneumococcal vaccine (revaccinate once if > 64 yrs & last vaccination > 5 yrs)
- Tight glycemic control as above reduces the risk of microvascular
  complications: retinopathy, nephropathy and neuropathy.
- **Lipid goals:** LDL < 100 mg/dL, HDL > 40 mg/dL and triglycerides < 150 mg/dL
  ➤ Statin therapy indicated for all DM patients with known coronary or
    cerebrovascular disease **and** for those >40 yrs with total cholesterol ≥135
    mg/dL **or** who have concomitant smoking, HTN, retinopathy, nephropathy,
    left ventricular hypertrophy, peripheral arterial or carotid artery disease
- **Hypertension goals:** blood pressure (BP) < 130/80 mmHg
  ➤ Goal BP < 125/75 mmHg for nephropathy with nephrotic-range proteinuria
- Aspirin 81 mg PO daily as secondary prevention of CV disease for history of
  coronary artery, cerebrovascular, carotid artery or peripheral vascular disease
  ➤ Aspirin for primary prevention of CV disease if ≥ 40 yrs **or** any cardiac risk
    factors (HTN, smoking, dyslipidemia, positive family history or nephropathy)
- Smoking cessation counseling and dietary reminders
- Discussion of contraception or preconception counseling in young women

Diabetic Nephropathy
- Initiate screening: Type 2 DM, at diagnosis; Type 1 DM after 5 years of disease.
- Consider other causes of nephropathy in absence of retinopathy.
- Screening for microalbuminuria:
  ➤ Urine random microalbumin (mcg albumin/mg creatinine)
  ➤ Microalbuminuria = 30-299 mcg/mg and overt nephropathy = ≥ 300 mcg/mg
  ➤ 24h urine for creatinine clearance/proteinuria yearly once pt has nephropathy
- Methods to delay progression of nephropathy
  ➤ Maintain BP<130/80 for microalbuminuria, <125/75 for overt nephropathy
    o Preferred order: ACEI (angiotensin converting enzyme inhibitor) > ARB
      (angiotensin receptor blocker) > β-blockers, verapamil or diltiazem
  ➤ Restrict protein to ≤ 0.8 gm/kg ideal body weight/day
- Referral to nephrologist when creatinine clearance < 60 mL/minute

Diabetic Retinopathy
- Screening guidelines are the same as for diabetic nephropathy.
- Laser photocoagulation surgery indicated for macular edema, severe
  nonproliferative diabetic retinopathy or any proliferative diabetic retinopathy.

Diabetic Neuropathy
- May present as burning, tingling, numbness or aching in hands or feet.
- Best screening tool is use of a Semmes-Weinstein 5.07 U monofilament tool
  tested at 6 areas on each foot: plantar skin over the 1st and 5th toes, the skin
  over the 1st, 3rd and 5th metatarsal heads and the area over the heel.
- Avoid prolonged walking, jogging and step exercises.
- Treatment of DM neuropathic pain (see section on neuropathic pain): best
  evidence for tricyclic antidepressants, gabapentin, carbamazepine or tramadol.
- Rule out other causes: alcohol, B12 deficiency, hypothyroidism, uremia,
  paraneoplastic, amyloidosis, dysproteinemias, sarcoidosis, arsenic, lead,
  mercury, herbicide or pesticide poisoning and meds (isoniazid, metronidazole,
  nitrofurantoin, cisplatin, vinca alkaloids [e.g., vincristine or vinblastine], taxanes,
  tacrolimus, statins, didanosine, zalcitabine, stavudine, hydralazine or
  amiodarone)

CV = cardiovascular, LDL = low-density lipoprotein, HDL = high-density lipoprotein

Cardiovascular Disease
- Noninvasive cardiac testing for abnormal resting ECG, typical or atypical chest pain, peripheral or carotid artery disease, ≥ 2 cardiac risk factors **or** age > 35 years, sedentary lifestyle and plans to begin vigorous exercise program
- Aspirin 81 mg PO daily for primary/secondary prevention as described above

Insulins*	Rapid acting		Short acting	Intermediate acting		Long acting	
Time (hr)	lispro	aspart	regular	NPH	lente	ultralente	glargine
Onset	0.25	0.5	0.5-1	1-2	2-4	4-8	1-2
Peak	0.5-1.5	1-3	2.5-5	4-12	7-15	10-30	"flat"
Duration	4-6	3-5	6-8	12-18	18-24	24-36	24-30
Appearance	clear	clear	clear	cloudy	cloudy	cloudy	clear

N/A = not applicable. * - Continuous subcutaneous insulin pumps can be considered in highly-motivated Type I DM patients instead of multi-dose insulin injection regimens

Oral Medications for Type 2 Diabetes Mellitus

Classes	Examples	Fall in HgbA₁C	Mechanism	Contra-indications	Side effects
Sulfonylurea	glipizide glimepiride glyburide	1.5-2.0	Insulin secretagogue	Sulfa allergy	Weight gain Hypoglycemia SIADH
Biguanide	metformin	1.5-2.0	Insulin sensitizer and ↓ gluconeo-genesis	crt >1.4 (♀) crt >1.5 (♂) acute CHF cirrhosis IV contrast alcoholic	Nausea, Anorexia, Metallic taste, B₁₂ deficiency
Thiazolidine-diones	pioglitazone rosiglitazone	1-2.0	Insulin sensitizer	CHF Cirrhosis	Hepatitis Edema Anemia
Meglitinides	repaglinide nateglinide	1.5-2.0	Short-acting insulin secretagogue	Hypersensi-tivity	Weight gain Hypoglycemia Headache
Alpha-glucosidase inhibitor	acarbose miglitol	0.5-1.0	Inhibits the conversion of disaccharides to glucose	crt > 2	Nausea, Diarrhea, Flatulence

crt = creatinine, SIADH = syndrome of inappropriate antidiuretic hormone secretion and IV = intravenous

Prevention of Type II Diabetes in Patients at Risk
- High-risk patients: those with the metabolic syndrome (see hyperlipidemia section), impaired glucose tolerance or a history of gestational diabetes
- Studies of diabetes prevention have found two effective methods:
  ➤ Lifestyle modification is the best method available and consists of aerobic exercise ≥ 30 minutes most days of the week & diet→≥ **5-10% weight loss**
    ○ 58% relative risk reduction for development of DM
  ➤ Metformin 500 mg PO bid most effective if 24-44 yrs old + BMI ≥ 35 kg/m².
    ○ Equally as effective as lifestyle modification in this subset of DM pts.
  ➤ Acarbose led to a 25% relative risk reduction for development of DM.
  ➤ Thiazolidinediones and angiotensin converting enzyme inhibitors may play a role in preventing the development of DM in high risk patients.

References: Diabetes Care, 2005; 28 (Supplement 1): S4-36. Lancet, 2003; 361: 2005-16. Lancet, 2004; 364: 685-96. Ann. Intern. Med., 2002; 136: 157. NEJM, 2002; 346: 393. Lancet, 2002; 359: 2072. NEJM, 2000; 342: 145. Ann. Intern. Med., 2004; 140: 644. NEJM, 2005; 352: 174 and NEJM, 2004; 351: 1106.

Obesity Equations and Definitions
- **Body Mass Index (BMI)** = weight (kg)/(height in meters)^2
- **Normal weight** = BMI 18.5 – 24.9
- **Overweight** = BMI 25 – 29.9
- **Obese** = BMI 30 – 39.9
- **Morbidly obese** = BMI ≥ 40
- Worse prognosis if waist circumference > 40 inches (♂) and > 35 inches (♀)

Relative Risk (RR) of Developing Medical Complications Because of Obesity

Category	RR in Women*	RR in Men+
Coronary Artery Disease	3.56	2.9
Type 2 Diabetes	61 (if BMI ≥ 35)	11.2
Hypertension	4.2	3.2
Cardiovascular mortality	4.1	2.9
Cancer mortality	2.1	1.6
Cholelithiasis	3.5	3.2
Osteoarthritis	18	Not available
Congestive heart failure	2	1.8
Stroke	2.4	2.1

* - data from the Nurses' Health Study and is the relative risk for ♀ with BMI ≥ 32 vs BMI < 21
± - data from the Framingham Heart Study or the Health Professionals Follow-up Study: BMI≥30 vs BMI<21

Other Obesity-related Medical Conditions
- Gout, metabolic syndrome, steatohepatitis, obstructive sleep apnea, cancers of the breast, endometrium, colorectum and prostate, depression, hyperlipidemia, obesity-hypoventilation syndrome, anovulatory cycles and abdominal striae.

Nonpharmacologic Interventions for the Management of Obesity
- Maintenance calories = caloric intake to maintain weight = 25 kcal/kg/day
- Maintenance calories – 500 kcal/day → weight loss about 0.5 kg/week.
- Reduce daily fat intake to 30 grams for each 1,000 kcal
- Increase fiber in diet and avoid soda, juices, alcohol and sweets.
- Utilize stimulus control techniques to alter eating behavior: eat at same time while seated at same place, eliminate distractions (e.g., TV), cook small portions, slow eating pace, take a drink of water between bites, chew many times with each bite and avoid second servings, midmeal or bedtime snacks.
- 30-45 minutes of aerobic exercise 3 - 5 times a week
- Behavioral therapy to develop adaptive thinking, stress reduction & self control.
- Self-help groups such as Take Off Pounds Sensibly & Overeaters Anonymous

Pharmacologic Interventions for the Management of Obesity
- Indicated for BMI ≥ 30 or ≥ 27 **and** two obesity-related medical problems
- Sibutramine 5 – 15 mg PO daily (side effects: dry mouth, constipation, hypertension, tachycardia, insomnia, seizures and headache)
- Orlistat 120 mg PO tid within 1 hour of meals (side effects: flatulence, fecal incontinence, steatorrhea, abdominal bloating, dyspepsia and oily spotting)
- Noradrenergic drugs for use ≤ 12 weeks (side effects same as for sibutramine)
  - ➢ Phentermine 8 mg PO tid or 15-37.5 mg PO daily (extended-release)
  - ➢ Some risk of pulmonary hypertension and valvular heart disease
- SSRIs: fluoxetine 10-40 mg PO qAM and sertraline 50-200 mg PO daily (side effects: sweating, tremor, nausea, fatigue, weakness, diarrhea and insomnia)
- Bupropion 200-450 mg/day (side effects: paresthesias, insomnia & dry mouth)
- Topiramate 25-400 mg/day (side effects: paresthesias, altered taste & acidosis)

Bariatric Surgery Candidates (Roux-en-Y Gastric Bypass or Gastric Banding)
- BMI ≥ 40 or ≥ 35 + 1 obesity-related medical problems
- Failed medical + dietary therapy, compliant and no history of substance abuse
- Mentally stable patients with realistic expectations.

References: NEJM, 2002; 346 (8): 591. NEJM, 2004; 350: 1075 and Ann Int Med, 2005; 142: 525-46. A website for details on obesity treatment is www.nhlbi.nih.gov/guidelines/obesity/prctgd_c.pdf

Risk Factors for Osteoporosis

- Menopausal women
- Low calcium intake
- Alcohol and tobacco abuse
- Chronic medications: GnRH analogues, glucocorticoids, anticonvulsants, heparin, tetracyclines, rifampin, retinoic acid derivatives, cyclosporine or Depo-Provera
- Sedentary lifestyle
- Low body weight (<127 pounds)
- Chronic amenorrhea
- Caucasian or Asian ethnicity
- Family history of osteoporosis
- Medical conditions: hyperthyroidism, inflammatory bowel disease, Celiac Sprue, malabsorptive states, hyperparathyroidism, Cushing's syndrome, hyperprolactinemia, chronic renal failure, hypercalciuria, hypogonadism, acromegaly, sarcoidosis and hematologic malignancies
- Low-trauma fracture after age 45

GnRH = gonadotropin releasing hormone

Who to screen for osteoporosis

- All women 65 years or older at 2-year intervals
- Postmenopausal women with any of the following:
  - ➢ History of fractures with minimal trauma
  - ➢ Family history of osteoporosis
  - ➢ Active cigarette smokers
  - ➢ Low body weight (< 127 pounds)
  - ➢ Radiological abnormalities suggestive of osteoporosis/osteopenia
  - ➢ Any high-risk medical condition or chronic medication use as above
- Elderly men with hypogonadism or history of fracture with minimal trauma

Diagnosis of Osteoporosis

- Dual-energy x-ray absorptiometry of spine/hip to assess bone mineral density.
  - ➢ Osteoporosis if the T-score is < - 2.5
  - ➢ Osteopenia if the T-score is -1 to -2.5
- Lumbar spine: 1.5x increased fracture risk per -1 standard deviation on T-score
- Hip: 2.7x increased fracture risk per -1 standard deviation on T-score

Work-up of Osteoporosis

- Lab tests: calcium, phosphorus, intact parathyroid hormone, 25-Vitamin D level, total protein, albumin, electrolytes, liver and renal panels, complete blood count and urinary calcium. Also, check a serum testosterone in men.
- Specific tests targeted for high-risk medical conditions if clinically suspected
- Spine radiographs for patients with height loss, back pain or spinal deformity.

Management of Osteoporosis

- Initiate treatment when the central T-score is ≤ -1.5 with risk factors or ≤ -2.0
- Oral elemental calcium 500 mg with each meal and Vitamin D 800 IU/day
- Weight-bearing exercise for 30 minutes at least 3 times per week.
- Smoking and alcohol cessation
- Bisphosphonates (alendronate 70 mg PO or risedronate 35 mg PO qweek)
- Hormone replacement therapy for less than 5 years is an option.
- Selective estrogen receptor modulators are excellent for the prevention of and second-line therapy to bisphosphonates for the treatment of osteoporosis.
- Parathyroid hormone (teriparatide) 20 mcg SQ daily for those at ↑ fracture risk
- Thiazide diuretics decrease bone loss and fracture risk in hypertensive menopausal women and in people with hypercalciuria.
- Nasal calcitonin 200 IU/day: analgesia for acute vertebral compression fracture.

Follow-up of Patients on Therapy

- Repeat Dual-energy x-ray absorptiometry (DEXA) scan every 2 years.
- In the future, may follow biochemical markers of bone turnover such as urinary N-telopeptide at baseline and after 3 months of therapy to guide therapy.

References: JAMA, 2001; 285: 785. Southern Med. J., 2004; 97 (6): 537-58. Arch Int. Med., 2002; 162: 2297.

Hypokalemia Causes
- Decreased potassium intake (intake < 40 mEq/day, extremely rare)
- Increased intestinal losses (vomiting, diarrhea or laxative abuse)
- Increased renal losses (diuretics, hyperaldosteronism, hypomagnesemia, amphotericin B therapy, corticosteroid, fludrocortisone or high-dose penicillin therapy, toluene intoxication ("glue sniffing"), osmotic diuresis (e.g., uncontrolled diabetes), Bartter's syndrome and Gitelman's syndrome).
- Type I (distal) or Type II (proximal) renal tubular acidosis
- Increased cellular shift into cells: alkalosis, insulin, high-dose β-agonist use, tocolytic agents, theophylline, chloroquine intoxication and severe hypothermia.
- Hypokalemic periodic paralysis (HPP)
- Increased blood cell production: Post-therapy with vitamin B_{12}, folate or granulocyte-macrophage colony-stimulating factor (GM-CSF).

Clues to Certain Etiologies of Hypokalemia
- Metabolic acidosis: renal tubular acidosis, chronic diarrhea or toluene abuse
- Metabolic alkalosis and normotensive: vomiting (low urine chloride) or diuretics, Gitelman's syndrome versus Bartter's syndrome (high urine chloride)
- Metabolic alkalosis + Hypertension: Conn's syndrome (↓ renin/↑ aldosterone) or licorice, ectopic corticotropin or Liddle syndrome (↓ renin/↓ aldosterone)
- Hypokalemic periodic paralysis: normal potassium between paralytic episodes, positive family history, thyrotoxicosis, normal acid-base status, transtubular potassium gradient <3.0 and urine potassium/creatinine ratio < 2.5

Treatment of Hypokalemia
- IV KCl for ventricular arrhythmias, digoxin toxicity, paralysis or severe myopathy
- PO KCl 20-80 mEq/day in divided doses for all other causes except:
  ➤ Hypokalemic periodic paralysis requires no more than 40 mEq PO KCl.
  ➤ Renal tubular acidosis is treated with K-citrate, K-bicarbonate or K-acetate.

Hyperkalemia Causes
- Increased transcellular shift out of cells: metabolic acidosis, insulin deficiency, increased tissue catabolism, β₂-blockade or digitalis intoxication.
- Cellular breakdown: crush injury, severe burns, rhabdomyolysis, hemolysis
- Pseudohyperkalemia from hemolyzed blood specimen, marked leukocytosis or marked thrombocytosis.
- Decreased urinary potassium excretion: hypoaldosteronism, renal failure and ureterojejunostomy.
- Type IV renal tubular acidosis
- Excessive potassium ingestion/administration
- Tumor lysis syndrome

Treatment of Hyperkalemia (mnemonic CBIGKDrop)
C – calcium (1 ampule calcium gluconate IV for ECG changes from hyperkalemia)
B – bicarbonate (1 ampule sodium bicarbonate IV)
I – insulin (10 units regular insulin subcutaneous or IV)
G – glucose (1 ampule of 50% dextrose unless patient already hyperglycemic)
K – kayexalate (15-30 grams PO or PR)
D(rop) – Dialysis

Electrocardiogram Changes with Hypokalemia and Hyperkalemia
- Hypokalemia: ST depression→ U waves
- Hyperkalemia: peaked T waves→ PR prolongation → QRS widening→ sinusoidal pattern

References: NEJM, 1998; 339: 451-8. Crit. Care Clinics, 2002; 18: 273-88. Arch Int Med., 2004; 164: 1561-6

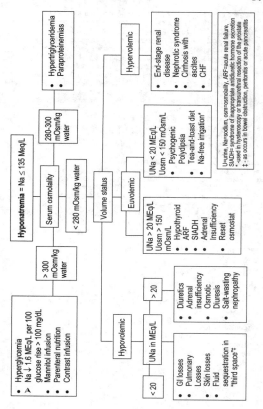

Hyponatremia = Na ≤ 135 Meq/L

Serum osmolality

- **> 300 mOsm/kg water**
  - Hyperglycemia
    - Na ↓ 1.6 MEq/L per 100 glucose rise > 100 mg/dL
  - Mannitol infusion
  - Parenteral nutrition
  - Contrast infusion

- **280–300 mOsm/kg water**
  - Hypertriglyceridemia
  - Paraproteinemias

- **< 280 mOsm/kg water** → Volume status

Volume status:

Hypervolemic
- End-stage renal disease
- Nephrotic syndrome
- Cirrhosis with ascites
- CHF

Euvolemic
- UNa < 20 MEq/L
  Uosm > 150 mOsm/L
  - Psychogenic Polydipsia
  - Tea-and-toast diet
  - Na-free irrigation*
- UNa > 20 MEq/L
  Uosm > 150 mOsm/L
  - Hypothyroid
  - ARF
  - SIADH
  - Adrenal Insufficiency
  - Reset osmostat

Hypovolemic
- UNa in MEq/L
  - < 20
    - GI losses
    - Pulmonary Losses
    - Skin losses
    - Fluid sequestration in "third space"‡
  - > 20
    - Diuretics
    - Adrenal insufficiency
    - Osmotic Diuresis
    - Salt-wasting nephropathy

U=urine, Na=sodium, osm=osmolality, ARF=acute renal failure, SIADH= syndrome of inappropriate antidiuretic hormone secretion
*=used in hysteroscopy or transurethral resection of the prostate
‡= as occurs in bowel obstruction, peritonitis or acute pancreatitis

Syndrome of Inappropriate Antidiuretic Hormone Secretion (SIADH)
- Diagnosis of exclusion; normal thyroid stimulating hormone and serum cortisol.
- Frequently associated with a low serum uric acid
- Causes: post-operative, central nervous system disorders, lung process (pneumonia, pulmonary embolus, lung cancer), delirium tremens, psychosis, cancer, medications (e.g., cyclophosphamide, opiates, chlorpropamide, clofibrate, selective serotonin reuptake inhibitors, phenothiazines, tricyclic antidepressants, vincristine, neuroleptics, nonsteroidal anti-inflammatory drugs, carbamazepine, indapamide, theophylline, amiodarone or general anesthesia)
- Treatment: remove offending meds; treat underlying condition; & fluid restrict
  - ➤ Can add demeclocycline 300-600 mg PO bid for chronic SIADH

Reset Osmostat (or "sick cell syndrome")
- Generally in patients with severe malnutrition, tuberculosis, AIDS, alcoholics, terminal cancer or pregnancy.
- Patients appropriately regulate serum osmolality around a reduced set point.

General Guidelines for the Treatment of Hyponatremia
- Hypovolemic, hypotonic hyponatremia: use isotonic saline until euvolemic
- Hypervolemic or hypotonic, euvolemic hyponatremia: free water restrict to 800-1000 mL daily in severe cases and 1500 mL daily in mild cases.
- Consider hypertonic saline +/- furosemide in the intensive care unit only for severe, symptomatic hyponatremia until Na $\geq$ 120 mEq/L
  - ➤ Use the formula below to determine the optimal intravenous drip rate
- Maximum correction of 1 mEq/L/hr and 8 mEq/L over 24 hours.
  - ➤ More rapid correction can lead to osmotic demyelination syndrome

Hypernatremia
- **Etiologies**
  - ➤ Extrarenal free water losses (skin, pulmonary or gastrointestinal)
  - ➤ Diabetes insipidus (central or nephrogenic)
  - ➤ Hypothalamic disorders (cancer, granulomatous diseases or cerebrovascular accidents)
  - ➤ Renal cause: osmotic diuresis (mannitol / glucose); postobstructive diuresis
  - ➤ Conn's or Cushing's syndromes
  - ➤ Excessive sodium administration
- **Clinical features**
  - ➤ Confusion, weakness, lethargy, and in severe cases coma
- **Treatment**
  - ➤ Initially volume replete dehydrated patients with isotonic saline
  - ➤ Once euvolemic, use the following equation to correct sodium:

$$\text{Change in serum Na} = \frac{[(\text{infusate Na} + \text{infusate K}) - \text{serum Na}]}{\text{Total body water (L)} + 1}$$

(after 1 liter infusate)

Total body water (L) = 0.6 x weight (kg) for ♂ and 0.5 x weight (kg) for ♀
  - ➤ Too rapid correction can lead to cerebral edema.

References: NEJM, 2000; 342 (20): 1493-9. NEJM, 2000; 342 (21): 1581-9 and American Family Physician, 2004; 69: 2387-94. Na = sodium and K = potassium

Etiologies of Hypothyroidism
- Thyroiditis syndromes (see table)
- Post-thyroidectomy or post-radioablation
- Panhypopituitarism: consider if low or low normal TSH and low FT4
- Medication-induced: amiodarone, antithyroid drugs, interferon-alpha, iodides, lithium, nitroprusside, phenylbutazone or sulfonylureas
- Chronic iodine deficiency

Category	Hashimoto's thyroiditis	Painless postpartum thyroiditis	Painful subacute thyroiditis	Painless sporadic thyroiditis	Painful suppurative thyroiditis
Onset	Usually 30-50 years	≤ 4 months postpartum	20-60 years	Usually 30-40 years	Children + 20-40 years
anti-TPO antibodies	High titers in 90%	High titers	Low titer or absent	High titers	Absent
ESR	Normal	Normal	High	Normal	High
24 hour - ^{123}I uptake	Variable*	< 5%	< 5%	< 5%	Normal or low

anti-TPO = anti-thyroid peroxidase antibody, ESR = erythrocyte sedimentation rate, ^{123}I = iodine 123,
* - uptake is high in rare cases of hashitoxicosis and otherwise is low

Clinical Presentation
- Signs: dry skin, coarse hair, hair thinning, delayed relaxation of reflexes, galactorrhea, growth failure, irregular menses, infertility, hypothermia, bradycardia, myxedema, mental slowing, eyebrow loss, deep, hoarse voice, constipation, weight gain, periorbital edema and macroglossia
- Symptoms: cold intolerance, fatigue, weakness, myalgias and confusion
- Complications: myxedema coma, pericardial effusion, heart block, hypertension infertility, dementia and carpal tunnel syndrome
- Labs: hyponatremia, hyperlipidemia and elevated creatinine phosphokinase

An Approach to the Patient with Suspected Hypothyroidism

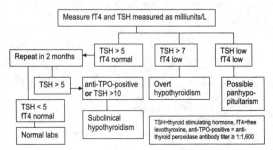

Management of Hypothyroidism
- Mean oral replacement dose of levothyroxine = 1.7 mcg/kg/day
- If patient has cardiac disease, start with levothyroxine 25-50 mcg PO daily
- If no cardiac disease, start with expected replacement dose (~100 mcg/day)
- Check TSH level q6 weeks and adjust dose until TSH 1-2.5 milliunits/L

Management of Subclinical Hypothyroidism
- Recommend therapy for TSH > 10 or anti-TPO antibody titer ≥ 1:1,600
- Desire TSH 1 - 2.5 milliunits/L

Screening for Hypothyroidism
- All women > 60 years and those with autoimmune disorders every 2-3 years
- All patients with suspicious symptoms
- Unexplained infertility, depression, dementia, hyperlipidemia, hyponatremia

Hyperthyroidism
Etiologies of Hyperthyroidism
- Graves disease: TSH receptor antibody/thyroid stimulating immunoglobulin +
- Toxic multinodular goiter or toxic thyroid nodule
- Hyperthyroid phase of thyroiditis (Hashitoxicosis, postpartum, lymphocytic or de Quervain's/Subacute thyroiditis)
- Thyroid stimulating hormone-secreting pituitary adenoma (very rare)
- Struma ovarii
- Thyrotoxicosis factitia (from exogenous thyroid hormone ingestion)
- Thyrotoxicosis of gestational trophoblastic disease
- Metastatic follicular thyroid cancer
- Amiodarone-induced hyperthyroidism (rare)
- Radiocontrast dye

Clinical Presentation of Hyperthyroidism
- Signs: diaphoresis, fine resting tremor, hyperreflexia, diarrhea, muscle weakness and wasting, diffuse goiter, irregular menses, infertility, insomnia, weight loss despite good appetite, mental slowing, warm, moist skin, onycholysis, hair loss and sinus tachycardia
- Symptoms: nervousness, hyperactive, irritability, insomnia, palpitations, heat intolerance, pruritus, loss of libido and fatigue
- Complications: atrial fibrillation, periodic paralysis, CHF and rarely psychosis

Manifestations Characteristic of Graves' Disease
- Ophthalmopathy: exophthalmos, lid retraction, lid lag +/- retrobulbar pain
- Infiltrative dermopathy: typically localized to the anterolateral aspect of the shin
- Associated with autoimmune diseases
- Typically diagnosed clinically
- Thyrotropin-receptor antibodies will be positive in 80% of patients and ^{123}I uptake scan will show diffuse uptake if etiology is in question.

References: NEJM, 2000; 343 (17): 1236-48, NEJM, 2001; 345 (7): 512-6, NEJM, 2001; 345: 260-5. NEJM, 2003; 348: 2646-55 and NEJM, 1996; 335: 99-107.

An Approach to Patients with Suspected Hyperthyroidism

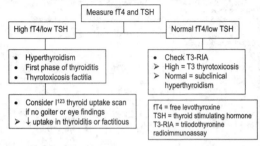

```
                    ┌─────────────────────┐
                    │ Measure fT4 and TSH │
                    └─────────────────────┘
      ┌──────────────┐                    ┌──────────────────┐
      │ High fT4/low TSH │                │ Normal fT4/low TSH │
      └──────────────┘                    └──────────────────┘
```

- Hyperthyroidism
- First phase of thyroiditis
- Thyrotoxicosis factitia

- Check T3-RIA
  ➤ High = T3 thyrotoxicosis
  ➤ Normal = subclinical hyperthyroidism

- Consider I123 thyroid uptake scan if no goiter or eye findings
  ➤ ↓ uptake in thyroiditis or factitious

fT4 = free levothyroxine
TSH = thyroid stimulating hormone
T3-RIA = triiodothyronine radioimmunoassay

Treatment Options for Hyperthyroidism
- If thyroid gland ≤ 2x normal and soft, mild-moderate hyperthyroidism, children or pregnant or lactating women, recommend using antithyroid drugs.
  ➤ Methimazole 10 - 40 mg PO daily or propylthiouracil 50 -100 mg PO tid
  ➤ Follow thyroid function tests q4-6 weeks until euthyroid then q2 months x 3 then q4-6 months. Watch for agranulocytosis, rashes and hepatotoxicity.
  ➤ Trial for 12-18 months then discontinue and monitor for hyperthyroid relapse
- If thyroid >2x normal, multinodular, hard, severe exophthalmos, atrial fibrillation, or relapse, recommend radioiodine ablation (pretreat with antithyroid drugs).
- Subtotal thyroidectomy for pregnant patients intolerant of antithyroid drugs, pediatric Graves' disease or patients refusing I131 therapy.
- Propranolol is an adjunctive agent for tachycardia, tremors & nervousness.

Treatment of Graves' Ophthalmopathy
- Graves' ophthalmopathy followed with exophthalmometer
- Use artificial tears or eye ointment at night
- Smoking cessation
- Prednisone 40-80 mg PO daily until condition stable (especially prior to I131)
- Avoid bright lights and dust

Treatment of Graves' Dermopathy
- 0.02% fluocinolone ointment applied each night under occlusion

Subclinical Hyperthyroidism
- Asymptomatic patient and non-nodular thyroid disease → follow.
- Patients symptomatic with osteoporosis or cardiac disease or have nodular thyroid disease → consider low-dose antithyroid drugs to normalize TSH.
- If symptoms resolve with therapy, can consider I131 radioiodine ablation.
- Consider referral to endocrinologist to help manage this condition.

References: NEJM, 2000; 343 (17): 1236-48, NEJM, 2001; 345 (7): 512-6, NEJM, 2001; 345: 260-5. NEJM, 2003; 348: 2646-55. NEJM, 2005; 352: 905-17 and NEJM, 1996; 335: 99-107.

Epidemiology
- Palpable thyroid nodule ≥ 1 cm in 4-7% of U.S. population: 5% are malignant

Risk Factors for malignancy
- ♂>♀, age < 20 or > 60, history of head or neck radiation, positive family history of thyroid CA, hoarseness, dysphagia, dysphonia, cervical lymphadenopathy and a nodule that is > 4 cm, nontender, hard, fixed or rapidly growing

Management of the Solitary Thyroid Nodule

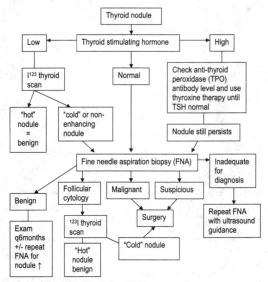

Management of Multinodular Goiters (MNG)
- Toxic multinodular goiters should be treated with ^{131}Iodine therapy
- Nontoxic MNG - FNA of any dominant nodule ≥ 1.5 cm and consider subtotal thyroidectomy for compressive symptoms or multiple high risk factors as above.

Management of Thyroid Incidentalomas
- Ultrasound-guided FNA of nodule >15 mm or 8-15 mm + ≥ 1 cancer risk factors
- Serial ultrasounds q6-12 months if thyroid nodule < 8 mm or no risk factors

References: NEJM, 2004; 351: 1764. JAMA, 2004; 292: 2632-42. Amer. Fam. Physician, 2003; 67:559.

Etiologies of Ascites
- Classification based on serum-ascites albumin gradient (SAAG)
- SAAG ≥ 1.1 gm/dL = portal hypertension (97% accuracy)

High SAAG (≥ 1.1 gm/dL)	Low SAAG (< 1.1 gm/dL)
• Cirrhotic ascites	• Peritoneal carcinomatosis
• Alcoholic hepatitis	• Peritoneal tuberculosis
• Right-sided congestive heart failure	• Pancreatic ascites
• Multiple liver metastases	• Biliary ascites
• Fulminant hepatic failure	• Nephrotic syndrome
• Budd-Chiari syndrome	• Lupus serositis
• Portal vein thrombosis	• Bowel infarction or obstruction
• Veno-occlusive disease	• Postoperative lymphatic leak
• Fatty liver of pregnancy	
• Myxedema	

Evaluation of Ascites
- Diagnostic paracentesis for all new-onset ascites and send peritoneal fluid for:
  - Protein, albumin, glucose, cell count, lactate dehydrogenase (LDH) & culture (place fluid directly into blood culture bottles for optimal yield).
  - If SAAG low, consider placing a PPD test and sending fluid for cytology

General Management of Cirrhotic Ascites
- Dietary restriction to < 2 grams sodium daily essential for successful control
- No need for fluid restriction unless severe hyponatremia with Na ≤ 125 MEq/L
- Avoid aspirin, NSAIDS and Cox-2 inhibitors and no role for bed rest

Management of Moderate Volume Cirrhotic Ascites
- Spironolactone 50-200 mg PO qAM or amiloride 5-10 mg PO daily

Management of Large Volume Cirrhotic Ascites
- Diuretic therapy (keep spironolactone/furosemide ratio approximately 5:2)
  - Begin spironolactone 100 mg PO qAM and furosemide 40 mg PO qAM
  - Double dosages q3-5days until urine Na >urine K + weight loss 1 lb/d or maximal doses of spironolactone 400 mg/furosemide 160 mg PO qAM.
  - Monitor for encephalopathy, renal insufficiency and electrolyte imbalances.

Management of Refractory Ascites (Diuretic-resistant Ascites)
- Large volume paracentesis q2-4 weeks +/- infusion of 8-10 gm albumin for each liter of ascitic fluid if more than 5 liters of ascitic fluid is removed.
- Alternative is a transjugular intrahepatic portosystemic shunt (TIPS procedure).
- Evaluate all patients with ascites for liver transplantation (60-70% 5 yr mortality)

Spontaneous Bacterial Peritonitis (SBP)
- **Clinical Features:** abdominal pain, fever, encephalopathy or asymptomatic
- **Diagnosis:** ascitic fluid neutrophils ≥ 250 or monomicrobial bacterial growth
  - Secondary bacterial peritonitis likely if ascitic white blood count >10,000/μL, glucose<50 mg/dL, LDH>250 U/L, protein>1 gm/dL or polymicrobial growth.
- **Treatment:** cefotaxime 2 gm IV q12h preferred
  - Ofloxacin 400 mg PO bid x 5 days consideration for uncomplicated SBP
  - Albumin 1.5 gm/kg IV on day 1 then 1 gm/kg IV on day 3 had a 19% absolute mortality ↓ and decreases the risk of hepatorenal syndrome.
- **Prophylaxis:** norfloxacin 400 PO mg daily or TMP-SMX DS 1 tablet PO daily.
  - Indicated for prior SBP, if ascitic fluid protein ≤ 1 gm/dL or Tbili > 2.5 mg/dL.
  - Norfloxacin 400 mg PO bid or ofloxacin 400 mg IV daily x 7d for acute variceal bleed. Improves survival and decreases the risk of SBP.

Na = sodium, K = potassium, TMP-SMX DS = trimethoprim-sulfamethoxazole DS, Tbili = total bilirubin
References: Hepatology, 2004; 39(3): 1-16. NEJM, 2004; 350: 1646-54. Mayo Clin Proc, 2000; 75: 501-9.

Definition: increased frequency (>3/day) and liquidity of stools for ≥ 4 weeks.
History
- Family history of diarrhea (inflammatory bowel disease or celiac disease)
- Follows ingestion of dairy products (lactose intolerance) or "sugar-free" foods (sorbitol-induced osmotic diarrhea)
- Recent travel (aeromonas, giardiasis, cryptosporidiosis or amebiasis)
- Previous intestinal surgery (consider "dumping syndrome")
- Abdominopelvic radiation (radiation enteritis)
- Systemic illnesses (hyperthyroidism, diabetic enteropathy, Whipple's disease, carcinoid syndrome or systemic mastocytosis)
- AIDS (opportunistic infections of colon)
- Abdominal pain out-of-proportion to tenderness (ischemic colitis)
- Crampy lower quadrant pain with altered bowel habits (irritable bowel syn.)
- Voluminous, malodorous stool (malabsorption)
- Nocturnal diarrhea (consider secretory process)
- Bloody stools: infectious colitis, ischemic colitis, inflammatory bowel disease (see page 51) or colon cancer
- Antibiotic usage in last 8 weeks, recent hospitalization or recent systemic chemotherapy (consider *Clostridium difficile* colitis)

Categories of Chronic Diarrhea

Category	Malabsorption	Inflammatory	Secretory	Osmotic
Stool osmotic gap (mOsm/kg)*	Not Applicable	Not Applicable	< 50 mOsm/kg	>125 mOsm/kg
Fecal leukocytes	Absent	Present	Absent	Absent
Hemoccult	Negative	+ or -	Negative	Negative
Nocturnal BMs	No	Possible	Yes	No

*-stool osmotic gap = 290 − 2 x (stool(sodium) + stool(potassium)), BM = bowel movement

Work-up of Chronic Diarrhea
- **Routine labs:** complete blood count, chem 7 and thyroid stimulating hormone
- **Malabsorptive diarrhea**
  ➢ Typical findings: anemia, decreased serum iron, folate, calcium, magnesium, cholesterol, albumin and carotene +/- vitamin B₁₂.
  ➢ 72 hour quantitative stool fat > 6 grams diagnostic of steatorrhea
  ➢ Etiologies: pancreatic exocrine insufficiency (screen with bentiromide or pancreolauryl tests), celiac disease (screen with antiendomysial or transglutaminase antibodies), lactose intolerance (check Lactose tolerance test with 50 gram test dose and measure serum glucose at 0, 60 and 120 minutes) or Whipple's disease (upper endoscopy with small bowel biopsy).
- **Inflammatory diarrhea**
  ➢ Stool for ova and parasites on 3 consecutive days
  ➢ Stool for clostridium difficile toxin if recent antibiotics or chemotherapy
  ➢ If no infectious cause, flexible sigmoidoscopy or colonoscopy to evaluate for inflammatory bowel disease, collagenous colitis, ischemic colitis or colon CA
- **Secretory diarrhea**
  ➢ Stool for aeromonas, microsporidia, cryptosporidia and ova + parasites
  ➢ Check stool for giardia antigen by enzyme-linked immunoassay test.
  ➢ Rule out thyrotoxicosis or diabetic enteropathy (nocturnal diarrhea)
- **Osmotic diarrhea**
  ➢ Stool for laxatives
  ➢ D-xylose test positive and stool pH < 5.6 in carbohydrate malabsorption
  ➢ Examine diet and meds for magnesium- or sorbitol-containing substances.
- **Irritable bowel syndrome** is a diagnosis of exclusion (see page 52)

References: Gastroenterology, 1999; 116: 1464. NEJM, 1995; 332: 725.

Definition: cirrhosis is the end stage of liver injury characterized by diffuse, hepatic fibrosis and replacement of the normal lobular architecture with abnormal nodules.

Etiologies of Cirrhosis in the United States
- Listed in order of prevalence: hepatitis C virus, alcohol, cryptogenic (primarily nonalcoholic steatohepatitis from obesity or diabetes), hepatitis B virus, hemochromatosis, Wilson's disease, α_1-antitrypsin deficiency & autoimmune hepatitis

Diagnosis of Cirrhosis
- Gold standard is a percutaneous liver biopsy
- Presumptive diagnosis by abnormal labs, imaging studies and exam findings
  - Imaging studies: ultrasound or radionuclide liver/spleen scan

Child-Turcotte-Pugh Scoring System for Cirrhosis Classification

Categories	1 point	2 points	3 points
Albumin (gm/dL)	>3.5	2.8-3.5	<2.8
Bilirubin (mg/dL)	<2.0	2.0-3.0	>3.0
International Normalized Ratio (INR)	< 1.7	1.7 – 2.3	> 2.3
Presence of ascites	None	Diuretic-controlled	Diuretic-resistant
Encephalopathy	None	Mild	Severe

Class A = 5 - 7 points, Class B = 8 -10 points, Class C = >10 points

Clinical Features that May be Present in Cirrhosis
- General: muscle wasting, hepatic fetor and testicular atrophy
- Skin: jaundice, spider angiomata and palmar erythema.
- Thorax: gynecomastia and pleural effusion (hepatic hydrothorax)
- Extremities: Dupuytren's contracture, white nails and clubbing
- Abdomen: ascites, caput medusae and splenomegaly
- Neurologic: confusion, decreased level of consciousness and asterixis

Work-up of Cirrhosis
- Labs: complete blood count, chem 7, liver panel and prothrombin time
- Labs to consider: Hepatitis B and C virus serologies, iron studies, antimitochondrial and anti-smooth muscle antibodies, serum ceruloplasmin, alpha$_1$-antitrypsin level & a percutaneous liver biopsy if diagnosis equivocal
- Imaging studies: abdominal ultrasound +/- duplex of portal vein blood flow

Complications of Cirrhosis
- **Gastroesophageal varices**
  - Octreotide 50 mcg/hr IV drip x 3 d after endoscopic variceal band ligation
  - Transjugular intrahepatic portosystemic shunt is a bridge to transplantation
  - Prophylaxis with propranolol 40 mg PO or nadolol 20-40 mg PO daily then titrated up to decrease resting pulse 25%
- **Ascites and spontaneous bacterial peritonitis** (see ascites section, page 45)
- **Hepatic Encephalopathy**
  - Precipitants: intestinal bleed, medications, high protein intake or infection
  - Treatments: lactulose; add oral neomycin +/- oral metronidazole if resistant
- **Hepatorenal syndrome:** diagnosis of exclusion, serum creatinine > 1.5 mg/dL and urinary indices mimic prerenal azotemia (urine sodium < 10 mEq/L)
  - No sustained renal improvement after fluid challenge and stopping diuretics
- **Hepatopulmonary syndrome:** dyspnea and deoxygenation accompanying change from a recumbent to a standing position and usually clubbing is present
  - Diagnosis with radioisotope perfusion lung scan
- **Hepatic Hydrothorax:** virtually always right-sided plus effusion +/- ascites
  - 2 gm/day sodium restriction and diuretics as per large volume ascites
  - Transjugular intrahepatic portosystemic shunt for diuretic-resistant effusions

Treatment of Decompensated Cirrhosis is an orthotopic liver transplant.

References: Hepatology, 2004; 39(3): 1-16. NEJM, 2004; 350: 1646-54. BMJ, 2003; 326: 751-2.

Clinical presentation
- Acute diarrheal illness: ≥ 3 loose bowel movements/day (< 2 weeks duration)
- Most cases are self-limited, of viral etiology, and last less than 48 hours.
- Bacterial etiology more likely if any of the following are present:
  ➢ Profuse watery diarrhea with dehydration
  ➢ Dysenteric signs: stool containing blood, mucus or pus and fever >101ºF
  ➢ Tenesmus or severe abdominal cramping pain
  ➢ Passage of ≥ 6 unformed stools/day for >48 hours
  ➢ Diarrhea in patients who are over 65 years or immunocompromised
  ➢ Presence of fecal leukocytes or fecal lactoferrin

History
- Exposure to ill contacts
- Recent travel to a developing area
- Ingestion of undercooked beef, pork, eggs or poultry, shellfish or unpasteurized dairy products
- Recent contact with turtles, reptiles or ducklings (Salmonella)
- Recent antibiotics in last 2 months or chemotherapy (*Clostridium difficile* colitis)
- Attends or employed at day care center or nursing home
- Occupation as a food handler, veterinarian or chronic caregiver
- Medical conditions: immunocompromised, HIV-positive or prior gastrectomy
- History of receptive anal intercourse
- Medication side effect (e.g., sorbitol, antacids, colchicine, antibiotics & laxatives)

Work-up Based on Category of Diarrhea
- No testing if diarrhea <48h & no dehydration **or** fever>101º **or** blood/pus in stool
- **Community-acquired or Traveler's Diarrhea**
  ➢ Stool studies if dehydration, blood/pus in stool, tenesmus or fever > 101º
  ➢ Stool culture for salmonella, shigella, campylobacter and E. coli 0157:H7 + shiga toxin if history of nonfebrile bloody diarrhea or hemolytic-uremic syn.
  ➢ Stool for clostridium difficile toxin if recent antibiotics or chemotherapy
  ➢ Stool cultures for vibrio if recent ingestion of shellfish
- **Nosocomial Diarrhea** (onset > 3 days after hospitalization)
  ➢ Stool for clostridium difficile toxin
  ➢ Check for salmonella, shigella, campylobacter +/- E. coli 0157:H7 if immunocompromised, neutropenic or suspected systemic enteric infection.
- **Persistent Diarrhea** (> 7 days)
  ➢ Check fecal leukocytes as screen for inflammatory diarrhea
  ➢ Consider stool studies for giardia, cryptosporidium, cyclospora and isospora
  ➢ If HIV-positive, add stool for microsporidia and blood cultures for mycobacterium avium complex and consider flexible sigmoidoscopy
- **Treatment**
- Oral rehydration solutions (ORS) based on World Health Organization (WHO)
  ➢ WHO-ORS or Rehydralyte solutions contain the optimal compositions.
  ➢ Home mix: ½ tsp salt, ½ tsp baking soda, 8 tsp sugar in 1 liter of water.
- Antimotility agents if patients are nontoxic and there is absence of fever, blood in stool or fecal leukocytes (e.g., loperamide or bismuth subsalicylate).
- Empiric antibiotics if severe community-acquired or traveler's diarrhea
  ➢ Oral quinolone x 5 days (7 days for *Yersinia enterocolitica*) is first choice
  ➢ Trimethoprim-sulfamethoxazole as second choice or in children
- Empiric antibiotics for severe nosocomial diarrhea or persistent diarrhea
  ➢ Metronidazole 500 mg PO tid x 10 days (Clostridium difficile or giardia)

References: NEJM, 2004; 350: 38-47 and Gastroenterol. Clin. In America, 2003; 32: 1249-67.

Indications for Testing and Treatment of Helicobacter pylori (H. pylori)
- Peptic ulcer disease (duodenal or gastric ulcers)
- Ulcer-like dyspepsia
- Chronic active or atrophic gastritis
- Mucosa-associated lymphoid tissue lymphoma
- Controversial although advised for nonulcer dyspepsia, use of chronic NSAIDS and gastroesophageal reflux disease requiring long-term acid suppression
- Recent resection of gastric cancer or first-degree relative with gastric cancer
  ➢ Gastric cancer occurs more commonly in patients infected with Helicobacter pylori compared with age-matched, uninfected counterparts.

Noninvasive Testing for Helicobacter pylori (H. pylori)

Test	Sensitivity	Specificity	Test for cure
Urea breath test (not for < 6 yrs old)	95%	95%	Yes
H. pylori serum IgG by ELISA	90-93%	95-96%	No
H. pylori whole blood IgG by ELISA	50-85%	75-100%	No
H. pylori stool antigen test‡	89-98%	92-95%	Yes

ELISA = Enzyme Linked Immunosorbent Assay, IgG = immunoglobulins

‡ = Test of cure should be done 4 weeks post-therapy and off proton pump inhibitor for ≥ 1 week

Preferred Treatment Regimens for Helicobacter pylori
- Favor treatment with any regimen for a 10-14 day course‡

Treatment regimen	Cure rate (%)
PPI* + metronidazole 500 mg bid + clarithromycin 500 mg bid	80-84%
PPI* + amoxicillin 1000 mg bid + clarithromycin 500 mg bid	80-86%
PPI daily + bismuth subsalicylate 525 mg qid + metronidazole 500 mg tid + tetracycline 500 mg qid	83-95%
bismuth subsalicylate 525 mg qid + metronidazole 250 mg qid + tetracycline 500 mg qid + H₂-blocker x 2 weeks	> 80%

*-PPI=proton pump inhibitor: oral omeprazole 20 mg bid, lansoprazole 30 mg bid or esomeprazole 40 mg daily

‡ - 10 day course for all PPI-based regimens and 14 day course for H₂-blocker and bismuth-based regimens

Bismuth subsalicylate = Pepto Bismol

PPI or H₂ blockers therapy generally continues for at least 2 weeks beyond antibiotic treatment

- Some reports that clarithromycin tid is more effective than bid dosing

Indications for Esophagogastroduodenoscopy
- New-onset dyspepsia if ≥ 50 years or associated gastrointestinal bleed
- Alarm signs: unintentional weight loss, anemia, early satiety or dysphagia
- Dyspepsia refractory to appropriate medical therapy
- Dyspepsia which recurs within 3 months of a complete 2 month treatment course for ulcer-like dyspepsia

References: Ann. Intern. Med., 2002; 136: 280-7. NEJM, 2002; 347: 1175-86. NEJM, 2001; 345: 784-9.

Hepatitis is classified into cholestatic, hepatocellular injury or infiltrative patterns.
- **Cholestasis**: alkaline phosphatase and gamma-glutamyl transpeptidase elevated more so than the elevation of the liver transaminases.
- **Hepatocellular injury**: liver transaminases ↑ > alkaline phosphatase ↑.
- **Infiltrative diseases of the liver**: usually cause marked elevations of alkaline phosphatase with disproportionately low bilirubin levels.

Cholestatic Pattern	Conditions Causing Hepatocellular injury	Medication-induced Hepatocellular injury
• Gallstones	• Alcoholic hepatitis	• acetaminophen
• Hepatocellular carcinoma	• Autoimmune hepatitis	• allopurinol
• Primary biliary cirrhosis	• Chronic viral hepatitis	• amiodarone
• Primary sclerosing cholangitis	• Nonalcoholic steatohepatitis (diabetes and obesity)	• angiotensin-converting enzyme inhibitors
• Venoocclusive disease	• Congestive hepatopathy	• cyclophosphamide
• Budd-Chiari syndrome	• Wilson's disease	• dapsone
Medications	• Hemochromatosis	• diclofenac
• allopurinol	• Alpha₁-antitrypsin deficiency	• fluconazole
• amoxicillin-clavulanate	• Ischemic hepatitis	• griseofulvin
• androgenic steroids		• halothane
• azathioprine	**Infiltrative Diseases Affecting Liver**	• heparin
• benzodiazepines	• Sarcoidosis	• hydralazine
• carbamazepine	• Tuberculosis	• isoniazid
• chlorpromazine	• Deep fungal infections	• ketoconazole
• cyclosporine	• Hepatocellular carcinoma	• labetalol
• erythromycin	• Metastatic cancer to the liver	• methotrexate
• estrogens	• Leukemic infiltrate	• methyldopa
• felbamate	• Lymphoma	• minocycline
• fluoroquinolones	**Herbal hepatotoxins**	• nefazodone
• flutamide	• amanita mushrooms	• nevirapine
• gold	• chaparral leaf	• nifedipine
• Histamine₂-blockers	• comfrey	• penicillins
• haloperidol	• germander	• phenobarbital
• mercaptopurine	• gordolobo herbal tea	• phenytoin
• methimazole	• greasewood	• piroxicam
• naproxen	• jin bu huan	• primidone
• niacin	• margosa oil	• procainamide
• nitrofurantoin	• mistletoe	• quinidine or quinine
• penicillamine	• oil of cloves	• rifampin
• phenothiazines	• pennyroyal (squawmint)	• ritonavir
• propoxyphene	• skullcap	• statins
• propylthiouracil	• valerian root	• stavudine
• pyrazinamide	• yerba herbal tea	• sulfonamides
• sulfasalazine		• tamoxifen
• sulfonylureas		• thiazolidinediones
• sulindac		• trazodone
• terbinafine		• valproic acid or divalproate
• tetracycline		• venlafaxine
		• verapamil
		• zidovudine

References: NEJM, 2000; 342: 1266-71. Gastroenterology, 2002; 123: 1364-84 and AFP, 2005; 71: 1105-10

Features	Ulcerative Colitis (UC)	Crohn's Disease (CD)
Fever	Occasionally	Common
Abdominal pain	Varies	Common
Diarrhea	Very common	Occasionally
Rectal bleeding	Very common	Occasionally
Weight loss	Occasionally	Common
Malnourished	Occasionally	Common
Perianal disease	Absent	Occasionally
Abdominal mass	Absent	Common
Growth failure	Infrequent	Common
Colonic involvement	Exclusively	Common
Ileal involvement	Absent	Common
Rectal involvement	Very common	Occasionally
Esophagus/duodenum/jejunum	Absent	Infrequent
Strictures or fistulas	Absent / rare	Common
Perforation	Infrequent	Infrequent
Cancer	Common	Occasionally
Extraintestinal manifestations*	Rare	Common
Endoscopic Findings		
Friability	Very common	Occasionally
Aphthous/linear ulcers	Absent	Common
Cobblestone appearance	Absent	Common
Pseudopolyps	Common	Occasionally
Distribution	Continuous in colon	Segmental distribution
Laboratory Findings		
p-ANCA antibodies	70% of patients	Rare
Saccharomyces cerevisiae Ab	Rare	≥ 50% of patients

p-ANCA = perinuclear antineutrophil cytoplasmic antibodies and Ab = antibodies
* - Arthralgias/arthritis, erythema nodosum, pyoderma gangrenosum, oral ulcers, episcleritis, uveitis or iritis
Table adapted from NEJM, 2002; 347: 417-29.

Medical Treatment of Inflammatory Bowel Disease
- Avoid narcotics, anticholinergics, antimotility agents and NSAIDS
- Rule out infectious colitis for any flare of CD or UC

5-Aminosalicylic Acid Derivatives for both mild-moderate CD and UC
- Sulfasalazine or olsalazine or balsalazide for colonic involvement
- Mesalamine formulations: Oral Asachol or Pentasa and Rowasa enemas
  - Asachol PO for distal ileum and colon
  - Pentasa for distal stomach and small bowel involvement by Crohn's disease
  - Rowasa enemas for distal colon and rectum

Corticosteroids for Moderate-Severe CD and UC
- Prednisone 40 mg PO daily for moderate CD and UC
- Hydrocortisone enemas or foam for ulcerative proctitis or distal UC
- Methylprednisolone 40 mg IV daily for severe CD or UC

Immunomodulating Drugs
- Azathioprine 2-2.5 mg/kg PO daily or 6-mercaptopurine 1.5 mg/kg PO daily for steroid-dependent or refractory CD or UC
- Methotrexate 25 mg SQ qweek for moderate, steroid-dependent CD
- Consider cyclosporine 4 mg/kg IV infusion x 1 for severe, refractory UC

Oral Antibiotics
- Metronidazole 500-750 mg tid or ciprofloxacin 500 mg bid for mild-moderate CD

Anti-Tumor Necrosis Factor Agents
- Infliximab 5 mg/kg IV infusion for severe, refractory or perianal, fistulizing CD

References: NEJM, 2002; 347: 417-29. AFP, 2003; 68: 707-14. Gastro Clin. N. Amer, 2004; 32: 191-250.

Rome II Criteria for Irritable Bowel Syndrome (IBS)
- At least 12 weeks of the preceding year with abdominal discomfort characterized by 2 or 3 of the following features:
  - Relieved with defecation
  - Abnormal frequency of defecation
    1. > 3 times per day or < 3 times per week
  - Change in consistency of the stool
    1. Hard/lumpy or loose/watery stools in > 25% of defecations
    2. Passage of mucus in > 25% of defecations
- IBS is a diagnosis of exclusion after all organic etiologies have been ruled out.

Other criteria to increase the diagnostic accuracy and subtype IBS
- Abnormal stool passage
  - Straining, fecal urgency or incomplete evacuation in > 25% of defecations
- Abdominal fullness or bloating > 25% of the time

Diagnostic Studies for IBS
- Complete blood count and erythrocyte sedimentation rate for all
- Electrolytes, thyroid stimulating hormone, stool for ova and parasites and giardia antigen for diarrhea-prone IBS patients
- For severe diarrhea, thyroid function tests, anti-endomysial or transglutaminase antibodies (celiac sprue), stool for ova and parasites +/- colonoscopy
- Sigmoidoscopy or colonoscopy for patients > 50 yrs or those with "alarm signs"

"Alarm" Signs and Clinical Features that Make the Diagnosis of IBS Unlikely
- Weight loss, fever, anorexia, dysphagia, anemia, leukocytosis, elevated erythrocyte sedimentation rate, chronic, severe diarrhea or GI bleeding
- Pain that is progressive, awakens the patient from sleep or prevents sleep
- Presence of an abdominal mass or organomegaly

Principles of Treatment
- **Dietary modification**
  - For pain-predominant or diarrhea-prone IBS, eliminate dairy products, fructose and sorbitol and foods that increase gas (e.g., beans, onions, celery, carrots, raisins, cabbage, broccoli and cauliflower).
  - Limit fat intake and dietary triggers that may be worsening symptoms
  - Increase fiber intake for constipation-prone IBS
- **Psychotherapy** and lifestyle modification to ameliorate psychosocial stressors.
- **Daily aerobic exercise** and good sleep hygiene
- Validate patient's symptoms and remain non-judgmental

Medications for Irritable Bowel Syndrome
- **Abdominal cramps or Pain-predominant IBS**
  - Antispasmodic agents may offer marginal benefit.
    1. Dicyclomine 10-20 mg PO qid, hyoscyamine 0.125–0.25 mg PO q4h, belladonna 0.3-1.2 mg PO qid or clidinium bromide 2.5-5 mg PO qid
  - Tricyclic antidepressants
    1. 10-75 mg qhs of amitriptyline, desipramine, clomipramine or doxepin
- **Irritable Bowel Syndrome with Diarrhea**
  - Loperamide 4 mg PO x 1 then 2 mg PO after each unformed stool
  - Cholestyramine 4 gm PO qAC can be an adjunct for refractory diarrhea
  - Alosetron 0.5-1 mg PO daily-bid for women with severe symptoms
    1. Observe carefully for obstipation or ischemic colitis
- **Irritable Bowel Syndrome with Constipation**
  - Milk of magnesia, lactulose and polyethylene glycol-based solutions
  - Tegaserod 6 mg PO bid for women with severe symptoms and for ≤ 12 wks
- **Other agents that may be beneficial for IBS**
  - Peppermint oil, clonidine, leuprolide and simethicone

References: Gut, 1999; 45(supplement 2): 43. NEJM, 2003; 349: 2136-46. Amer. J. Gastroenterology, 2002; 97 (11) Supplement: S1-S5.

Gastroenterology: Upper Abdominal Pain 53

Categories	Peptic Ulcer Disease	Biliary Colic	Gastritis	GERD
Character of pain	• Burning • Sharp	• Crampy • Sharp	• Dull • Burning	• Burning
Radiation of pain	• Penetrating ulcers radiate to back	• Right scapula	• None	• Retrosternal chest to throat
Exacerbating factors	• Alcohol • NSAIDS • Excessive caffeine	• Fatty foods	• Alcohol • NSAIDS	• Supine • Fatty foods • Chocolate • Alcohol
Alleviating factors	• Antacids	• None	• Antacids	• Upright position
Risk Factors	• Smoking • NSAIDS • Salicylates • Steroids • Stress • Alcohol • Age > 60 y • H. pylori infection • + Family history	• Female • Middle age • Obese • Positive family history	• Same as in ulcer disease • H. pylori infection	• Obese • Pregnancy • Alcohol • Smoking
Nocturnal pain	• DU usually 12 – 2 AM	• No	• No	• Yes if supine
Relationship with meals	• DU 2-5 hrs after meal • GU pain 30-60 min. after meals	• Pain 30 - 180 min. after meals	• Pain soothed by bland meals	• Postprandial pain in supine position
Antacids help	• Yes	• No	• Yes	• Yes
Associated symptoms	• Anorexia • Nausea • Bloating • Belching	• Nausea • Vomiting • Anorexia	• Nausea	• Acid taste in mouth • Hoarseness • Dry cough
Diagnostic tests	• EGD • UGI study 2nd option	• Abdominal ultrasound	• EGD	• EGD • Esophageal pH probe

H. pylori = Helicobacter pylori, DU = duodenal ulcer, GU = gastric ulcer, UGI study = Upper GI contrast study
EGD = esophagogastroduodenoscopy, GERD = gastroesophageal reflux disease

Category	18-25 yr	26-39 yr	40-49 yr	50-64 yr	≥ 65 yr
Health maintenance exam	q5 yr	q2-3 yr	q1-2 yr	Annually	Annually
Ht, Wt, BP and BMI	q2-4 yr	q2-3 yr	q1-2 yr	q1-2 yr	q1-2 yr
Clinical breast exam	q3 yr	q2-3 yr	Annually	Annually	Annually
Self breast/ testicular exam	Monthly	Monthly	Monthly	Monthly	Monthly
Digital rectal exam	-	-	q3-4 yr	Annually	Annually
Pelvic exam + pap smear[1]	q1-3 yr	q1-3 yr	q1-3 yr	q1-3 yr	-
Chlamydia and gonorrhea screen[2]	q 6 mo.	Annually	-	-	-
Mammogram[3]	-	-	Annually	Annually	Annually
Fecal occult blood testing	-	-	-	Annually	Annually
Colon CA screen[4]	-	-	-	q5-10 yr	q5-10 yr
Osteoporosis test[5]	-	-	-	-	q2 yr
Prostate CA screen[6]	-	-	-	-	?annually
Depression screen	with HME	with HME	with HME	with HME	with HME
Lipoprotein levels[7]	q5 yr	q5 yr	q5 yr	q5 yr	q5 yr
Fasting glucose	-	-	q3 yr	q3 yr	q3 yr
Thyroid stimulating hormone[8]	-	-	-	-	q2 yr
HIV, gonococcal & VDRL screening[9]	q1-2 yr	q1-3 yr	q1-3 yr	-	-

HME = Health maintenance exam, Ht = Height, Wt = Weight, BP = blood pressure, BMI = body mass index, CA = cancer, HIV = Human Immunodeficiency virus, VDRL = Venereal Disease Research Laboratory test

1 – Annual screening starts at age 18 or when sexually active. If no cervical cancer risk factors, no history of abnormal pap smears and 3 consecutive normal paps, can screen q3 years and then can stop screening at age 65 with a history of normal pap smears or earlier after hysterectomy performed for a benign indication.

2 – Screen all sexually active women 18-25 q6 months and annually in women over age 25 years if practicing unprotected sex with multiple partners

3 – United States Preventive Services Task Force (USPSTF) states that there is insufficient evidence to recommend for or against screening mammography in women over 70 years old.

4 – Colonoscopy every 10 years or flexible sigmoidoscopy and air-contrast barium enema every 5 years with annual fecal occult blood testing for either method starting at age 50 years.

5 – Screen with dual-energy x-ray absorptiometry to assess bone mineral density. May screen postmenopausal women with osteoporosis risk factors or elderly men with hypogonadism

6 – USPSTF does **not** recommend routine prostate-specific antigen, digital rectal exam or transrectal ultrasound tests for prostate cancer screening, although some societies advocate an annual digital rectal exam and state that prostate-specific antigen screening is controversial.

7 – Start screening at age 20

8 – May offer to women in this age group

9 – Should be offered to sexually promiscuous patients and to homosexual men

Category	18-25 yr	26-39 yr	40-49 yr	50-64 yr	≥ 65 yr
Tetanus toxoid (dT)	q10 yr	q10 yr	q10 yr	q10 yr	q10 yr
MMR vaccine[1]	1 dose if not pregnant, nonimmune and born after 1957				
Menactra (meningococcal vaccine)	1 dose at 11-12 years, catch-up vaccination at high school entry or for freshman college dormitory students				
Varicella vaccine	1 dose if not pregnant without prior chickenpox or zoster				
Influenza vaccine[2]	-	-	-	-	Annually
Pneumovax[3]	-	-	-	-	Single dose
Calcium intake/day[4]	1,200	1,200	1,200	1,200	1,500
Vitamin D 800 IU/d	yes	yes	yes	yes	yes
Get-up-and-go test (fall prevention)	-	-	-	-	Annually
Hearing impairment	-	-	-	-	Annually

Counseling topics and Examinations for every health maintenance visit
- Nutritional assessment and weight loss counseling for obese patients
- Injury prevention: seat belt and helmet use, firearms in house, water safety
- Substance abuse screening
- Smoking cessation counseling
- Safe sex counseling
- Encourage regular exercise
- Complete skin exam with every health maintenance exam

1 – MMR = measles mumps and rubella vaccine
2 – Annually for all people ≥ 65 or with chronic cardiopulmonary disease, renal failure, pregnant, diabetes, sickle cell disease, asplenia or immunocompromised
3 – Single dose for all people ≥ 65 or earlier for those with chronic cardiopulmonary disease, renal failure, DM, sickle cell disease, asplenia or are immunocompromised
4 – Daily calcium intake expressed in milligrams of elemental calcium (% elemental calcium in different calcium salts: calcium carbonate, 40%; calcium chloride, 27%; calcium phosphate, 23%; calcium citrate, 21%; calcium lactate, 13% and calcium gluconate, 9%)

Modified from recommendations by the American Academy of Family Physicians, The Advisory committee on Immunization Practices, American Cancer Society, the National Cancer Institute (www.cancer.gov), U.S. Preventive Services Task Force Guide to Clinical Preventive Services, 2005 (www.ahcpr.gov/clinic/uspstfix.htm) and the Centers for Disease Control

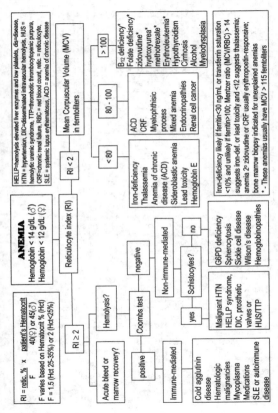

HELLP=hemolysis elevated liver enzymes and low platelets, dis=disease, HTN = hypertension, DIC=disseminated intravascular hemolysis, HUS = hemolytic uremic syndrome, TTP=thrombotic thrombocytopenic purpura, CRF=chronic renal failure, RBC = red blood count, retic. = reticulocyte, SLE = systemic lupus erythematosus, ACD = anemia of chronic disease

ANEMIA
Hemoglobin < 14 g/dL (δ)
Hemoglobin < 12 g/dL ($\female$)

$RI = retic. \% \times \dfrac{\text{patient's Hematocrit}}{F}$

F 40($\female$) or 45(δ)

F varies based on Hematocrit % (Hct)
F = 1.5 (Hct 25-35%) or 2 (Hct <25%)

Reticulocyte index (RI)

RI < 2

Mean Corpuscular Volume (MCV) in femtoliters

> 100
- B12 deficiency*
- Folate deficiency*
- zidovudine*
- hydroxyurea*
- methotrexate*
- Erythroleukemia*
- Hypothyroidism
- Cirrhosis
- Alcohol
- Myelodysplasia

80 - 100
- ACD
- CRF
- Myelophthisic process
- Mixed anemia
- Endocrinopathies
- Renal cell cancer

< 80
- Iron-deficiency
- Thalassemia
- Anemia of chronic disease (ACD)
- Sideroblastic anemia
- Lead toxicity
- Hemoglobin E

Iron-deficiency likely if ferritin<30 ng/mL or transferrin saturation <10% and unlikely if ferritin>100; Mentzer ratio (MCV/RBC) > 14 suggests thalassemia and <12 suggests iron-def.; anemia 2° zidovudine or CRF usually erythropoetin-responsive; bone marrow biopsy indicated for unexplained anemias
* These anemias usually have MCV > 115 femtoliters

RI ≥ 2

Hemolysis?

negative

no
- G6PD deficiency
- Spherocytosis
- Sickle cell disease
- Wilson's disease
- Hemoglobinopathies

Coombs test

Non-immune-mediated

Schistocytes?

yes
- Malignant HTN
- HELLP syndrome,
- DIC, prosthetic
- valves or
- HUS/TTP

positive

Acute bleed or marrow recovery?

Immune-mediated
- Cold agglutinin disease
- Hematologic malignancies
- Mycoplasma
- Medications
- SLE or autoimmune disease

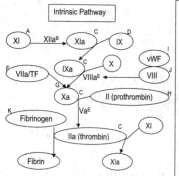

Intrinsic Pathway

A = FXI deficiency
B = FXII deficiency
C = Antithrombin III action
D = FIX deficiency (Hemophilia B or Christmas disease)
E = Proteins C & S action
F = Tissue Factor (TF) or extrinsic pathway
G = TF pathway inhibitor
H = prothrombin deficiency
I = vWF (von Willebrand's factor) binds to FVIII to ↓ FVIII concentration and activity
J = FVIII deficiency or (Hemophilia A)
K = fibrinogen deficiency or dysfibrinogenemia

Coagulation Studies for Various Bleeding Diatheses

Disorder	PTT	PTT with mixing study	PT	Other tests
vWD	↑	NL	NL	RCA + RIPA decreased and low vWD antigen
Hemophilia A	↑	NL	NL	RCA NL and FVIII ↓
Hemophilia B	↑	NL	NL	decreased FIX
Inhibitors to fibrinogen, II, V or X	↑	↑	↑	PT ↑ with mixing study
Inhibitors to VIII, IX, XI or XII	↑	↑	NL	Direct inhibitor testing
FVII deficiency	NL	NL	↑	decreased FVII
FXI deficiency	↑	NL	NL	decreased FXI
FXII deficiency	↑	NL	NL	decreased FXII
Prothrombin deficiency	↑	NL	↑	decreased prothrombin
Fibrinogen deficiency	↑	NL	↑	↓ fibrinogen, ↑ TCT
Vitamin K deficiency	↑	NL	NL/↑	Normal TCT
DIC	↑	NL	↑	↓ PLT, ↑ TCT, ↓ fibrinogen, ↑ D-Dimer

vWD = von Willebrand's disease, Roman numerals refer to specific clotting factors, RCA = ristocetin cofactor activity, RIPA = ristocetin-induced platelet aggregation, PTT = partial thromboplastin time, PT = prothrombin time, TCT = thrombin clotting time, NL = normal, BT = bleeding time, PLT = platelets, Fib = fibrinogen, FSP = fibrin split products and DIC = disseminated intravascular coagulation

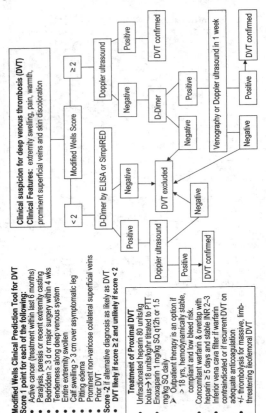

Clinical suspicion for deep venous thrombosis (DVT)
Clinical Features: extremity swelling, pain, warmth, prominent superficial veins and skin discoloration

Modified Wells Clinical Prediction Tool for DVT
Score 1 point for each of the following:
- Active cancer (treatment within last 6 months)
- Paralysis, paresis or recent extremity casting
- Bedridden ≥ 3 d or major surgery within 4 wks
- Tenderness along deep venous system
- Entire extremity swollen
- Calf swelling > 3 cm over asymptomatic leg
- Pitting edema
- Prominent non-varicose collateral superficial veins
- Prior DVT

Score -2 if alternative diagnosis as likely as DVT
- **DVT likely if score ≥ 2 and unlikely if score < 2**

Treatment of Proximal DVT
- Unfractionated heparin 80 units/kg bolus→18 units/kg/hr titrated to PTT
- Enoxaparin 1 mg/kg SQ q12h or 1.5 mg/kg SQ daily
  ➤ Outpatient therapy is an option if > 18 yrs, hemodynamically stable, compliant and low bleed risk.
- Concomitant warfarin & overlap with heparin ≥ 5 days and stable INR 2–3
- Inferior vena cava filter if warfarin contraindicated or if recurrent DVT on adequate anticoagulation
- +/- thrombolysis for massive, limb-threatening ileofemoral DVT

Modified Wells Score

< 2 → D-Dimer by ELISA or SimpliRED
- Positive → Doppler ultrasound
  - Positive → DVT confirmed
  - Negative → DVT excluded
- Negative → DVT excluded

≥ 2 → Doppler ultrasound
- Positive → DVT confirmed
- Negative → D-Dimer
  - Positive → Venography or Doppler ultrasound in 1 week
    - Positive → DVT confirmed
    - Negative → DVT excluded
  - Negative → DVT excluded

Testing Recommendations for Thrombophilia in Venous Thrombosis
- **Strongly thrombophilic states**
  - ➤ Idiopathic VTE<50 yr, Recurrent VTE or first-degree relative with VTE<50 yr
- **Weakly thrombophilic states**
  - ➤ Idiopathic VTE ≥ 50 yrs and no family history of thrombophilia
- **Timing for testing of hypercoagulable states**
  - ➤ Can check for Factor V Leiden and prothrombin gene mutation immediately
  - ➤ Check the other lab tests after anticoagulation completed and patient has been off of warfarin for at least two weeks.

Clinical Conditions	Tests to Consider Checking
Strongly thrombophilic states	APC resistance by PCR, prothrombin gene mutation, anticardiolipin antibody, lupus anticoagulant, & levels of plasma homocysteine, antithrombin III , protein C, ↑ FVIII and protein S
Weakly thrombophilic states	APC resistance by PCR, prothrombin gene mutation, anticardiolipin antibody, lupus anticoagulant, and plasma homocysteine level
DVT in unusual site	Levels of Proteins C and S and antithrombin III
Recurrent miscarriages/stillbirths	Anticardiolipin antibody and lupus anticoagulant
VTE during pregnancy or with use of oral contraceptive pills or HRT	APC resistance by PCR, levels of antithrombin III , proteins C & S & prothrombin gene mutation

HRT = hormone replacement therapy, APC = activated protein C and PCR = polymerase chain reaction

Suggested Work-up for Acquired Hypercoagulable States after VTE event
- Thorough history and exam (including breast, pelvic and rectal exam), fecal occult blood testing, urinalysis, complete blood count with peripheral blood smear, chemistry panel, chest x-ray, mammogram (♀>40 yrs), prostate specific antigen (♂ > 50 yrs) and colonoscopy (> 50 yrs) to evaluate for malignancy.
- Urinalysis and serum albumin to screen for nephrotic syndrome
- Inquire about GI symptoms that may represent inflammatory bowel disease.
- Examine patient for orogenital ulcers, uveitis & skin lesions (Behcet's disease).
- Inquire about the use of hormonal medications, tamoxifen or raloxifene.

Conditions Associated with Premature Arterial Thrombosis
- Antiphospholipid syndrome
- Hyperhomocysteinemia
- Elevated lipoprotein(a) levels

Screening Asymptomatic Family Members for Genetic Thrombophilia
- No consensus about screening family members of patients with thrombophilia
- Consider screening family members who are contemplating pregnancy or treatment with hormonal contraception or hormone replacement therapy.
- No role for long-term anticoagulation of asymptomatic patients with inherited thrombophilia and no history of a deep venous thrombosis/pulmonary embolus.

Indefinite Anticoagulation in High-Risk Patients with Thrombophilia
- At least two unprovoked venous thromboembolic events
- One spontaneous life-threatening thrombotic event
- One spontaneous thrombosis at an unusual site
- Idiopathic VTE with active cancer, antiphospholipid syndrome or antithrombin III deficiency

References: Ann Int Med, 2001; 135: 367-73. Clin. in Chest Med., 2003; 24: 153-70. NEJM, 1998; 338: 1169.

Definition: any white blood count >11,000 per µL is elevated, but typical work-ups are not initiated unless white blood count persistently elevated > 15-20,000 per µL.

Causes of Leukocytosis

Spurious	Secondary
• Mixed cryoglobulinemia • Platelet clumping (0.1% of blood draws) **Primary** • Hereditary neutrophilia • Chronic idiopathic neutrophilia • Myeloproliferative disorders ➤ Chronic myelogenous leukemia ➤ Polycythemia vera ➤ Essential thrombocythemia ➤ Agnogenic myeloid metaplasia • Acute and chronic lymphocytic leukemias • Down syndrome	• Infection • Stress reaction • Chronic anxiety • Post-traumatic stress disorder • Severe burns or electric shock • Major operation or trauma • Myocardial infarction • Cigarette smoking • Meds [glucocorticoids, lithium, catecholamines, β-agonists, granulocyte/ macrophage-colony stimulating factor (GM-CSF) and all-trans retinoic acid] • Solid tumors (e.g., lung, renal cell and breast cancer) • Heat stroke • Chronic hemolysis (e.g., sickle cell or hemoglobin SC disease) • Asplenia • Recent vaccination or envenomation • Pregnancy • Sweet's syndrome

Causes of Severe Leukocytosis > 50,000/µL
• **Chronic myelogenous leukemia**
  ➤ Leukocyte alkaline phosphatase (LAP) low and positive Philadelphia chromosome [or positive polymerase chain reaction or fluorescence in-situ hybridization (FISH) test for the bcr-abl translocation]
• **Leukemoid reaction** from sepsis, metastatic cancer, all-trans retinoic acid or GM-CSF therapy
  ➤ Serum leukocyte alkaline phosphatase normal or high

How the Complete Blood Count Differential Can Narrow the Possibilities
• Presence of Dohle bodies, toxic granulations or cytoplasmic vacuoles
  ➤ 80% sensitivity for chronic inflammatory or infectious process
• Presence of polycythemia suggests polycythemia vera especially with eosinophilia, thrombocytosis, microcytic indices and usually high LAP
• Thrombocytosis
  ➤ Infection, chronic inflammation, malignancy or essential thrombocythemia
• Monocytosis can be from steroid use, pregnancy, asplenia, tuberculosis or chronic myelomonocytic leukemia
• Hypereosinophilic syndromes: absolute eosinophil count > 1,500/mm³ for > 6 months and end-organ dysfunction
  ➤ Etiologies include hypereosinophilic syndrome, eosinophilic leukemia, Churg-Strauss syndrome, eosinophilic gastroenteritis, eosinophilic pneumonia or helminthic infections (ascariasis, hookworms, strongyloides, trichinosis, visceral larva migrans, loiasis, onchocerciasis, schistosomiasis, clonorchiasis, paragonimiasis, fascioliasis and fasciolopsiasis)

Absolute Neutrophil Count (cells/mm³)	Risk of Bacterial Infection
> 1000	No significant risk
500-1000	Some infection risk if ANC<750. Outpatient therapy unless ill or febrile
200-500	Significant risk of infection. Usually inpatient management
< 100	Very high risk of infection

Etiologies of Neutropenia

Acquired		Congenital
Bacterial infection	Rickettsial infection	Chediak-Higashi syndrome
Leukemia	Viral: HBV, HCV, HIV, EBV	Cyclic neutropenia
Felty's syndrome*	Hemodialysis	Shwachman-Diamond-Oski syn.
Acute respiratory distress syndrome	Drug-induced	Severe infantile agranulocytosis
Autoimmune	Systemic lupus erythematosus	Reticular dysgenesis
B₁₂ deficiency	Myelodysplastic syndrome	
Aplastic anemia	Chronic idiopathic	
	Alcoholism	
	Chemotherapy	
	Folate deficiency	
	Transfusion rxn	

HBV/HCV = Hepatitis B or C virus, HIV = human immunodeficiency virus, EBV = Epstein Barr virus, * - Felty's syndrome = rheumatoid arthritis with splenomegaly and neutropenia, rxn = reaction

Drug-induced Neutropenia*

acetazolamide	dapsone‡	IV immune globulin	quinine or quinidine‡
amiodarone	ethosuximide	macrolides	spironolactone
amphotericin B#	flecainide	methimazole	sulfasalazine#
ACE inhibitors#	flucytosine‡	NSAIDS	sulfonamides#
azathioprine#	foscarnet#	penicillamine	Thiazide diuretics‡
carbamazepine#	furosemide	semisynthetic PCN	ticlopidine#
cephalosporins‡	ganciclovir#	phenothiazines#	tolbutamide
chloramphenicol‡	gold salts#	phenytoin‡	tricyclic antidepressants
chloroquine‡	H₂-blockers#	procainamide#	valproic acid‡
chlorpropamide	isoniazid	propranolol	vancomycin
clozapine#	isotretinoin	propylthiouracil#	zidovudine#

* - Drug-induced neutropenia usually resolves 1-3 weeks after stopping offending drug, H₂-blockers = Histamine₂-receptor antagonists and PCN = penicillins, # - prominent incidence, ‡ - rare incidence

Outpatient Management of Fever and Neutropenia in Patients with Cancer

- Empiric antibiotics if ANC<500 cells/mm³ and oral temperature≥38.3°C (101 °F)
- Check blood, urine and sputum cultures (if cough), a chest x-ray, complete blood count with differential, chemistry panel and stool for clostridium difficile toxin in patients with diarrhea. Lumbar puncture only if meningismus present.
- Outpatient management if patient at "low risk" for serious infection: nontoxic; age<60 years; both absolute neutrophil and monocyte counts ≥100 cells/mm³; normal chest x-ray, normal liver and renal panels; none of the following: intravenous catheter site infection, abdominal pain, hypotension, hypoxia, vomiting, diarrhea, chronic lung disease, neurologic or mental status changes, prior fungal infection; malignancy is in remission; neutropenia duration <7 days; signs of bone marrow recovery; peak temp.<39.0°C and community-acquired.
  - ➢ Multinational Association for Supportive Care in Cancer predictive model score ≥ 21 also predicts "low risk" neutropenic patients (www.mascc.org).
- Ciprofloxacin 500 mg PO bid + amoxicillin-clavulanate 875 mg PO bid
- If an etiologic agent is identified, tailor antibiotics based on culture sensitivities.
- If no etiologic agent is found, antibiotics are continued for 7 days if afebrile for 48 hours and ANC ≥ 500 cells/mm³.
- If ANC < 500 cells/mm³ after 7 days of antibiotic therapy and patient is stable, continue oral antibiotics until patient afebrile for 5 days.

References: JAMA, 1994; 271: 935. CID, 2002; 34: 730-51 and CID, 2004; 39:S32-67

Clinical Features of Pulmonary Embolism (PE):
Dyspnea, pleuritic chest pain, cough, hemoptysis, tachycardia, tachypnea, fever or pleural rub

Low PTP and D-Dimer <=500 ng/mL rules out a pulmonary embolism

Wells Clinical Prediction Tool for PE

Clinical Characteristics	Points
- Signs/symptoms of DVT	3
- Alternative diagnosis less likely then PE	3
- Heart rate >100	1.5
- Immobilization or surgery in last 4 weeks	1.5
- Prior venous thromboembolic event (VTE)	1.5
- Hemoptysis	1
- Cancer treatment or palliation in last 6 months	1

Low pretest probability < 2 points
Intermediate pretest probability 2-6 points
High pretest probability > 6 points

Flowchart:

Intermediate or High PTP or Low PTP with D-Dimer > 500 ng/mL → Choose lung imaging study

- Multidetector CT pulmonary angiogram → Positive → PE confirmed; Negative → Low or interm. PTP → PE excluded; High PTP → DUS‡ → Positive → VTE event confirmed; Negative → PE excluded

- V/Q scan:
  - Normal → Low PTP → PE Excluded; Interm PTP → Observe if DUS‡ negative; High PTP → Pulmonary angiogram# if DUS‡ negative
  - Low probability → Low PTP → PE Excluded; Interm or High PTP → Pulmonary angiogram# if DUS‡ negative
  - Interm. probability → Low PTP → Pulmonary angiogram# if DUS‡ negative; Interm or High PTP → PE confirmed
  - High probability → PE confirmed

Key: * - D-Dimer by ELISA or new generation latex agglutination assay <=500 ng/mL is negative ‡ - DUS = duplex ultrasound test of extremity # - Multidetector CT and traditional pulmonary angiograms are equivalent. PTP = pretest probability, V/Q scan = ventilation/perfusion scan. Interm = intermediate

References: AFP, 2004; 69: 2829-36. Ann Intern Med, 2004; 140: 589-602. Am. Heart Hosp, 2003: 1: 281-8. Am J Med, 2004; 116: 291-9. NEJM, 2003; 349: 1227-35. NEJM, 2004; 351: 268-77. JAMA, 2005; 293: 2012-7 and NEJM, 2005; 352: 1760-8.

Definition: Platelet count < 150,000 cells/μL (abbreviated as 150K)
Clinical Presentation: asymptomatic or petechiae, purpura, ecchymoses, epistaxis, menorrhagia, hematuria, GI bleed or spontaneous intracranial bleeds
Risks of Complications at Different Platelet Counts
- > 50K: major surgery safe
- 20 – 50K: risk of major bleeding low
- 10 – 20K: risk of mild-mod. bleeding (low risk for spontaneous hemorrhage)
- < 10K: high risk for spontaneous hemorrhage (especially if < 5K)
- Consider platelet transfusion if platelets < 5-10K or active bleeding (avoid in hemolytic uremic syndrome [HUS], thrombotic thrombocytopenic purpura [TTP] and try to avoid in antiphospholipid antibody syndrome, heparin-induced thrombocytopenia or severe idiopathic thrombocytopenic purpura).
  - ➢ 1 unit random donor platelets usually increases platelet count ~10K
  - ➢ 1 unit single donor platelets usually increases platelet count ~50K

Etiologies
- **Pseudothrombocytopenia** (platelet clumping in 0.1% of all blood draws)
- **Decreased Platelet Production**
  - ➢ Congenital causes (e.g., May-Hegglin, Bernard-Soulier and aplastic anemia)
  - ➢ Myelodysplasia (> 60 years) or lymphoproliferative disorders
  - ➢ Meds/Toxins: alcohol, thiazide diuretics, estrogens, ganciclovir and chemotherapy or radiation therapy
  - ➢ Vitamin deficiencies: B₁₂ or folate
  - ➢ Infection: sepsis, tuberculosis, measles, HIV, rubella, mumps, parvovirus, varicella virus, hepatitis B virus and hepatitis C virus
- **Immune-mediated Platelet Destruction** (most common mechanism)
  - ➢ Idiopathic thrombocytopenic purpura (ITP): diagnosis of exclusion with isolated thrombocytopenia, normal peripheral blood smear and spleen size
  - ➢ SLE, antiphospholipid antibody syndrome or transfusion reaction
  - ➢ Meds (likely): abciximab, cephalosporins, clopidogrel, gold, heparins, inamrinone, penicillins, quinidine, quinine, rifampin, rifabutin, trimethoprim-sulfamethoxazole and valproate
  - ➢ Meds (less likely): acetaminophen, allopurinol, amiodarone, amphotericin B, aspirin, carbamazepine, colchicine, danazol, didanosine, digoxin, dipyridamole, disopyramide, ethambutol, fluconazole, furosemide, hydroxychloroquine, indinavir, interferons, isoniazid, NSAIDs, penicillamine, phenothiazines, phenytoin, procainamide, ranitidine, spironolactone, sulfasalazine, ticlodipine and vancomycin
  - ➢ Infection: cytomegalovirus, toxoplasmosis, HIV and Epstein-Barr virus
- **Non-immune-mediated Platelet Destruction**
  - ➢ Disseminated intravascular coagulopathy, HUS/TTP, vasculitis, prosthetic valve, Hemolysis Elevated Liver enzymes Low Platelets (HELLP syndrome) or malignant hypertension
- **Splenic sequestration** (platelets usually > 40K)
  - ➢ Portal hypertension, Gaucher's disease, lymphoma/leukemias, severe CHF
- **Gestational** (5% of all pregnancies in late 3ʳᵈ trimester. Platelets usually >70K)
- **Dilutional**: Usually follows massive blood transfusion

Work-up
- Good history/exam assessing spleen size, any lymphadenopathy & med list
- Examine peripheral blood smear for platelet clumping and schistocytes
- Are other cell lines and differential normal?
- Check mean platelet volume (MPV) – usually high with platelet destruction
- Labs: complete blood count with differential and coagulation studies (other labs will depend on most likely etiologies as above)
- Anti-platelet antibodies **not** useful for diagnosing routine or classic ITP
- Consider bone marrow biopsy if etiology unclear at any age or patient > 60 yrs

References: Mayo Clin. Proc, 2004; 79: 504. Ann Int Med, 2001; 134: 346. Lancet, 1997; 349: 1531-6.

Risk Factors for Venous Thromboembolic Events (VTE)

Advanced age > 75	Obesity
Prolonged immobility	Chronic congestive heart failure
Recent trauma or severe burns	Inflammatory bowel disease
Previous deep venous thrombosis or pulmonary embolus	Abdominal, orthopedic, pelvic or brain surgery (major surgeries) in last 4 weeks
Active cancer	Nephrotic syndrome
Stroke or paralysis	Pregnancy or oral contraceptive pill use
Inherited hypercoagulable state	Behcet's syndrome
Family history of venous thromboembolic events or thrombophilia	
Medications: tamoxifen, raloxifene, thalidomide, emcyte or systemic chemotherapy	

Treatment of Deep Venous Thrombosis or Pulmonary Emboli

- Unfractionated heparin 80 units/kg bolus→18 units/kg/hr titrated to PTT
- Enoxaparin 1 mg/kg SQ q12h or 1.5 mg/kg SQ daily
  - ➤ Avoid low molecular weight heparins (LMWH) when serum creatinine >3.0
  - ➤ For VTE with cancer, use LMWH for initial 3 - 6 months of anticoagulation.
- Start warfarin after adequate heparinization and overlap with heparin at least 5 days and stable INR 2-3
- Inferior vena cava filter if warfarin contraindicated or if recurrent deep venous thrombosis or pulmonary embolus on adequate anticoagulation
- Consider thrombolysis for a massive, limb-threatening ileofemoral DVT or in a hemodynamically unstable patient with a massive pulmonary embolus.
- Graded 40 mmHg compression stockings to extremity for 2 years after DVT

Duration of Anticoagulation for Venous Thromboembolic Events

Underlying Condition or Risk Factor(s)	Duration
First episode of DVT or PE with reversible risk factors*	3 - 6 months
First episode of idiopathic DVT or PE	6 -12 months
First episode‡ of VTE with: active cancer, antiphospholipid syn., AT III deficiency or recurrent, idiopathic or life-threatening VTE	12 months-to-life
Symptomatic isolated calf vein DVT with reversible cause	6 – 12 weeks

* - trauma, immobilization, estrogen use, pregnancy or recent surgery. AT III = antithrombin III
‡ - duration unclear for Factor V Leiden, Protein C or S deficiency, prothrombin gene mutation or↑ Factor VIII

Prophylaxis for Venous Thromboembolic Events in Hospitalized Patients

Level of Risk	Options for Prophylaxis
Low Risk Age < 40, minor surgery, no risk factors	Early ambulation
Moderate Risk Minor surgery with risk factors or Minor surgery in 40 - 60 year old patients Major surgery, no risk factors	enoxaparin 40 mg SQ daily or heparin 5,000 units SQ q8h (starting 1-2 hours preop) or pneumatic compression stockings
High Risk Minor surgery if patient > 60 years Major surgery if > 40 years Risk factors in patients > 40 years High risk medical inpatients	enoxaparin 40 mg SQ daily or heparin 5,000 units SQ q8h or dalteparin 5,000 units SQ daily (start 1-2 hours preop) PLUS pneumatic compression stockings
Highest Risk Major surgery if pt > 40 and prior VTE event, cancer* or thrombophilic state Hip or knee arthroplasty or fracture repair* Acute spinal cord injury Neurosurgical malignancy surgery‡	enoxaparin 40 mg SQ daily or dalteparin 5,000 units SQ daily or fondaparinux 2.5 mg SQ daily# (start 8-12 hours preop except for neurosurgery cases‡) PLUS pneumatic compression stockings

‡ - Start anticoagulation within 24 hours postop and continue for at least 7 days after operation
* - Continue anticoagulation for 30 days after hip arthroplasty or abdominal/pelvic cancer surgeries
# - Has been shown to be superior to enoxaparin for VTE prophylaxis after major orthopedic operations

References: Chest, 2004; 126 (3S): 401S-28S. Chest, 2004; 126(2): 501-8. Circulation, 2001; 103: 2453-60.

General Points about Cancer of Unknown Primary
- Primary site identified by work-up in only 40% of patients
- Extensive search for the primary site should be undertaken only if it is expected to alter the overall management of the patient.
- Identifying the cell type is more important than identifying the site of origin as this may alter the chemotherapy regimen used.
- **Work-up of all patients**: a thorough history and exam, complete blood count, chemistry panel, immunohistochemistry and **thorough pathologic review is critical** and usually a CT scan of the chest, abdomen and pelvis

Histological Categories of Cancer of Unknown Primary Site
- Adenocarcinoma – 80% of all cases
- Poorly-differentiated carcinoma (non-adenocarcinoma) – 5-10%
- Poorly-differentiated neoplasm - < 5%
- Squamous cell carcinoma – 5%
- Neuroendocrine carcinoma - < 5%

Adenocarcinoma of Unknown Primary Site (AUP)
- Pancreas, hepatobiliary, lung, gastric and colon are all relatively common
- Breast and prostate uncommon
  - ➢ An isolated axillary node adenocarcinoma in a woman is likely breast cancer
- **Work-up of AUP in Addition to General Work-up Above**
  - ➢ A urinalysis, fecal occult blood testing and prostate specific antigen in men and a urinalysis, fecal occult blood testing and a mammogram in women.
  - ➢ Abdominal CT scan with careful assessment of stomach, pancreas and liver
  - ➢ Positron emission tomography scan using 18-F-fluorodeoxyglucose has proven to be of additional benefit **if results would alter management**.
  - ➢ No role for CEA, CA 19-9, CA 15-3, CA 125, human chorionic gonadotrophin or alpha-fetoprotein in diagnostic work-up of AUP

Poorly-differentiated Carcinoma of Unknown Primary Site (PDCUP)
- Melanoma 10%, lymphoma 5%, neuroendocrine tumor 4%, prostate CA 1%
- **Work-up of PDCUP in Addition to General Work-up Above**
  - ➢ CT scan of the chest and abdomen, human chorionic gonadotrophin and alpha-fetoprotein (extragonadal germ cell tumor) and immunohistochemistry

Poorly-differentiated Neoplasms of Unknown Primary Site (PDNUP)
- Non-Hodgkin's lymphomas account for 34-66% of all PDNUP
- Most of the other cases are from poorly-differentiated carcinomas and a small percentage are from melanomas and sarcomas.
- **Work-up of PDNUP in Addition to General Work-up Above**
  - ➢ Immunohistochemical staining, electron microscopy +/- cytogenetic analysis of tissue can differentiate lymphoma, sarcoma, melanoma or carcinoma

Squamous Cell Carcinoma of Unknown Primary Site (SCCUP)
- **Upper or mid-cervical lymph node involvement**
  - ➢ Fiberoptic nasopharyngolaryngoscopy to rule out primary head/neck cancer Chest/neck CT scan. Fine needle aspiration of involved lymph nodes.
- **Lower cervical or supraclavicular lymph node involvement**
  - ➢ Primary lung cancer more likely than head and neck cancer
  - ➢ CT scan of thorax and neck and if unrevealing a bronchoscopy.
- **Inguinal lymph node involvement**
  - ➢ 99% are primary in anorectal or genital areas
  - ➢ Anoscopy and careful exam of either penis or vulva/vagina/cervix.

CEA = carcinoembryonic antigen, CA = cancer antibody

References: Ann Oncol., 1990; 1: 119. J Clin. Oncol., 1991; 9: 1931. J. Clin Oncol., 1995; 13: 274.

Malignant Spinal Cord Compression
- Patients with known cancer who develop lower extremity neurologic deficits have cord compression until otherwise proven
- Prostate, lung and breast cancers most commonly cause cord compression.
- Thoracic > Lumbar > Cervical spine and 30% pts with multiple sites involved.
- Management involves hospital admission, dexamethasone 40 mg IV x 1 then 10 mg IV q6h, emergent MRI of entire spine and radiation oncology consultation.

Brain Metastases
- Clinical presentation: headache (50%), focal weakness (40%), cognitive impairment (75%), gait disturbance (25%), seizure (15%) and behavioral changes (30%)
- Most common cancers: lung > breast > melanoma > colon > germ cell
- Management: dexamethasone 20 mg IV x 1 then 10 mg IV q6h
- Radiation oncology and neurosurgery consultations

Superior Vena Cava Syndrome
- Clinical presentation: dyspnea (75%), cough, facial swelling and plethora and venous distension of neck and chest wall (70%)
- Causes: lung and breast cancer, lymphoma and mediastinal germ cell tumor
- Must also rule out malignant pericardial effusion with tamponade
- Tissue diagnosis via bronchoscopy, mediastinoscopy or thoracotomy
- Radiation oncology consultation

Altered Mental Status in Known Cancer Patient
- Differential diagnosis: brain mets, meningitis, stroke, paraneoplastic, hypoxia, hypercalcemia, hyponatremia (usually SIADH) or medication effect
- **Treatment of hypercalcemia**: isotonic saline + bisphosphonates (pamidronate 60-90 mg IV x 1 over 2-24h or zoledronic acid 4 mg IV x 1 over 15-60 minutes)
  ➤ Other treatments include calcitonin, steroids, plicamycin or gallium nitrate.
- **Treatment of SIADH**: fluid restriction and demeclocycline 300-600 mg PO bid

Hyperviscosity Syndrome
- Clinical presentation: mucosal bleeding, visual changes, headache, confusion, altered mental status, ataxia, vertigo and seizures
- Causes: Waldenstrom's macroglobulinemia, myeloma and leukemias
- Treatment: urgent plasmapheresis and hematology consultation

Selected Chemotherapy Toxicities
- Taxanes: peripheral neuropathies, myopathies & heart conduction problems
- Mitomycin C: hemolytic uremic syndrome
- 5-fluorouracil and camptosar: severe diarrhea or mucositis
- Bleomycin: malignant hyperthermia, pneumonitis or severe skin rash
- Thalidomide, estramustine and tamoxifen: venous thromboembolic event
- Oxaliplatin: cold-induced neuropathy
- Capecitabine and liposomal doxorubicin: palmar-plantar erythrodysesthesias

Other General Rules of Thumb for Clinical Oncology
- Dyspnea in a cancer patient: consider pulmonary embolus, malignant pleural effusion or post-obstructive pneumonia
- Neutropenia (ANC<500) plus fever is infection until proven otherwise
- Never use granulocyte colony stimulating factors and chemotherapy or radiation therapy concurrently

Diagnosis

- Acute symptoms (cough +/- sputum, dyspnea, +/- fever, +/- chest pain)
- Exam: pulmonary rales or ronchi +/- egophony or tactile fremitus
- Chest x-ray almost always with an infiltrate (unless severe dehydration)

Pneumonia Patient Outcome Research Team (PORT) Prediction Rule

- Exclusion criteria: Age < 18, HIV+, admission within last 7 days

Characteristic	score	Comorbid Disease	score	Exam Findings	score	Laboratory Findings	score
Age	Age	Cancer	+30	AMS	+20	pH < 7.35*	+30
Female	-10	Liver disease	+20	RR ≥ 30	+20	BUN ≥ 30	+20
Nursing home resident	+10	CHF	+10	SBP < 90	+20	Na < 130	+20
		Cerebrovascular disease	+10	T ≤ 35°C or T ≥ 40°C	+15	Glucose > 250 mg/dL	+10
		Renal disease	+10	Pulse≥ 125	+10	Hct < 30%	+10
						PaO₂< 60	+10
						Pl. effusion	+10

CHF = congestive heart failure, AMS = altered mental status, RR = respiratory rate, SBP=systolic blood pressure, Pl. = pleural, Na = sodium, PaO₂ = partial pressure arterial oxygen, * - pH from arterial blood sample, BUN = blood urea nitrogen, T = temperature and Hct = hematocrit

Risk Class	PORT score	Mortality (%)	Recommended care	* - patient
I*	N/A	0.1	Outpatient	< 50 years &
II	≤ 70	0.6	Outpatient	no worrisome
III	71-90	0.9 – 2.8	Outpatient or inpatient	predictors as
IV	91-130	8.2 – 9.3	Inpatient	in table
V	>130	27.0 – 29.2	Inpatient	above

Recommended Diagnostic Studies for Outpatient treatment

- Posteroanterior and lateral chest radiograph: examine for infiltrate/effusion
- Pulse oximetry
- Complete blood count, electrolytes, renal panel, +/- sputum culture and gram stain +/- pretreatment blood cultures x 2

Empiric Outpatient Antibiotic Treatment for Community-acquired Pneumonia

- Outpatient therapy (patient < 65 years, **no** recent antibiotics or comorbidities*)
  - ➤ Macrolide antibiotic (azithromycin 500 mg PO daily, clarithromycin 500 mg PO bid or erythromycin 500 mg PO qid) **or**
  - ➤ Doxycycline 100 mg PO bid
- Outpatient therapy (patient > 65 years or comorbidities* & **no** recent antibiotics)
  - ➤ Oral respiratory fluoroquinolone (levofloxacin 500 mg daily, gatifloxacin 400 mg daily, moxifloxacin 400 mg daily **or** gemifloxacin 320 mg daily)
  - ➤ New macrolides: azithromycin or clarithromycin as dosed above
- Outpatient therapy (pt > 65 yrs or comorbidities* **and** recent antibiotics ≤ 3 mo.)
  - ➤ Respiratory fluoroquinolone
  - ➤ New macrolide antibiotic and ß-lactam‡
- Duration of therapy is typically 7-10 days for outpatient therapy.

* - comorbidities include chronic obstructive pulmonary disease, CHF, diabetes, chronic renal failure or cancer
‡ - PO amoxicillin 1 gm tid, amoxicillin-clavulanate XR 2 gm bid, cefpodoxime 400 mg bid, cefuroxime 500 mg bid or cefprozil 500 mg bid

References: Arch Int Med, 2004; 164: 502-8. CID, 2003; 37: 1405-33 and CID, 2004; 38: S328-40.

Condition	Clinical Features	Diagnosis	Empiric Therapy
Amebiasis: diarrhea *Entamoeba histolytica* Lancet, 2003; 361: 1025.	Chronic diarrhea or dysentery +/- weight loss	Stool for ova and parasites or *E. histolytica* antigen will be positive	Metronidazole 750 mg PO tid x 10 days followed by either paromomycin 500 mg PO tid x 7 days **or** Iodoquinol 650 mg PO tid x 20 days.
Amebiasis: Extraintestinal *Entamoeba histolytica* NEJM, 2003; 348: 1563.	Right upper quadrant abdominal pain, fevers, chills, anorexia, nausea, (hepatic abscess usually right lobe & solitary)	*E. histolytica* antibody titers positive Abscess aspirate "anchovy paste" appearance and sterile	Abscess drainage an option for size > 5 cm, left hepatic lobe or refractory to antibiotics at 5 d
Balanitis	Multiple red papules and thick white exudate on glans of penis	Clinical diagnosis. Potassium hydroxide prep of exudate positive for hyphae Check blood sugar	Topical antifungal cream to penile glans bid **or** fluconazole 150 mg PO x 1 for refractory cases
Bites (animal) NEJM, 1999; 340: 85 and 138	Historical evidence of animal bite	Amoxicillin-clavulanate 875 mg PO bid x 5 days (prophylaxis) or x 10 days (treatment). **Alternative:** ciprofloxacin 500 mg PO bid **or** trimethoprim-sulfamethoxazole 5 mg/kg PO bid (for children) **and** clindamycin 300 mg PO qid x 10 days Give tetanus toxoid if none in last 5 years.	
Blepharitis	Inflammation of the lid margin with erythema, scaling and yellow crusting	Clinical diagnosis. Exclude seborrheic blepharitis or ocular rosacea	Use 50:50 solution of baby shampoo to lid margin followed by warm compresses bid-tid. No role for antibiotics.

Condition	Clinical Features	Diagnosis	Empiric Therapy
Acute Bronchitis Ann Intern Med, 2001; 134: 518-20	Acute cough < 3 weeks, +/- sputum production. Majority of cases from respiratory viruses including influenza. Rarely pertussis.	Exclude cough asthma and pneumonia (**Unlikely if:** pulse <100, respiratory rate < 24, temperature < 38°C and no consolidative exam findings)	No role for antibiotics unless pertussis suspected. Consider empiric antivirals if influenza suspected & < 48 hrs of symptoms (see influenza)
Brucellosis (**Notifiable infection to state**) MMWR, 2001; 50 (RR-2): 1-72.	Fevers, chills, diaphoresis, weakness, headache, myalgias, arthralgias, weight loss and bloody diarrhea Incubation period: 7-21 days	Ingestion of unpasteurized milk, goat cheese or contaminated meats. Positive blood culture (slow growing and may take 3 - 4 weeks) or positive brucella serologies	Doxycycline 100 mg PO bid and rifampin 600-900 mg PO daily x 6 weeks (>8 years) **or** trimethoprim-sulfamethoxazole 5 mg/kg trimethoprim PO q12h and rifampin 15 - 20 mg/kg PO daily x 6 weeks (< 8 years)
Cat Scratch Disease (*Bartonella henselae*) Infectious Disease Clin. Of N. Amer., 1998; 12: 137.	Papular/pustular lesion forms at puncture site with regional lymphadenopathy. Infrequent: fevers, nausea, splenomegaly or conjunctivitis. Usually a self-limited disease	Clinical diagnosis. Positive serology by immunofixation or by polymerase chain reaction testing or positive Warthin-Starry stain on tissue sample.	Generally antibiotics not needed. In severe cases can use azithromycin 500 mg or 10 mg/kg PO x 1 then 250 mg or 5 mg/kg PO daily x 4 days.
Cellulitis Immunocompetent patient NEJM, 2004; 350 (4): 904-12.	Erythema, warmth, tenderness and swelling of affected area. +/- Fever, leukocytosis & indistinct borders. Consider MRSA (methicillin-resistant staph aureus) if infection refractory.	Clinical diagnosis. Risk factors include chronic edematous states, morbid obesity, venous/lymphatic obstruction and skin puncture	Cephalexin 250-500 mg PO qid **or** erythromycin 500 mg PO qid x 7-14 d & extremity elevation. Trimethoprim-sulfamethoxazole DS 1 tab PO bid for refractory infections (covers most MRSA)

Condition	Clinical Features	Diagnosis	Empiric Therapy
Mild/Moderate Cellulitis Immunosuppressed by diabetes, AIDS or cancer CID, 2004; 39 (S2): S83-122.	Erythema, warmth, swelling and tenderness of affected area. +/- fever, chills, leukocytosis or systemic toxicity. Consider MRSA (methicillin-resistant staph aureus) if infection refractory.	Clinical diagnosis. Deep venous thrombosis can mimic signs of cellulitis and may need to be excluded	Amoxicillin-clavulanate 875 mg PO bid **or** clindamycin 450 mg PO qid **+ either** levofloxacin or moxifloxacin or gemifloxacin x 10 -14 days. Extremity elevation.
Cellulitis Erysipelas CID, 1996; 23: 1091.	Bright red, tender, edematous, raised border and sharp demarcation. 80% involves legs. Marked lymphatic involvement	Clinical diagnosis. β-hemolytic group A streptococcal cellulitis which is frequently rapidly spreading	Penicillin VK 500 mg PO qid **or** dicloxacillin 500 mg PO qid **or** erythromycin 500 mg PO qid x 10 -14 days.
Chancroid (*Haemophilus ducreyi*) MMWR, 2002; 51 (RR-6): 1-80.	Red papule of genital area → a painful ulcer with gray-yellow exudate. 2/3 with painful inguinal lymphadenitis. Sexually transmitted	Pleomorphic gram negative coccobacilli. Positive culture or polymerase chain reaction (PCR) test of exudates.	Ceftriaxone 250 mg IM x 1 **or** azithromycin 1 gm PO x 1 **or** ciprofloxacin 500 mg PO bid x 1 -3d. Treat sex partners as well.
Chlamydia (urethritis or cervicitis) AFP, 2002; 65 (4): 673-6	Asymptomatic. Dysuria, urinary frequency or cervical/urethral discharge. Sexually transmitted.	Nucleic acid amplification test on urine or an endocervical or urethral swab.	Doxycycline 100 mg PO bid **or** erythromycin 500 mg PO qid x 7d **or** azithromycin 1 gm PO x 1.
Cholera (*Vibrio cholerae*) **Notifiable to state** (Adapted from the CDC guidelines for the management of cholera)	Asymptomatic or profuse watery diarrhea with "rice water" stool, vomiting, often severe dehydration. Source: contaminated water, or undercooked fish/shellfish.	Stool culture positive **or** Stool gram stain with curved gram-negative rods **or** Vibrios identified by dark field microscopy of stool specimen	**If >12 yrs**, use ciprofloxacin 1 gm PO x1 **or** doxycycline 300 mg PO x 1. **If < 12 yrs**, erythromycin 10 mg/kg PO tid x 3 days **or** azithromycin 20 mg/kg up to 1 gm PO x 1. Oral rehydration.

Condition	Clinical Features	Diagnosis	Empiric Therapy
Coccidiomycosis (Pulmonary) CID. 2000; 30: 658-61.	High risk: African-American, pregnant, Filipino or immunosuppressed patients. Subclinical infection 50-65%, 30% have self-limited pneumonitis with fatigue, cough, headache, myalgias, and 5% with reticulonodular or cavitary pneumonia. Mild hypercalcemia	Elevated coccidioidomycosis complement fixation (CF) titers. Eosinophilia in 25%. Chest x-ray with interstitial or reticulonodular infiltrates, cavities or effusions	**Mild** pneumonia: supportive care **Moderate** pneumonia: fluconazole 400 mg PO daily **or** itraconazole 200 mg PO bid x 3-12 months. **Severe** pneumonia: Amphotericin B 2 gms IV total dose then fluconazole 400 mg PO daily x 12 mo.
Coccidiomycosis (Extrapulmonary) CID. 2000; 30: 658-61.	Nonmeningeal: maculopapular, erythema multiforme or erythema nodosum rash, arthritis, osteomyelitis **versus** meningitis. Indicators of severity: weight loss > 10%, night sweats > 3 wks, pulmonary infiltrates > 50% of lungs or symptoms >2 months.	Elevated coccidioidomycosis CF titers (usually >1:32). Cocci spherules in tissue biopsy, positive bone scan or cerebrospinal fluid with lymphocytic pleocytosis and high coccidioidomycosis titers.	Fluconazole 400-800 mg PO daily for lifetime. For meningitis, may use fluconazole 800-1,000 mg PO daily **or** amphotericin B 2-2.5 grams total IV load initially then fluconazole 400-800 mg PO daily indefinitely.
Cystitis (uncomplicated) Mayo Clin Proc. 2004; 79: 1048-54. CID. 2004; 38: 1150-8. CID. 2004; 39: 75-80.	Dysuria, urinary frequency, suprapubic pain and no fever or significant flank pain	Midstream urine with positive leukocyte esterase & nitrite **or** ≥10⁴ bacteria/mm³ **or** positive gram stain of unspun urine.	Trimethoprim-sulfamethoxazole double-strength 1 tab PO bid **or** nitrofurantoin 100 mg PO qid x 7d oral fluoroquinolone x 3 d **in refractory cases only**
Cystitis or bacteriuria in pregnancy	Same presentation and diagnostic criteria as cystitis		Nitrofurantoin 100 mg PO qid **or** cephalexin 250 mg PO qid **or** trimethoprim-sulfamethoxazole double-strength 1 tab PO bid (14-36 wks pregnant) **or** amoxicillin 250 mg PO tid x 5-7days

Condition	Clinical Features	Diagnosis	Empiric Therapy
Diverticulitis (mild-moderate) Dis Col Rectum 2000; 43:289 Am J Gastro 1999; 94: 3110	Lower quadrant abdominal pain (left much more common than right) +/- fever, nausea, vomiting, anorexia or constipation	Clinical diagnosis, mild-mod. tenderness on exam. CT scan with diverticula and inflammation of pericolic fat	Ciprofloxacin 500 mg PO bid + metronidazole 500 mg PO qid **or** amoxicillin-clavulanate 875 mg PO bid x 7-10 d + clears
Epididymo-orchitis Med. Clinics of N. Amer., 2004; 88: 495. MMWR, 2002; 51 (RR-6): 1-80. J. Urology, 1995; 154: 209-13.	Scrotal pain, testicular and epididymal swelling & tenderness +/- dysuria and/or urinary frequency. Usually a sexually-transmitted disease if < 35 years old.	Clinical diagnosis. Urine may show sterile pyuria. Urethral discharge may test positive for gonorrhea or chlamydia.	**Age<35:** ceftriaxone 250 mg IM + doxycycline 100 mg PO bid x 10 days **or** ofloxacin 300 mg PO bid x 10 days. **Age>35:** fluoroquinolone x 21 d
Gastroenteritis (mild)	≥3 unformed stools daily, duration <14 days, recent travel, ill contacts. Usually viral in etiology.	+/- Fecal leukocytes +/- Occult blood +/- Positive stool cultures	Oral rehydration solutions + antimotility agents if afebrile and mild symptoms
Gastroenteritis (moderate-severe) CID 2001; 32: 331-51. Am J Gastro 1997; 92: 1962	≥3 unformed stools daily, duration <14 days, recent travel, ill contacts, fever, abdominal cramps, anorexia, nausea and/or vomiting	Fecal leukocytes present, +/- tenesmus, bloody diarrhea or dehydration. Positive stool cultures	Ciprofloxacin 500 mg PO bid x 3 - 5 days. For severe symptoms, oral/IV rehydration and avoid antimotility agents
Traveler's Diarrhea Ann Int Med, 2005; 142: 805.	Clinical diagnosis manifested by ≥3 unformed stools/day + one of following: nausea, vomiting, abdominal pain, fever or blood in stools. Stool cultures are rarely required to make a diagnosis. High risk areas: Asia, Africa, Mexico, Central and South America.		**Mild-moderate:** oral rehydration **Severe:** ciprofloxacin 500 mg PO bid x 2d +/- antimotility meds **Prophylaxis:** rifaximin 200 mg PO bid x 2 weeks
Giardiasis (Giardia lamblia) CID, 1997; 25: 545-50.	Transmission person-to-person or waterborne. Asymptomatic carriers or chronic watery diarrhea, malaise, steatorrhea + abdominal cramps	Positive stool ova and parasites exam or fecal enzyme-linked immunosorbent assay for giardia antigen	Metronidazole 250 mg PO tid x 5 days **or** furazolidone 100 mg PO qid x 7-10 days.

Condition	Clinical Features	Diagnosis	Empiric Therapy
Gonorrhea (*Neisseria gonorrhea*) urethritis/cervicitis	Asymptomatic carrier or urethral or cervical discharge. May also have dysuria, urinary frequency or pelvic pain.	Positive endocervical/urethral swab culture or nucleic acid amplification test of urine or endocervical/urethral swab	Ceftriaxone 125 mg IM x 1 preferred **or** ofloxacin 400 mg PO x 1 **or** ciprofloxacin 500 mg PO x 1 (if fluoroquinolone resistance low) **Treat for chlamydia as well**
Disseminated Gonococcal Infection MMWR, 2002; 51 (RR-6); 1-80.	Monoarticular arthritis, fever, tender skin vesiculopustules. Rarely heart, bone, liver or meninges involved	As above or isolating organism from joint, skin or blood	Ceftriaxone 1 gm IV/IM daily **or** ciprofloxacin 400 mg IV q12h until improved x 24 – 48 hours then ciprofloxacin 500 mg PO bid x 7d
Granuloma inguinale (*Calymmatobacterium granulomatis*)	Subcutaneous nodules/papules in genital area erode into painless granulating ulcers with rolled edges	Wright stain of tissue smear **or** tissue biopsy with Donovan bodies **or** culture of organism	Trimethoprim-sulfamethoxazole DS 1 tab PO bid **or** doxycycline 100 mg PO bid x 3-4 weeks
Hordeolum (stye)	Infection of superficial sebaceous glands → mass along lid margin	Clinical diagnosis	Warm compresses bid-tid. Rarely excision required
Herpes Simplex Virus (HSV) (labialis or gingivostomatitis)	Painful vesicles or shallow ulcers of lip and/or mouth. Self-resolves in 7-14 days.	+ serologic type-specific HSV antibodies with clinical features **or** blister fluid HSV culture +	**Primary infection:** acyclovir 400 mg PO tid x 7d. **Recurrent:** 5% acyclovir or 1% penciclovir q3h as needed
Herpes Simplex Virus (HSV) (genitals) MMWR, 2002; 51 (RR-6);	Usually asymptomatic or painful vesicles or ulcers in genital area. Primary episode may have fever, myalgias and lymphadenopathy	Diagnosis as above **Primary outbreak:** acyclovir 400 mg PO tid **or** valacyclovir 1 gm PO bid **or** famciclovir 250 mg PO tid x 7-10 days.	**Recurrent outbreaks:** acyclovir 400 mg PO tid **or** famciclovir 125 mg PO bid **or** valacyclovir 500 mg PO bid x 5 days (7-10 d if HIV+) **Prophylaxis:** PO acyclovir 400 mg bid **or** valacyclovir 500 mg daily **or** famciclovir 250 mg bid if > 6 episodes in 12 months.

Condition	Clinical Features	Diagnosis	Empiric Therapy
Impetigo	Contagious, skin infection. Primary lesion bullous or vesicular and usually with golden crust +/- itching	Clinical diagnosis. Lesions may become superinfected and if so appropriate therapy for cellulitis needed	Mupirocin ointment tid **or** erythromycin 250 mg PO qid **or** cephalexin 250 mg PO qid x 10 days and antibacterial soap.
Influenza Prevention NEJM, 1999; 341: 1387	Abrupt onset of fever, headache, myalgias, malaise, cough, sore throat during winter months. Mild cases self-resolve in 5-7 days. Severe cases with influenza pneumonia or secondary bacterial pneumonia	Disease occurs in outbreaks. Isolation of virus in tissue culture or rapid detection of viral antigens by immunologic assays from throat/nasal swabs or sputum.	Influenza vaccination for high-risk: > 50, diabetes, renal failure, pregnancy, immunosuppressed, institutionalized, heart and lung disease or household contacts. Zanamivir 2 puffs inhaled daily **or** oseltamivir 75 mg PO daily during peak influenza season or in house-hold contacts of index cases. **Avoid zanamavir in lung diseases.**
Influenza Treatment Lancet, 2000; 355: 1845 BMJ, 2003; 326: 1235.	Clinical features and diagnosis are same as above. All treatment should be started ≤ 48h of symptoms Influenza A treatment: amantadine **or** rimantadine 100 mg PO bid or 5 mg/kg/d to 75 mg PO bid (>1 year) x 7 days. Influenza A/B treatment: zanamivir 2 puffs inhaled bid **or** oseltamivir 75 mg PO bid or 2 mg/kg PO bid (ages 1-12 years) x 5 days.		
Leptospirosis (*Leptospira interrogans*) CID, 1995; 21: 1. (Severe icteric form is Well's disease)	Ingestion of contaminated water or infected animal tissue. Abrupt fever, rigors, myalgias, cough, headache, aseptic meningitis, nausea or diarrhea **Well's disease:** severe icteric form with acute renal failure.	**Risk groups:** farmers, ranchers, military, trappers. Positive blood/cerebrospinal fluid cultures or serologies.	**Mild infection:** doxycycline 100 mg PO bid **or** ampicillin 500 mg PO qid x 7 days. **Well's disease:** penicillin G 1.5 million units IV q6h or ceftriaxone 1 gm IV daily x 7days.

Condition	Clinical Features	Diagnosis	Empiric Therapy
Listeriosis (*Listeria monocytogenes*) CID, 1997; 24: 1.	Fever, chills, meningitis symptoms, gastroenteritis or shock. In pregnancy with intact membranes can cause chorioamnionitis or preterm labor.	Positive culture from cerebrospinal fluid, blood or amniotic fluid.	Ampicillin 2 gm IV q4h + gentamicin 2 mg/kg IV q8h **or** trimethoprim-sulfamethoxazole 20 mg/kg/d IV ÷ qid x 14 days (immunocompetent) or x 3 - 8 weeks (immunocompromised or meningitis).
Lyme Disease (*Borrelia burgdorferi*) Early disease CID, 2000; 31(S1): S1-14.	After tick bite, erythema chronicum migrans, 1st or 2nd-degree heart block, Bell's palsy, headache, arthralgias, fever, lymphadenopathy	Antibody positive by enzyme-linked immunoassay after 2-4 weeks, polymerase chain reaction testing in joint fluid or culture from skin biopsy.	Doxycycline 100 mg PO bid **or** amoxicillin 500 mg PO tid x 14-21 d. In endemic areas consider doxycycline 200 mg PO x 1 for worrisome tick bites.
Lyme Disease (*Borrelia burgdorferi*) Late disease NEJM, 2001; 345: 85, 115-25	Lyme arthritis: large joints affected and arthritis is oligoarticular. Neuroborreliosis: meningitis, acute radiculopathy or encephalopathy Carditis: complete heart block	As above with cerebrospinal fluid	Oral regimen as above x 28 - 60 days ceftriaxone 2 gm IV daily **or** penicillin G 4 million units IV q4h x 14 - 28 days for Lyme arthritis Ceftriaxone 2 gm IV daily **or** penicillin G 4 million units IV q4h x 14-28 d **or** oral regimen as above x 21 d (carditis).
Lymphogranuloma venereum (*Chlamydia trachomatis*) MMWR, 2002; 51 (RR-6): 1-80.	Incubation period 3-30 d. Painless papule/pustule→ small shallow ulcer→ painful inguinal lymph nodes (buboes)→ proctocolitis (late stage)	Positive culture of lymph node aspirate or infected tissue **or** >1:64 complement fixation antibody titer	Doxycycline 100 mg PO bid x 21 d **or** erythromycin 500 mg PO qid x 21 d Avoid excision since sinus tracts may develop.

Condition	Clinical Features	Diagnosis	Empiric Therapy
Odontogenic infections	Uncomplicated dental infections present as dental caries and periodontitis with toothache and sensitivity to cold	Clinical diagnosis. Rule out parapharyngeal or other dental abscess. X-rays can rule out periapical abscess	Extract tooth + give amoxicillin-clavulanate 875 mg PO bid or penicillin VK 500 mg PO qid x 10 days
Otitis Externa	Otalgia, ear pruritus +/- hearing impairment. Ear canal swollen & erythematous with yellowish debris. Risks: swimming and ear devices	Clinical diagnosis. Treat with hydrocortisone/polymyxin/neomycin suspension 4 drops qid or cipro/hydrocortisone suspension 3 drops bid x 5-7days. If severe in immunosuppressed patient, ciprofloxacin 750 mg PO bid x 7-10 d. Ear wick for very edematous ear canals.	
Acute Otitis Media (AOM) Pediatrics, 2004; 113: 1412.	Most cases are in children < 5 years and follow a viral upper respiratory infection. Otalgia, fever, irritability, ↓ hearing. Red, bulging tympanic membrane suggests bacterial cause	Red tympanic membrane with ↓ mobility, middle ear effusion and acute symptoms. Reserve antibiotics for severe infections, < 6 mths or if pt unimproved in 2d	amoxicillin 80 mg/kg/d PO ÷bid or clarithromycin 7.5 mg/kg PO bid x 10 d (<2 yr) or 5 - 7 d (>2 yrs) or azithromycin 10mg/kg PO x 1d → 5 mg/kg/d PO x 4d.
Otitis Media with effusion (OME) Pediatrics, 2004; 113: 1412.	Patient usually has no systemic symptoms, but may have decreased hearing.	Fluid behind non-inflamed tympanic membrane whose mobility is decreased. Fluid persisting > 3 months after AOM	Consider tympanostomy tubes if hearing impaired and speech delayed. Antibiotics not shown to be helpful in this condition.
Resistant otitis media	Resistant otitis media if AOM with unimproved symptoms ≥ 3 days on appropriate antibiotics	Symptoms of AOM should be much improved within 72 hrs on antibiotics. Uninfected fluid may persist in middle ear for 3 months	Amoxicillin-clavulanate 90 mg/kg/d PO ÷ tid or cefuroxime 30 mg/kg/d PO ÷ bid x 10 d or ceftriaxone 50 mg/kg/d IM x 3d

Condition	Clinical Features	Diagnosis	Empiric Therapy
Recurrent otitis media (recurrent OM) NEJM, 2004; 344: 403.	≥ 3 episodes acute otitis media (AOM) in 6 months or ≥ 4 episodes acute otitis media in 12 months.	Patient must have proven resolution after each episode of AOM to make diagnosis of recurrent OM	Suppressive antibiotics with amoxicillin 40 mg/kg PO daily **or** sulfisoxazole 50 mg/kg PO qhs. May need tympanostomy tubes
Pelvic inflammatory disease (PID) MMWR, 2002; 51(RR-6): 1.	**Risk factors:** multiple sexual partners, prior history, no condoms and poverty. Lower abdominal pain < 2 weeks, onset during or just after menses, dyspareunia, cervical motion and adnexal tenderness +/- fever or purulent vaginal discharge	Clinical +/- leukocytosis, high sedimentation rate, positive chlamydia or gonorrhea test or laparoscopic evidence of salpingitis	Levofloxacin 500 mg PO bid + metronidazole 500 mg PO bid **or** ceftriaxone 250 mg IM x 1 + doxycycline 100 mg PO bid x 14 days (if outpatient therapy). **Partner(s) must be evaluated**
Streptococcal pharyngitis JAMA, 2004; 291: 1587-95[*] [* discusses Centor score]. CID, 2002; 35: 113-25.	Sudden sore throat, tonsillar exudates, tender cervical adenopathy, fever and headache. Absent cough or rhinorrhea. Winter-spring and usually 5-15 years	Gold standard is throat culture. Rapid antigen test 10-20% false negative rate	Bicillin LA 1.2 MU IM x 1 **or** PO: penicillin VK 500 mg bid **or** erythromycin 500 mg x10 d. Empiric antibiotics if Centor Score ≥ 4[*]
Acute prostatitis JAMA, 1999; 282: 236.	Suprapubic, perineal and/or testicular pain, irritative and/or obstructive urinary symptoms, fever, malaise, myalgias and/or hematospermia	Tender, edematous prostate, pyuria and leukocytosis. No cystitis.	< 35 yrs: Treat as per PID > 35 yrs: PO fluoroquinolone **or** trimethoprim-sulfamethoxazole DS 1 tab PO bid x 4-6 weeks
Acute pyelonephritis AFP, 2005; 71: 933-42. CID, 1999; 29: 745-58.	Cystitis symptoms, fever, flank pain and tenderness, abdominal pain, nausea, vomiting, and anorexia. Inpatient management if pregnant or severe symptoms	Urine with marked pyuria usually with leukocyte casts, leukocytosis, positive urine culture	14 days of PO fluoroquinolone **or** cefpodoxime 400 mg PO bid +/- ceftriaxone 2 gm IV/IM x 1. Amoxicillin-clavulanate 875 mg PO bid is an alternative in most areas.

Condition	Clinical Features	Diagnosis	Empiric Therapy
Scabies and Head lice NEJM, 2002; 346: 1645. J. Derm., 2001; 28: 481.	Scabies: severely pruritic papules, worse at night in finger web spaces, wrists, elbows, knees, axillae, penis and umbilicus Head lice: itchy scalp	Scabies: Clinical diagnosis. Microscopic exam of skin scraping: mites/eggs/feces. Head lice: nits on hairshafts (comb out nits after meds)	**For scabies:** 5% permethrin cream apply from neck down → wash off in 8-12h or ivermectin 200 mcg/kg PO q2weeks x 2. **For head lice:** 1% permethrin liquid x 10 minutes then wash off.
Acute rhinosinusitis NEJM, 2004; 351: 902. CID, 2004; 39; S151-8.	Purulent rhinorrhea, postnasal drip, facial pain, "sinus" headache, sinus tenderness, maxillary toothache with unilateral predominance and opaque transillumination of affected sinus. Duration ≤ 4 weeks	Clinical Diagnosis. Coronal sinus CT scan with mucosal thickening or sinus fluid or Waters view sinus x-rays with air/fluid levels or sinus opacification	Antibiotics when symptoms > 7 days despite supportive therapy. Amoxicillin 500-1000 mg PO tid or TMP/SMX DS 1 tab PO bid x 10 days. If refractory or severe infection: Amoxicillin-clavulanate XR 2000 mg PO bid x 10-14 days.
Syphilis **(primary and secondary)** AFP, 2003; 68: 283-90. MMWR, 2003; 52: 1117.	Sexually-transmitted disease. Primary syphilis: genital area papule → painless ulcer (chancre) Secondary syphilis: maculopapular rash on body with palms/soles +/- condyloma lata, lymphadenopathy or "moth-eaten" alopecia	Darkfield microscopy or direct fluorescent antibody testing of chancre or skin/genital lesions or positive VDRL or RPR test confirmed by positive FTA test.	**Primary or non-neuro secondary or latent syphilis of <1 year duration:** benzathine penicillin 2.4 million units IM x 1 or x 3 if HIV +. **Latent syphilis (> 1 year):** benzathine penicillin 2.4 million units IM qweek x 3 **or** doxycycline 100 mg PO bid x 28 days.
Syphilis **(tertiary)** NEJM, 1992; 326: 1060	Cutaneous or visceral gummas (mass lesions in brain or viscera), aortitis or neurosyphilis (stroke, meningitis or asymptomatic)	Serologic testing as above. Cerebrospinal fluid (CSF) with lymphocytes, + CSF VDRL +/-↓glucose/↑protein	**Neurosyphilis:** penicillin G 4 million units IV q4h x 10 – 14 days. Gummas or aortitis: benzathine penicillin 2.4 million units IM qweek x 3

VDRL = venereal disease research laboratory, RPR = rapid plasma reagin, FTA = fluorescent treponemal antibody test, TMP/SMX = trimethoprim-sulfamethoxazole

Condition	Clinical Features	Diagnosis	Empiric Therapy
Trichinosis (*Trichinella spiralis*) Prog Clin Parasitol, 1994; 4: 117.	Eating undercooked infected pork. **Intestinal stage:** asymptomatic or abdominal cramps, vomiting, diarrhea. **Muscle stage:** subungual splinter, conjunctival and retinal hemorrhages, chemosis, myalgias, weakness. **Late complications:** arrhythmias, myocarditis, meningoencephalitis or pneumonia	Positive antibody enzyme-linked immunoassay test after > 3 weeks infestation or biopsy of symptomatic muscle near tendinous insertion identifying trichinella larvae. Elevated creatinine phosphokinase and lactate dehydrogenase.	Mild infections self-limited and do not require meds. Infection of brain, heart or lungs: albendazole 400 mg PO bid **or** mebendazole 400 mg PO tid x 14 days + prednisone 40-60 mg PO daily x 7 days then taper of over 7 days
Vaginitis (*Bacterial vaginosis*) MMWR, 2002; 51 (RR-6): l-80. CID, 2002; 35 (S2): 135.	Asymptomatic vaginal discharge or occasionally vaginal and/or vulvar pruritus	Any 3 of the following: • watery vaginal discharge • "clue cells" on wet mount • "fishy" odor when discharge mixed with potassium hydroxide • vaginal pH >4.5	Metronidazole 500 mg PO bid **or** clindamycin 300 mg PO bid x 7days **or** 2% clindamycin or 0.75% metronidazole cream 1 applicator intravaginally qhs x 5-7 d. Treat partner if he has balanitis or exudate on glans. Use clindamycin in pregnancy
Vaginitis (Yeast)	Asymptomatic or commonly a pruritic, thick, "cheesy", white vaginal discharge	Potassium hydroxide prep of discharge with fungal hyphae	Antifungal azole* cream or vaginal suppository qhs x 1-7d **or** fluconazole 150 mg PO x 1
Vaginitis (*Trichomonas vaginalis*) MMWR, 2002; 51 (RR-6): l-80.	Asymptomatic or commonly with frothy, malodorous vaginal discharge*, "strawberry cervix" and/or vaginal/vulvar pruritus	Wet prep of discharge with trichomonads. Vaginal pH > 5	Metronidazole 2 gm PO x 1 **or** Tinidazole 2 gm PO x 1 Must treat patient **and** partner.

* = antifungal azoles that are available as creams or suppositories: clotrimazole, miconazole, miconazole and terconazole; butoconazole and ticoconazole and ficoconazole are only available as creams

Condition	Clinical Features	Diagnosis	Empiric Therapy
Warts Anogenital MMWR, 2002; 51 (RR-6): 1-80.	Sexually-transmitted. Human papilloma virus-related. Appearance pink, painless, verrucous growths often coalescing in anogenital area	Clinical diagnosis. 5% acetic acid applied to penis/scrotum can identify subclinical flat warts that can transmit human papilloma virus	**Patient applied:** podofilox cream bid x 3 consecutive days/week x 4 wks **or** 5% imiquimod cream applied for 6-10 hours 3x/week ≤ 16 weeks. **Physician-applied:** 25% podophyllin x 4 hr qweek **or** cryotherapy q2week
Warts Cutaneous	Dome-shaped gray-brown hyperkeratotic papules on extremities. Flat or filiform growths on face. Cut edge reveals black dots representing thrombosed capillaries	Clinical diagnosis. Differential diagnosis includes calluses or corns (which retain their skin lines). Warts lack skin lines.	Topical salicylic acid, electrocautery or cryotherapy for common and filiform warts. 0.025% Retin A or 5% Efudex cream qhs for flat facial warts

Complications of HIV Infection by CD₄ count

CD₄ count	Complications of HIV Infection by CD₄ count	
	Infectious	**Non-infectious**
> 500	Acute retroviral syndrome or recurrent vaginal candidiasis	Lymphadenopathy, Guillain-Barre, aseptic meningitis
200-500	Pneumonia, sinusitis, pulmonary tuberculosis (Tb), thrush, zoster, Kaposi's sarcoma, cryptosporidiosis, Oral Hairy Leukoplakia	B-cell or Hodgkin's lymphoma, anemia, idiopathic thrombocytopenic purpura, cervical dysplasia, cervical cancer or mononeuritis multiplex
50-200	Pneumocystis carnii pneumonia, disseminated herpes simplex, toxoplasmosis, cryptococcosis, histoplasmosis, coccidiomycosis or Tb, microsporidiosis & prog. multifocal leukoencephalopathy	HIV wasting, HIV dementia, central nervous system lymphomas, immunoblastic lymphoma, HIV cardiomyopathy, peripheral neuropathy, myelopathy or polyradiculopathy
< 50	Disseminated cytomegalovirus/Mycobacterium avium complex	

Estimated Risk of Infective Endocarditis with Various Cardiac Conditions

High Risk	Moderate Risk	Negligible Risk
• Prosthetic valve • Prior bacterial endocarditis • Cyanotic congenital heart disease • Systemic-to-pulmonary shunts or conduits	• Noncyanotic congenital ht. disease • Mitral valve prolapse & mitral regurgitation • Acquired valvular heart disease • Hypertrophic cardiomyopathy	• Mitral valve prolapse & **no** mitral regurgitation • Innocent murmur • Prior coronary bypass • Prior rheumatic fever • Cardiac pacemaker • Atrial septal defect • Post-op ASD, VSD or PDA

ASD = Atrial septal defect, VSD = ventricular septal defect, PDA = patent ductus arteriosus

Bacterial Endocarditis Prophylaxis for Various Procedures

Endocarditis Prophylaxis Indicated	Endocarditis Prophylaxis Not Indicated

• Dental extractions or cleaning
• Dental implants
• Periodontal procedures
• Cleaning with gingival or mucosal bleeding
• Subgingival surgery
• Orthodontic banding
• Root canal operations
• Tonsillectomy/adenoidectomy
• Rigid bronchoscopy
• Surgery involving respiratory mucosa
• Variceal sclerotherapy
• Esophageal stricture dilatation
• Endoscopic retrograde cholangiopancreatography
• Biliary tract surgery
• Surgery involving GI mucosa
• Prostate surgery
• Cystoscopy
• Urethral dilatation
• Open heart surgery
• Urethral catheterization if urinary tract infection present
• Vaginal delivery with chorioamnionitis
	• Restorative dentistry
	• Placement of oral appliances
	• Suture removal from mouth
	• Cardiac catheterization or angioplasty
	• Endotracheal intubation
	• Flexible bronchoscopy *
	• Tympanostomy tubes
	• Trans-esophageal echocardiogram*
	• Upper/Lower endoscopy*
	• Vaginal hysterectomy*
	• Uncomplicated vaginal delivery*
	• In absence of infection:
	  ➢ Sterilization operations
	  ➢ Cesarean section
	  ➢ Intrauterine device insertion or removal
	  ➢ Therapeutic abortion
	  ➢ Uterine dilatation and curettage
	  ➢ Skin biopsy
	  ➢ Circumcision
	  ➢ Laparoscopy
	• Defibrillator or pacemaker insertion

*- prophylaxis may be given to high-risk patients

References: JAMA, 1997; 277: 1794-1801 and NEJM, 1995; 332 (1): 38-44.

Prophylaxis for Bacterial Endocarditis in Adults

For dental, oral, respiratory tract or esophageal procedures	
Standard prophylaxis	amoxicillin 2 gm PO 1 hour before procedure
Unable to take oral meds	ampicillin 2 gm IM/IV 30 minutes before procedure
Penicillin-allergic	clindamycin 600 mg PO or cephalexin 2 gm PO or azithromycin 500 mg PO or clarithromycin 500 mg PO 1 hour before procedure
Penicillin-allergic and unable to take oral meds	clindamycin 600 mg IV or cefazolin 1 gm IM/IV 30 minutes before procedure
For genitourinary and gastrointestinal procedures (excluding the esophagus)	
High-risk patients	ampicillin 2 gm IV/IM plus gentamicin 1.5 mg/kg (up to 120 mg) IM/IV 30 minutes before procedure; ampicillin 1 gm IV/IM or amoxicillin 1 gm PO 6 hrs after procedure
High-risk patients allergic to penicillin	vancomycin 1 gm IV over 1-2 hours plus gentamicin 1.5 mg/kg (up to 120 mg) IV 30 minutes before procedure.
Intermediate-risk patients	amoxicillin 2 gm PO or ampicillin 2 gm IV/IM 30 minutes before procedure
Intermediate-risk patients allergic to penicillin	vancomycin 1 gm IV over 1-2 hours completed within 30 minutes of procedure.

Prophylaxis for Bacterial Endocarditis in Children

For dental, oral, respiratory tract or esophageal procedures	
Standard prophylaxis	amoxicillin 50 mg/kg PO 1 hour before procedure
Unable to take oral meds	ampicillin 50 mg/kg IM/IV 30 minutes before procedure
Penicillin-allergic	clindamycin 20 mg/kg PO or cephalexin 50 mg/kg PO or azithromycin 15 mg/kg PO or clarithromycin 15 mg/kg PO 1 hour before procedure
Penicillin-allergic and unable to take oral meds	clindamycin 20 mg/kg IV or cefazolin 25 mg/kg IM/IV within 30 minutes of procedure
For genitourinary and gastrointestinal procedures (excluding the esophagus)	
High-risk patients	ampicillin 50 mg/kg IV/IM plus gentamicin 1.5 mg/kg (up to 120 mg) IV/IM 30 minutes before procedure. Then, ampicillin 25 mg/kg IV/IM or amoxicillin 25 mg/kg PO 6 hours after procedure
High-risk patients allergic to penicillin	vancomycin 20 mg/kg IV over 1-2 hours plus gentamicin 1.5 mg/kg (up to 120 mg) IV both completed within 30 minutes of procedure.
Intermediate-risk patients	amoxicillin 50 mg/kg PO or ampicillin 50 mg/kg IV/IM 30 minutes before procedure
Intermediate-risk patients allergic to penicillin	vancomycin 20 mg/kg IV over 1-2 hours completed within 30 minutes of procedure.

References: JAMA, 1997; 277: 1794-1801 and NEJM, 1995; 332 (1): 38-44.

Baseline Diagnostic Screening Studies for HIV-positive Patients

Test	Whom to test	Frequency of testing
HIV-1 serology	All patients	Baseline only
Total CD₄ count	All patients	Every 3-4 months
HIV-1 RNA by PCR	All patients	Every 3-4 months
Complete blood count	All patients	As needed
Full chemistry panel	All patients	As needed
Fasting lipid panel	All patients	Baseline then as needed
VDRL	All patients	Annually
Urine NAAT for gonorrhea/chlamydia	All patients	Baseline and at least annually
Vaginal trichomonas swab	Women	Baseline and then annually
Purified protein derivative (PPD) skin test	If no history of positive PPD or tuberculosis	Annually
Toxoplasma antibody titer	Sulfa-allergic patients	Baseline if CD₄<200 cells/µL
Varicella zoster antibody titer	Unknown history of chickenpox infection	Baseline
Hepatitis B virus antigen and antibody tests	All patients (vaccinate those nonimmune)	Baseline
Anti-CMV IgG antibodies	All patients	Baseline (for transfusions)
Hepatitis C virus antibody	History of intravenous drug use or transfusion	Baseline
G6PD level	Certain ethnic groups*	Baseline
Pap smear	All women	Every 6 - 12 months

G6PD = Glucose-6-phosphate dehydrogenase, VDRL = venereal disease research laboratory, NAAT = nucleic acid amplification test, RNA = ribonucleic acid, PCR = polymerase chain reaction, CMV = cytomegalovirus, * - African-Americans and those of Mediterranean, Indian and Southeast Asian descent

Vaccinations

- Influenza vaccine yearly
- Hepatitis A Virus vaccine series
- Pneumovax q10 years
- HBV vaccine series
- Tetanus q10 years

When to Consider Initiation of Highly-Active Antiretroviral Therapy

- Symptomatic HIV infection or AIDS-defining illness
- Asymptomatic HIV infection if < 350 CD₄ T cells/mm³
- Asymptomatic HIV infection if quantitative HIV-1 RNA > 100,000 copies/mL
- Needle stick prophylaxis
- Compliant, motivated and capable individuals

Prophylaxis for Opportunistic Infections in Patients with AIDS

Infection	CD₄ count	Preferred medication prophylaxis
Pneumocystis carinii pneumonia	< 200 cells/ µL	trimethoprim-sulfamethoxazole DS 1 tablet PO daily **or** dapsone 100 mg PO daily
Toxoplasma gondii	< 100 cells/ µL	trimethoprim-sulfamethoxazole DS 1 tablet PO daily **or** (oral doses of dapsone 50 mg daily + pyrimethamine 50 mg & leucovorin 25 mg qwk)
Mycobacterium avium complex	< 50 cells/ µL	azithromycin 1200 mg PO qwk **or** clarithromycin 500 mg PO bid **or** rifabutin 300 mg PO daily
History of salmonellosis	Any	Consider chronic ciprofloxacin 500 mg PO daily for history of severe salmonella septicemia
Varicella zoster	Any	Varicella zoster immune globulin 1.25 mL x 5 vials IM within 96 hrs of exposure
+ PPD skin test	Any	isoniazid 300 mg PO daily and pyridoxine 50 mg PO daily x 9 months

Note: Would recommend that HIV-positive patients be cared for in collaboration with an HIV specialist as the spectrum of disease is broad & rapidly changing. Check www.hivatis.org or www.aidsinfo.nih.gov/guidelines or www.iasusa.org for details of HIV practice guidelines. References: CID, 2004; 39: 609-29.

84   Adverse Side Effects with Antiretroviral Therapy

Drug				
Abacavir[1] *Ziagen*	Nausea vomiting	5-15%	Insomnia	2-7%
	Fever, Rash	3 & 7%	Diarrhea	1-12%
	Dizziness	5-10%	Hypersensitivity	3-5%
Adefovir dipivoxil	Nephrotoxicity	3-5%	Diarrhea	5%
	AST/ALT/CK elevation	2-4%	Nausea	5-8%
Amprenavir[3] *Agenerase*	Rash	18%	Headache	7-44%
	Nausea	10-33%	Vomiting	15%
Atazanavir[3]	Hyperbilirubinemia	35-47%	Hyperglycemia	3-5%
			1st-degree AV block	< 1%
Delavirdine[2] *Rescriptor*	Rash	10-18%	Fatigue	3-5%
	Headache	3-11%	Diarrhea	4%
Didanosine[1] *Videx, ddI*	Diarrhea	15-28%	Periph. Neuropathy	2-20%
	Pancreatitis	5-9%	AST/ALT elevation	6-10%
Efavirenz[2] *Sustiva*	CNS effects	52%	AST/ALT elevation	2%
	Rash	5-10%		
Emtricitabine[1]	Hyperpigmentation	5-10%	Headache, nausea	5-10%
Fosamprenavir[3]	Rash		Headache,	
	Diarrhea, vomiting	19%	hyperglycemia	
	Hyperlipidemia		AST/ALT elevation	
Hydroxyurea *Hydrea, Doxia*	↓ WBC, platelets, Hgb	All 15%	Stomatitis, rash	8 & 6%
	Nausea, headache	5 & 12%	AST/ALT elevation	2%
Indinavir[3] *Crixivan*	Nephrolithiasis	3-5%	Abdominal pain	9%
	Elevated bilirubin	10%	Headache	6%
	Nausea	12%	Vomiting, diarrhea	4 & 5%
Lamuvidine[1] *Epivir, 3TC*	Headache, fatigue	8 & 4%	Nausea, insomnia	4% each
Nelfinavir[3] *Viracept*	Diarrhea	14-32%	Nausea	3-7%
Nevirapine[2] *Viramune*	Rash	17-24%	Fever	5-10%
	Nausea	7-11%	AST/ALT/GGT high	3-8%
	Headache	7-10%	Steven Johnson's	0.5%
Ritonavir[3] *Norvir*	Nausea, Headache	26 & 5%	Asthenia	9-14%
	Diarrhea	13-21%	Perioral dysesthesia	3-6%
	Altered taste	5-15%	Hyperlipidemia	2-8%
	Anorexia, Vomiting	3-15%	AST/ALT elevation	5-6%
Saquinavir[3] *Fortovase, Invirase*	Diarrhea	20%	Headache	5%
	Nausea, abd. Pain	11 & 9%	Fatigue	5%
	Dyspepsia, flatulence	8 & 8%	AST/ALT elevation	2-6%
Stavudine[1] *Zerit, d4T*	Periph. Neuropathy	13-24%	GI upset	4-6%
	AST/ALT elevation	5-10%	Headache	3-5%
Tenofovir[1]	Asthenia	7-11%	Headache	5-8%
	Diarrhea & Vomiting	11 & 6%	AST/ALT elevation	2-4%
Zalcitabine[1] *Hivid, ddC*	Periph. Neuropathy	10-30%	Stomatitis	2-17%
	Rash	10-20%		
Zidovudine[1] *Retrovir, AZT, ZDV*	Headache	12-18%	Myopathy/Myalgia	6-18%
	Neutropenia	2-31%	Fatigue, Anemia	2-7%
	Nausea or vomiting	4-26%	Insomnia	4-5%

1 Nucleoside reverse transcriptase inhibitors (NRTIs), 2 Nonnucleoside reverse transcriptase inhibitors (NNRTIs), 3 Protease inhibitors. AST = aspartate aminotransferase, ALT = alanine aminotransferase, CK = creatinine phosphokinase, CNS = central nervous system, WBC = white blood count, Hgb = hemoglobin, GGT = gamma glutamyl transpeptidase, abd. = abdominal, GI = gastrointestinal and periph. = peripheral AV = atrioventricular. Reference: Clin Infect Dis 2000; 30 (Suppl 2): S96 & www.aidsinfo.nih.gov/guidelines
Adapted with permission from the Tarascon Adult Emergency Pocketbook, 3rd Ed., Tarascon Publishing.

Typical Cerebrospinal Fluid Parameters

	Normal	Bacterial	Viral	Fungal	Tb	Abscess
WBC/ml	0-5	> 1000[1]	< 1000	100-500	100-500	10-1000
%PMN	0-15	> 80[1]	< 50	< 50	< 50	< 50
%lymph	> 50	< 50	> 50	> 80	↑ Monos	varies
Glucose	45-65	< 40	45-65	30-45	30-45	45-60
Ratio[2]	0.6	≤ 0.4	0.6	< 0.4	< 0.4	0.6
Protein[3]	20-45	> 150	50-100	100-500	100-500	> 50
Pressure[4]	6-20	20-50	Variable	> 20	> 20	variable

1 – early meningitis may have lower numbers, 2 – CSF/blood glucose ratio, 3 – mg/dl,
4 - opening pressure in cm H₂0. Adapted from EM Reports 1998; 19:94.

General Guidelines for Meningitis Treatment

- Perform blood cultures and lumbar puncture as quickly as possible
- Start empiric antibiotics +/- adjunctive dexamethasone as soon as lumbar puncture completed or prior to CT scan if this precedes a lumbar puncture
- Adjunctive dexamethasone administered prior to or concurrent with antibiotics
  - ➢ 0.15 mg/kg IV q6h x 2-4 d for H. influenzae meningitis in infants & children
  - ➢ 10 mg IV q6h x 4 days for adult pneumococcal meningitis
- No role for rapid bacterial antigen testing or Limulus lysate assays
- **Duration of IV antibiotics:** 7 days for *N. meningitidis* or *H. influenzae*, 10-14 days for *S. pneumoniae*, 14-21 days for *streptococcus agalactiae* and 21 days for aerobic gram-negative bacilli or *listeria monocytogenes*

Indications for CT scan of Head prior to Lumbar Puncture

Age ≥ 60 years	History of recent stroke	Immunosuppressed state[1]
Seizure in last week	Altered level of consciousness	Dysphasia or aphasia
Gaze or facial palsy	Cognitive impairment[2]	Focal extremity weakness
Papilledema	Focal cerebral infection	CNS mass lesion

1 – HIV infection, chronic steroids or post-transplantation
2 – Inability to answer 2 consecutive questions or follow 2 consecutive commands.

Cerebrospinal Fluid Tests to Differentiate Adult Bacterial vs Viral Meningitis

- Individual predictors of bacterial meningitis with 99% accuracy: CSF glucose <34 mg/dL, CSF/blood glucose <0.23, CSF protein >220 mg/dL, CSF with >2000 leukocytes/mm³ or CSF neutrophils >1180/ mm³
- Normal serum C-reactive protein has a 99% negative predictive value to rule out bacterial meningitis
- CSF lactate ≥4 mmol/L predicts bacterial meningitis in postop neurosurgical pts.

Empiric Antibiotic Therapy for Bacterial Meningitis

Clinical Condition / Age	Empiric Antibiotic Therapy
< 1 month	ampicillin 200 mg/kg/d + cefotaxime 150-200 mg/kg/d
1 - 23 months	vancomycin 60 mg/kg/d* + ceftriaxone 80-100 mg/kg/d
2 – 50 years	vancomycin 30-45 mg/kg/d* + ceftriaxone 2 gm IV bid
> 50 years	vancomycin 30-45 mg/kg/d* + ceftriaxone 2 gm IV bid + ampicillin 2 gm IV q4h
Basilar skull fracture	vancomycin 30-45 mg/kg/d* + ceftriaxone 2 gm IV bid
Penetrating trauma, CSF shunt, post-neurosurgical	vancomycin 30-45 mg/kg/d * + cefepime 2 gm IV q8h **or** ceftazidime 2 gm IV q8h

* - Maintain serum trough levels 15-20 mcg/mL and give vancomycin as divided doses q8-12h

References: Infectious Disease Clinics of North America, 1999; 13 (3): 579-94. CID, 2004; 39: 1267–84.

Screening for Tuberculosis (Tb)
- Positive PPD (purified protein derivative) test is evidence of prior tuberculosis infection, but not necessarily evidence of active tuberculosis disease.

Whom to Screen:
- Children at 12 months and at preschool age and pregnant patients
- High-risk subgroups: patients > 65 yrs, gastrectomy, gastric bypass, immunosuppressed (HIV-positive, diabetes, renal failure, chronic steroid/immunosuppressive therapy, head/neck or hematologic malignancies), silicosis, organ transplant patients, malabsorptive syndromes, alcoholics, intravenous drug users, close contacts of patients with active pulmonary tuberculosis, immigrants from endemic areas, medically underserved, low socioeconomic class, and residents/employees of long-term care facilities, jails and hospitals
  ➢ High-risk patients should be screened annually
- Chronic cough, hemoptysis, unexplained weight loss, fevers or sweats

PPD Test Positive if (measure induration in transverse axis only)
- ≥ 5 mm: close contacts with active Tb, HIV-positive or chest x-ray findings consistent with old tuberculosis
- ≥10 mm: all high-risk patients as above (excluding those in 5 mm category)
- ≥15 mm: all other patients
- Interpret irrespective of prior bCG (bacillus Calmette-Guerin) vaccine

Management of Positive PPD
- Check chest x-ray for evidence of active or old infection.
- Abnormal chest x-ray → 3 morning sputa for acid-fast bacilli smear and culture.
- Treat for latent Tb infection if PPD and acid-fast bacilli smear negative x 3
- If acid-fast bacilli smear or culture positive, treat as active tuberculosis

Latent Tuberculosis infection
- Isoniazid (INH) 5 mg/kg/d up to 300 mg PO daily
- Pyridoxine 1-2 mg/kg/d to 50 mg PO daily: minimizes INH-induced neuropathy
- Duration 6 months (adults), 9 months (children) and 9-12 months HIV+

Active Pulmonary Tuberculosis
- Symptoms: cough, fever, sweats, weight loss, anorexia and malaise
- Generally start 4 drug therapy x 2 months then continue 2 drugs (based on acid-fast bacilli sensitivities) x 4 months
  ➢ For isoniazid-containing regimens, add pyridoxine to minimize neuropathy.
- Monitor for adverse med reactions and monthly sputum samples
- Patients **not** infectious if: adequate meds x 2-3 weeks, good clinical response and sputum acid-fast bacilli smear negative x 3

Medication	Monitoring	Adverse reactions
isoniazid	Liver panel	Hepatitis, neuropathy
rifampin	Liver panel	Orange urine and secretions, GI upset, hepatitis and rash
pyrazinamide	Liver panel, uric acid	GI upset, hepatitis, gout, arthralgias
ethambutol	Visual acuity	Optic neuritis
streptomycin	Hearing, renal panel	Ototoxicity common

Reference: Am Fam Physician, 2000; 61: 2667-82.

Definitions:
- Acute renal failure: The rapid decline in the glomerular filtration rate with retention of nitrogenous waste products & creatinine ↑ over hours to days.
- Oliguria: urine output < 400 ml/day
- Anuria: urine output < 100 ml/day

Classification and Causes of Acute Renal Failure (ARF):
- **Causes of prerenal azotemia**
  - ➤ Hypovolemia
  - ➤ Distributive shock (sepsis, anaphylaxis or neurogenic)
  - ➤ Decreased effective circulating volume (chronic CHF, sepsis, nephrotic syndrome, decompensated cirrhosis or "third spacing" of fluids)
  - ➤ Decreased cardiac output (cardiogenic shock or pericardial tamponade)
  - ➤ Chronic hypercalcemia causing renal vasoconstriction
- **Causes of postrenal or obstructive nephropathy**
  - ➤ Bilateral ureteral obstruction
  - ➤ Bladder outlet obstruction (benign prostatic hyperplasia, bladder stone or cancer of the cervix, bladder or prostate)
  - ➤ Neurogenic bladder
  - ➤ Urethral stricture
  - ➤ Meds: acetazolamide, acyclovir, indinivir, sulfadiazine, topiramate and triamterene
- **Intrinsic ARF:** acute glomerulonephritis, tubular necrosis or interstitial nephritis
- **Causes of acute glomerulonephritis (AGN)**
  - ➤ Systemic illnesses: systemic lupus erythematosus, Wegener's granulomatosis, Goodpasture's disease and polyarteritis nodosa
  - ➤ Henoch Schonlein purpura or Immunoglobulin A (IgA) nephropathy
  - ➤ Infectious: hepatitis B virus, hepatitis C virus, endocarditis, HIV and post-streptococcal
  - ➤ Malignancy
  - ➤ Mixed cryoglobulinemia (often hepatitis C virus-related)
  - ➤ Medications (rare): allopurinol, hydralazine, penicillamine, gold or cytokine therapy
- **Causes of acute tubular necrosis (ATN)**
  - ➤ Ischemia from renal hypoperfusion
  - ➤ Medications/toxins: aminoglycosides, amphotericin B, arsenic, carboplatin, cisplatin, chromium, contrast dyes, cyclosporine, foscarnet, ifosfamide, methotrexate, methoxyflurane, oxaliplatin, pentamidine, plicamycin, rifampin, tetracyclines and trimetrexate
  - ➤ Pigment-related: severe hemolysis or rhabdomyolysis
  - ➤ Cast nephropathy from multiple myeloma
- **Acute interstitial nephritis (AIN)**
  - ➤ Medications (90% of AIN): acyclovir, adefovir, allopurinol, azathioprine, carbamazepine, cephalosporins, cidofovir, cimetidine, cyclosporine, erythromycin, ethambutol, fluoroquinolones, furosemide, lithium, NSAIDS, penicillins, phenobarbital, phenytoin, ranitidine, sulfas, tacrolimus, tetracyclines, thiazide diuretics, vancomycin and some Chinese herbs (such as aristolochic acid)
  - ➤ Infection
  - ➤ Lymphomatous or leukemic infiltration of interstitium

- **Other nephrotoxic agents:** cytarabine and melphalan (via tumor lysis syndrome), gemcitabine and mitomycin (hemolytic uremic syndrome), interleukin-2 (vascular leak syndrome), gallium nitrate, IV immune globulin, nitrosoureas and streptozocin (unclear etiologies for acute renal failure)
- **Causes of pseudo-renal failure** (benign elevation of serum creatinine)
  ➤ Cimetidine, glucocorticoids and trimethoprim

Clinical Presentation of ARF
- Asymptomatic
- Fatigue, lethargy and generalized weakness
- Palpitations or arrhythmia-related syncope
- Congestive heart failure or anasarca
- Uremia: somnolence, pericarditis, asterixis, nausea, anorexia or pruritus

Urinary Studies in ARF

Subtype	Urinary sediment	UNa (mmol/L)	Protein (mg/dL)	FENa (%)	FEurea* (%)
Prerenal	Bland	< 20	0	< 1	< 35
Postrenal	Bland	Usually >20	0	> 1	> 35
AGN	RBC casts	< 20	≥100	< 1	< 35
ATN	Gran. casts	> 20	30-100	> 1‡	> 35
AIN	WBC casts	> 20	30-100	> 1	> 35

U = urine, crt = creatinine, BUN = blood urea nitrogen, Na = sodium, RBC = red blood cells,
WBC = white blood cells, Gran. = granular
FENa = fractional excretion of sodium = (UNa x Serum crt)/(Ucrt x Serum Na) x 100
FEurea = fractional excretion of urea = (Uurea x Serum crt)/(Ucrt x BUN) x 100
* - more useful measure when patient receiving diuretics
‡ - contrast nephropathy and pigment-induced nephropathy cause ATN and may have a FENa < 1

Work-up of ARF
- Thorough history and physical and careful investigation of medication history
- Calculate FENa or FEurea using equations above and check urinary sediment
- Place a foley catheter & measure the postvoid residual after urine studies done.
- Renal ultrasound (for size and to check for hydronephrosis/hydroureter)
- Labs to consider depending on classification of ARF and likely causes: urine eosinophils (present in 30% of AIN), complete blood count, electrolytes, renal panel, calcium, phosphate, hepatitis B and C virus serologies, HIV test, anti-streptolysin O titer, anti-glomerular basement membrane antibody, antineutrophil cytoplasmic antibody, antinuclear antibody, complement studies, serum cryoglobulins, blood cultures, serum and urine protein electrophoreses
- When to perform a renal biopsy
  ➤ There is no unanimous consensus about this issue.
  ➤ Reasonable approach is to biopsy patients with an active urinary sediment or who have an unexplained intrarenal process (AGN, ATN or AIN)

Indication for Acute Dialysis (mnemonic AEIOU)
- **A** – Acidosis: persistent arterial pH < 7.2 refractory to medical therapy
- **E** – Electrolytes: severe hyperkalemia refractory to medical therapy
- **I** – Intoxications or overdoses
- **O** – fluid Overload
- **U** – Uremia

References: NEJM, 1996; 334 (22): 1448-60. NEJM, 1997; 336 (12): 870-1. J. Amer. Soc. Neph., 1999; 10 (8): 1833-9. J. Amer. Soc. Neph., 1998; 9 (4): 710-8, J. Amer. Soc. Neph., 1998; 9 (3): 506-15. AFP, 2000; 61: 2077-88 and AFP, 2003; 67 (12): 2527-39.

Definition of Chronic Kidney Disease (CKD)
- Structural or functional kidney abnormalities for ≥ 3 months
  - ➤ Hematuria, proteinuria or abnormal kidneys by imaging studies
- Glomerular filtration rate (GFR) < 60 mL/min./1.73m² for ≥ 3 months

Classification of Chronic Kidney Disease
- Native versus transplanted kidneys
- Diabetic versus nondiabetic etiologies of chronic kidney disease

National Kidney Foundation Stages of Chronic Kidney Disease

Stage	Description	GFR (mL/min./1.73m²)	Action
1	Kidney damage (NL GFR)	≥ 90	Treat comorbid conditions, slow progression & CVD risk reduction
2	Mild ↓ GFR	60 - 89	Estimate/slow disease progression
3	Moderate ↓ GFR	30 - 59	Treat disease complications
4	Severe ↓ GFR	15 - 29	Definite referral to nephrologist* Prepare for dialysis/transplantation
5	Renal failure	< 15	Dialyze if uremic or GFR < 10

CVD = cardiovascular disease and GFR = glomerular filtration rate (expressed in mL/min/1.73m²)

* - Nephrology referral can be made at any stage & should be made if a clinical action plan cannot be made.

Select Etiologies of CRF (diabetes and hypertension account for 66% of all cases)

• Diabetes mellitus	• Hypertension	• Polycystic kidney disease
• Glomerulonephritis	• Alport's syndrome	• Medullary sponge kidney
• Reflux nephropathy	• Myeloma kidney	• Analgesic nephropathy
• Sarcoidosis	• Amyloidosis	• Chronic obstructive uropathy
• Lupus nephritis	• IgA nephropathy	• Hypercalcemic nephropathy

Screening for Chronic Kidney Disease in Adults
- Risk factors for CKD: Age ≥ 60, family history of CKD, history of low birth weight, racial or ethnic minority status, low income, diabetes, HTN, autoimmune disease, recurrent UTIs, nephrolithiasis and history of obstructive uropathy
- All patients with risk factors for CKD should be screened annually
- Screen with urine albumin-to-creatinine ratio and estimation of GFR
  - ➤ First morning voided specimen is optimal but random specimen is adequate.
  - ➤ Urine albumin-to creatinine > 30 mg/gm = microalbuminuria (abnormal)
  - ➤ Urine albumin-to creatinine > 300 mg/gm = albuminuria/overt proteinuria
- MDRD (Modification of Diet in Renal Disease) equation for estimating GFR
  - ➤ GFR (mL/min./1.73 m²) = 186 x serum creatinine (mg/dL) x age (years) x 0.742 (women) x 1.212 (if African-American)
- Urinalysis and microscopy to assess for hematuria, pyuria and casts.

Monitoring Patients with Chronic Kidney Disease
- Follow urine protein-to-creatinine (mg/gm) ratio once overt proteinuria develops.
- Monitor GFR and degree of proteinuria at each periodic health evaluation

Work-up of Chronic Renal Failure (CRF)
- History of any systemic diseases or medication usage that may cause CRF?
- Renal ultrasound to assess size and cortical appearance of kidneys
  - ➤ Kidneys tend to be small and cortex exhibits increased echogenicity
- Urinalysis with microscopic exam
- Urine protein-per-creatinine ratio (measured in mg of protein per gm of creatinine) correlates with the grams of proteinuria in 24 hours.
- **Labs:** complete blood count, full chemistry panel, HIV and hepatitis B and C virus serologies, intact parathyroid hormone level (iPTH), lipid panel & other labs based on clinical evaluation.

Clinical Presentation of Chronic Renal Failure
- Asymptomatic
- Uremia: anorexia, nausea, fatigue, pruritus, encephalopathy, bleeding diathesis, lassitude or pericarditis
- Pulmonary edema +/- anasarca

Typical Lab Findings of Chronic Renal Failure

Normocytic anemia	Hyperkalemia	Anion gap acidosis
High blood urea nitrogen (BUN) and creatinine	Hypocalcemia
Mild hyponatremia	Hypermagnesemia	Hyperphosphatemia

Management of Chronic Kidney Disease
- **Blood pressure:** keep BP < 130/80 or < 125/75 for overt proteinuria
  - Best agents are ACEIs or ARBs for proteinuric kidney disease
    - Use caution starting these if serum creatinine >3 mg/dL and need to follow potassium, BUN and creatinine closely during titration period.
  - Verapamil and diltiazem also decrease proteinuria
  - Diuretics are needed in most patients for blood pressure control
- **Anemia:** epoetin alpha 40-60 units/kg subcutaneous qweek-to-3x/week to maintain hemoglobin 11-12 mg/dL.
- **Access:** refer patient to surgeon for dialysis access when CrCl < 25 mL/min.
  - Protect arm most suitable for access from venipunctures, IVs or BP checks.
- **Metabolic acidosis:** maintain serum bicarbonate > 20 mmol/L with sodium bicarbonate 0.5-1 MEq/kg/d
  - May use diuretics to control sodium and fluid retention
- **Dietician consult:** low sodium, potassium, phosphate and protein diet
- **Vitamins:** initiate multivitamin 1 tablet PO daily and folate 1 mg PO daily
- **Hyperphosphatemia treatments:** calcium acetate 667 mg 1-3 tabs PO tid with meals (or calcium carbonate), but avoid if hypercalcemic
  - Restrict dietary phosphate intake
  - Sevelamer 800-1600 mg PO tid with meals (use if patient hypercalcemic)
  - Lanthanum 250-500 mg PO tid with meals; max = 3 grams/day
  - Goal calcium 8.4 - 9.5 mg/dL, phosphate 3.5 - 5.5 mg/dL and calcium-phosphate product < 55
- **Vitamin D analogs:** calcitriol 0.25-2 mcg PO daily or paricalcitol 0.04-0.1 mcg/kg IV 3x/week or doxercalciferol 2-6 mcg IV/PO 3x/week titrated to iPTH.
  - Use only if serum calcium < 9.5 mg/dL and phosphate < 5.5 mg/dL.
  - Goal iPTH: Stage 3 (35-70 pg/mL), Stage 4 (70-110), Stage 5 (150-300)
- Strict glucose and lipid control (HgbA1c < 7% & serum LDL < 100 mg/dL)
- Reduced dose of renally-cleared drugs as appropriate.
- Consider GI prophylaxis with famotidine 20 mg PO daily
- **Avoid:** meperidine, fleets enemas, milk of magnesia, magnesium citrate, magnesium-aluminum antacids, nitrofurantoin, NSAIDs, COX 2-inhibitors and caution with digoxin and antiarrhythmics
- **Lifestyle changes:** smoking cessation, weight loss and lipid control
- **Vaccinations:** hepatitis B, influenza, tetanus and pneumovax
- **Indications for dialysis:** Estimated GFR<10 mL/min/1.73 m², symptoms/signs of uremia, malnutrition or HTN, hyperkalemia or acidosis refractory to treatment

HgbA1c = glycohemoglobin, LDL = low-density lipoprotein, iPTH = intact parathyroid hormone, COX 2 = cyclo-oxygenase type 2, CrCl = creatinine clearance
References: Mayo Clin. Proc., 1999; 74: 269-73. NEJM, 1998; 339: 1054-62 and 1448-56. AFP, 2004; 70: 869-76 and 1091-7 and Am. J. Kidney Dis., 2002; 39 (S1): S1-266. See www.kidney.org or www.kdoqi.org.

Folstein Mini-Mental Status Exam

Score	Orientation, Registration, Attention, Recall, Language/praxis
5	What is the year, season, date, day, and month?
5	Where are we (city, state, country, hospital, and floor)?
3	Name 3 objects: one second to say each. Ask patient for all 3 after you have said them. 1 point for each correct answer.
5	Serial 7s backward from 100 (stop after 5X) or spell WORLD backwards
3	Ask 3 objects above to be repeated. 1 point for each correct answer
2	Show pencil & watch and ask subject to name them
1	Ask patient to repeat "no ifs, ands, or buts."
3	Obey: "Take this paper in your right hand, fold in ½, put it on floor (or bed)"
1	Read & obey written command: "Close your eyes"
1	Write any sentence with a noun, verb (sentence must be sensible)
1	Copy design below: Copy must contain all angles and 2 must intersect
Total = 30 points	

A score ≤ 23 is abnormal (dementia)   *J Psychiat Res 1975; 12: 189.*

Additional tests of cognitive function

- Clock test: have the patient draw the face of a clock with all of the numbers and then make the clock demonstrate the time 11:10 (implying but not mentioning that they add the hands of the clock). This tests visual-spatial function.
- Ask questions to investigate judgment & insight to check frontal lobe function.

Differentiating Between Delirium, Dementia, and Acute Psychosis

Feature	Delirium	Dementia	Psychosis
Age of onset	Any	Usually older	13-40 years
Psychiatric history	Usually absent	Usually absent	Present
Emotion	Labile	Normal or labile	Flat affect
Vital signs	Abnormal	Normal	Normal
Onset	Sudden	Gradual	Sudden
24h course	Fluctuates	Stable	Stable
Consciousness	Altered or depressed	Clear	Clear
Attention	Disordered	OK unless severe	Can be disordered
Cognition	Disordered	Impaired	Selective
Hallucinations	Visual or sensory	Rare	Auditory
Delusions	Fleeting	Rare	Sustained, grand
Orientation	Impaired	Often Impaired	May be impaired
Psychomotor	↑ or ↓ or Shifting	Normal	Variable
Speech	Incoherent	Perseveration, difficulty finding words	Normal, slow or rapid
Involuntary move	Asterixis or tremor	Often absent	Usually absent
Physical illness or drug toxicity	Drug toxicity	Either (esp. Alzheimer's)	Neither

Emerg Med Clin North Am 2000; 18: 243.

Adapted with permission from the Tarascon Adult Emergency Pocketbook, 3rd Ed., Tarascon Publishing.

The Diagnosis of Delirium Requires the Following 3 Conditions:
- Disturbance of consciousness: decreased awareness of environment, poor attention span leading to poor information recall
- Cognitive change: confusion, disorientation or language impairment
- Sudden onset, fluctuating severity and transient in nature

Commonly Seen Associated Findings
- Alterations in sleep-wake cycle
- Mood lability
- Hallucinations or visual misperceptions

Risk Factors for Delirium
- Advanced age, dementia, comorbid medical disorder, psychiatric disorder, polypharmacy, depression, social isolation or a history of substance abuse

Diagnosis
- Patients must meet above-mentioned clinical characteristics
- Confusion Assessment Method reliable tool to detect delirium (Refer to Annals Internal Med. 1990; 113: 941 for details of this tool.)

Categories	Specific Etiologies (mnemonic = AEIOUMITS)
Alcohol (or illicit drug)	Alcohol or illicit drug intoxication or withdrawal
Endocrine/Electrolytes/ Environmental	Electrolytes: ↑/↓ sodium, hypercalcemia ↑/↓ thyroid, ↑/↓ cortisol, hyperthermia or hypothermia
Infection/Infarct	Myocardial infarction, hypertensive encephalopathy, hyperviscosity, any infection
Oxygen (gases)	Hypoxia, hypercarbia or carbon monoxide poisoning
Uremia	Usually blood urea nitrogen > 100 mg/dL
Metabolic/Mental (Psychiatric) or Meds (see below)	B$_{12}$ deficiency, Wilson's disease, Wernicke's and/or Korsakoff's syndrome, hepatic encephalopathy or psychiatric (diagnosis of exclusion)
Insulin	Severe hypoglycemia or hyperglycemia
Trauma/Toxins/TTP	Head trauma, toxins (organophosphates, etc.) or Thrombotic thrombocytopenic purpura
Seizures, **S**pace-occupying lesion, **S**troke	Stroke, intracranial bleed, brain tumor, hydrocephalus or seizure
Commonly Implicated Medications	
Anticholinergics, amiodarone, amphotericin B, anticonvulsants, antihistamines, antiparkinsonian meds, aspirin, ß-blockers, cephalosporins, chlorpromazine, colchicine, digoxin, disopyramide, fluoroquinolones, GI antispasmodics, histamine receptor$_2$ blockers, metoclopramide, methyldopa, neuroleptics, nifedipine, NSAIDS, opiates, penicillins, pentamidine, procainamide, prochlorperazine, promethazine, quinidine, sedatives, steroids, sympathomimetics, theophylline, tricyclic antidepressants, tuberculosis meds, zalcitabine, zidovudine and zolpidem	

Treatment of Delirium
- Discontinue all nonessential medications and treat underlying condition(s).
- Detailed history, exam and lab evaluation for above conditions
- Low-dose haloperidol (2.5 - 5 mg IM) for agitation or psychotic symptoms
- Quiet room with familiar objects, family/friends to calm and reorient patient
- Use sensory aids to correct visual or auditory impairments
- Maintain consistent caregivers and constantly reorient/reassure patient.
- Avoid overstimulation and change lighting to cue day and night.

References: Emer. Med. Clin. N. Amer., 2000; 18 (2): 243-52. Amer. Fam. Physician. 1997; 55 (5): 1773-80.

Definition of Dementia: Acquired cognitive impairment severe enough to interfere with daily functioning and showing at least 3 of the following areas of deficiency: memory, language, visuospatial skills, complex cognition, emotion or personality.
- Folstein Mini-Mental Status Exam (MMSE) < 24/30 indicative of dementia
  ➢ Less accurate for age < 50, low level of education or non-caucasions
- Must rule out delirium and depression (see corresponding sections)

Functional Assessment Staging (FAST) Scale to Stage Alzheimer's disease
- Developed for Alzheimer's but principles applicable to all types of dementia

FAST	Timing*	MMSE	Characteristics and Abilities
Stage 1	N/A	28-30	No problems. Normal adult
Stage 2	N/A	26-28	Forgetful of names and location of objects
Stage 3	0-7 yrs	24-26	Poor job function and concentration deficit
Stage 4	7-11 yrs	14-23	↓ ability to travel, handle finances, plan activities or perform complex task. Withdrawal + denial common
Stage 5	11-13	5-13	Difficulty choosing proper clothing, no recall of some names or numbers important to patient
Stage 6	13-15	0-5	Needs assistance putting on clothes, bathing and toileting. May forget spouse's name. Disoriented. +/- delusions, obsessions, anxiety or loss of will.
Stage 7	15-17	0	Verbal abilities lost→ unable to sit→ unable to smile→ unable to lift head up→ unable to swallow

* - timing is the number of years into the disease when most patients will be in the various stages.
Stage 4 = mild dementia, Stage 5 = moderate dementia, Stage 6 = severe dementia, Stage 7 = end-stage

Alzheimer's Dementia (AD: 60-70% of dementias)
- Gradually progressive deterioration following FAST stages as above
- Personality changes (extreme passivity→ severe hostility)
- Psychotic symptoms: 50% with delusions and 25% with hallucinations
- Mood disorders: 40% depressed or anxious
- Parkinsonism: 30% can develop Parkinsonian features

Vascular Dementia (20 - 30% of dementias)
- Stepwise progression of cognitive decline that usually follows a stroke
- Urinary incontinence and gait disturbance common

Parkinson's (Lewy Body) Dementia (~5% of dementias)
- Parkinson's features (see corresponding section)
- Graphic, recurrent hallucinations and delusions common

Frontal Lobe Dementia (1 - 3%, e.g. Pick's disease)
- Impaired initiation, goal setting and planning more than memory loss
- Apathy, disinhibited behavior and neglect of hygiene and grooming
- Language impairments (logorrhea, echolalia and palilalia)

Reversible Dementias (2 % of dementias are fully reversible)

B₁₂ deficiency	Hypothyroidism	HIV dementia	Neurosyphilis
Normal pressure hydrocephalus (triad of dementia, ataxia and urinary incontinence)			

Treatment of Dementia
- Recommend driving restriction when at FAST stage ≥ 4 (www.alz.org)
- Cholinesterase inhibitors improve cognition in mild-moderate dementia
  ➢ Beneficial for AD, vascular dementia and Lewy body dementias
  ➢ Donepezil 5 mg PO daily x 4 weeks titrated to 10 mg PO daily
  ➢ Rivastigmine 1.5 mg PO bid titrated q2weeks to 6 mg PO bid
  ➢ Galantamine 4 mg PO bid titrated q4weeks to 12 mg PO bid
- Memantine 5 mg PO daily titrated qweek to 10 mg PO bid for mod.-severe AD
- No benefit for NSAIDS, steroids, gingko biloba, selegiline or estrogen therapy.
- Low-dose haloperidol 0.5-2 mg PO bid best for psychosis or agitation.
- Citalopram or sertraline best tolerated antidepressants for depression
- Trazodone, carbamazepine or valproic acid for aggressive behavior & insomnia

References: NEJM, 2004; 351: 56. Ann. Int. Med. 2003; 138: 925-37 and Neurology, 2001; 56: 1133-66.

Motor level	Motor function
C1-2	neck flexion
C3	side neck flexion
C4	spontaneous breathing
C5	shoulder abduction/deltoid
C6	biceps (elbow flexion), wrist extension
C7	triceps, wrist flexion
C8	thumb ext, ulnar deviation
C8/T1	finger flexion
T1-T12	intercostal and abdominal muscles

Motor level	Motor function
T7-L1	abdominal muscles
T12	cremasteric reflex
L1/L2	hip flexion, psoas
L2/3/4	hip adduction, quads
L4	foot dorsiflexion, foot inversion
L5	great toe dorsiflexion
S1	foot plantar flexion, foot eversion
S2-S4	rectal tone

Causes in Primary Care Setting: Peripheral vestibular disorder 40%, central vertigo 10%, basilar migraine 1%, psychogenic 15%, presyncope or orthostasis 5%, disequilibrium 2%, multifactoral 15% and idiopathic 12%

Assessment of Vertigo		
Characteristics	**Central Vertigo**	**Peripheral Vertigo**
Onset	Subacute/insidious	Abrupt
Timing	More continuous	Paroxysmal
Positional worsening	No	Yes
Nystagmus	Often reverses direction	Always unidirectional
Nystagmus type	Any direction possible	Horizontal / rotational
Visual fixation	No effect	Suppresses
Other neuro deficits*	Usually present	Absent
Postural instability	Severe	Mild-moderate
Ear findings‡	Absent	Can be present
Headache	May be present	Absent
Dix-Hallpike test	No habituation	Habituation common

*Neuro deficits: ataxia, nausea, diplopia, dysarthria, weakness/numbness of face or extremities
‡ Ear findings: hearing loss or tinnitus

Causes of Central Vertigo
- Posterior fossa stroke, vertebrobasilar insufficiency, cerebellopontine angle tumor or multiple sclerosis
- Work-up: magnetic resonance imaging/angiogram of posterior fossa

Benign Paroxysmal Positional Vertigo (BPV)
- Clinical presentation: Symptom duration < 1 minute, head movement provokes and symptoms are fatigable
- Diagnosis: Dix-Hallpike or Nylen Barany maneuver
- Treatment: Epley's maneuvers (see www.charite.de/ch/neuro/englishL.htm)

Labyrinthitis or Vestibular neuronitis
- Clinical presentation: prolonged episode of peripheral vertigo
- Treat with steroids +/- antivirals and symptomatic therapy (as needed)
  ➤ Diazepam 5-10 mg PO q6h prn or meclizine 25 mg PO q6h prn
  ➤ Acyclovir 400 mg PO 5x/day x 10 days may be of benefit
  ➤ Prednisone 60 mg PO daily x 10 days then taper off over 10 days.

Meniere's disease
- Clinical features: unilateral tinnitus, hearing loss, vertigo & aural fullness
- Symptomatic treatment same as for labyrinthitis
- Restrict sodium < 1,800 mg/day, caffeine and tobacco
- Hydrochlorothiazide 25 mg PO daily or acetazolamide 250 mg PO bid

Psychogenic
- Clinical features: Associated with mood or somatization disorders
  ➤ Hyperventilation can replicate symptoms

Presyncope
- Clinical presentation: near fainting and work-up same as syncope
- Chronic orthostasis can be treated with fludrocortisone 0.1-0.3 mg PO bid or midodrine 10 mg PO tid and mandates a careful work-up to determine etiology.

Disequilibrium
- Sense of imbalance while walking, common in elderly, usually multifactorial
- Risk factors: peripheral neuropathy, visual impairment, arthritis, cervical spondylosis, Parkinson's disease, mood disorder, ischemic heart disease, polypharmacy (especially anticholinergic meds) and hearing impairment

References: South Med J 2000; 93: 160. AFP, 2005; 71: 1115-30 and Med Clin N Amer, 2003; 87: 609-41

Most Common Final Cause of Falls in Elderly Patients			
Accident/Environmental	31%	Visual impairment	2%
Weakness, balance, gait disorder	17%	Syncope	0.3%
Dizziness or vertigo	13%	Unknown	5%
Drop attack	9%	Other (acute illness, arthritis,	15%
Postural/Orthostatic hypotension	3%	pain, drugs, seizure & confusion)	

Clin Geriatric Med, 2002; 18: 146.

Evaluation of Elderly Patients Presenting After a Fall			
Functional History Concerning a Fall		**Key Physical Exam Findings**	
C	Caregiver and housing adequate	I	Inflammation joints (or immobility)
A	Alcohol (and withdrawal)	H	Hypotension or orthostasis
T	Treatment (meds, compliance)	A	Auditory or visual abnormalities
A	Affect (depression)	T	Tremor
S	Syncope	E	Equilibrium (disequilibrium)
T	Teetering (dizziness or vertigo)	F	Foot problems
R	Recent medical or surgical illness	A	Arrhythmia, heart block or valve
O	Ocular problems	L	Leg-length discrepancy
P	Pain or problems with mobility	L	Lack of conditioning
H	Hearing impairment	I	Illness – general/medical
E	Environmental hazards (e.g. stairs)	N	Nutrition (weight loss?)
		G	Gait disturbance

Am Fam Phys 2000; 61: 2159.

Get Up & Go Test for Geriatric Mobility

Test: get up out of a standard armchair, walk 3 m (10 ft), turn, walk back to chair and sit down. Ambulate with or without an assistive device & follow above 3 step command. One practice trial & 3 actual trials are performed with 3 trials averaged.

	Seconds	Rating
Get Up and Go	< 10	Freely mobile
Predictive	10 - 19	Mostly independent
Results	20 – 29	Variable mobility
	≥ 30	Impaired mobility

Am Fam Physician 2000; 61: 2159.

Probability of Falling in Patients ≥ 75 Years Old

Specific Risk Factor	Total Number of Risk Factors	Probability of Falling per Year
Sedative use		8%
Cognitive impairment	No risk factors	8%
Lower extremity disability	1 risk factor	19%
Palmomental reflex	2 risk factors	32%
Abnormal balance/gait	3 risk factors	60%
Foot problems	≥4 risk factors	78%

N Engl J Med 1988; 1701.

Other references: NEJM, 2003; 348: 45. J Amer Geriatrics Soc, 2001; 49: 666 and AFP, 2005; 72: 81-8.
Adapted with permission from the Tarascon Adult Emergency Pocketbook, 3rd Edition, Tarascon Publishing.

Headache Syndromes	Location	Characteristics	Duration	Associated Symptoms	Exacerbating factors	Relieving factors
Tension	Global Bilateral	♀ > ♂, band-like pain or bilateral tightness	Variable min.-hours	Mood disorders common	Stress	Relaxation Biofeedback
Cluster	Retroorbital Periorbital Unilateral	Abrupt onset Deep and stabbing People are restless	5-180 min. Headache clusters	Ipsilateral lacrimation rhinorrhea, eye redness, miosis, ptosis & sweating	Alcohol use and supine position	
Migraines	70% unilateral	Rarely starts >40 years Gradual onset, pulsating quality ♀ > ♂, + family history + Migraine triggers	4 – 72 hours	Nausea, vomiting, photophobia phonophobia and/or aura (classical)*	Activity, exertion, bright light, loud noise, and valsalva	Rest Darkness Quiet
Temporal Arteritis	Temporal Frontal	Tender temporal artery (33%) & age>55	Variable severity	Myalgias, fatigue, ipsilateral blindness, ↑ erythrocyte sedimentation rate, sweats, & polymyalgia rheumatica		
Trigeminal Neuralgia	Trigeminal nerve area	Paroxysms of shock-like or stabbing pain in cheeks and jaw	Seconds – < 2 minute		Brushing teeth Touching face Wind on face	None
Subarachnoid Hemorrhage	Global	Sudden onset of "worst headache of my life"	Constant and severe	+/- Loss of consciousness vomiting, meningismus and photophobia	Darkness	Bright light
Medication Rebound	Global	Chronic analgesic overuse > 3x/week	Hours	Analgesic abuse mood disorders	Not applicable	Stopping medication

* - Aura = fully reversible visual scotomata, fortification spectra or oscillating lines, focal numbness or paresthesias, dysphasia, epigastric discomfort, fear or a bad smell developing gradually over 5 minutes

Indications for Neuroimaging in Patients with Nonacute Headache
- Focal neurologic exam
- Sudden onset of the "worst headache of my life"
- Headache exacerbated by coughing, sneezing or straining
- Headache with early AM worsening or awakening patient from sleep
- New headache starting after the age of 40 years or in young children
- Progressively worsening daily headache
- Presence of altered mental status, nuchal rigidity, fever or papilledema
- New headache in HIV-positive patients or those with known cancer
- Work-up of worrisome headaches
  ➤ Consider head CT **with contrast** or MRI with gadolinium in HIV-positive patients, those with known cancer or for chronic progressive headaches to assess for brain tumors or brain mets, lymphoma, infection, multiple sclerosis, arteriovenous malformations or hydrocephalus.
  ➤ If head CT normal, consider a lumbar puncture to rule out early subarachnoid hemorrhage, meningitis or pseudotumor cerebri

Treatment Options for Tension Headaches
- **Abortive therapy** typically with acetaminophen or NSAIDS
- nortriptyline or amitriptyline 10-75 mg PO qhs can be used prophylactically
- Avoid ergots, caffeine, butalbital & opiates for potential of abuse & dependence

Treatment Options for Cluster Headaches
- Have patient breathe100% oxygen at 7-10 L/min. by mask for 15-20 minutes
- **Abortive agents**: dihydroergotamine 1 mg IM or 0.5 mg nasal spray bilaterally, sumatriptan 6 mg SQ or 20 mg intranasally, zolmitriptan 5-10 mg PO or 1 mL of 10% lidocaine placed in each nostril using a cotton swab for 5 minutes
- **Prophylactic agents**

verapamil 120 – 160 mg PO tid	lithium 300 mg PO bid - tid
valproic acid 250-1000 mg PO bid	topiramate 25 – 200 mg PO daily
Start prednisone 50-80 mg PO daily x 5 d then taper off over 10-12 days	

Treatment Options for Migraine Headaches
- **Abortive agents**
  ➤ **Mild headaches**: aspirin 800-1000 mg PO or NSAIDS
  ➤ **Moderate headaches**: triptans, ergotamine + caffeine 2 tabs PO at onset then 1 tab PO q30 min. prn (max 6 tabs/day), dihydroergotamine 1 mg IM or SQ q1hr (max 3 mg/day) or 1 spray in each nostril q15 minutes x 2 prn (max 6 sprays/day), isometheptene + dichloralphenazone + acetaminophen 2 caps PO at onset then 1 tab PO q1h prn (max 5 caps/day) or butorphanol 1 spray in nostril and may repeat once after 1 hour prn **(high abuse potential)**.

> **Severe headaches: triptans**

	Daily maximum dose
almotriptan 6.25-12.5 mg PO q2hr prn migraine	25 mg
eletriptan 20-40 mg PO q2hr prn migraine	80 mg
frovatriptan 2.5 mg PO q2hr prn migraine	7.5 mg
naratriptan 1-2.5 mg PO q4hr prn migraine	5 mg
rizatriptan 5-10 mg PO q2hr prn migraine*	30 mg
sumatriptan 25-100 mg PO q2hr prn migraine	200 mg
6 mg SQ q1hr prn migraine	12 mg
5-20 mg intranasally q2hr prn migraine	40 mg
zolmitriptan 1.25-2.5 mg PO q2hr prn migraine	10 mg

* - Rizatriptan may be the best oral triptan for aborting migraine headaches (NEJM, 2002; 346: 257)

> All triptans available as tablets, rizatriptan and zolmitriptan also available as disintegrating tablets, sumatriptan and zolmitriptan available as a nasal spray and sumatriptan can be administered SQ or as a suppository as well.
> Contraindications: ischemic heart disease, uncontrolled HTN or focal neurologic findings.

- **Prophylactic agents**
  > Indicated for ≥ 3 attacks/month, incapacitating or complicated migraines
  > **Highest efficacy:** propranolol 40-120 mg PO bid, timolol 20-30 mg PO daily, amitriptyline 25-150 mg PO qhs, divalproex sodium 250-750 mg PO bid, sodium valproate 400-750 mg PO bid, gabapentin 100-1,200 mg PO tid
  > **Moderate efficacy:** metoprolol 100-200 mg PO daily, atenolol 50-200mg PO daily, nadolol 20-160 mg PO daily, topiramate 50-200 mg PO bid, nortriptyline 10-60 mg PO qhs or riboflavin (vitamin B2) 400 mg PO daily

Treatment Options for Temporal Arteritis
- Prednisone 40-60 mg PO daily x 2-4 weeks and decrease dose 10% q1-2 weeks to minimum effective dose (duration may be as long as 1-2 yrs)
  > Follow clinical symptoms & erythrocyte sedimentation rate at least monthly
  > Methylprednisolone 1 gram IV daily x 3 days for impending visual loss

Treatment Options for Trigeminal Neuralgia

• carbamazepine 200-600 mg PO bid is the **most effective medication.**	
• valproic acid 300-600 mg PO bid	• gabapentin 300-1200 mg PO tid
• lamotrigine 200-400 mg PO daily	• topiramate 100-200 mg PO bid
• baclofen 10-20 mg PO tid	• clonazepam 1-2 mg PO tid

- Magnetic resonance imaging/angiogram focusing on the cerebellopontine angle indicated to rule out a mass or multiple sclerosis if any of the following present: age<40, sensory loss, bilateral symptoms or poor response to medical therapy
- Surgical options for trigeminal neuralgia refractory to medical therapy
  > Microvascular decompression surgery for vascular compression of trigeminal nerve.
  > Radiofrequency rhizotomy

Treatment of Analgesic Rebound Headaches
- Completely eliminate analgesics +/- temporary dihydroergotamine therapy
- Severe cases need inpatient treatment for detoxification.

References: Neurology, 2000; 54: 1553. Neurology, 2000; 55: 754 and NEJM, 2002; 347(4): 261-71. Cephalgia, 2002; 22: 491-512. Ann. Int. Med, 2002; 137: 840-9. American Family Physician, 2005; 71: 717-24. NEJM, 2002; 346: 257 and Southern Med. J., 2004; 97: 1069-77.

Root	Disc	Muscles	Weakness	Reflex loss
C4	C3-4	Trapezius, scalene	Shoulder shrugging	None
C5	C4-5	Deltoid, biceps, brachioradialis	Shoulder abduction, external rotation of arm, elbow flexion	Biceps, brachioradialis
C6	C5-6	Brachioradialis, biceps, pronator teres, extensor carpi radialis	Elbow flexion, arm pronation, finger and wrist extension	Biceps, brachioradialis
		Radial nerve injuries produce similar findings except brachioradialis function is normal		
C7	C6-7	Triceps, pronator teres, extensor digitorum	Elbow extension , finger and wrist extension	Triceps
C8	C7-T1	Flexor digitorum, flexor/abductor pollicis, interossei	Long flexors of fingers, intrinsics of hand (finger abduction, palmar abduction of thumb)	Finger flexor
		Ulnar nerve injuries similar but also weaken thumb adductor		
T10	T9-10		Beevor's sign (sit-up → umbilicus pulled upwards)	
L2	L1-2	Iliopsoas	Hip flexion	Cremaster
L3	L2-3	Iliopsoas, adductors	Hip flexion, thigh adduction	Knee jerk
L4	L3-4	Quadriceps, sartorius, tibialis anterior	Knee extension, ankle dorsiflexion and inversion	Knee jerk
		Femoral nerve injury limited to knee extension; associated hip flexion and adduction weakness localizes to plexus		
L5	L4-5	Glutei, hamstrings, tibialis, extensor hallux/digiti, peronei	Thigh adduction and internal rotation, knee flexion, plantar and dorsiflexion of ankle and toes	None
		Deep peroneal nerve weakness limited to ankle/toe extensors; posterior tibial nerve lesions weaken foot inversion		
S1	L5-S1	Gluteus maximus, hamstrings, soleus, gastrocnemius, extensor digitorum, flexor digitorum	Hip extension, knee flexion, plantar flexion of ankle and toes	Ankle jerk
S2	S1-2	Interossei	Cupping and fanning of toes	

Epidemiology: 1% of population over 60, but 10% of cases have onset < 50 years

Causes of Parkinsonism: Parkinson's disease, vascular parkinsonism, dementia with Lewy bodies, progressive supranuclear palsy and multiple system atrophy, carbon monoxide, cyanide or MPTP*-induced, dementia pugilistica, drug-induced (the "typical" neuroleptics, prochlorperazine, promethazine and metoclopramide)

Clinical Features	Exam Findings
"Pill-rolling" tremor	Coarse, asymmetric, stress ↑ and intention ↓ tremor
Rigidity	Cogwheeling and typically asymmetric
Bradykinesia	Decreased automatic movements, micrographia, decreased arm swing, masked facies and flat affect
Gait/postural instability	Festinating gait, flexed posture, decreased postural reflexes and en bloc turning
Autonomic abnormalities	Hyperhidrosis, constipation, urinary urgency/frequency, orthostatic hypotension and sexual dysfunction
Dermatologic	Seborrheic dermatitis
Neuropsychiatric	Dementia (40%), psychosis and depression (50%)
Sleep disorders	Restless legs, nocturnal rigidity, insomnia, parasomnias and excessive daytime sleepiness all quite common

Treatment of Early Parkinson's Disease (rating scale at www.wemove.org)
- **Medications that may be neuroprotective**
  - ➤ High-dose coenzyme Q10 therapy and possibly selegiline therapy.
- **Dopamine agonists for young, healthy patients with 1ˢᵗ 4 features above**
  - ➤ Pramipexole, ropinirole, bromocriptine, pergolide and cabergoline
  - ➤ Complications: psychosis, nausea, orthostasis, leg edema and sedation
- **Anticholinergics for young patients with tremor as major problem**
  - ➤ Benztropine mesylate, biperiden and trihexyphenidyl
  - ➤ Helps tremor and sialorrhea, but follow for anticholinergic side effects
- **Carbidopa-levodopa is best therapy for elderly & more severe symptoms**
  - ➤ Complications: dyskinesia, dystonia, psychosis and motor fluctuations
- **Amantadine**
  - ➤ Effective for early, mild disease and to suppress dyskinesias
  - ➤ Complications: anticholinergic side effects, edema and insomnia
- **Catechol-O-methyltransferase (COMT) inhibitors** (entacapone or tocapone)
  - ➤ Decreases "off" time and enhances motor response to levo-dopamine
  - ➤ Complications: dyskinesias and urine discoloration

Managing Complications of Parkinson's Disease or Therapy
- **Motor fluctuations or "on/off" phenomenon**
  - ➤ Add dopamine agonist or COMT inhibitor
  - ➤ Dietary protein restriction as high protein decreases levodopa absorption.
  - ➤ Surgery (thalamotomy, pallidotomy or bilateral deep brain stimulation of subthalamic nuclei)
- **Dyskinesias or dystonias**
  - ➤ Change to controlled release carbidopa-levodopa and stop selegiline
  - ➤ Decrease carbidopa-levodopa and add dopamine agonist
- **Cognitive impairment**: minimize anticholinergics and dopamine agonists
- **Delirium/Psychosis**: minimize doses of carbidopa-levodopa, anticholinergics, selegiline and/or dopamine agonists
  - ➤ Trial of low-dose quetiapine or clozapine (use caution in the very elderly pt)
- **Urinary Urgency or Incontinence**: Trial of oxybutynin or tolterodine
- **Depression**: trial of selective serotonin reuptake inhibitor or venlafaxine
- **Constipation**: minimize anticholinergics & ↑ fluid/fiber intake & stool softeners
- **Orthostatic hypotension**: ↑ salt/fluid intake, use fludrocortisone or midodrine

* - MPTP = methyl-4-phenyl-1,2,3,6-tetrahydropyridine

References: Lancet, 2004; 363: 1783-93. Ann Int. Med, 2004; 138: 651-8 and Am J. Med, 2004; 117: 412-9.

- **Definition:** involuntary activity, perception or behavior as a result of abnormal neuronal discharges in the cerebral cortex

Classification of Seizures

Seizure Type	Consciousness impaired	Tongue biting or Incontinence	Aura (*)	Hyperventilation triggers	Automatisms (**)	Postictal Duration
Simple Partial Seizure	No	No	Yes	No	No	Seconds
Complex Partial Seizure	Yes	No	Yes 1st	No	Yes (after aura)	Minutes–Hours
Secondary Generalized Partial Seizure	Yes	Yes	Yes 1st	No	Possibly	Minutes–Hours
Absence Seizure	Yes	No	No	Yes	No	Seconds
Grand mal seizure	Yes	Yes	No	No	No	Minutes–Hours

* - jerking movements, epigastric discomfort, fear, bad smell, focal sensory or psychic symptoms
** - facial grimacing, gesturing, chewing, lip smacking, snapping fingers, walking, undressing, etc.

- **Differential Diagnosis:** migraines, syncope, transient ischemic attack, pseudoseizures, sleep disorder, conversion disorder and movement disorders
- **Etiologies:** post-traumatic, severe hyponatremia, hypomagnesemia, hypoglycemia or hypocalcemia, congenital brain malformations, hyper- or hypothyroidism, dialysis disequilibrium syndrome, acute intermittent porphyria, severe hypoxia, carbon monoxide poisoning, meningitis, stroke, alcohol or benzodiazepine withdrawal states, medication side effect or idiopathic
- **Seizure Triggers:** strong emotions, intense exercise, flashing lights, fever, menses, lack of sleep and stress
- **History:** positive family history, history of head trauma, febrile seizures, birth complications, substance abuse, prior seizure, concomitant sinusitis or otitis media, fever/headache/neck stiffness, HIV-positive or known history of cancer
- **Work-up:** chemistry panel, drug screen, electroencephalogram, thyroid stimulating hormone, lumbar puncture for meningismus (or possible meningitis)
- **Imaging:** noncontrast head CT scan for head trauma, new severe headache and anticoagulated patients. MRI preferred for focal neuro deficits, persistently altered mental status, history of cancer, and possible AIDS
- **Risk Factors for Recurrent Seizures:** history of closed head injury, structural brain lesion, focal neuro exam, cognitive impairment, partial seizures, abnormal electroencephalogram (EEG) or positive family history
- **Indications for Chronic Antiepileptic Drug (AED) use**
  - ➢ Start after 1st seizure + 2 risk factors
  - ➢ Start after 2nd seizure
- **Miscellaneous:** check state requirements for mandatory Department of Motor Vehicles reporting (see www.efa.org)
- **Discontinuation of Therapy:** wean AED 25% every 2-4 weeks. Can attempt once seizure-free for **at least** 2-3 years. Increased risk of recurrent seizures if risk factors present (see above), abnormal EEG or abnormal neuroimaging.

References: Epilepsia 2001; 42: 1255. Epilepsia 2001; 42: 1387 and NEJM 2001; 344 (15): 1145.

Medication	Pt age (yrs)	AS	PS	GS	Starting Dose (mg)‡	Therapeutic Dose (mg)‡	Side effects/ monitoring
carbamazepine*	≥ 6		•		200 bid	400 tid*	Hyponatremia, osteopenia, hepatitis, rash, leukopenia/follow levels, liver panel and CBC
clonazepam#	> 10			•	0.5 tid	1-5 mg tid	Sedation, confusion, anemia and leukopenia
ethosuximide*	> 6	•			250 daily	250-750 bid*	GI upset, rarely depression, psychosis & leukopenia
felbamate*	≥ 2		•	•	400 tid	400-1200 tid	GI upset, insomnia, hepatitis, aplastic anemia/ CBC
gabapentin#	≥ 3		•		300 qhs	300-1200 tid	Somnolence, dizziness, weight gain and fatigue
lamotrigine*	≥ 2		•	•	50 daily	200 bid	Rash, headache, tremor, vomiting, insomnia, diplopia
levetiracetam#	≥ 16		•		500 bid	500-1500 bid	Somnolence, asthenia, headache, agitation & anxiety
oxcarbazepine*	≥ 4		•		300 bid	600 bid	Dizziness, diplopia, nausea, ataxia & hyponatremia
phenobarbital*	> 12		•	•	60 daily	150 daily*	Rash, sedation and cognitive delays/ follow levels
phenytoin*	> 16		•	•	1 gm load	300 daily*	Rash, gingival hyperplasia, mild hirsutism, hepatitis, osteopenia/ follow drug levels and liver panel
primidone#	≥ 8		•	•	100 qhs	250 tid-qid	Rash, sedation and cognitive delays/ follow levels
tiagabine#	≥ 12		•		4 mg daily	4-8 mg bid-qid	Dizziness, tremor, confusion and fatigue
topiramate#	≥ 2		•	•	25 daily	200 bid	Ataxia, confusion, dizziness, fatigue, paresthesias, acidosis, nephrolithiasis, weight loss & an ocular syn.
valproic acid*	> 10	•	•	•	250 tid	500 - 750 tid*	Weight gain, tremors, hair loss/ follow levels
zonisamide#	≥ 16		•	•	100 daily	200 daily	Fatigue, paresthesias, nephrolithiasis, anorexia, ataxia and hyperhidrosis

*= Approved for monotherapy, #= used as an adjunctive medication, ‡= oral doses, AS = absence seizures, PS = partial seizures including partial complex seizures with secondary generalization and GS = generalized seizures including tonic-clonic, tonic, clonic, myoclonic or atonic seizures. CBC = complete blood count. ¥= adjust based on serum drug levels. References: Arch. Neurology, 2004; 61:1361-5. JAMA, 2004; 291: 605-20. Postgrad. Med, 2004; 80:581-7 & Clinical Neuropharmacology, 2003; 1: 58.

Classification of Cerebrovascular Accidents (CVA)
- Hemorrhagic 15% (subarachnoid or intraparenchymal)
- Ischemic 85% (thrombotic 20%, lacunar 25%, cardioembolic 20%, cryptogenic 30% or other 5%)
  - Cryptogenic is most likely embolic and often paradoxical through PFO
  - Other causes: hypercoagulable states, dissection, vasculitis, endocarditis, complicated migraine, stimulant drugs, neurosyphilis, patent foramen ovale
  - Embolic: patients generally experience a sudden onset of maximal deficit
  - Thrombotic: patients generally have a stuttering or stepwise progression
  - Paradoxical embolus with sudden neuro deficits after a valsalva maneuver

Clinical Presentation of Strokes in Carotid Distribution	Vascular Area
Face and arms affected more than legs, aphasia, hemiparesis, hemianesthesia, contralateral homonymous hemianopsia and ipsilateral gaze deviation	MCA (dominant)
Face and arms affected more than legs, neglect, hemiparesis, hemianesthesia, contralateral homonymous hemianopsia and ipsilateral gaze deviation	MCA (nondominant)
Legs are affected more than face and arms, hemiparesis, hemianesthesia, incontinence, personality change and grasp/suck reflexes	ACA
Clinical Presentation of Strokes in Posterior Circulation	
Homonymous visual field deficit	PCA
Ipsilateral cranial nerve palsies and contralateral hemiparesis	Brainstem
Headache, vertigo, vomiting, ataxia, dysarthria and nystagmus	Cerebellum
Clinical Presentation of Penetrating Artery Strokes	
Hemiparesis where legs, arms and face are equally affected is a pure motor lacunar stroke	Internal capsule (IC)
Hemianesthesia where legs, arms and face are equally affected is a pure sensory lacunar stroke	Thalamus
Ipsilateral weakness and limb ataxia is an ataxia hemiparesis lacunar stroke	Midbrain
Clumsy hand-dysarthria lacunar stroke	Basis pontis
Hemiparesis and hemianesthesia where legs, arms and face are equally affected represents a sensorimotor lacunar stroke	IC or thalamus

MCA (Middle Cerebral Artery), ACA (Ant. Cerebral Artery), PCA (Post. Cerebral Artery)

Risk Factors: hypertension, ischemic heart disease, atrial fibrillation, diabetes, carotid artery stenosis, smoking, hyperlipidemia, obesity, age > 65 & alcohol abuse

Work-up
- Cardiac echocardiogram for thrombus in cardioembolic strokes
- Carotid duplex ultrasound for MCA or ACA strokes
- Noncontrast head CT: rule out an intracranial bleed or mass effect
- Magnetic resonance imaging/magnetic resonance angiogram or transcranial doppler study for suspected posterior fossa, internal capsule or thalamic strokes
- Electrocardiogram
- Complete blood count, chemistry panel, coagulation studies and lipid panel
- Holter monitor for history of palpitations: rule out atrial fibrillation/flutter

- **Patients < 50 years with few vascular risk factors:** drug screen, blood cultures, syphilis testing, cardiac echocardiogram with bubble study, lupus anticoagulant, anticardiolipin antibody, Factor V Leiden and prothrombin gene mutation, serum homocysteine level, ANA, duplex ultrasound of neck for posterior circulation strokes and sickle cell prep (if patient is African-American or of Mediterranean or Southeast Asian descent)

Prevention of Ischemic Strokes
- Keep tight glycemic control with glycohemoglobin (HgbA1c)< 7%
- Control hypertension with goal BP< 140/90 and < 130/80 in patients with diabetes or chronic kidney disease
- Statin therapy for primary and secondary prevention aiming for LDL<100 mg/dL
  ➢ Indicated for primary prevention if total cholesterol >240 mg/dL, for diabetics ≥ 40 years with total cholesterol ≥135 mg/dL or if 10-year coronary artery disease risk ≥ 20% based on Framingham risk score.
  ➢ Indicated for secondary prevention of strokes if total cholesterol ≥135 mg/dL
- Smoking cessation; regular aerobic exercise; limit alcohol intake, <1-2 drinks/d
- Aspirin 81-325 PO **or** clopidogrel 75 mg PO daily as first-line antiplatelet agent
  ➢ If CVA/TIA occurs while on aspirin or clopidogrel, change to the other agent **or** to aspirin + extended-release dipyridamole (25/200) 1 cap PO bid (may be marginally more effective than aspirin or clopidogrel, but expensive).
  ➢ Combined aspirin and clopidogrel offers no benefit **&** has a higher bleed risk versus aspirin alone for secondary prevention of CVA/TIA (MATCH trial).

- **Indications for Anticoagulation**
  ➢ Chronic or paroxysmal atrial fibrillation
  ➢ Hypercoagulable state causing premature arteriosclerosis
  ➢ Paradoxical embolus through a patent foramen ovale
  ➢ Vertebral dissection +/- and severe vertebrobasilar stenosis typically are indications for heparinization at the time of acute ischemic stroke in the vertebrobasilar territory **but would consult a neurologist**
  ➢ For all except vertebral dissection, anticoagulation usually delayed ≥ 3 days for a small stroke and ≥ 7 days for a large stroke.

- **Indications for Carotid Endarterectomy (CEA) or Carotid Artery Stenting**
  ➢ Definite benefit for symptomatic carotid artery stenosis (CAS) >70% (marginal benefit for stenosis 50-69%) in patients ≤ 80 years if perioperative stroke and mortality rate < 6%
  ➢ Option for asymptomatic CAS > 60% **in men** ≤ 80 yrs if perioperative risk ≤3%. 5-year stroke rate ↓ 6%, but **no** decrease in death or disabling CVAs.
- **Perioperative Stroke Risk Reduction**
  ➢ Wait at least 4 weeks after a stroke prior to elective surgery
  ➢ Noncardiac surgery can safely be performed in pts with asymptomatic CAS
  ➢ Perioperative stroke risk with coronary artery bypass graft surgery (CABG) & > 50% CAS is 3% if unilateral, 5% if bilateral and 7% if symptomatic CAS
    - Consider combined CEA and CABG for symptomatic CAS **or** high-grade asymptomatic bilateral CAS **and** symptomatic coronary disease
    - Consider carotid artery stenting or CEA for unilateral, asymptomatic high-grade CAS **prior to** CABG (controversial)
  ➢ Perioperative stroke risk with coronary artery bypass graft surgery and symptomatic vertobrobasilar stenosis is 6%

BP=blood pressure, LDL= low-density lipoprotein, HDL= high-density lipoprotein, PFO= patent foramen ovale
References: Chest, 2004; 126: S483-512. JAMA, 2004; 292: 1867-74. Mayo Clin Proc, 2004; 79: 1197 and 1330. Am J. Med, 2004; 117: 596-606. Mayo Clin Proc, 2004; 79: 223-9. Arch. Int. Med, 2004; 164: 950-6. Lancet, 2004; 363: 757-67 and Lancet, 2004; 364: 331-7 (MATCH trial).

Causes of Generalized Weakness
- **Electrolytes:** low levels of potassium, phosphate, magnesium or sodium or elevated levels of sodium or calcium
  - ➤ Periodic paralysis (look for hypokalemia or hyperthyroidism)
  - ➤ Depression
  - ➤ Medical problems: anemia, chronic ischemic or congestive cardiomyopathy, chronic obstructive pulmonary disease, adrenal insufficiency, thyroid disorders or cachexia of malignancy or AIDS

Patterns of Weakness
- Upper motor neuron (UMN): ↑tone, ↑DTRs, + Babinski sign and spastic
- Lower motor neuron (LMN): ↓ tone, ↓ DTRs, - Babinski sign, severe atrophy, fasciculations, fibrillations and flaccid paralysis
- Myopathic: mild atrophy, proximal weakness, normal DTRs, and - Babinski's

Weakness Syndromes

Location of Defect	Clinical Features	Diagnosis
Cortex	Contralateral hemiparesis/hemianesthesia and upper motor neuron pattern present	CT/MRI
Internal capsule	"pure motor" lacunar syndrome and + UMN	CT/MRI
Brainstem	Ipsilateral cranial nerve palsies, contralateral hemiparesis and + UMN	MRI
Spinal cord lesion	Sensory level, bilateral weakness & + UMN	Spinal MRI
Brown-Sequard syndrome	Hemiparesis, ipsilateral ↓ proprioception and contralateral ↓ pain/temp.	Spinal MRI
Radiculopathy	Back & dermatomal pain/weakness, ↓DTR	Spinal MRI
Anterior Horn cells (polio)	Asymmetric monoparesis, lower motor neuron pattern present & normal sensation	Clinical
Amyotrophic Lateral Sclerosis	Asymmetric combined LMN limb weakness + UMN bulbar palsies, progressive, familial	Clinical
Peripheral nerves	Nerve distribution, lower motor neuron pattern present	EMG/nerve conduction studies
NMJ [myasthenia gravis (MG), botulism (B) or Eaton-Lambert syndrome]	Fatigability, bulbar palsies (diplopia, ptosis, dysarthria, dysphagia), descending paralysis	+ edrophonium test & positive acetylcholine receptor Ab (MG), positive botulinum toxin* (botulism)
Guillain-Barre	Ascending symmetric weakness, absent/↓ DTRs, post-upper respiratory infection	Clinical
Myopathies	Proximal muscle weakness	EMG/Biopsy
PMR	Pain + stiff hip/shoulder girdles, ↑ESR > 50	Clinical
Rhabdomyolysis	Increased CK and sore muscles	↑ CK

NMJ = neuromuscular junction, MG = Myasthenia Gravis, EMG = electromyogram, DTR = deep tendon reflexes, ESR = erythrocyte sedimentation rate, CK = creatinine phosphokinase, PMR = polymyalgia rheumatica, MRI = magnetic resonance imaging and CT = computed tomography.
* - botulinum toxin from serum if food-borne and from tissue if wound botulism

Causes of Peripheral Neuropathies (mnemonic = MOVESTUPID)

Metabolic	B_{12}, thiamine, pyridoxine or folate deficiencies
Other	Rare familial disorders, Amyloidosis
Vasculitis	Systemic lupus erythematosus, Sjogren's, cryoglobulinemia, or polyarteritis nodosa
Endocrine	Diabetes or hypothyroidism
Syphilis or Sarcoidosis	
Tumor-related	Paraneoplastic
Uremia	Blood urea nitrogen usually > 100 mg/dL
Paraproteinemia	or porphyria or polycythemia vera
Infectious/idiopathic	Lyme disease, leprosy, mononucleosis, AIDS or chronic inflammatory demyelinating polyneuropathy

Drugs/Toxins: alcohol, amiodarone, arsenic, beta-lactams, chloroquine, carboplatin, cisplatin, colchicine, dapsone, didanosine, disulfiram, fluoroquinolones, herbicides, hydralazine, isoniazid, lead, mercury, metronidazole, niacin, nitrofurantoin, pentazocine, pesticides, phenytoin, statins, stavudine, suramin, tacrolimus, taxanes, thalidomide, vincristine, zalcitabine and zidovudine

Causes of Myopathies: postviral, polymyositis, dermatomyositis, inclusion body myositis, myotonic or limb-girdle muscular dystrophies, medications (statins, colchicine, steroids, amiodarone, methimazole, propylthiouracil, zidovudine, lamivudine, cimetidine, gemfibrozil, interferon, leuprolide acetate, penicillins and sulfonamides), alcohol, thyrotoxicosis or hyperparathyroidism

Work-up of Weakness
- Is the weakness generalized or fit one of the weakness syndromes above?
- **Evaluation of Generalized Weakness**
  - ➢ Assess for depression or chronic cardiopulmonary disease
  - ➢ Labs: chemistry 7 panel, magnesium, phosphate, calcium, thyroid stimulating hormone (TSH) level and complete blood count
  - ➢ Cosyntropin stimulation test for any suspicion of adrenal insufficiency
  - ➢ Consider a chest x-ray for adult smokers or those with a chronic cough

- **Evaluation of Weakness Syndromes**
  - ➢ Start with the diagnostic test of choice as outlined in the table above
  - ➢ For myopathies or myositis, check an erythrocyte sedimentation rate, creatine kinase, antinuclear antibody test, EMG & consider an open muscle biopsy of the affected muscle for routine pathology and electron microscopy.
  - ➢ For Guillain-Barre, a lumbar puncture will have few cells and a high protein

- **Evaluation of Peripheral Neuropathies**
  - ➢ Examine for any medication culprits
  - ➢ Routine labs: chemistry 7 panel, TSH, B_{12} and folate levels, serum protein electrophoresis and a venereal disease research laboratory (VDRL) test
  - ➢ Additional labs if the history and exam are suggestive: antinuclear antibody, anti-SSA and anti-SSB (Sjogren's syndrome A and B) antibodies, serum cryoglobulins, angiotensin converting enzyme level and HIV test

Reference: Emerg. Med. Clin. North America, 1999; 17 (1): 265-78 and AFP, 2005; 71: 1327-36.

Visual Acuity Screen

96	**20/800**
873	**20/400**
2 8 4 3 **O X X**	**20/200**
6 3 8 5 2 X O O	20/100
8 7 4 5 9 O X O	20/70
6 3 9 2 5 X O X	20/50
4 2 8 3 6 5 o x o	20/40
3 7 4 2 5 8 x x o	20/30
8 3 7 8 2 6 x o o	20/25

Hold card in good light 14 inches from eye. Record vision for each eye separately with and without glasses. Presbyopic patients should read through bifocal glasses. Myopic patients should wear glasses only.

Pupil Diameter (mm)

Rosenbaum pocket vision screen

Ophthalmology: Evaluation of the Red Eye

109

The Red Eye with No Pain
- Subconjunctival hemorrhage
  - ➤ Exam: sharply-circumscribed red area on sclera & patient has normal vision

The Red Eye with Deep Eye Pain
- **Corneal Ulcer**
  - ➤ Fluorescein staining with white spot on cornea
  - ➤ Remove contacts and treat ulcer with antibiotic ointment and eye patching
- **Scleritis**
  - ➤ Exam with tender eye & injection of conjunctival and deep episcleral vessels
  - ➤ Ophthalmology referral and search for a systemic rheumatologic condition.
- **Uveitis or Iritis**
  - ➤ Exam with mild decreased vision, circumcorneal conjunctival injection, miotic pupil, photophobia and slit lamp exam reveals cells and a "flare" in the anterior chamber (iritis) or cells in the vitreous humor (posterior uveitis).
  - ➤ Consider initiating cycloplegic drops and topical corticosteroids after ophthalmologic consultation and with follow-up appointment within 24 hours.
- **Periorbital or Orbital Cellulitis**
  - ➤ Exam with fever, lid swelling and erythema +/- proptosis and restricted eye movement (if orbit involved)
  - ➤ Mild-moderate infections: use cefuroxime 500 mg PO bid **or** cefixime 400 mg PO daily **or** amoxicillin-clavulanate 875 mg PO bid; severe infections with ceftriaxone 3 gm IV daily **or** ampicillin-sulbactam 3 gm IV q6h
  - ➤ Consider CT scan of orbit for proptosis or restricted eye movement to rule out an orbital abscess.
- **Acute Angle-Closure Glaucoma (medical emergency)**
  - ➤ Exam: markedly decreased vision, severe brow pain, nausea/vomiting, diffuse conjunctival injection, mid-dilated pupil, hazy cornea, "halos" around lights and increased intraocular pressure
  - ➤ Treatment options include: beta-blocker drops (e.g., timolol or betaxolol), acetazolamide 500 mg x 1 then 250 mg q6h (IV, IM or PO), apraclonidine, 1 drop q30 min. x 2, mannitol 1–1.5 mg/kg IV x 1 and 2-4% pilocarpine 1 drop q15 minutes x 4-8 doses and **immediate ophthalmology referral**

The Red Eye with Foreign Body Sensation or Irritation
- **Conjunctivitis**
  - ➤ Presence of clear discharge suggests viral conjunctivitis.
  - ➤ Presence of purulent discharge suggests bacterial conjunctivitis.
    - o Treat with antibiotic eye drops or ointment x 7 days.
  - ➤ No discharge consistent with allergic conjunctivitis.
    - o Treat with antihistamine eye drops (e.g., naphazoline/pheniramine, levocabastine or azelastine eye drops)
  - ➤ Dendrites on fluorescein staining suggest herpes simplex conjunctivitis.
    - o Treat with trifluridine drops, cycloplegic drops & ophthalmology referral
- **Corneal Laceration/Abrasion or Foreign Body**
  - ➤ History of trauma or exposure to foreign body. Pupil often constricted.
  - ➤ Foreign body can usually be removed with a sterile Q-tip.
  - ➤ Treat a laceration or abrasion with antibiotic ointment +/- eye patching.
- **Keratitis**
  - ➤ Exam: slightly decreased visual acuity, circumcorneal conjunctival injection, corneal opacification and positive fluorescein staining
  - ➤ Consider initiating topical steroids after ophthalmologic consultation.
- **Episcleritis**
  - ➤ Exam: Engorged, episcleral vessels and nodule adjacent to limbus, vision unaffected, dull achiness and tenderness on palpation
  - ➤ Often associated with an autoimmune disorder and is self-limited.

Reference: Amer. Family Physician, 1996; 53 (2): 565-74 and NEJM, 2000; 343: 345.

Mechanisms of visual impairment

Subtypes	Refractive error	Media opacity	Retina or optic nerve disease	Neurological insult
Mechanism	Image poorly focused	Opacity of eye tissue	Damaged retina or nerve	Abnormal brain tissue
Examples	• Myopia • Hyperopia • Astigmatism • Presbyopia • Hyperglycemia-induced lens swelling	• Cataract • Corneal ulcer or scar • Hyphema • Vitreous hemorrhage	• Retinal detachment • Retinal vein occlusion • Glaucoma • Optic neuritis • Optic nerve trauma • Macular degeneration • Ischemic optic neuropathy*	• Pituitary tumor¥ • CNS infarct • Brain tumor • Head trauma
Exam	Pinhole normalizes vision	No red reflex with ophthalmoscope	Relative afferent pupillary defect	Visual field cuts on confrontation

* - caused by temporal arteritis or retinal artery occlusion, ¥ - presents as bitemporal hemianopsia

Onset of visual loss
- **Sudden visual loss**: trauma, acute glaucoma, stroke or amaurosis fugax, hyphema, ischemic optic neuropathy, retinal vein occlusion, optic neuritis, vitreous hemorrhage, large corneal ulcer or retinal detachment
- **Transient visual loss**: migraine headaches or amaurosis fugax
- **Gradual visual loss**: refractive error, cataracts, chronic glaucoma, macular degeneration or expanding pituitary or orbital tumors

Treatment of Visual Impairment by Cause
- **Refractive error**
  ➢ Corrective lenses
- **Media opacity**
  ➢ Ophthalmology referral for definitive therapy
- **Retinal or optic nerve disease**
  ➢ Ophthalmology referral for retinal detachment, retinal vein occlusion, glaucoma, optic nerve injury or globe trauma
  ➢ Optic neuritis: prednisone 1 mg/kg PO daily x 11 days then taper
- **Neurological Insult**
  ➢ **Pituitary tumor with bitemporal hemianopsia**
     - Bromocriptine or cabergoline for microprolactinomas
     - Consider transphenoidal excision for macroprolactinomas
  ➢ **Brain tumor or head trauma**
     - Neurosurgical consult for possible excision or evacuation of clot.

References: NEJM, 2000; 343: 556-62 and Ophthalmologic Clin. N. Amer., 2003; 16: 269-87.

Epistaxis

Anterior Nosebleeds

- 80% occur within Kiesselbach's plexus located in the nasal vestibule.
- **Risk Factors:** arid places, rhinitis, nose picking, foreign body, facial trauma, anticoagulation, bleeding diathesis, Osler-Weber-Rendu disease, Wegener's granulomatosis and angiofibromas (young boys)
- **Work-up:** complete blood count, coagulation studies and bleeding time
- **Management:** compression of nostrils x 5 minutes and tilting head forward→ control hypertension→ apply cotton pledgets soaked with 4% cocaine, oxymetazoline **or** phenylephrine x 5-10 minutes→ cautery with silver nitrate stick **or** Biolife QR powder **or** haemostatic packing with Gel foam **or** Surgicel → Replace pledgets with nasal tampon or anterior nasal pack x 24–48 hours
- Consider antibiotic prophylaxis with trimethoprim-sulfamethoxazole DS or amoxicillin-clavulanate until nasal packing removed.

Posterior Nosebleeds

- **Risk Factors:** nasopharyngeal tumors, hypertension, coagulopathies or patients over 60 years.
- **Work-up as above**
- **Management:** admission→ control of hypertension→ tamponade posterior structures with 14 French foley catheter secured on nasal end with a clamp or with an Epistat catheter→ anterior nasal pack. Alternatively, a double balloon device can be used with one balloon tamponading the posterior structures and the other tamponading the anterior structures→ antibiotics as above and remove pack and catheter in 2-5 days.

Acute Hoarseness (< 2 weeks)

- **Etiologies:** Acute laryngitis, vocal strain, peritonsillar abscess or post-operative from anterior neck surgery
- **Therapy:** Treat peritonsillar infection if present, hydration, humidification and voice rest
- **Natural history:** Voice returns to normal within 1 week

Chronic Hoarseness (> 2 weeks)

- **History:** Duration, onset abrupt or insidious, smoking history, alcohol use, prior neck surgery or radiation therapy, occupation and reflux symptoms
- **Associated symptoms:** dyspnea, stridor, cough, hemoptysis, ear or throat pain, dysphagia, odynophagia or weight loss
- **Etiologies:** inhaled toxins, chronic gastroesophageal reflux, chronic sinusitis with postnasal drip, chronic vocal strain, vocal cord polyps or nodules, spasmodic dysphonia, vocal cord paralysis, laryngeal conversion disorder (psychogenic), laryngeal cancer or lung cancer
- **Work-up:** Direct laryngoscopy indicated
- **Treatments:** cigarette and alcohol cessation, voice rest and other treatments based on underlying disorder

Reference: Postgraduate Med 1996; 99: 83 and American Family Physician, 2005; 71: 305-11.

ENT COMBINATIONS (selected)	Decongestant	Antihistamine	Antitussive	Typical Adult Doses
OTC				
Actifed Cold & Allergy	PS	TR	-	1 tab or 10 mL q4-6h
Actifed Cold & Sinus¶	PS	CH	-	2 tabs q 6h
Allerfrim, Aprodine	PS	TR	-	1 tab or 10 mL q4-6h
Benadryl Allergy/Cold¶	PS	DPH	-	2 tabs q 6h
Benadryl-D Allergy/Sinus Tablets	PS	DPH	-	1 tab q 4-6 h
Claritin-D 12 hour (Claritin-D 24 hour)	PS	LO	-	1 tab q12h (or q24h)
Dimetapp Cold & Allergy Elixir	PS	BR	-	20mL q 4h
Dimetapp Multi-Symp Cold & Allergy¶	PE	CH	-	2 tabs q4h
Mucinex-DM Extended-Release	-	-	GU,DM	1-2 tab q12h
Robitussin CF	PS	-	GU, DM	10 mL q4h*
Robitussin DM, Mytussin DM	-	-	GU, DM	10 mL q4h*
Robitussin PE, Guaituss PE	PS	-	GU	10 mL q4h*
Drixoral Cold & Allergy	PS	DBR	-	1 tab q12h
Drixoral Cold & Flu¶	PS	DBR	-	2 tab q 12h
Triaminic Cold & Allergy	PS	CH	-	20 mL q4-6h‡
Triaminic Cough	-	-	DM	20 mL q4h‡
Rx Only				
Allegra-D12-hour (Allegra-D 24-hour)	PS	FE	-	1 tab q12h (or q24h)
Bromfenex	PS	BR	-	1 cap q12h
Clarinex-D 24-hour	PS	DL	-	1 tab daily
Deconamine	-	CH	-	1 tab or 10 mL tid-qid
Codeprex	-	CH	CO	10 mL q12h
Deconamine SR, Chlordrine SR	PS	CH	-	1 tab q12h
Deconsal II	PS	-	GU	1-2 tabs q12h
Dimetane-DX	PS	BR	DM	10 mL PO q4h
Duratuss	PS	-	GU	1 tab q12h
Duratuss HD©III	PS	-	GU, HY	10mL q4-6h
Entex PSE, Guaifenex PSE 120	PS	-	GU	1 tab q12h
Histussin D©III	PS	-	HY	5 mL qid
Histussin HC©III	PE	CH	HY	10 mL q4h
Humibid DM	PS	-	GU, DM	1 tab q12h
Hycotuss©III	-	-	GU, HY	5mL pc & qhs
Phenergan/Dextromethorphan	-	PR	DM	5 mL q4-6h
Phenergan VC	PE	PR	-	5 mL q4-6h
Phenergan VC w/codeine©V	PE	PR	CO	5 mL q4-6h
Poly-Histine Elixir	-	PT/PY/PH	-	10 mL q4h*
Robitussin AC©V	-	-	GU, CO	10 mL q4h*
Robitussin DAC©V	PS	-	GU, CO	10 mL q4h*
Rondec Syrup	PS	BR	-	5 mL qid*
Rondec DM Syrup	PS	BR	DM	5 mL qid*
Rondec Oral Drops	PS	CX	-	0.25 to 1 mL qid†
Rondec DM Oral Drops	PS	CX	DM	0.25 to 1 mL qid†
Rynatan	PE	CH	-	1-2 tabs q12h
Rynatan-P Pediatric	PE	CH, PY	-	2.5-5 mL q12h*
Semprex-D	PS	AC	-	1cap q4-6h
Tanafed	PS	CH	-	10-20 mL q12h*
Triacin-C, Actifed w/codeine©V	PS	TR	CO	10 mL q4-6h
Tussionex©III	PS	CH	HY	5 mL q12h

AC=acrivastine   DL=desloratadine   GU=guaifenesin   PR=promethazine
BR=brompheniramine   DM=dextromethorphan   HY=hydrocodone   PS=pseudoephedrine
CH=chlorpheniramine   DBR=dexbrompheniramine   LO=loratadine   PT=phenyltoloxamine
CO=codeine   DPH=diphenhydramine   PE=phenylephrine   PY=pyrilamine
CX=carbinoxamine   FE=fexofenadine   PH=pheniramine   TR=triprolidine

*5 mL/dose if 6-11 yo. 2.5 mL if 2-5yo. 1 mL/dose if 2-5yo. †1 mL/dose if 10-18 mo. ¾ mL if 7-9 mo. ½ mL if 4-6 mo. ¼ mL if 1-3 months old. ‡10 mL/dose if 6-11 yo. 5 mL. if 2-5 yo. 2.5 mL if 13-23 mo. 1.25 mL if 4-12 mo. ¶Also contains acetaminophen. Adapted with permission from the Tarascon Pharmacopoeia, 2006, Tarascon Publishing

History
- Onset (acute versus gradual) and progression of hearing loss, unilateral or bilateral hearing loss, auralgia or ear discharge, history of trauma including barotrauma, frequent ear infections or ear injury? Any associated tinnitus, vertigo or disequilibrium?, history of loud noise exposure? Any occupational noise hazards? Family history of hearing loss and at what age? Ototoxic medication exposure (aminoglycosides, azithromycin, chloroquine, carboplatin, cisplatin, erythromycin, 5-fluorouracil, interferons, loop diuretics, minocycline, NSAIDS, quinine, salicylates, tetracycline, vancomycin and zidovudine)

Hearing Screening Tests
- Weber test using a 512-hz tuning fork: lateralizes to good ear in sensorineural hearing loss and to bad ear in conductive hearing loss
- Rinne test: negative test (bone ≥ air) consistent with conductive hearing loss

Audiologic testing
- Assesses hearing at frequencies between 250 – 8000 Hertz
- Hearing impairment if >20 decibels: mild 20-40, mod 40-60, severe>60 decibels

Tympanometry
- Decreased mobility: suggests fluid in middle ear
- Negative pressure: corresponds to retracted tympanic membrane

Causes of Conductive Hearing Loss in Adults

History	Exam Findings	Diagnosis
Sudden, painless hearing loss	Cerumen or foreign body impaction	Canal occlusion
Sudden, painful hearing loss	Swollen canal with yellow debris	Otitis externa
	Inflamed tympanic membrane (TM) and fluid in middle ear	Acute otitis media (OM)
Gradual, painless hearing loss	Normal TM and fluid in middle ear	Chronic OM
	Normal otoscopic exam	Otosclerosis
	Benign mass with characteristic features on otoscopic exam	Osteoma, glomus tumor, exostosis
	Retracted or perforated TM with chronic drainage	Cholesteatoma

Causes of Sensorineural Hearing Loss in Adults

Diagnosis	History	Audiogram/ Exam
Presbycusis	Elderly patient/ normal exam	Bilateral high-frequency loss
Noise-induced hearing loss	Gradual hearing loss, tinnitus and noise exposure	Bilateral high-frequency loss
Autoimmune hearing loss	Rapidly progressive, bilateral, impairment may fluctuate	Abnormal pattern and poor speech discrimination
Perilymph fistula	Sudden, unilateral, tinnitus, vertigo, follows head trauma	Unilateral abnormality. Nystagmus with positive pneumatic pressure
Meniere's disease	Sudden, fluctuating unilateral hearing loss & vertigo, tinnitus	Unilateral low-frequency hearing loss
Acoustic neuroma	Gradual unilateral hearing loss and tinnitus	Unilateral abnormality

Treatment/Prevention
- Consideration of hearing aids
- Surgical excision of cholesteatomas, exostoses or tumors
- Low sodium diet; avoid caffeine/alcohol & a thiazide trial for Meniere's disease.
- Ear plugs or hearing protection should be worn with any noise blasts or with chronic noise exposure > 85 decibels time-weighted average

References: AFP, 2003; 68: 1125-32 and Medical Clinics of N. America, 1999; 83: 139-49.

Rhinitis Definition: Rhinorrhea, nasal itching, sneezing, congestion, inflammation of the nasal mucosa and possibly postnasal discharge

Allergic Rhinitis: affects up to 25% of the U.S. population
- Associated conditions: postnasal drip, eczema, asthma, sinusitis, eustachian tube dysfunction and conjunctivitis
- Common allergens:
  - ➤ Tree, grass or weed pollens and fungi **(seasonal)**
  - ➤ Dust mites, cockroaches, animal dander and fungi **(perennial)**.
- Risk Factors: family history of atopy, males>females, early introduction of formula, smoke exposure in infancy, birth during pollen season, history of asthma (25-50% concomitant) or eczema (30% association)
- Clinical Features: nose rubbing, "allergic salute", transverse nasal crease, "allergic shiners" or Denie-Morgan lines under eyes, itchy palate, nasal polyps, edematous nasal mucosa with faint bluish hue or pallor, irritability, fatigue, mouth breathing and snoring
- Diagnosis: Clinical and/or confirmed presence of allergen-specific IgE by hypersensitivity skin testing. Nasal smear with eosinophilia.
  - ➤ Skin test panel: tree and grass pollens, mold, dust mites & animal dander
- Allergic rhinitis treatment: Allergen avoidance strategies (see www.aaaai.org)

Meds	Sneezing	Rhinorrhea	Congestion	Nasal itch	Eye itch
Antihistamines*	++	++	+	+++	+
Nasal steroids	+++	+++	+++	++	++
Nasal cromolyn	+	+	+	+	no effect
Decongestant#	no effect	-	+ - ++++	no effect	no effect
Nasal ipratropium	no effect	+++	+++	no effect	no effect
Antileukotrienes	no effect	+	++	no effect	++

* - oral or nasal, # - nasal formulation used < 3-5 d & has 4+ congestion control vs 1+ control for oral forms
  - ➤ Immunotherapy for symptoms refractory to avoidance & medication therapy.

Non-Allergic Rhinitis Syndromes
- Exam: Nasal turbinates of nonallergic rhinitis erythematous and boggy
- All distinguished from allergic rhinitis by negative skin testing

Vasomotor Rhinitis
- Exacerbated by rapid changes in temperature, humidity, strong odors or alcohol
- azelastine 2 sprays in each nostril bid effective for vasomotor rhinitis

Infectious Rhinitis: symptoms of the common cold (viral or bacterial infections)

Non-Allergic Rhinitis with Nasal Eosinophilia Syndrome (NARES)
- Perennial symptoms, 50% with sinusitis, 33% with nasal polyps and 15% with asthma. Poor response to antihistamines

Hormonal: pregnancy, hypothyroidism and oral contraceptive pill

Rhinitis Medicamentosa: abuse of cocaine or vasoconstrictor nasal sprays

Gustatory Rhinitis: IgE-mediated condition exacerbated by certain tastes

Atrophic Rhinitis: elderly, *Klebsiella ozaenae* colonization, pt. smells a foul odor

Mechanical: foreign body, nasal polyps or deviated nasal septum

Granulomatous: Wegener's granulomatosis (c-antineutrophil cytoplasmic antibody or biopsy +) or sarcoidosis (high angiotensin converting enzyme level or biopsy +)

Treatment: steroid nasal sprays can benefit all types of non-allergic rhinitis
- Nasal saline irrigation, increased fluids and decreased caffeine/alcohol intake.
- Ipratropium bromide nasal spray as adjunct therapy for profuse rhinorrhea
- Treat underlying condition for mechanical & granulomatous rhinitis

Ann Int Med, 2004; 140: 278-89. J. Allergy & Clin. Immunology, 2004; 114: S155-S212. Institute for Clinical Systems Improvement Rhinitis guidelines, 2003 & AHRQ guidelines at www.ahrq.gov/clinic/rhininv.htm

History: duration, prior ear disease, noise exposure, hearing status, medications, history of prior neck injury, quality of tinnitus, exacerbating/relieving factors, associated mood disorder or insomnia

The Different Causes of Tinnitus with Suggested Evaluation and Treatment

Hearing impairment: noise-induced, presbycusis, congenital, ototoxic meds (see below), Meniere's disease, otitis media or externa and cerumen impaction.
- **Work-up:** otoscopic ear exam, audiogram and tympanometry
- **Treatment:** hearing aids or cochlear implants for refractory cases

Otosclerosis: often conductive hearing loss
- **Treatment:** surgery to correct conductive defect

Vascular
- Pulsating/humming quality. Head position or exertion changes pitch or intensity
- **Etiologies:** arteriovenous (AV) fistulas, glomus tumors, arterial bruits or venous hum (can occur with systemic hypertension or pseudotumor cerebri)
- **Work-up**
  - ➤ Auscultate for bruits
  - ➤ Compression of ipsilateral internal jugular vein can suppress venous hum
  - ➤ MRI/MRA to rule out a dural AV fistula or skull-based glomus tumor
- **Treatment:** selective embolization or excision/ligation depending on etiology

Middle Ear Spasmodic Activity
- Clicking quality
- **Etiologies:** middle ear disease or multiple sclerosis
- **Work-up:** tympanometry and otoscopy
- **Treatment:** middle ear surgery or botulinum injections

Eustachian Tube Dysfunction
- Ocean wave quality. Occurs because eustachian tube has impaired patency.
- Frequently occurs after marked weight loss or radiation treatment to nasopharynx
- **Treatment:** Topical nasal steroids or antihistamines

Ototoxic Medications
- Aminoglycosides, amphotericin B, aspirin, azithromycin, chloramphenicol, chloroquine, carboplatin, cisplatin, cyclooxygenase-2 inhibitors, erythromycin, hydroxychloroquine, local anesthetics, loop diuretics, mefloquine, methotrexate, nitrogen mustard, quinidine, quinine, heterocyclic antidepressants, minocycline, NSAIDs, salicylates, sulfonamides, tetracyclines, vancomycin and zidovudine

Temporomandibular Joint Dysfunction
- **Treatment:** stop chewing gum/bruxism and use of custom-fitted oral devices

Whiplash/craniocervical injury
- **Treatment:** physical therapy and soft cervical collar

Acoustic Neuroma and Cerebellopontine Angle Tumors
- Hearing loss and intermittent vertigo
- **Work-up:** MRI of posterior fossa and auditory canal
- **Treatment:** surgical resection

Barotrauma to Ear

Infections: neurosyphilis, Lyme disease, meningitis or chronic otitis media

Meniere's disease: low-pitched tinnitus, hearing loss, aural fullness and vertigo

Endocrine Etiologies: vitamin B12 deficiency or hypothyroidism
- **Treatment:** vitamin B12 or thyroid replacement therapy

Other therapies: tinnitus retraining therapy, biofeedback, masking devices and consider tricyclic antidepressants if associated mood disorder is present.

Reference: NEJM, 2002; 347: 904-10 and American Family Physician, 2004; 69: 120-8.

Classification of pain syndromes
- Acute pain lasts less than 6 months & chronic pain lasts longer than 6 months.
- **Nociceptive or somatic pain**: pain in response to tissue injury or irritation
  - Examples include lacerations, abrasions, contusions, sprains or strains.
  - Responds well to topical therapies and non-opioid analgesics (page 119).
- **Inflammatory pain**: pain in response to tissue inflammation
  - Examples include rheumatoid arthritis or crystal-induced arthritis.
  - Responds well to NSAIDS, COX-2 inhibitors, salicylates and potentially immunomodulating drugs (e.g., corticosteroids) +/- opioids.
- **Neuropathic pain**: pain from a lesion in or dysfunction of the nervous system.
  - Examples include trigeminal neuralgia, post-herpetic neuralgia, peripheral neuropathy from DM, AIDS or multiple sclerosis & phantom limb syndrome.
  - Patients often have dysesthesias, allodynia, hypalgesia or hyperalgesia.
- **Visceral pain**: pain from stimulation of visceral nociceptors which course alongside autonomic nerve fibers. Thus, visceral pain often accompanied by autonomic symptoms: nausea, vomiting, sweating, bradycardia +/- hypotension
  - Examples include ischemic bowel, renal colic, biliary colic, myocardial infarction, small bowel obstruction, sickle cell crisis and appendicitis.
  - Responds well to NSAIDS, opioids and potentially antispasmodics.
- **Functional pain**: pain from the abnormal central processing of normal stimuli.
  - Examples include fibromyalgia and irritable bowel syndrome
  - Less responsive to non-opioid or opioid analgesics. A multidisciplinary approach and nonpharmacologic techniques essential in these syndromes.

General principles of chronic pain treatment
- Successful control often requires a multidisciplinary approach using pharmacologic and psychiatric interventions and adjunctive physical modalities.
- Medications are prescribed by a single physician and filled at a single pharmacy.
- Addiction to opioids prescribed properly is rare.
- The most appropriate assessment of pain severity is the patient's self report.
  - Abnormal vital signs or exam findings are **not** a good indicator of pain severity in chronic pain, although they are useful indicators in acute pain.

Nonpharmacologic interventions
- Improving sleep hygiene, regular exercise, physical therapy, heating packs, acupuncture, cognitive-behavioral therapy to address mood disorders, improve coping skills and discuss psychosocial stressors, teach relaxation techniques and develop realistic treatment goals.
  - Electrical stimulation: transcutaneous electrical nerve stimulation and spinal cord stimulation modalities can help refractory neuropathic or functional pain

Stepwise approach to medication management of acute or chronic pain
- Mild pain: acetaminophen, NSAIDS and salicylates
- Moderate pain: add low-dose opioids often as combination pills (hydrocodone, codeine, pentazocine or tramadol) and/or adjuvant medications
- Severe pain: long-acting opioids (morphine SR, oxycodone CR, methadone or fentanyl patch) and adjuvant medications (based on specific pain syndrome).
- Aggressive bowel regimen for chronic opioid therapy
- Neuropathic pain management (see page 118). Least opioid responsive.
- Pain meds should be initially titrated to effect then given on a scheduled basis.

Adjuvant treatments for inflammatory pain syndromes
- Epidural steroid injections for cervical or lumbar radiculopathy
- Systemic corticosteroids and radiation therapy for cancer pain related to vasogenic edema or metastatic bone lesions

References: Mayo Clin Proc, 2004; 79: 1533-45. NEJM, 2003; 348: 1243-55. NEJM, 2003; 349: 1943-53. Ann Int Med, 2004; 140: 441-51, Lancet, 1999; 353: 1865-69 and 2004 Pain Guidelines at www.icsi.org

OPIOIDS*	Approximate equianalgesic		Starting dose: adults>50 kg		Starting dose: children/adults 8-50 kg	
	IV/SC/IM	PO	IV/SC/IM	PO	IV/SC/IM	PO
Opioid Agonists						
morphine	10 mg q3-4h	†30 mg q3-4h †60 mg q3-4h	5-10 mg q3-4h	15 mg q3-4h 30 mg q8-12h#	0.1 mg/kg q3-4h	0.3 mg/kg q3-4h
codeine	n/r	200 mg q3-4h	n/r	30 mg q3-4h	n/r	0.5 mg/kg q3-4h
fentanyl‡	0.1 mg q1h	n/a	50 mcg q1h	n/a	n/r	n/a
hydromorphone	1.5 mg q3-4h	7.5 mg q3-4h	1-2 mg q3-4h	2 mg q3-4h	0.015 mg/kg q3-4h	0.03 mg/kg q3-4h
hydrocodone	n/a	30 mg q3-4h	n/a	10 mg q3-4h	n/a	0.2 mg/kg q3-4h
levorphanol	2 mg q6-8h	4 mg q6-8h	2 mg q6-8h	2 mg q6-8h	0.02 mg/kg q6-8h	0.04 mg/kg q6-8h
meperidine§	75 mg q3h	300 mg q2-3h	100 mg q3h	n/r	0.75 mg/kg q2-3h	n/r
oxycodone	n/a	20 mg q3-4h	n/a	10 mg q3-4h or q8-12h#	n/a	0.1 mg/kg q3-4h
oxymorphone	1 mg q3-4h	n/a	1 mg q3-4h	n/a	n/r	n/r
Opioid Agonist-Antagonist and Partial Agonist						
buprenorphine	0.3-0.4 mg q6-8h	n/a	0.4 mg q6-8h	n/a	0.004 mg/kg q6-8h	n/a
butorphanol	2 mg q3-4h	n/a	2 mg q3-4h	n/a	n/r	n/a
nalbuphine	10 mg q3-4h	n/a	10 mg q3-4h	n/a	0.1 mg/kg q3-4h	n/a
pentazocine	30 mg q3-4h	50 mg q3-4h	n/r	50 mg q4-6h	n/r	n/r

*Approximate dosing. All PO dosing with immediate-release preparations. Individualize all dosing, especially in the elderly, children, and patients with chronic pain, opioid tolerance, or hepatic/renal insufficiency. Not available = "n/a". Not recommended = "n/r". Methadone is excluded due to poor consensus on equivalence. #- Dosing with sustained-released or controlled-release preparations such as morphine SR (MS Contin) or Oxycodone CR (Oxycontin). †30 mg with around the clock dosing, and 60 mg with a single dose or short-term dosing (i.e., the opioid-naive). §Doses should be limited to <600 mg/24 hrs and total duration of use <48 hrs; not for chronic pain. ‡ Transdermal fentanyl conversion: 25 mg/day IV morphine = fentanyl 50 mcg/hour q3days. Adapted from the 1992 AHCPR guidelines, www.ahcpr.gov, the NEJM, 2003; 349: 1943-53 and Principles of Analgesic Use in the Treatment of Acute Pain and Cancer Pain. 5th Edition. American Pain Society, 2003.

Medication	Starting oral adult dose	Titration / Usual oral daily dose range in mg	Numbers needed to treat (NNT₅₀)*
Antiepileptics			
carbamazepine	100 mg bid	200 mg q7d / 1000-1600¥	2.6 - 3.3
clonazepam#	0.5 mg daily	0.5 mg q3-5d / 5-20	-
gabapentin‡	300 mg qhs	300 mg q7d / 1800-3600	3.2 - 4.1
lamotrigine	50 mg daily	100 mg q14d / 200-600	2.1
oxcarbazepine	300 mg daily	300 mg q7d / 1200-2400¥	-
phenytoin	100 mg daily	100 mg q7d / 300-500¥	2.1
topiramate	25 mg daily	25 mg q7d / 400-800	-
valproic acid	250 mg bid	250 mg q7d / 1500-3000¥	-
Tricyclic Antidepressants			
amitriptyline	10 mg qhs	10 mg q7d / 50-150¥	2.3 - 3.0
desipramine	25 mg qhs	25 mg q7d / 75-200¥	2.3 - 3.0
doxepin	10 mg qhs	10 mg q7d / 75-150	2.3 - 3.0
nortriptyline	10 mg qhs	10 mg q7d / 25-75¥	2.3 - 3.0
Selective Serotonin Reuptake Inhibitors (SSRIs)			
paroxetine	10 mg daily	10 mg q7d / 20-60	6.7
citalopram	10 mg daily	10 mg q7d / 20-60	6.7
Other Antidepressants			
bupropion	100 mg daily	100 mg q7d / 200-400	-
duloxetine	20 mg daily	20 mg q14d / 20-60	-
venlafaxine	37.5 mg daily	37.5 mg q7d / 150-300	-
Topical Anesthetic Creams			
capsaicin	0.25% tid	Use up to 0.75% 5 times/d	5.3 - 5.9
5% lidoderm	1 patch bid	Use up to 3 patches bid	4.4
Muscle Relaxants			
baclofen	5 mg bid	5 mg q7d / 15-60	1.4
tizanidine	2 mg qhs	2 mg q7d / 12-24	-
Non-opioid analgesics			
clonidine	0.1 mg bid	0.1 mg q7d / 0.2-0.6	-
dextromethorphan	30 mg bid	30 mg q7d / 60 mg q6h	1.9#
tramadol	50 mg bid	50 mg q7d / 200-400	3.1 - 3.4
Opioid analgesics (as extended-release or controlled-release formulations)			
morphine	15 mg bid	15 mg q7d / 60-360	-
oxycodone	20 mg bid	10 mg q7d / 20-160	2.5
methadone	2.5 mg bid	2.5 mg q7d until qid/10-80	-

* - NNT₅₀ is the number needed to treat to decrease the neuropathic pain severity ≥ 50% in 1 patient
‡ -gabapentin + sustained-release morphine more effective than either agent alone (NEJM, 2005; 352: 1324)
# - data supporting the efficacy of SSRIs, benzodiazepines and dextromethorphan for neuropathic or functional pain syndromes is sparse.
¥ - Titrate drug dosage to therapeutic serum drug levels
References: NEJM, 2003; 348: 1243-55. NEJM, 2003; 349: 1943-53. Mayo Clin. Proc., 2004; 79: 1533-45, Pain, 1999; 83: 389. Pain, 2003; 106: 151. Anesthesiology, 2002; 96: 1053. Neurology, 2001; 57: 1583 and the pain management guidelines of the Institute for Clinical Systems Improvement at www.icsi.org.

Medication	Usual Oral Adult Dose	Max Daily Adult Dose	Usual Oral Pediatric Dose
acetaminophen	650 mg q4-6h	4000 mg	10-15 mg/kg q4-6h
Salicylates†			
aspirin	650 mg q4-6h	4000 mg	N/R for <19 years*
diflunisal	500 mg q12h	1500 mg	N/R
salsalate	500 mg q4h	3000 mg	N/R
trilisate	1000-1500 mg q12h	3000 mg	N/R
Nonsteroidal Anti-inflammatory Drugs (NSAIDS)¥			
diclofenac	50 mg q8h	150 mg	N/R
etodolac	200-400 mg q6-8h	1200 mg	N/R
flurbiprofen	50-100 mg bid-tid	300 mg	N/R
ibuprofen	400-800 mg q6-8h	3200 mg	10 mg/kg q6-8h
indomethacin	25-50 mg q8h	200 mg	0.3-1 mg/kg q6-8h
ketoprofen	25-75 mg q6-8h	300 mg	N/R
ketorolac#	10 mg PO q6-8h 30 mg IV/IM q6h (<65 y) 15 mg IV/IM q6h (>65 y)	120 mg (<65 y) 60 mg (>65 y)	0.5 mg/kg PO/IV/IM q6h (max 100 mg/day)
meclofenamate	50-100 mg q4-6h	400 mg	N/R
meloxicam	7.5 mg daily	15 mg	N/R
mefenamic acid	250 mg q6h#	1250 mg	N/R
nabumetone	500-1000 mg bid	2000 mg	N/R
naproxen	250-500 mg bid	1000 mg	5-10 mg/kg q12h
naproxen sodium	275-550 mg bid	1100 mg	5-10 mg/kg q12h
oxaprozin	1200 mg daily	1800 mg	10-20 mg/kg daily
piroxicam	20 mg daily	20 mg	N/R
sulindac	150-200 mg q12h	400 mg	N/R
tolmetin	200-600 mg tid	1800 mg	N/R
Cyclooxenase-2 (COX-2) Inhibitors‡			
celecoxib	100-200 mg bid	400 mg	N/R

* - salicylate use during a viral illness < 19 years is associated with Reye's syndrome

- duration of use limited to 5 days. Ketorolac only NSAID available in a parenteral formulation.

‡ - Celecoxib has the same GI toxicity as nonselective NSAIDS, increases platelet aggregation and can cause papillary necrosis of the kidneys. Rofecoxib (Vioxx) and valdecoxib (Bextra) were voluntarily withdrawn from the market for their association with an increased risk of MI and stroke.

† - salicylates as a class are associated with increased risk of gastritis or peptic ulcer disease, irreversible inhibition of platelet aggregation, potential papillary necrosis of kidneys and can exacerbate asthma.

¥ - NSAIDS as a class are associated with increased risk of gastritis or peptic ulcer disease, reversible inhibition of platelet aggregation, potential papillary necrosis of kidneys and can cause fluid retention, elevated blood pressure and can offset the antiplatelet action of aspirin.

Adapted from the Principles of Analgesic Use in the Treatment of Acute Pain and Cancer Pain, 5th Edition. American Pain Society, 2003 and American Family Physician, 2005; 71: 913-18.

Diagnosis of Asthma
- Episodic wheezing, chest tightness, dyspnea or cough
- Symptoms often worsened by certain allergens, exercise, infection or cold air.
- History of allergic rhinitis or eczema
- Family history of asthma, allergic rhinitis, eczema or recurrent sinusitis
- Exam with hyperexpansion of chest, wheezing, prolonged expiratory phase
- For children under age 5, > 3 wheezing episodes in past year for > 1 day and sleep interrupted **AND** risks (atopic dermatitis or parents with asthma **OR** any two: allergic rhinitis, >4% peripheral eosinophilia or wheezing apart from colds)

Reversible Airflow Obstruction on Spirometry
- FEV_1 < 80% predicted or FEV_1/FVC < 65%
- FEV_1 increases ≥ 12% and 200 mL with inhaled β_2-agonist

FEV_1 = forced expiratory volume in 1 second, FVC = forced vital capacity

Exclude Alternative Diagnoses
- COPD, CHF, airway obstruction, vocal cord dysfunction, pulmonary embolism, cough due to ACEI or cystic fibrosis or inhaled foreign body in small children

Classification of Asthma Severity* (Select most severe factor before treatment)

Class	Days with symptoms	Nights with symptoms	PEF or FEV_1**	PEF variability
Mild intermittent	≤ 2/week	≤ 2/month	≥ 80%	< 20%
Mild persistent	3-6/week	3-4/month	≥ 80%	20-30%
Mod. Persistent	Daily	≥ 5/month	> 60%-< 80%	> 30%
Severe persistent	Daily	Most	≤ 60%	> 30%

Mod. = moderate, PEF = Peak expiratory flow, variability = daily variability over 1-2 weeks
* Same criteria used for children under 5 although spirometry not possible
** % personal best for PEF, % predicted for FEV_1; may not correlate with symptoms

Predicted PEF (liters/min) for Nonsmoking Patients Am Rev Resp Dis, 1963; 88: 644

Age (yrs)	Women (height in inches)					Men (height in inches)					Child (height in inches)	
	55	60	65	70	75	60	65	70	75	80	44	160
20	390	423	460	496	529	554	602	649	693	740	44	160
30	380	413	448	483	516	532	577	622	664	710	48	214
40	370	402	436	470	502	509	552	596	636	680	52	267
50	360	391	424	457	488	486	527	569	607	649	56	320
60	350	380	412	445	475	463	502	542	578	618	60	373
70	340	369	400	432	461	440	477	515	550	587	64	427

Risk Factors for Death in Asthmatics

Sudden severe attacks	Prior intubation/ICU stay	≥ 2 ER/hospitalizations/yr
Hospital/ER in last month	Recent systemic steroids	>2 albuterol canisters/mo.
Heart/psychiatric disorder	Illicit drug use	Low socioeconomic class

Trigger Avoidance/Control
- Possible triggers: smoke, allergens, medications (β-blocker, aspirin, NSAIDS)
- Exercise-induced: starts during and peaks 5-10 minutes after exercise; nonpharmacologic treatment + inhaled β_2-agonist prophylaxis first
- Allergic rhinitis: control with intranasal steroids, allergen avoidance
- Gastroesophageal reflux: raise head of bed, avoid bedtime snack, medications

Stepwise Approach to Asthma Management
- Gain control early with oral steroids or high-dose inhaled steroids
- Step down therapy every 1-2 months to least medications necessary
- Never use salmeterol or formoterol alone without an inhaled steroid
- Consider anti-IgE therapy if severe allergic asthma with elevated serum IgE.

- For children under 5, follow the same therapeutic principles
  - ➤ Inhaled corticosteroids preferred initial med; benefits > stunted growth risk
  - ➤ If no response in 4-6 weeks, reconsider diagnosis and therapy

Class	Preferred meds	Additional medications
Mild intermittent	SA β2-agonist* prn	
Mild persistent	Low dose inhaled steroids (see table)	mast cell stabilizers, leukotriene receptor blockers, theophylline SR# (adults only)
Moderate persistent	LA β2-agonists and low-medium dose inhaled steroids; medium dose as monotherapy in kids	leukotriene receptor blockers +/- theophylline SR# (only as last resort)
Severe persistent	high dose inhaled steroids (see table) + LA β2-agonists‡	Oral steroids +/- theophylline SR# (only as last resort)

*SA = short-acting β2-agonists: albuterol and levalbuterol used for breakthrough symptoms in all classes.
‡LA = long-acting β2-agonists: salmeterol and formoterol. #Theophylline SR titrated to level 5-15 mcg/mL.

INHALED STEROIDS: ESTIMATED COMPARATIVE DAILY DOSES*

Drug	Form	ADULT			CHILD (≤12 yo)		
		Low	Medium	High	Low	Medium	High
beclomethasone MDI	40 mcg/puff	2-6	6-12	>12	2-4	4-8	>8
	80 mcg/puff	1-3	3-6	>6	1-2	2-4	>4
budesonide DPI	200 mcg/dose	1-3	3-6	>6	1-2	2-4	>4
	Soln for nebs	-	-	-	0.5 mg	1 mg	2 mg
flunisolide MDI	250 mcg/puff	2-4	4-8	>8	2-3	4-5	>5
fluticasone MDI	44 mcg/puff	2-6	6-15	>15	2-4	4-10	>10
	110 mcg/puff	1-2	3-6	>6	1	1-4	>4
	220 mcg/puff	1	2-3	>3	n/a	1-2	>2
fluticasone DPI	50 mcg/dose	2-6	6-12	>12	2-4	4-8	>8
	100 mcg/dose	1-3	3-6	>6	1-2	2-4	>4
	250 mcg/dose	1	2	>2	n/a	1	>1
triamcinolone MDI	100 mcg/puff	4-10	10-20	>20	4-8	8-12	>12

*MDI=metered dose inhaler. DPI=dry powder inhaler. All doses in puffs (MDI) or inhalations (DPI). Reference: http://www.nhlbi.nih.gov/guidelines/asthma/execsumm.pdf. Table used with permission from the 2006 Tarascon Pocket Pharmacopoeia, Tarascon Publishing.

Asthma Action Plan (AAP) for Patients Older than 5 Years
- Green zone (doing well): PEF≥ 80% → Continue maintenance medications
- Yellow zone (worsening asthma): PEF ≥ 50% - < 80%
  Use albuterol 2-4 puffs q4hrs x 1-2 days; follow peak flows frequently; and if deterioration persists oral prednisone 1 mg/kg/day up to 60 mg/day x 3-10 days
- Red zone (medical emergency that needs evaluation): PEF < 50%
  Add albuterol 4-6 puffs or 2.5-5 mg nebulized q20 minutes x 3 then q1-2 hours +/- inhaled ipratropium; oral prednisone 1 mg/kg/day up to 60 mg/day x 3-10 d

Asthma Action Plan for Babies-Adapted from National Jewish Medical & Research Center AAP
Zones harder to classify; consider symptom complex:
- Green: no early warning signs or symptoms
- Yellow: fussy or restless, runny/stuffy nose, grunting with/poor feeding, dark circles under eyes, cough (night > day), noisy breathing and tachypnea
- Red: very fussy, prefers sitting > lying down, noisy breathing (wheezing may be quiet), accessory muscle use/retractions, gray/blue starting periorally or hypoxic

Adapted from 2002 National Asthma Education & Prevention Program- www.nhlbi.nih.gov/guidelines/asthma
Other references: AFP, 2004; 70: 893-898; 1061-6. AFP, 2005; 71: 1959-68. The Lancet, 2004; 363: 271-5 and JAMA, 2004; 292: 367-76.

Definition
- Chronic cough lasts ≥ 8 weeks duration

Etiologies of Chronic Cough
- 85-90% of cases in non-smokers who do not use ACEIs are caused by postnasal drip, cough variant asthma or gastroesophageal reflux.
- Up to 40% of patients have multifactorial causes for their chronic cough.
- Other common causes of chronic cough include: chronic bronchitis, eosinophilic bronchitis, chronic sinusitis, postviral bronchospasm and angiotensin converting enzyme inhibitor (ACEI)-induced cough
- Less common causes of chronic cough: bronchiectasis, lung cancer, interstitial lung disease, occult CHF ("cardiac asthma"), foreign body, pulmonary embolus, pulmonary infection (typical or atypical bacteria, tuberculosis, coccidiomycosis, histoplasmosis, pertussis) or psychogenic cough
- Warning signs warranting immediate diagnostic evaluation: unintentional weight loss, hemoptysis, night sweats and an immunocompromised state.

Evaluation and Treatment of the Common Causes of Chronic Cough
- **Postnasal drip:** symptoms of rhinitis, frequent throat clearing, itchy throat or palate, although some are asymptomatic. Exam may reveal edematous nasal turbinates and a glistening, "cobblestone" appearance of the oropharynx.
  - ➢ Empiric trial of an oral antihistamine-decongestant, nasal corticosteroids or ipratropium nasal spray for 3-4 weeks.
- **Cough variant asthma:** atopic history or family history of eczema, allergies or asthma, history of cough triggers (e.g., exercise, cold exposure, environmental allergens or animal dander). Only manifestation of asthma in up to 55% of pts.
  - ➢ Consider an empiric trial of inhaled steroids and albuterol for 8 weeks.
  - ➢ Test with routine spirometry and if normal a methacholine challenge test that is normal effectively rules out cough-variant asthma.
- **Gastroesophageal reflux (GERD):** history of heartburn, dyspepsia or sour taste in the mouth exacerbated by meals and the supine position. Up to 75% of patients with GERD-induced cough have no reflux symptoms.
  - ➢ Nonpharmacologic interventions: diet high in protein and avoid bedtime snacks, fatty foods, chocolate, excess alcohol, caffeine and citrus fruits, smoking cessation and elevate head of the bed 6 inches.
  - ➢ Empiric trial of proton pump inhibitor or moderate-high dose H_2-blockers (e.g., ranitidine 150-300 mg bid or famotidine 20-40 mg bid) for 2 months.
  - ➢ Esophageal pH probe testing usually not necessary but solidifies diagnosis.

Evaluation of Less Common Causes of Chronic Cough
- **Initial studies and interventions to consider**
  - ➢ Chest x-ray, place a PPD test and stop ACEI therapy
  - ➢ Investigate for toxic occupational exposures
  - ➢ Smoking cessation counseling
  - ➢ Pulmonary function tests if chronic bronchitis a consideration
  - ➢ X-rays or coronal CT scan of sinuses to rule out chronic sinusitis
  - ➢ Induced sputum for eosinophils > 3% and normal methacholine challenge test indicates eosinophilic bronchitis→ treat with inhaled steroids x 14 days.
- **Second-tier diagnostic studies**
  - ➢ High-resolution CT scan of chest to evaluate for interstitial lung disease or bronchiectasis if chest x-ray abnormal and high clinical suspicion.
  - ➢ Bronchoscopy indicated if high suspicion for lung cancer or foreign body.

References: Archives Internal Medicine, 1998; 158: 1222. NEJM, 2000; 343: 1715-21. Thorax, 2004; 59: 342-6. BMJ, 2003; 326: 261 and Eur. Resp. Journal, 2004; 24: 481-92.

Diagnosis of Chronic Obstructive Pulmonary Disease (COPD)

History
- Persistent usually progressive exertional dyspnea worse with lung infections
- Chronic cough usually worse in morning with any pattern of sputum production
- Risks: Smoking (80%); smoke, occupational, chemical or pollution exposure; chronic lung infections; α-1 antitrypsin deficiency (age<45, strong family history)

Exam
- Expiratory wheezing, prolonged expiration and/or decreased air movement
- Anteroposterior dimension of thorax often enlarged ("barrel chest")
- Breathing through pursed lips in severe disease
- Consider secondary polycythemia with ruddy face, Cor pulmonale if leg edema

Spirometry: airflow obstruction not fully reversible
- FEV_1/FVC < 70% predicted and postbronchodilator FEV_1 < 80%

   FEV_1 = forced expiratory volume in 1 second, FVC = forced vital capacity

Exclude other diagnoses: asthma, heart failure, bronchiectasis or tuberculosis

Therapy for Stable COPD (lung function declines with time even with therapy)
- No role for oral steroids in stable disease
- Trial of oral steroids does not predict response to inhaled steroids

Stage*	Spirometry	Therapy
All	No Smoking! Influenza and pneumococcal vaccines and exercise	
0 (at risk)	Normal	
I (mild)	FEV_1/FVC < 70% FEV_1 ≥80% predicted	Short-acting or long-acting bronchodilator(s)** prn
II (moderate)	50%≤ FEV_1 < 80%	Scheduled long-acting bronchodilator(s)** and pulmonary rehabilitation⁺
III (severe)	30%≤ FEV_1 < 50%	Add inhaled steroids for symptom relief if > 3 exacerbations in last 2-3 years
IV (very severe)	FEV_1<30% or <50% + chronic resp failure	As for Stage III; oxygen⁺⁺ (improves survival!); consider bullectomy/transplant#

*FEV_1 used to stratify severity but BODE index (Body mass index, airway obstruction, dyspnea, exercise capacity on 6 min. walk) better to assess risk of death-see http://content.nejm.org/cgi/reprint/350/10/1005.pdf
**bronchodilators (anticholinergics> β₂-agonists >> methylxanthines) - use combination therapy if monotherapy inadequate; long-acting bronchodilators (e.g., tiotropium and salmeterol) are preferred but are more expensive than short-acting bronchodilators (e.g., ipratropium and albuterol).
⁺aerobic exercise, good nutrition and education. resp = respiratory
⁺⁺PaO_2<55 mm Hg/O_2 sat≤88% (PaO_2≤60 mm Hg if pulmonary hypertension, polycythemia or cor pulmonale)
#bullectomy or lung-volume reduction surgery best for upper lobe emphysema and low exercise capacity.
Lung transplantation indicated for idiopathic emphysema or α-1 antitrypsin deficiency

Therapy for Acute Exacerbations (↑ in dyspnea, sputum volume and purulence)
- Assess with chest x-ray, sputum culture, oximetry or arterial blood gas
- Admit for severe exacerbations: respiratory acidosis, need for ventilation, PEF< 100L/min, FEV_1 < 1L or < 40% predicted, or serious comorbidities
- Medical management
  - ➤ Combined albuterol and ipratropium via MDI or nebulizer q1-4hr
  - ➤ Antibiotics* x 5-10 days for exacerbations associated with purulent sputum
  - ➤ Systemic steroids with prednisolone 30-40 mg/day (or prednisone 40-60 mg PO daily) x 10 days if FEV_1 < 50% predicted
  - ➤ Oxygen if hypoxia; noninvasive positive-pressure ventilation if acute respiratory acidosis (pH ≤ 7.35) and no contraindications

*typically amoxicillin, doxycycline, or trimethoprim-sulfamethoxazole; severe exacerbation = most benefit.
References: Global Initiative for Chronic Obstructive Lung Disease Pocket Guide to COPD Diagnosis, Management and Prevention, 2004 at www.goldcopd.com. NEJM 2004; 350:1005-12; 2689-97. NEJM 2002; 346:988-94. JAMA 2003; 290:2301-16. Lancet, 2004; 364: 883-95 and Lancet, 2003; 362: 1053-61.

Test	Transudate	Exudate[‡]
Specific gravity	< 1.016	≥ 1.016
PF protein (gm/dL)	< 3.0	≥ 3.0
PF protein/serum protein	< 0.5	≥ 0.5
PF LDH (IU)	< 200	≥ 200 or > 2/3 upper limit of labs normal range
PF LDH/serum LDH	< 0.6	≥ 0.6
PF glucose (mg%)	> 60	≤ 60*

PF = pleural fluid, LDH = lactate dehydrogenase, IU = international units
* - glucose < 60 suggests cancer, tuberculosis, empyema or effusion from rheumatoid lung
‡ - only one test needs to be abnormal to classify effusion as an exudate

Causes of Transudative Effusions

• Constrictive pericarditis	• Hepatic hydrothorax	• Nephrotic syndrome	• Severe hypo-albuminemia
• Urinothorax	• Heart Failure	• Peritoneal dialysis	• Superior vena cava syndrome

Evaluation of Exudative Effusions

Diagnosis	PF appearance	Diagnostic Pleural Fluid Testing
Empyema	Purulent	Pleural fluid pH<7.2*, ↑ WBC[‡], + culture
Malignant	+/- Bloody	Positive pleural fluid cytology
Chylothorax	Milky	Triglycerides > 110 mg/dL
Pancreatitis	-	High amylase
Uremia	-	Very high BUN (usually > 100 mg/dL)
Sarcoidosis	-	High angiotensin converting enzyme level
Lupus pleuritis	-	Positive pleural fluid ANA
Rheumatoid lung	Yellow-green	Characteristic cytology, glucose< 30 mg%
Ovarian hyper-stimulation syn.	-	Fertility medication use
Meig's syndrome	-	+ Ascites and ovarian fibroma
Amebic abscess	Anchovy paste	+ Amebic titers and + liver abscess
Pulmonary embolus	Bloody	+ Ventilation/perfusion scan
Tuberculosis	Bloody	+ Acid fast bacilli on pleural biopsy and < 5% mesothelial cells in pleural fluid

* - fluid for pleural fluid pH should be collected in an arterial blood gas tube and kept on ice
‡ - ↑ WBC = elevated pleural fluid white blood count. Cell count should be collected in a purple top tube.
Any effusion that develops during pneumonia treatment should be aspirated and analyzed.

Contraindications to Diagnostic Thoracentesis

- International normalized ratio > 2.0 or partial thromboplastin time > twice normal
  ➤ Can perform thoracentesis if coagulopathy corrected prior to procedure.
- Platelets < 25,000 cells/mL
- Caution if creatinine > 6 mg/dL
- Small volume of pleural fluid: <1 cm fluid that layers out on decubitus CXR.
  ➤ Thoracentesis can be done if free-flowing fluid >1 cm on decubitus CXR.

References: Chest, 1997; 111: 970. Semin. Respir. Crit. Care Med., 1995; 16: 269.

Lung volumes in a healthy individual

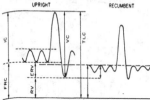

Abbreviations
ERV= expiratory reserve vol.
FEF$_{25-75\%}$=forced expiratory flow from 25-75%VC
FEV$_1$= forced expiratory volume in 1 second
FRC= functional residual capacity
FVC= forced vital capacity
IC= inspiratory capacity
RV= residual volume
TLC= total lung capacity
VC= vital capacity

Spirometry Patterns

Flow-Volume Loop

- **Normal:** FVC, FEV$_1$, PEFR and FEF$_{25-75\%}$ > 80% predicted; FEV$_1$/FVC > 95% predicted ♦ Can be seen with intermittent disease (e.g. asthma), pulmonary emboli and pulmonary vascular disease

- **Obstructive:** Obstruction to airflow prolongs expiration ♦ FEV$_1$/FVC < 95% predicted and increased airway resistance ♦ Differential diagnosis: asthma, COPD, bronchiectasis, cystic fibrosis, bronchiolitis, proximal airway obstruction

Expired Volume vs Time

- **Restrictive:** Reduced volumes without changes in airway resistance ♦ Decreased VC and TLC, FEV$_1$ and FVC decreased proportionately (FEV$_1$/FVC ratio > 95% pred) ♦ Must confirm lung volumes by helium dilution or plethysmography (reduced FVC on spirometry not specific for restrictive disease, although normal FVC predicts normal TLC) ♦ Differential diagnosis: interstitial disease, CHF, pleural disease, pneumonia, neuromuscular disease, chest wall abnormalities, obesity and lung resection

- **Bronchodilator response:** Positive if FVC or FEV$_1$ increase 12% *and* ≥ 200 mL

- **Poor effort:** Most reliably diagnosed by technician performing test rather than spirometric values. Forced expiratory time (FET) < 6 seconds suggests inadequate expiration.

Grading of PFT abnormalities

Obstruction	% Predicted FEV$_1$
Mild	70 - 100%
Moderate	60 - 69%
Mod-severe	50 - 59%
Severe	35 - 49%
Very Severe	< 35%

Restriction	% Predicted TLC#	% Predicted FVC
Mild	70% - LLN*	70% - LLN*
Moderate	50 - 69%	60 - 69%
Mod-severe		50 - 59%
Severe	< 50%	35 - 49%
Very Severe		< 35%

\# TLC superior to FVC in assessing restrictive disease
* LLN= lower limits of normal

Diffusion capacity (DL$_{CO}$)

- Expensive, imprecise and generally not very helpful. Measured value needs to be adjusted for hemoglobin and alveolar ventilation (V$_A$). Most useful for (1) evaluating pulmonary vascular disease (2) diagnosing pulmonary hemorrhage (3) assessing change in collagen-vascular or drug-related pulmonary disease.
- **Reduced:** emphysema, interstitial lung disease, pulmonary embolism, pulmonary vascular disease, lung resection or severe congestive heart failure
- **Increased:** pulmonary hemorrhage or mild congestive heart failure
- **Normal:** asthma, chronic bronchitis, chest wall and pleural abnormalities or neuromuscular disease

Mechanical upper airway obstruction

- Most reliably diagnosed by contour of flow-volume loop and reproducibility (see below). If suspected, alert technician to emphasize performance of inspiratory limb.
- **Variable extrathoracic:** vocal cord paralysis or vocal cord dysfunction ♦ rheumatoid arthritis ♦ post-intubation vocal cord adhesions ♦ burns
- **"Fluttering" of the expiratory limb of flow-volume loop:** obstructive sleep apnea
- **Variable intrathoracic:** non-circumferential tracheal tumors which make walls "floppy" ♦ relapsing polychondritis ♦ tracheomalacia following surgery ♦ mainstem bronchus tumors
- **Fixed upper airway obstruction:** benign stricture after prolonged intubation ♦ tracheal tumor ♦ goiter ♦ small endotracheal or tracheostomy tube ♦ bilateral stenosis of mainstem bronchi (rare)

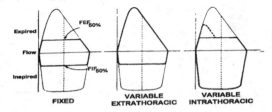

FIXED   VARIABLE EXTRATHORACIC   VARIABLE INTRATHORACIC

Pulmonary Function Testing is adapted with permission from the Tarascon Internal Medicine and Critical Care Pocketbook, 3rd Edition, Tarascon Publishing

Risk factors for perioperative pulmonary complications

- Smoking within 8 weeks of surgery
- Poor general health (ASA > 2)
- Inability to exercise, chronic cough, or unexplained dyspnea
- Abnormal lung exam (wheezing or prolonged expiration)
- Thoracic, abdominal aortic aneurysm or upper abdominal surgery
- Chronic obstructive pulmonary disease or significant airway obstruction
- Elevated arterial carbon dioxide pressure ($PaCO_2$)
- Surgery lasting > 3 hours
- General anesthesia
- Long-acting neuromuscular blockade

Note: obesity by itself does not appear to increase risk

Pre-operative risk stratification

- Few patients have an absolute pulmonary contraindication to surgery.
- Pre-operative spirometry should **not** be used to prevent surgery but rather as a tool to optimize preoperative lung function. Appropriate if the patient has:
  - Asthma or COPD and airflow obstruction has not been optimized.
  - Unexplained dyspnea or cough who will undergo major surgery (as above)
  - Patient will be undergoing lung resection.

- **Respiratory Failure Index**

Factor	Score	Factor	Score
Type of surgery		Albumin < 3 gm/dL	9
AAA repair	27	BUN > 30 mg/dL	8
Thoracic	21	History of COPD	6
Neuro, upper abdomen, peripheral vascular	14	Partially or dependent functional status	7
Neck	11	Age > 70	6
Emergency surgery	11	Age 60-69	4

Class	Points	Incidence of post-operative respiratory failure
1	≤ 10	0.5%
2	11-19	1.8%
3	20-27	4.2%
4	28-40	10.1%
5	> 40	26.6%

Interventions to reduce perioperative risk

- Smoking cessation: beneficial if patient quits ≥ 8 weeks prior to surgery
- Inhaled ipratropium 4 puffs qid for COPD; ß–agonists for wheezing
- Oral or inhaled steroids if COPD or asthma and pulmonary function not optimal (no increase risk of infections, but potential for adrenal suppression if ≥ 20 mg/day prednisone for ≥ 3 weeks).
- Defer elective surgery for acute exacerbations of pulmonary disease
- Consider shorter procedures (<3 hrs), laparoscopic approach & spinal/epidural or regional anesthesia rather than general anesthesia for high-risk patients.
- Avoid long-acting neuromuscular blockers (e.g., pancuronium).
- Post-operative deep breathing exercises or incentive spirometry beneficial.
- Epidural analgesia and nerve blocks for post-op pain control

AAA = Abdominal aortic aneurysm, ASA = Anesthesia Society of America class, COPD = chronic obstructive pulmonary disease and BUN = blood urea nitrogen
References: NEJM, 1999; 340: 937-44. Med Clin N Am, 2003; 87: 153-73 and Ann Surg, 2000; 232: 242-53.
Preoperative pulmonary evaluation is adapted with permission from the Tarascon Internal Medicine and Critical Care Pocketbook, 3rd Edition, Tarascon Publishing

Insomnia
- **Definition:** subjective report of difficulty initiating or maintaining sleep, early awakening and interrupted or non-restorative sleep.
- **Assessment of Insomnia**
  - Identify nature of the sleep problem and if any daytime consequences exist.
  - Frequency of complaint (chronic insomnia = occurrence > 2-3 times/week)
  - Any contributing factors? (any medical or psychological conditions, stressors, medication history, substance abuse, chronic pain, nocturia or nocturnal events: nightmares, sleep paralysis, night sweats or hot flashes?)
  - Any negative cognition (e.g., "I'll never get to sleep" or "If I can't sleep…I can't function"…or…"my life will fall apart" or "I can't sleep without a pill."
- **Treatment of Chronic Insomnia**
  - **Primary treatment is cognitive-behavioral therapy** which includes: go to bed only when sleepy, use the bed only for sleep, avoid naps, maintain a regular sleep-wake schedule, avoid caffeine, tobacco, stimulants and alcohol after lunch, avoid excessive fluids after dinner, avoid lying in bed awake for longer than 20 minutes, practice progressive muscle relaxation to initiate sleep, identify maladaptive and distorted cognitions and replace these with positive, adaptive beliefs. Keep a sleep diary or log.
  - **Recommended meds for short-term insomnia treatment (≤12 weeks)**

Name	Dose given at bedtime	Indication
doxylamine	25-50 mg PO	Mainly for sleep onset >maintenance
temazepam	7.5-30 mg PO	Mainly for sleep maintenance
trazodone	50-150 mg PO	For sleep onset or maintenance*
zolpidem	5-10 mg PO	Mainly for sleep onset >maintenance
zaleplon	5-10 mg PO	Mainly for sleep onset >maintenance

* - especially effective in association with SSRI therapy

  - **Medications for long-term insomnia treatment:** eszopiclone 2-3 mg PO at bedtime for both sleep onset and sleep maintenance

Narcolepsy
- **Definition:** a sleep disorder characterized by excessive daytime sleepiness and a tendency to transition suddenly from wakefulness into REM sleep. Associated with cataplexy (abrupt loss of muscle tone without loss of consciousness precipitated by extreme emotion), sleep paralysis & hypnogogic hallucinations (vivid dream-like states occurring at the onset of sleep).
- **Pharmacologic Treatments**

Name	Oral Dosages	Indication
dextroamphetamine	5-50 mg bid	Excessive daytime sleepiness
methylphenidate	10-30 mg bid	Excessive daytime sleepiness
modafinil	200-400 mg/d; daily or bid	Excessive daytime sleepiness
clomipramine	10-150 mg qAM or qhs	Cataplexy
fluoxetine	20-80 mg qAM	Cataplexy
protriptyline	5-60 mg qAM or qhs	Cataplexy
sodium oxybate*	4.5-9 gm/d (qPM and qhs)	Cataplexy
venlafaxine XR	75-150 mg qAM	Cataplexy

* - Also known as gamma-hydroxybutyrate (or GHB) and has been associated with abuse (e.g., "date rape")
References: Ann. Neurol., 2003; 53: 154 and Lancet, 2004; 364: 1959-73.

Definitions Related to Obstructive Sleep Apnea (OSA)
- Apnea is the cessation of airflow for at least 10 seconds
- Apnea index is number of apneas per hour of sleep
- Hypopnea is reduction in airflow > 50% + oxygen saturation decreases > 4%
- Respiratory disturbance index (RDI) = apneas + hypopneas per hour of sleep
- Obesity-Hypoventilation syndrome is a subset of obstructive sleep apnea.
  ➤ Patients have chronic daytime hypoxemia and hypercapnia.

Risk Factors for Obstructive Sleep Apnea
- Central obesity (body mass index > 29), postmenopausal women, men>40 yrs, alcoholics, hypothyroidism, sedating med use, micrognathia, acromegaly, macroglossia, tonsillar hypertrophy, adjusted neck circumference ≥ 43 cm (add 4 cm for HTN, 3 cm for habitual snorer and 3 cm for nocturnal choking/gasping.

Clinical Features of Obstructive Sleep Apnea
- **Symptoms**: Restless and nonrestorative sleep, daytime hypersomnolence, morning headaches, cognitive impairment, mood disorders and irritability, decreased libido, impotence, hearing impairment, night sweats, morning dry mouth, sore throat and nocturnal drooling
- **Signs**: Loud snoring, obesity, short and thick neck, excessive pharyngeal tissue, large uvula, sleepiness and hypertension
- Cor pulmonale or left ventricular dysfunction occurs in 30% of people with OSA.

Diagnosis of Obstructive Sleep Apnea
- Nocturnal polysomnography in a sleep lab is the gold standard for diagnosis.
- Apnea-hypopnea index ≥5, ↑daytime somnolence & oxygen desaturation< 90%

Classification of Obstructive Sleep Apnea
- Mild OSA: RDI of 5 -14 +/- minimum oxygen saturation > 79%.
- Moderate OSA: RDI of 15 - 29 +/- minimum oxygen saturation > 69%.
- Severe OSA: RDI ≥ 29 +/- minimum oxygen saturation > 70%.

Treatment Options for Obstructive Sleep Apnea
- Weight reduction, sleep on side and minimize alcohol, narcotics and sedatives
- Nasal continuous positive airway pressure (CPAP) for patients with only OSA
  ➤ Compliance major issue: only 50-80% of patients used mask ≥ 3-4 hrs/night
  ➤ Bilevel positive airway pressure (BiPAP) more appropriate for obesity-hypoventilation syndrome by providing pressure support ventilation
- Uvulopalatopharyngoplasty gives significant improvement in < 50% of patients.
- Tracheotomy
- Tongue-retaining/mandibular-advancing devices suboptimal compared to CPAP
- Protriptyline is not useful for OSA; the side effects outweigh its small benefit.

Restless Legs Syndrome (RLS)
- **Clinical features**: akathisia (irresistible need to move one's legs) and uncomfortable paresthesias of legs occurring at rest, relieved by movement and worse at night. Usually associated with periodic limb movements while asleep.
- **Common coexisting diseases**: iron deficiency (supplemental iron helps RLS), DM, rheumatoid arthritis, fibromyalgia, uremia, pregnancy, Parkinson's disease
- **Treatment Options for restless legs syndrome**

Name	Oral Dosages	Side Effects
Sinemet 25/100 mg	½ -1 tablet qhs	nausea, vomiting, orthostatic
pramipexole*	0.125 qhs-0.75 mg qhs	hypotension, hallucinations for all
ropinirole*	0.25–2.5 mg qhs	*=↑ fluid retention and rhinorrhea
clonazepam	0.25–2 mg qhs	tolerance, dependence & sedation
gabapentin	200–600 mg qPM & qhs	sedation, dizziness and fatigue
pergolide	0.05-0.5 mg qPM & qhs	nausea, diarrhea and dyskinesias
opiates (various formulations given qhs)		sedation, constipation and nausea

References: Ann Intern Med., 2005; 142: 187-97. NEJM, 2003; 348: 2103-9 and NEJM, 2002; 347: 498-504

Epidemiology: occurs in 40-50% in men age 50-60 yrs and ~ 80% if ≥ 80 yrs

Clinical Presentation
- Asymptomatic
- Irritative symptoms: urinary frequency, nocturia and urinary urgency
- Obstructive symptoms: hesitancy, weak urinary stream, intermittent urinary stream, and sensation of incomplete bladder emptying.
- Hematuria or dysuria (urinary tract infection)
- Bladder outlet obstruction with postrenal azotemia
- American Urological Association has developed a urinary symptom score that evaluates the frequency of the 7 irritative and obstructive symptoms as above.
  ➢ Each symptom is scored on a scale of 0 to 5 based on symptom frequency: not at all (0), less than 20% of the time (1), less than 50% of the time (2), 50% of the time (3), more than 50% of the time (4) or almost always (5)
  ➢ Score 0 – 7 = mild, 8 – 19 = moderate and ≥ 20 = severe symptoms

Physical Exam
- Typically find a diffusely enlarged, nontender prostate with no discrete nodules
- Rarely, patients have a normal-sized prostate

Lab Evaluation
- Urinalysis to check for blood or evidence of infection and serum creatinine.
- Prostate specific antigen (PSA) level not recommended for routine screening.

Pharmacologic Treatments for Benign Prostatic Hyperplasia (BPH)
- Generally initiated for men with moderate-severe urinary symptom scores
- Stop anticholinergic and sympathomimetic meds +/- calcium channel blockers.
- Combined α_1-blockers and 5-α-reductase inhibitors reduce the rate of clinical progression more than either agent alone.
- **Nonselective alpha$_1$ blockers** (inexpensive generics available)
  ➢ Doxazosin 1-8 mg PO qhs **or** terazosin 1-10 mg PO qhs
  ➢ Alpha blockers are better than 5-α-reductase inhibitors for symptom control.
  ➢ Side effects: postural hypotension, dizziness, fatigue and weakness
- **Selective alpha$_{1A}$ blockers** (no generics available)
  ➢ Tamsulosin 0.4 mg PO daily or alfuzosin 10 mg PO daily taken with food.
  ➢ Less orthostatic hypotension than nonselective alpha-blockers
- **5-alpha-reductase inhibitors**
  ➢ Finasteride 5 mg PO daily or dutasteride 0.5 mg PO daily
  ➢ Induce an 80-90% reduction in serum dihydrotestosterone
  ➢ Greater efficacy the larger the initial prostate size
  ➢ Side effects: decreased libido, ejaculatory dysfunction and impotence

Surgical Treatments for Benign Prostatic Hyperplasia
- Indications: failed medical therapy, recurrent UTIs, recurrent hematuria, renal failure, acute urinary retention, bladder calculi or severe urinary symptom score.
- Transurethral resection of the prostate (TURP): most common surgical procedure for BPH
  ➢ Symptom improvement in 90% of patients
  ➢ Complications: retrograde ejaculation (50%), impotence (5-10%), urethral stricture (4%) and urinary incontinence (6% with partial & 1% with complete)
- Other surgical options: transurethral incision of the prostate, transurethral microwave thermotherapy or needle ablation of prostate & laser prostatectomy.

Reference: AFP, 2002; 66: 77-88. Lancet, 2003; 361: 1359-67 and NEJM, 2003; 349: 2449-51.

Definition of Hematuria: ≥ 5 red blood cells per high powered field.

Etiologies of Transient Hematuria in Adults
- Vigorous exercise, sexual intercourse, trauma or vaginal contamination

Etiologies of Persistent Hematuria in Adults and Children

- Infections: cystitis, pyelonephritis, prostatitis, urethritis, renal tuberculosis
- Alport's syndrome*
- Benign familial hematuria*
- Cancer: bladder, kidney or urethral
- Coagulopathy, overanticoagulation
- Foreign body: urethra or bladder
- Goodpasture's syndrome
- Henoch-Schonlein purpura*
- Hypercalciuria
- Hyperuricosuria

- Glomerular causes: IgA nephropathy, hereditary nephritis, thin basement membrane disease, glomerulonephritis
- Loin pain-hematuria syndrome
- Medullary sponge kidney
- Nephrolithiasis or ureterolithiasis
- Polycystic kidney disease
- Renal arteriovenous malformation
- Renal infarction
- Renal vein thrombosis
- Sickle cell disease*
- Thrombocytopenia

* - causes of hematuria occurring primarily in children

Work-up of Microscopic Hematuria in Children
- AAP recommends a screening urinalysis at age 4-5 yr & then between 11-21 yr
- Confirm hematuria with urinalysis and microscopic exam weekly x 2
- Check urinalysis and urine sediment for associated proteinuria (≥100 mg/dL), dysmorphic red blood cells or red blood cell casts = a glomerular etiology.
- Parents and siblings also have hematuria = benign familial hematuria
- Family history of stones: urine calcium/creatinine ratio >0.21 x 2 warrants a 24 h urine for calcium > 4 mg/m^2/day = hypercalciuria
- Hearing screen in young boys with hearing impairment (Alport's syndrome)
- Hemoglobin electrophoresis or sickle cell prep for those at risk
- Labs: renal panel, complete blood count, prothrombin time, partial thromboplastin time +/- C3, C4 and anti-streptolysin O titer if clinically indicated.
- Urine culture to rule out infection

Work-up of Microscopic Hematuria in Adults
- Routine screening urinalyses are not recommended in adults.
- If urine dipstick positive for "blood" x 2, check a microscopic exam of urine.
- Examine urinary sediment for dysmorphic red blood cells or red blood cell casts both of which suggest a glomerular source of hematuria.
  - ➤ Check for renal insufficiency and significant persistent proteinuria (urine protein/creatinine ratio > 0.5 or 24h urine with >500 mg protein).
  - ➤ For glomerular bleeding, nephrology consult and renal biopsy are indicated.
- Helical CT scan for nonglomerular bleeding: assess kidneys for stones/cancer.
- First morning urine for cytology +/- acid-fast bacilli culture (if indicated) x 3 days.
- Cystoscopy indicated for positive urine cytology or if patient ≥ 40 with risk factors for bladder or transitional cell cancer (tobacco abuse or history of exposure to benzenes, aromatic amines, aniline dyes or cyclophosphamide).
- For unexplained hematuria, consider 24 hr urine for calcium and uric acid

IgA = immunoglobulin A, AAP = American Academy of Pediatrics, C3 and C4 are complements 3 and 4

References: NEJM, 2003; 348: 2330-8. Urol Clin N Amer, 2004; 31: 559-73 and Med Clin N Amer, 2004; 88: 329-43 and American Family Physician, 2001; 63: 1145-54.

Clinical Presentation
- Asymptomatic
- Flank pain radiating to the groin associated with nausea, vomiting and ileus.
- 90% with hematuria

Risk Factors for Nephrolithiasis

• Distal renal tubular acidosis	• Hypertension
• Positive family history of stones	• Hyperthyroidism
• Gout or secondary hyperuricemia	• UTI with urease-positive bacteria*
• Hot climate and dehydration	• Obesity
• Primary hyperparathyroidism	• Vitamin D intoxication

- Diet: low calcium, high sodium, high animal protein and low fluid intake
- Meds: acyclovir, indinavir, sulfadiazine, topiramate, triamterene & zonisamide

* - proteus, klebsiella and pseudomonas, UTI = urinary tract infection

Work-up of Nephrolithiasis
- Stone analysis
- Examine medication list for any offending medications
- **Labs for calcium stones**
  - ➢ Serum calcium, phosphate, potassium, magnesium, bicarbonate (screen for renal tubular acidosis), intact parathyroid hormone & vitamin D metabolites.
  - ➢ 24 hr urine for calcium, citrate, uric acid, oxalate, sodium and creatinine.
- **Urate stones:** serum uric acid, CBC and 24 hr urine for uric acid and creatinine
- **Staghorn calculi:** 24 hr urine for cystine and creatinine and check urine pH

General Management of Nephrolithiasis
- Drink 2-3 liters of noncaffeinated beverages daily (preferably water)
- NSAIDS and often opiates for symptomatic therapy of ureteral colic
- Stones < 5 mm have a good chance of spontaneous passage

Management of Calcium Nephrolithiasis
- Diet: low sodium, low animal protein, normal calcium and avoid grapefruit juice and dark sodas.
- Thiazide diuretics or indapamide can minimize hypercalciuria
- Parathyroid surgery for primary hyperparathyroidism
- Low oxalate diet and pyridoxine 50-100 mg PO daily for hyperoxaluria
- Potassium citrate (+/- magnesium) 30-60 MEq PO daily for hypocitraturia

Management of Urate Stones
- Allopurinol 300-600 mg PO daily for hyperuricosuria
- Potassium citrate 10-30 MEq PO tid with meals (titrated to urine pH ≥ 6.5-7)
- Low purine diet

Management of Struvite or Staghorn Calculi
- Surgical removal of stone and fluid intake should exceed 3 liters/day.
- Struvite stones: long-term antibiotic prophylaxis
- Staghorn calculi: potassium citrate for urine pH ≥ 7.5 and tiopronin 300-500 mg PO tid or penicillamine 125-250 mg PO qid + pyridoxine 50 mg PO 2x/week

Interventional Techniques for Nephrolithiasis and Ureterolithiasis
- Symptomatic renal stones: > 2 cm usually requires percutaneous nephrostolithotomy and < 2 cm can be treated with ESWL
- Proximal ureteral stones: 5-20 mm can be treated with ESWL or flexible ureteroscopy and >2 cm often require percutaneous nephrostolithotomy
- Mid-distal ureteral stones: usually treated by ureteroscopy and stenting.

ESWL = extracorporeal shock wave lithotripsy and CBC = complete blood count

References: Am J. Kidney Dis., 2005; 45: 422-8. NEJM, 2002; 346: 77-84 and Endo Metab Clin N Amer, 2002; 31: 1051-64.

Causes of Transient Incontinence (mnemonic is DIAPPERS)
- **D** – Delirium
- **I** – Infection of urinary tract
- **A** – Atrophy of genitourinary tract
- **P** – Pharmaceuticals (e.g., diuretics, caffeine, alcohol, +/- alpha$_1$-blockers, benzodiazepines, hypnotics, tranquilizers, antidepressants and laxatives)
- **P** – Psychological conditions
- **E** – Endocrine disorders (e.g., diabetes mellitus, diabetes insipidus or hyperparathyroidism)
- **R** – Restricted mobility (e.g., stroke, movement disorders, arthritis or visual impairment)
- **S** – Stool impaction

Causes of Established Urinary Incontinence
- **Genuine Stress Urinary Incontinence (GSUI)**
  - ➢ Caused by weakness of the muscles of the urethral sphincter or pelvic floor.
  - ➢ Hallmark is the loss of urine with increased intra-abdominal pressure as occurs with coughing, sneezing, laughing, running or position changes.
  - ➢ Provocative stress test: have patient vigorously cough with full bladder in recumbent and, if needed, upright position→ loss of urine indicates GSUI.
  - ➢ Bonney test: perform provocative stress test while elevating bladder neck and it is positive if there is no loss of urine.
  - ➢ Q-tip test: place sterile Q-tip in distal urethra and have patient valsalva. A change of the angle > 30° is positive and suggests urethral hypermobility.
- **Urge Incontinence**
  - ➢ Most common cause of urinary incontinence in patients over 60 years.
  - ➢ Hallmark is sudden onset of urinary urgency followed by loss of urine.
  - ➢ Definitive diagnosis by identifying detrusor instability by cystometrogram.
- **Overflow Incontinence**
  - ➢ Causes include bladder outlet obstruction (BOO) or a neurogenic bladder.
  - ➢ Causes of BOO: prostatism, cervical cancer, urethral stricture or bladder CA
  - ➢ Neurogenic bladder: diabetic neuropathy, sacral cord lesions or medications
  - ➢ Diagnosis by elevated by postvoid residual > 150-200 mL
- **Functional Incontinence**
  - ➢ Patients unable to maintain continence because of cognitive, physical or emotional problems.

Treatment of Urinary Incontinence
- **Nonpharmacologic Interventions**
  - ➢ Bladder retraining with timed voids at progressively longer intervals for UI
  - ➢ Avoid caffeine and alcohol
  - ➢ Kegel exercises, pessaries, bladder retraining and timed voiding for GSUI
  - ➢ Absorbent pads or condom catheters can help to ensure dryness.
- **Pharmacologic therapy**
  - ➢ Urge incontinence: oral oxybutynin 2.5-5 mg bid-tid, tolterodine 1-2 mg bid, doxepin 25-75 mg daily, dicyclomine 10-20 mg tid or flavoxate 100 mg tid
  - ➢ Stress urinary incontinence: topical estrogens for atrophic vaginitis or pseudoephedrine 15-30 mg PO tid (if available), imipramine 25 mg PO daily or midodrine 10 mg PO tid
  - ➢ Imipramine 10-25 mg PO tid for mixed incontinence from GSUI and UI
  - ➢ Neurogenic bladder: bethanechol 10-50 mg PO tid
  - ➢ Prostatism with bladder outlet obstruction: Oral terazosin 1-10 mg qhs, doxazosin 1-8 mg qhs, tamsulosin 0.4 mg qhs or alfuzosin 10 mg daily
- **Surgery for stress incontinence:** retropubic colposuspension or suburethral sling procedures or tension-free vaginal tape application

References: Southern Med J., 2001; 94: 952-7. AFP, 2000; 62: 2433-44 and JAMA, 2004; 291: 986-99.

Common Causes of Abnormal Vaginal Bleeding in Premenopausal Women

Premenarchal	Reproductive Years*	Perimenopausal
• Foreign body	• Anovulation#	• Anovulation#
• Trauma	• Pregnancy	• Endometrial cancer
• Precocious puberty	• Cervical/endometrial polyp	• Cervical cancer/polyp
• Sexual abuse	• Cervical cancer	• Endometrial polyp
• Urethral prolapse	• Adenomyosis	• Adenomyosis
• Vaginal or vulvar tumors	• Bleeding diathesis	• Fibroids
	• Hyper-/Hypothyroidism	• Severe cirrhosis
	• Fibroids	• Uremia
	• Cervicitis‡	• Cervicitis‡
	• Copper IUD	
	• Progestin breakthrough bleeding (can occur at any age)	

*- In postmenarchal adolescents, the common etiologies are pregnancy, anovulation and bleeding diatheses.
\# - causes of anovulation: hypothalamic-pituitary axis immaturity, polycystic ovary syndrome, congenital adrenal hyperplasia, anorexia nervosa/bulimia, hyperprolactinemia, pituitary adenomas, thyroid disorders, cirrhosis, medications (metoclopramide, phenothiazines or tricyclic antidepressants) or idiopathic
‡ - gonorrhea, chlamydia or trichomonal infections.

An Approach to Work-up of Abnormal Vaginal Bleeding
• **Pregnant vs non-pregnant**
• **Ovulatory vs Anovulatory Bleeding**
  ➢ Favoring ovulatory cycles: regular menses, molimina symptoms, Mittelschmerz, basal body temperature increase mid-cycle, mid-luteal serum progesterone > 5 ng/mL, luteinizing hormone surge noted by ovulation kit
• **Menorrhagia vs Metrorrhagia vs Post-coital bleeding**
  ➢ Menorrhagia (heavy menstrual bleeding) is typically caused by fibroids, adenomyosis, bleeding diathesis or thyroid, chronic liver or renal disease.
  ➢ Metrorrhagia is irregular, non-menstrual uterine bleeding that is typically caused by cervical/endometrial polyps or cancer, cervicitis or anovulation.
  ➢ Post-coital bleeding: cervicitis, cervical polyps, prolapsed myomas or cancer
• **Postmenopausal bleeding** is endometrial or cervical cancer until proven otherwise. Can occur during 1st 6-12 months of hormone replacement therapy.

Lab Evaluation
• Pregnancy test (if positive consider miscarriage or ectopic pregnancy)
• Complete blood count and thyroid stimulating hormone (+/- coagulation studies)
• Endometrial biopsy in all anovulatory women and those > 35 years
• Cervical cultures for gonorrhea, chlamydia and a saline prep for trichomonas
• Pelvic ultrasound can assess for fibroids; its use to assess endometrial stripe is **not** a substitute for endometrial biopsy in symptomatic postmenopausal women.
• Saline-sonohysterography or hysteroscopy for unexplained abnormal bleeding to evaluate for an endometrial polyp or submucous fibroid.
• Pap smear and a biopsy of any suspicious cervical, vaginal or vulvar lesion

Treatment Options for Various Conditions
• **Anovulatory bleeding**: correction of underlying cause, cyclic oral progesterone or combined oral contraceptive pills (OCPs)
  ➢ Clomiphene indicated for anovulatory women desiring pregnancy
• **Endometrial polyps**: hysteroscopic excision is the best option.
• **Fibroids**: hysterectomy, myomectomy, uterine artery embolization, depot leuprolide monthly to shrink or hysteroscopic resection of submucous fibroids
• **Menorrhagia treatments**: nonsteroidal anti-inflammatory drugs, combined OCPs, medroxyprogesterone 10 mg PO daily x 10 d/mo or 150 mg IM q13 wks, progesterone-releasing IUD, hysterectomy or endometrial ablation procedure.
• **Severe menometrorrhagia**: trial of the equivalent of one 35 mcg ethinyl estradiol OCP tablet tid x 7 days then 1 active tab daily x 21 days or admission for either IV conjugated estrogen 25 mg q4h x 24h or a dilatation and curettage.

References: AFP, 2004; 69: 1915-32, Ob and Gyn Clinics, 2000; 27: 219-337 & Ob Gyn, 2002; 99: 663-70.

Evaluation of Primary Amenorrhea (absence of menarche by age 14 in the absence of secondary sexual characteristics or by age 16 in their presence)
- **History**
  - ➢ Any signs of pubertal development: presence of a growth spurt, axillary/pubic hair or breast development?
  - ➢ Family history of amenorrhea or delayed puberty?
  - ➢ Any symptoms of hyperandrogenism or virilization? (e.g., hirsutism, acne, central obesity, male-pattern baldness, clitoromegaly and deepened voice)
  - ➢ Recent stress, weight change, strenuous exercise or dietary changes?
  - ➢ Galactorrhea, headache or visual field deficits?
  - ➢ Examine medication list for those that cause hyperprolactinemia
- **Exam**
  - ➢ Any secondary sexual characteristics?
  - ➢ Any hirsutism, acne, androgenic alopecia, acanthosis nigricans or virilization? (polycystic ovary syndrome or androgen secreting tumor)
  - ➢ Pelvic exam to determine the presence or absence of Mullerian structures
  - ➢ Presence of an imperforate hymen or a transverse vaginal septum?
  - ➢ Physical features of Turner syndrome?
- **Lab Testing if Pelvic Exam is Normal**
  - ➢ Pregnancy test
  - ➢ Follicle stimulating hormone (FSH): low in hypothalamic amenorrhea and elevated in gonadal dysgenesis (may present with normal female phenotype or ambiguous genitalia and absent secondary sexual characteristics)
  - ➢ Prolactin: hyperprolactinemia from pituitary adenoma or medications
  - ➢ Thyroid stimulating hormone: high in hypothyroidism
  - ➢ Serum testosterone: 80-200 ng/dL→ polycystic ovary syndrome (PCOS).
  - ➢ Dehydroepiandrosterone sulfate (DHEAS): 330-700 mcg/dL→ PCOS.
- **Lab Testing if Uterus is Absent**
  - ➢ Karyotype: 46, XY in androgen insensitivity syndrome and vanishing testes syndrome and 45, XO in Turner syndrome
  - ➢ Serum testosterone: high in androgen insensitivity syndrome and very low in vanishing testes syndrome or Mullerian agenesis

Evaluation of Secondary Amenorrhea
- **Definition:** the absence of menses for at least 3 cycles or for 6 months.
- **Step 1:** exclude pregnancy, hypothyroidism or hyperprolactinemia
  - ➢ Pituitary MRI for all unexplained hyperprolactinemia to rule out an adenoma.
- **Step 2:** progestational challenge test using medroxyprogesterone acetate 10 mg PO daily x 5 days.
  - ➢ A withdrawal bleed suggests chronic anovulation. No bleeding→ step 3.
  - ➢ For signs of hyperandrogenism check a serum testosterone and DHEAS to evaluate for PCOS, an adrenal tumor or androgen-secreting ovarian tumor
- **Step 3:** conjugated estrogen 1.25 mg PO daily x 21 days and add medroxyprogesterone acetate 10 mg PO daily on days 16-21.
  - ➢ No withdrawal bleed suggests a disorder of the outflow tract or uterus (e.g., Asherman's syndrome or cervical stenosis).
  - ➢ Check FSH and luteinizing hormone (LH) if a withdrawal bleed occurs.
    - o High levels indicate premature ovarian failure
    - o Low-normal levels indicate hypothalamic amenorrhea
- **Premature ovarian failure work-up**
  - ➢ A karyotype to rule out Turner syndrome if the patient is ≤ 30 years.
- **Work-up of unexplained hypothalamic amenorrhea**
  - ➢ Cranial MRI to rule out a hypothalamic mass

References: Obstet Gyn Clin N. Amer. 2003; 30: 287-302 and Amer. Fam. Physician, 1999; 60: 209-24.

History
- Duration mass has been present
- Painful or asymptomatic?
- Change in size or consistency over time and relationship to menstrual cycle.
- Associated skin changes or nipple discharge

Risk Factors for Breast Cancer (RR = relative risk)
- Family history of breast or ovarian cancer in first-degree relative (RR = 2.6)
- Personal history of breast cancer or atypical hyperplasia (RR = 3-5)
- Female sex (RR = 150)
- Age over 70 (RR = 17 vs age 30-34)
- Nulliparous
- Age at first live birth > 30 (RR 1.9-3.5)
- Age of menarche < 12 (RR = 1.5)
- Age of menopause ≥ 55 (RR = 2 vs menopause < 45)
- Postmenopausal body mass index (BMI) > 30 (RR = 1.6 vs BMI < 23)
- Current use of estrogen replacement therapy (RR = 1.2-1.4)
- Positive for Breast Cancer Genes 1 or 2 (BRCA1 or BRCA2) (RR 4-7)
- Individual breast cancer risk calculated with a tool at http://bcra.nci.nih.gov/brc/

Screening Guidelines for Breast Cancer
- Self-breast exams monthly beginning at age 20-30
- Clinical breast exam (CBE) for all women q3 years beginning age 20-30.
- CBE annually for all women starting at age 40
- Screening mammogram every 1-2 years beginning at age 40 and annually after age 50 if the life expectancy is at least 10 years.
  ➢ Mammography risks: each mammogram has 10% risk of a false positive result which can cause unnecessary anxiety and breast biopsies.
- Start screening 5-10 years earlier for positive family history of breast cancer.

Genetic Testing for BRCA1 and BRCA2 Genes
- Recommended if ≥ 10% risk of finding a gene mutation or if a first-degree relative has breast cancer and is positive for the BRCA1 or BRCA2 gene.
- Risk of BRCA 1 or 2 gene mutations at http://astor.som.jhmi.edu/brcapro/.

Suggested Algorithm for Evaluation of a Breast Mass
- In women < 40, breast ultrasound to determine if mass cystic or solid
- Women ≥ 40 require a diagnostic mammogram
- Fine needle aspiration (FNA) of cysts with pathologic analysis if fluid is bloody or blood-tinged (non-bloody fluid can be discarded).
  ➢ If fluid benign and mass disappears, repeat breast exam in 4-6 weeks.
  ➢ A residual mass, recurrence of mass, bloody cyst fluid or malignant cytology should be referred for diagnostic mammogram and excisional biopsy.
- Triple test score of solid masses using: clinical breast exam, imaging, and either FNA cytology or core needle biopsy.
  ➢ Women under 40 should be imaged using a breast ultrasound and those 40 or older need a diagnostic mammogram
  ➢ Each test scores as benign, suspicious or malignant
  ➢ If all 3 tests suggest benign disease, the chance of cancer is 0.7% and patient can be followed with a clinical breast exam in 3-6 months.
  ➢ If any test is suspicious for cancer, patient referred for an excisional biopsy.
  ➢ If the FNA of a solid mass is nondiagnostic, refer for a core-needle biopsy.
  ➢ If all tests suggest malignancy, patient is referred for definitive therapy.
  ➢ Women with a non-palpable suspicious breast mass detected by screening mammogram should undergo a stereotactic needle biopsy.

References: NEJM, 2001; 344: 276, Mayo Clin. Proc., 2001; 76 (6): 641-7, NEJM, 2003; 348: 1672-80, Ann Int Med, 2002; 137: 344-60. AFP, 2005; 71: 1731-8 and Mayo Clin Proc, 2004; 79: 810-6.

Adapted from the 2002 Guidelines of the American Society for Colposcopy and Cervical Pathology
Algorithms for management of cytologic and histologic cervical abnormalities available at www.asccp.org

Management of Cytologic Abnormalities
Options for Atypical Squamous Cells (ASC)
- Atypical Squamous Cells possibly High-grade Squamous Intraepithelial Lesion (ASC – H) evaluated by colposcopic examination.
- Options for Atypical Squamous Cells of Undetermined Significance (ASC – US)
  ➤ Repeat pap smear in 4-6 months and colposcopy for persistent ASC – US
  ➤ Colposcopy if HPV DNA testing* positive for high-risk subtypes
    o Resume annual pap smears if testing is negative for high-risk subtypes.
Low-grade Squamous Intraepithelial Lesions (LSIL)
- Most conservative option is colposcopy with endocervical sampling
- Management options may vary if pt. pregnant, adolescent or postmenopausal.
Options for High-grade Squamous Intraepithelial Lesions (HSIL)
- Colposcopy with endocervical sampling
- "See and treat" using a diagnostic excisional procedure* if lesion(s) seen.
Options for Atypical Glandular Cells (AGC)
- Endometrial biopsy indicated for atypical endometrial cells.
  ➤ Consider an endometrial biopsy for any endometrial cells on pap & age≥40
- Other subcategories require both colposcopy with endocervical sampling and an endometrial biopsy for age > 35 years or abnormal vaginal bleeding.
Management of Histologic Abnormalities
- Desire cytolopohistologic correlation (i.e., pap smear, cervical biopsy histology and colposcopic exam findings all correlate).
  ➤ Discrepancies require a review of original cytology and histology.
  ➤ For worrisome cytolopohistologic discrepancies (e.g., HSIL with low-grade histology), consider repeat colposcopy or a diagnostic excisional procedure.
- Diagnostic excisional procedure* for: unsatisfactory colposcopies; endocervical curettage (ECC) is positive; lesion extends > 5 mm up the endocervical canal.
Options for Cervical Intraepithelial Neoplasia 1 (CIN 1)
- Follow with q6 month pap smears or HPV DNA testing at 1 year → if normal pap smear x 2 or high-risk HPV negative then return to annual pap smears.
  ➤ Repeat colposcopy for any pap smear ≥ASC-US or if high-risk HPV positive
- Consider cryotherapy if high-risk patient and satisfactory colposcopy.
- Diagnostic excisional procedure preferred for recurrent CIN 1 or unsatisfactory colposcopy or if endocervical curettage is positive.
Options for Cervical Intraepithelial Neoplasia 2 or 3 (CIN 2 or CIN 3)
- Diagnostic excisional procedure* can be used for all cases of CIN 2 or CIN 3
  ➤ Preferred treatment modality for recurrent CIN 2 or CIN 3
- Ablative therapy if colposcopy is satisfactory, the lesion does not extend up the endocervical canal > 5 mm and not recurrent disease.
- Post-treatment follow up: q4-6 mo. pap smears or perform HPV DNA testing at ≥ 6 months→if normal pap smear x 3 or high-risk HPV negative→annual paps
  ➤ Repeat colposcopy for: pap smear ≥ ASC-US or if high-risk HPV positive
Options for Adenocarcinoma In-situ or AGC "favor neoplasia"
- Diagnostic excisional procedure (cold-knife conization preferred)
Management of Cervical Intraepithelial Neoplasia in Pregnancy
- Endocervical curettage contraindicated
- Colposcopic examination performed for same indications as above.
- Cervical biopsies performed only if high-grade lesion seen

HPV= Human Papilloma Virus, ‡can be performed on same thin prep pap smear, *- includes laser conization, cold-knife and loop electrosurgical conization or loop electrosurgical excision procedure (i.e., LEEP).
References: JAMA, 2002; 287 (16): 2120-9. NEJM, 1996; 334 (16): 1030-7, NEJM, 2003; 348: 489-90, American Journal of Obstetrics and Gynecology, 2003; 189 (1): 295-304 and JAMA; 2002; 287: 2114-19.

Method	Non-contraceptive benefits	Absolute Contraindications* *Disadvantages in italics*	Failure rate ideal use *(typical use)*
Combined Oral Contraceptive Pills (OCPs)	• Regular menses • Decreased menstrual flow • Decreased acne • Decreased endometriosis • Decreased risk of: ➤ Ovarian CA/cysts ➤ Endometrial CA ➤ Fibrocystic changes of the breast ➤ Dysmenorrhea ➤ Ectopic pregnancy	• Smoker >35 years; • Uncontrolled HTN; • H/O stroke,TIA, CAD; • Thrombotic disorder; h/o VTE • DM w/ end organ damage, other cardiovascular risk factors; • Migraine w/ focal neurological symptoms; • Breast CA; • Endometrial CA; • Hepatic adenoma/CA; • Severe cirrhosis	3 per 1,000 patients per year *(8% for typical use)*
Micronor	• No ↓ breast milk • Decreased dysmenorrhea and menstrual flow • Preferred for smokers	• Undiagnosed vaginal bleeding • *Irregular bleeding* • *Can increase acne and ovarian cysts* • *Must use at same time daily*	5 per 1,000 patients per year *(8% typical use)*
Ortho Evra	• Compliance weekly • Cycle regularity • Noncontraceptive benefits as OCPs	• Same OCP contraindications • *Unrecognized detachment* • *Skin irritation*	3 per 1,000 pts per year *(8% typical use)*
NuvaRing (etonogestrel/ethinyl estradiol vaginal ring)	• Less nausea than OCPs • Same noncontraceptive benefits as OCPs • Can remain in place for 3 weeks	• Contraindications same as OCPs • *Requires vaginal insertion/removal* • *No STD protection* • *Unrecognized ring loss* • *Very costly*	3 per 1,000 patients per year *(8% typical use)*
Condoms	• STD protection • Readily available • No delay in fertility once discontinued	• *Less spontaneity* • *Can break or fall off* • *Can decrease sexual sensitivity*	2% ideal failure rate *(15% typical failure rate)*
Diaphragm	• No delay in fertility once discontinued • Can remain in place for 4-5 hours	• *Requires vaginal insertion* • *Less spontaneity* • *Physician visit for fitting* • *↑Vaginal/bladder infections*	6% ideal failure rate *(16% typical failure rate)*

Method	Advantages	Absolute Contraindications* *Disadvantages*	Failure rate ideal use (typical use)
Natural Family Planning	• Free • No side effects • Self awareness	• *Requires motivation* • *No STD protection* • *Periodic abstinence*	2-9% ideal use (25% typical use)
Spermicide	• Readily available • Some ↓ STD risk	• *Nonoxynol 9 may increase HIV transmission* • *High failure rate* • *Less spontaneity*	15% ideal use (29% typical use)
Intrauterine Device (IUD) Mirena (M) ParaGard (P)	• Prolonged efficacy ➤ 5 yr - Mirena ➤ 10 yr-Paraguard • Decreased menstrual flow (Mirena) • Decreased dysmenorrhea (Mirena) • Lactation not disturbed • ↓ ectopic preg.	Uterine anomalies; active PID; postpartum endometritis or septic abortion in last 3 mo; uterine or ovarian or cervical cancer; unresolved abnormal pap smear; genital bleeding of unknown etiology; AIDS; high risk sexual behavior; genital infection; cirrhosis; history of ectopic pregnancy. **(Only Mirena)** acute hepatitis **or** hepatoma **or** breast cancer	**ParaGard:** 0.6% ideal use (0.8% typical use) **Mirena:** 0.1% ideal use (0.1% typical use)
Tubal ligation (TL)	• Permanent • No compliance needed	• Ambiguous about decision • *High initial cost* • *Risks of surgery* • *No STD protection* • *Post-TL regret*	0.5 % ideal failure rate (0.5% typical failure rate)
Vasectomy (V)	• Permanent • Office procedure	• Ambiguous about decision • *Sexual dysfunction* • *Anxiety about their virility* • *High initial cost* • *No STD protection* • *Post-vasectomy regret*	0.1 % ideal failure rate (0.15% typical failure rate)
Depo-provera (medroxy-progesterone acetate)	• Quarterly injections • ↓ sickle cell crises, PID risk, endometrial CA **and** ovarian cysts	• Undiagnosed vaginal bleeding • Breast CA • Liver disease or tumor • H/O stroke or CAD • DM with end-organ disease	0.3% ideal failure rate (3% typical failure rate)

CA = cancer, STD = sexually transmitted disease, VTE = venous thromboembolic event, PID = pelvic inflammatory disease, irreg. = irregular, trans. = transmission and poss. = possible, wt = weight, dis=disorder IUP = intrauterine pregnancy, TIA= transient ischemic attack, CVA= stroke, CAD= coronary artery disease
* Pregnancy and history of hypersensitivity is contraindication to all methods except natural family planning
Reference: Managing Contraception, 2005 edition, available at www.managingcontraception.com

ORAL CONTRACEPTIVES* Monophasic	Estrogen (mcg)	Progestin (mg)
Norinyl +50, Ortho-Novum 1/50, Necon 1/50	50 mestranol	1 norethindrone
Ovcon-50	50 ethinyl estradiol	
Demulen 1/50, Zovia 1/50E ¥		1 ethynodiol
Ovral, Ogestrel #		0.5 norgestrel
Norinyl 1+35, Ortho-Novum 1/35, Necon 1/35, Nortrel 1/35	35 ethinyl estradiol	1 norethindrone
Brevicon, Modicon, Necon 0.5/35, Nortrel 0.5/35		0.5 norethindrone
Ovcon-35		0.4 norethindrone
Previfem ¥		0.18 norgestimate
Ortho-Cyclen, MonoNessa, Sprintec-28 ¥		0.25 norgestimate
Demulen 1/35, Zovia 1/35E, Kelnor 1/35 *		1 ethynodiol
Loestrin 21 1.5/30, Loestrin Fe 1.5/30, Junel 1.5/30, Junel 1.5/30 Fe, Microgestin Fe 1.5/30	30 ethinyl estradiol	1.5 norethindrone
Cryselle, Lo/Ovral, Low-Ogestrel #		0.3 norgestrel
Apri, Desogen, Ortho-Cept #		0.15 desogestrel
Levlen, Levora, Nordette, Portia #		0.15 levonorgestrel
Yasmin¥ · ‡		3 drospirenone
Loestrin 21 1/20, Loestrin Fe 1/20, Junel 1/20, Junel Fe 1/20, Microgestin Fe 1/20	20 ethinyl estradiol	1 norethindrone
Alesse, Aviane, Lessina, Levlite, Lutera #		0.1 levonorgestrel
Progestin-only		
Micronor, Nor-Q.D., Camila, Errin, Jolivette, Nora-BE	none	0.35 norethindrone
Ovrette #		0.075 norgestrel
Biphasic (estrogen & progestin contents vary)		
Kariva, Mircette#	20/10 eth estrad	0.15/0 desogestrel
Ortho Novum 10/11, Necon 10/11	35 eth estradiol	0.5/1 norethindrone
Triphasic (estrogen & progestin contents vary)		
Cyclessa, Velivet¥	25 ethinyl estradiol	0.100/0.125/0.150 desogestrel
Ortho-Novum 7/7/7, Necon 7/7/7, Nortrel 7/7/7	35 ethinyl estradiol	0.5/0.75/1 norethindr
Tri-Norinyl		0.5/1/0.5 norethindr
Enpresse, Tri-Levlen, Triphasil, Trivora-28 #	30/40/30 ethinyl estradiol	0.5/0.75/0.125 levonorgestrel
Ortho Tri-Cyclen, Trinessa, Tri-Sprintec, Tri-Previfem¥	35 eth estradiol	0.18/0.215/0.25 norgestimate
Ortho Tri-Cyclen Lo¥ · ‡	25 eth estradiol	
Estrostep Fe ‡	20/30/35 eth estr	1 norethindrone

‡-These oral contraceptive pills are **NOT** available in generic form. #-high androgenicity. ¥-low androgenicity. *All: Not recommended in smokers. Increase risk of thromboembolism, stroke, MI, hepatic neoplasia & gallbladder disease. Nausea, breast tenderness, & breakthrough bleeding are common transient side effects. Effectiveness reduced by hepatic enzyme-inducing drugs such as certain anticonvulsants and barbiturates, rifampin, rifabutin, griseofulvin, & protease inhibitors. Coadministration with antibiotics or St. John's wort may decrease efficacy. Consider an additional form of birth control in above circumstances. See product insert for instructions on missing doses. Most available in 21 and 28 day packs. **Progestin only**: Must be taken at the same time every day. Because much of the literature regarding OC adverse effects pertains mainly to estrogen/progestin combinations, the extent to which progestin-only contraceptives cause these effects is unclear. No significant interaction has been found with broad-spectrum antibiotics. The effect of St. John's wort is unclear. No placebo days, start new pack immediately after finishing current one. Available in 28 day packs. Readers may find the following website useful: www.managingcontraception.com.
Adapted with permission from the Tarascon Pocket Pharmacopoeia, 2006, Tarascon publishing.

Summary based on recommendations by the U.S. Preventive Services Task Force, the American College of Obstetricians and Gynecologists and the North American Menopause Society.

Overview of Hormone Replacement Therapy (HRT)
- Estrogen is the most effective treatment of menopausal vasomotor symptoms and urogenital atrophy.
- Based on the results of the Women's Health Initiative (WHI) and the Heart and Estrogen/Progestin Replacement Studies (HERS/HERS II), there is no indication for HRT as primary or secondary prevention of cardiovascular disease.

Women's Health Initiative: Effect of conjugated equine estrogen & progestin[1]
- A RCT of Prempro (0.625/2.5 mg) daily versus placebo in over 16,000 women.
- The study was prematurely terminated after 5.2 years of follow-up because of a significantly increased risk in the treatment arm of cardiovascular events, breast cancer, stroke and venous thromboembolic events (VTE).
  ➤ The absolute risk of an adverse event was 19 additional events per 10,000 person years using Prempro versus placebo.
- Cardiovascular events (nonfatal MI, coronary heart disease deaths, need for revascularization procedures): 7 additional cases per 10,000 person years
- Stroke: 8 additional cases per 10,000 person years
- Venous thromboembolism: 18 additional cases per 10,000 person years
- Breast Cancer: 8 additional cases per 10,000 person years
- Osteoporotic fractures: 5 fewer fractures per 10,000 person years
- Colorectal cancer: 6 fewer cases per 10,000 person years.

Women's Health Initiative: Effect of conjugated equine estrogen alone[2]
- A RCT with over 10,000 women aged 50-79 with a prior hysterectomy
- Conjugated equine estrogen 0.625 mg/day vs placebo for average of 6.8 years
- No difference in cardiovascular events (nonfatal MI or cardiac deaths)
- Stroke: 12 additional cases per 10,000 person years
- Hip fracture: 6 fewer cases per 10,000 person years
- Trends in study that were **not** statistically significant
  ➤ Venous thromboembolism: 7 additional cases per 10,000 person years
  ➤ Breast cancer: 7 fewer cases per 10,000 person years

Heart and Estrogen/Progestin Replacement Studies[3]
- A RCT investigating 2,763 women with known CAD using continuous estrogen-progestin therapy vs placebo with 6.8 years average follow-up.
- No decrease in the risk of cardiovascular events with the use of HRT.

Clinical Event	Hazard Ratio (95% confidence interval)		
	HERS (Prempro)	WHI (Prempro)	WHI (CEE alone)
Cardiac events	0.99 (0.8-1.22)	**1.29 (1.02-1.63)**	0.91 (0.75-1.12)
Stroke	1.23 (0.89-1.7)	**1.41 (1.07-1.85)**	**1.39 (1.1-1.77)**
VTE events	**2.79 (0.89-8.75)**	**2.13 (1.39-3.25**	1.34 (0.87-2.06)
Breast cancer	1.3 (0.77-2.19)	**1.26 (1-1.59)**	0.77 (0.59-1.01)
Colon cancer	0.69 (0.32-1.49)	**0.63 (0.43-0.92)**	1.08 (0.75-1.55)
Hip fracture	1.1 (0.49-2.5)	**0.66 (0.45-0.98)**	**0.61 (0.41-0.91)**
Death	1.08 (0.84-1.38)	0.98 (0.82-1.18)	1.04 (0.88-1.22)

Bold indicates statistically significant differences
RCT = randomized controlled trial, CAD = coronary artery disease, CEE = conjugated equine estrogen, VTE = venous thromboembolic events
References: 1. JAMA 2002; 288: 321. 2. JAMA, 2004; 291: 1701-12 and 3. JAMA, 2002; 288: 49

Definition: inability to conceive after 12 months of unprotected intercourse.
Etiologies of Infertility
- Male factor, anovulation, tubal disease, endometriosis, uterine factor, cervical factor or unexplained infertility

History of Infertile Couples
- Obstetric history including prior uterine surgery or ectopic pregnancy
- History of sexually transmitted diseases, endometritis, pelvic surgery, dysmenorrhea, deep dyspareunia or chronic pelvic pain (endometriosis)?
- Menstrual and contraception history
- Any symptoms of ovulation? (regular menses, premenstrual molimina, dysmenorrhea or Mittelschmerz)
- History of oily skin, acne, hirsutism, oligomenorrhea, acanthosis nigricans or central obesity? (polycystic ovary syndrome or PCOS)
- Investigate for tobacco, alcohol or illicit drug use and prescribed medication use
- Has the man ever fathered any children?
- History of galactorrhea or amenorrhea? (hyperprolactinemia)
- Maternal age (work-up may be initiated earlier for advanced maternal age)

Initial Evaluation of Infertility
- Labs: check a thyroid stimulating hormone, prolactin and day 3 follicle stimulating hormone (FSH) if anovulatory or oligomenorrheic.
  - Day 3 FSH > 15 microIU/L is abnormal and > 10 portends poor prognosis.
- Serum testosterone, dehydroepiandrosterone sulfate (DHEAS), luteinizing hormone (LH), follicles stimulating hormone (FSH) and 75 gram 2 hour glucose tolerance test if any clinical evidence of hyperandrogenism (especially if obese)
- Various tests that indicate ovulation occurring
  - Ovulation predictor kits testing for salivary glucose or urine LH surge
  - Serum progesterone on day 21 of 28 day cycle ≥ 3 ng/mL
  - Basal body temperature charting with consistent rise of 0.4°F x 12-15 days.
- Semen analysis after abstinence x 5 d, no lubricants or saliva (normal values):
  - Semen volume ≥ 2 mL, sperm concentration ≥ 20 million/mL, ≥ 50% with progressive motility and ≥ 30% with normal morphology
  - For oligospermia, check prolactin, testosterone and FSH levels
- Postcoital test to assess for any cervical factor of little clinical utility.
- Hysterosalpingogram to assess for uterine abnormalities (septum, submucous fibroids or synechiae) or tubal obstruction.
- For unexplained infertility
  - Consider laparoscopy to rule out endometriosis or tubal adhesions

Treatment Options for Women by Primary Care Physicians
- Hyperprolactinemia can be treated with dopamine agonists.
- Hypothyroidism can be treated with levothyroxine.
- Empiric trial of clomiphene citrate 50 mg PO daily on days 5-9 of menstrual cycle for anovulation (attempt no more than 3 ovulatory cycles)
  - May increase in increments of 50 mg daily after each cycle to 150 mg daily.
  - Infertility from PCOS benefits from weight loss and metformin 500 mg PO tid
- Oligospermia: avoid anabolic steroid, alcohol, narcotic, tobacco, cocaine and marijuana use, prolonged hot tub exposure and lubricant use with intercourse.
  - Stop spironolactone, alpha-blockers, cimetidine, colchicine, tetracycline, sulfasalazine and avoid exposure to pesticides or organic solvents.
  - Referral for varicocele repair if one is present
- Referral to an infertility specialist for persistent infertility despite above treatment

References: NEJM, 2001; 345: 1388, AFP, 2003; 67: 2165-72 and ACOG Practice Bulletin #34, Feb., 2002.

- The causes of a pelvic mass are myriad and include GI sources (e.g., colon cancer, fecal impaction, diverticular or appendiceal abscesses), genitourinary sources (e.g., pelvic kidney or a distended bladder) or gynecologic sources.
  - ➤ The colon can be evaluated by lower endoscopy and/or barium enema.
  - ➤ If a distended bladder is suspected, urinary catheterization will resolve the mass and further investigation of the underlying cause can be undertaken.
  - ➤ Pelvic ultrasound can identify gynecologic abnormalities or a pelvic kidney.

Gynecologic Causes of a Pelvic Mass by Age Group
Premenarchal girls
- Newborns and infants with adnexal masses almost always from follicular cysts that will spontaneously regress within 6 months.
- Prepubertal children age 2-15 years with adnexal masses have an 80% risk of a malignant ovarian neoplasm (~85% of these are germ cell tumors).
- Most common childhood abdominal tumors: Wilms' tumors & neuroblastomas

Adolescence
- An imperforate hymen causes hematocolpos and a vaginal septum can cause hematometrium.
- Virtually all ovarian cysts are physiologic cysts and tend to be unilocular, thin-walled simple cysts < 10 cm in diameter.
- Other causes of a pelvic mass: benign teratomas, paratubal cysts, hydrosalpinx, uterine fibroids or pregnancy.

Premenopausal women
- Pregnancy
- Physiologic follicular cysts of the ovary
- Polycystic ovary syndrome: patient classically obese, hirsute, infertile from anovulation, has multicystic ovaries on ultrasound and usually has elevated serum testosterone, dehydroepiandrosterone sulfate levels and LH/FSH ≥ 3.
- Uterine fibroids (~30% of reproductive aged women with this condition).
- Endometrioma: patients may have dysmenorrhea, dyspareunia or pelvic pain.
- If 20-40 y.o., solid adnexal tumors usually benign teratomas or dysgerminomas.
- Tubal masses: hydrosalpinx, pyosalpinx or tuboovarian abscesses.

Postmenopausal Women
- Malignant ovarian neoplasm: 40-60% of all ovarian masses are malignant.
  - ➤ Only complaints may be nonspecific gastrointestinal symptoms: abdominal bloating, abdominal fullness, dyspepsia or early satiety
- Metastatic carcinoma: most commonly breast, endometrial and gastric cancers.
- GI or genitourinary sources of pelvic masses must be ruled out in this group.
- Endometrial hyperplasia or cancer: presents as postmenopausal bleeding.

ACOG Guidelines for Management of Adnexal Masses in Premenopausal Pts.
- Size < 10 cm, unilateral, mobile simple cyst with no ascites
  - ➤ Recheck bimanual exam and ultrasound in 4-6 weeks.
  - ➤ Birth control pills can suppress formation of new follicular cysts during the period of adnexal cystic mass observation.
  - ➤ Surgical exploration for unchanged or enlarging mass, for all solid masses, complex cysts, cysts > 10 cm, bilateral masses and if ascites present.

Management of Adnexal Masses in Postmenopausal Women
- Perform a pelvic ultrasound, serum tumor marker CA-125 and bimanual exam.
- Surgical exploration for a symptomatic mass, solid or complex cystic mass, cystic mass > 3 cm, an unchanged or increasing size during observation or an elevated serum CA-125 > 65 U/mL with a suspicious adnexal mass.
- Asymptomatic masses with a normal exam, normal pap smear, normal CA-125 level and simple, unilateral cyst ≤ 3 cm on ultrasound can be followed with serial ultrasound exams every few months.

LH = luteinizing hormone, FSH = follicle stimulating hormone

References: Obstet. Gynecol., 2002; 100: 1413, Cancer, 1994; 74: 1398 & Obstet. Gynecol., 1988; 71: 319.

Vaginitis
- Microscopy of saline (NS) + potassium hydroxide (KOH) preps of discharge

Categories	Yeast Vaginitis	Bacterial Vaginosis	Trichomonas
Microscopy	Hyphae on KOH	Clue cells on NS	Trichomonads on NS
Discharge	Thick + white	Watery, positive "whiff" test*	Frothy + malodorous
Vaginal pH	< 5	5 - 7	5 - 7
Symptoms	Itching and burning	Foul discharge	Itching and burning
DNA hybrid-ization‡	Sensitivity – 80% Specificity – 98%	Sensitivity – 94% Specificity – 81%	Sensitivity – 90% Specificity – 100%
Preferred treatment	• Antifungal vaginal cream#, tablet or suppositories daily x 1-7d • Fluconazole 150 mg PO x 1	• Metronidazole 500 mg PO bid x 7d • 5 d metronidazole 0.75% gel 5 gm intravaginal daily • 7 d 2% clindamycin cream 5 gm intravaginal daily	• Metronidazole 2 gm PO x 1 • Metronidazole 500 mg PO bid x 5 d • Tinidazole 2 gm PO x 1 • Treat partner as well

*-"fishy" odor with application of potassium hydroxide solution
‡ - office assays like Affirm VIP III can test for all three types of infection
# - Antifungal medications available in different preparations all administered intravaginally daily for 1-7 days.

Infectious Diseases of the Vulva
- **Herpes Simplex Virus**
  - Presents as intermittent painful vesicles or ulcerations
  - **Treatment of first episode**: acyclovir 400 mg PO tid, famciclovir 250 mg PO tid or valacyclovir 1000 mg PO bid x 7-10 days
  - **Treatment of recurrent episodes**: acyclovir 400 mg PO tid, famciclovir 125 mg PO bid or valacyclovir 500 mg PO bid x 5 days
  - **Prophylaxis for frequent genital herpes**: acyclovir 400 mg PO bid, famciclovir 250 mg PO bid or valacyclovir 500 mg PO daily
- **Condyloma accuminata (genital warts)**
  - Treat with physician-applied weekly treatments of podophyllin, cryotherapy or trichloroacetic acid or patient-applied 0.5% podofilox gel bid for 3 consecutive days per week or 5% imiquimod cream applied 3 times weekly
  - Extensive disease may require electrocautery or laser excision
- **Molluscum contagiosum**
  - Presents as clustered umbilicated flesh-colored papules
  - Treat with dermal curettage, liquid nitrogen or serial podophyllin applications
- **Pubic lice**
  - Presents as pruritic papules on vulva with nits on pubic hair
  - Treat with either 1% permethrin rinse or pyrethrins/piperonyl butoxide shampoo applied for 10 minutes then rinse off. Use a fine comb for nits.
- **Tinea cruris**
  - Presents as a pruritic, erythematous plaque with scaling and raised borders
  - Topical antifungal bid-tid prn rash
- **Erythrasma** (caused by *Corynebacterium minutissimum*)
  - Reddish brown rash that illuminates coral red under Wood's lamp.
  - Treat with erythromycin 250 mg PO qid x 14 days

Vulvovaginal Masses
- **Bartholin's cyst**: cyst of inner aspect of lower vaginal vestibule
  - Symptomatic or infected cyst can be treated with Word catheter placement.
- **Sebaceous cyst**: cyst on the anterior half of the labia majora
  - Infected cysts generally treated with incision and drainage.
- **Pelvic relaxation**: cystocele, rectocele, enterocele or uterine prolapse
  - Surgical correction is usually necessary if the patient is symptomatic.

- **Benign tumors of the vulva**
  - Fibromas: firm mass of labia majora usually 1-10 cm in diameter.
  - Lipomas: mass of labia majora with rubbery consistency
  - Hidradenoma: < 2 cm sessile, pinkish-gray nodules on vulva.
  - Syringoma: < 5 mm flesh-colored/yellow, subcutaneous papules on vulva
- **Vulvar hematoma**: tender, purplish vulvar mass that occur following vaginal delivery, straddle injuries or blunt trauma
  - Non-expanding hematomas < 10 cm treated conservatively with ice packs
  - Large or expanding or very symptomatic hematomas require evacuation.

Noninfectious Causes of Vulvar Discomfort
- **Vulvodynia**: idiopathic vulvar burning discomfort that may be focal or diffuse
  - Treat with 0.3 mg conjugated estrogen cream applied daily x 4 weeks
  - Nortriptyline or amitriptyline 10-50 mg PO qhs or gabapentin
- **Contact/irritant dermatitis**
  - Eliminate allergen. Apply low-potency steroid ointment (e.g. hydrocortisone or triamcinolone) bid for 2-4 weeks then twice a week for 3-4 weeks then off.
- **Lichen planus**: 5 P's (purple, polygonal, planar, pruritic papules)
  - Very high-potency steroid ointment daily x 3 - 6 weeks then 2x/week maintenance or prednisone 40 mg PO daily tapered over 4 weeks or griseofulvin 250 mg PO bid x 4 - 6 months.
- **Acanthosis nigricans**: thickened, brown, velvety plaques in inguinal folds.
  - May be a cutaneous sign of diabetes mellitus or glucose intolerance
- **Lichen sclerosis**: white, atrophic plaque, wrinkled surface and usually itchy
  - Confirm diagnosis by vulvar biopsy with immunofluorescence
  - Very high-potency topical steroids (e.g., clobetasol or halobetasol) daily for 6-12 weeks then decrease frequency to 1-3 times/week as maintenance.
  - Intralesional steroids can be beneficial in refractory cases
- **Hyperplastic dystrophy**: lichenified, white or red plaque with overlying scale
  - Commonly the result of neurodermatitis with chronic scratching
  - Low-medium potency topical steroids, antihistamines and behavioral modification to stop scratching
- **Hyperplastic dystrophy with atypia**: 5% will progress to vulvar carcinoma
  - Treat with topical 5-fluorouracil
- **Endometriosis**: blue, red or purple subcutaneous lesions usually in sites of healed obstetrical lacerations.
- **Bowenoid papulosis of vulva**: multiple brown or violaceous vulvar papules that are histologically identical to vulvar carcinoma-in-situ
  - Treat with local excision or laser ablation
- **Vulvar intraepithelial neoplasia**: frequently multifocal white, red, pink, gray or brown patches or plaques that may be asymptomatic, itch or burn.
  - Diagnosis is by direct or colposcopically-directed biopsy
  - Referral for wide local excision, skinning vulvectomy or laser ablation
- **Vulvar carcinoma**
  - Refer to Gyn oncologist for a radical vulvectomy and inguinal lymphadenectomy
- **Paget's disease of vulva**: well-demarcated, hypopigmented scaling plaque
  - Treat with wide local excision and investigate for anogenital adenocarcinoma.
- **Psoriasis**: well-demarcated, erythematous plaques with silvery scale
  - Initial therapy with low-potency topical steroids and calcipotriene ointment
  - tazarotene gel qhs can be used for refractory cases

Note: all vulvar lesions of unclear etiology must be biopsied (punch biopsy sufficient)
References: Dermatology Clinics, 1992; 10: 297. AFP, 2000; 62(5): 1095-1104. AFP, 2004; 70: 2125-40. Clinical Ob Gyn, 1999; 42: 221. Obstet Gynecol, 1998; 92: 962 and Obstet Gynecol, 2002; 100: 145-63.

Initial Prenatal Visit

- Medical, surgical, social, family and obstetrical history and do complete exam
- Pap smear, cervical cultures for gonorrhea and chlamydia
- Consider a varicella antibody test if pt unsure about prior varicella infection.
- Urinalysis for proteinuria and urine culture for asymptomatic bacteriuria
- Order prenatal labs to include a complete blood count, blood type, antibody screen, rubella titer, VDRL, hepatitis B surface antigen and an HIV test.
- An Ob ultrasound for dating in all women presenting after 16 weeks gestational age, unsure last menstrual period, for size/dates discrepancy on exam or for inability to hear fetal heart tones by 12 gestational weeks.
- Offer genetic testing and counseling to all women with singleton pregnancies who will be ≥ 35 years at delivery, to women with twins who will be ≥ 33 years at delivery and to those who have a personal or family history of birth defects.
- Prenatal testing offered for: sickle cell anemia (African descent), thalassemia (African, Mediterranean, Middle Eastern, Southeast Asians), Canavan's disease & Tay-Sachs (Ashkenazi Jews), cystic fibrosis (Caucasians & Ashkenazi Jews) and Fragile X syndrome (family history of nonspecified mental retardation).
- Place a tuberculosis skin test for all medium-to-high risk patients.
- Consider a 1 hour 50 gram glucose tolerance test for certain high-risk groups:
  ➤ History of gestational DM, macrosomia, unexplained stillbirth or malformed infant, BMI>30, glucosuria≥ 2+, high-risk ethnic group, family history of DM
  ➤ If test is normal, repeat the screen at 24-28 weeks gestation.
- Obtain an operative report in all women who have had a prior cesarean to determine if they are candidates for a vaginal birth after c-section (if applicable).
- Psychosocial risk assessment for mood disorders, substance or spousal abuse.
- Influenza vaccination if patient in 2nd or 3rd trimester during October-March.
- Start prenatal vitamins with iron and folate and 1,200 mg elemental calcium/day starting at 4 weeks preconception and continued until 6 weeks postpartum.

Frequency of Visits for Uncomplicated Pregnancies

- Every 4 weeks until the patient is 28 gestational weeks
- Every 2 weeks between 28-36 gestational weeks
- Weekly after 36 gestational weeks

Antepartum lab testing

- Offer alpha-fetoprotein/triple marker screen between 15-20 gestational weeks.
- 1 hour 50 gram glucose tolerance test in all women between 24-28 weeks.
- Rh immune globulin 300 mcg IM for all Rh-negative women with negative antibody screens between 26-28 weeks.
- Rectovaginal swab for group B streptococcal testing between 35-37 weeks.

Follow-up Visits

- Assess weight, fundal height, blood pressure, urine for glucose and protein, fetal heart tones, edema, discuss labor precautions & ask about regular uterine contractions, leakage of fluid, vaginal bleeding or decreased fetal movement.

Prenatal Counseling

- Cessation of smoking, drinking alcohol or use of any illicit drugs.
- Avoid cat litter boxes, hot tubs and initiation of any strenuous exercise program
- Proper nutrition and expected weight gain: National Academy of Sciences advises weight gain 28-40 pounds (prepregnancy BMI < 20), 25-35 pounds (BMI 20-26), 15-25 pounds (BMI 26-29) and15-20 pounds (BMI ≥ 30).
- Benefits of breast versus bottle feeding
- Discuss postpartum contraceptive options (including tubal sterilization)
- Discuss analgesia and anesthesia options & offer prenatal classes at 24 weeks
- Discuss repeat c-section versus vaginal birth after cesarean (if applicable).
- Discuss the option of circumcision if a boy is delivered
- Avoid air travel and long train or car trips past 36 weeks

Adapted from American College of Obstetricians and Gynecology 2002 Guidelines for Prenatal Care, American Family Physician, 2005; 71: 1307-22 and guidelines at www.maternitycarecalendar.com

Tests for Antepartum Fetal Surveillance
- **Nonstress test (NST)**
  - A **reactive NST** has two accelerations (at least 15 beats per minute above the baseline lasting 15 seconds) in a 20 minute period.
  - The stillbirth rate within 1 week of a reactive NST is 1.9 per 1,000.
  - A **nonreactive NST** warrants further testing with either a CST or BPP.
- **Biophysical Profile (BPP)**
  - Assigns a score of 0 or 2 for each of 5 parameters: an NST, an ultrasound assessment of fetal breathing movements, gross fetal movement, fetal tone, and amniotic fluid assessment: a score of 8 or 10 is a normal BPP.
    - Stillbirth rate within 1 week of a normal BPP or MBPP is 0.8 per 1,000.
- **Modified BPP (MBPP):** consists of an NST and an AFI
  - Normal if there is a reactive NST and an AFI > 5
- **Contraction Stress Test (CST)**
  - Uterine contractions (UCs) induced with either pitocin or nipple stimulation.
  - A satisfactory test has at least 3 UCs in a 10 minute period.
  - A **positive CST** shows late decelerations after > 50% of UCs.
  - CST equivocal if late or variable decelerations occur with < 50% of UCs.
  - A **negative CST** demonstrates no late or significant variable decelerations.
    - The stillbirth rate within 1 week of a negative CST is 0.3 per 1,000.
  - An **equivocal CST** warrants a repeat CST in 24 hours or a full BPP.
  Contraindications to a CST: preterm labor, ruptured membranes, history of a classical cesarean section or placenta previa.
- **Timing of Delivery:** consult an Ob/Gyn specialist for the optimal timing of delivery for the conditions below (beyond the scope of this pocketbook)

Suggested Guidelines for Antepartum Fetal Surveillance

Indicator condition(s)	When to initiate testing	Frequency of testing/test
Postdates pregnancy	41 weeks	Twice weekly / MBPP
Decreased fetal movement	When it occurs	Single NST
Chronic hypertension	32 weeks	Twice weekly / MBPP
Preeclampsia	At diagnosis	Twice weekly / MBPP
Class A₁ GDM	40 weeks	Twice weekly / NST
Class A₂ or B GDM	32 weeks	Twice weekly / NST
DM with vascular disease	28-32 weeks*	Twice weekly / MBPP
Fetal growth restriction	At diagnosis	Twice weekly / MBPP‡
History of fetal demise	2 weeks before demise	Twice weekly / NST
Active substance abuse	32-34 weeks	Weekly / NST
Increased serum AFP	32-34 weeks	Weekly / NST
Multiple gestation	32 weeks	Weekly / NST /q3wk UTZ
Collagen vascular disease	28-32 weeks*	Twice weekly / MBPP
Oligohydramnios	At diagnosis	Twice weekly / MBPP
Thyroid disease	32-34 weeks*	Weekly / NST
Cholestasis of pregnancy	At diagnosis	Twice weekly / MBPP
Polyhydramnios	At diagnosis	Weekly / NST
Chronic renal disease	28-32 weeks*	Twice weekly / NST
Congestive heart failure	28 weeks	Twice weekly / NST
Major congenital anomalies	32 weeks	Twice weekly / NST
Isoimmunization	28 weeks	Twice weekly / NST
Thrombophilias	32 – 34 weeks	Twice weekly / MBPP

GDM = gestational diabetes, *-initiate testing earlier if poor disease control, AFP = alpha-fetoprotein, ‡ = consider qweek umbilical artery doppler, UTZ= ultrasound. References: ACOG Practice Bulletin No. 9, 1999.

Constipation/Hemorrhoids
- Increase exercise, 8-10 glasses of water daily and increase fiber intake
- Docusate 100 mg PO bid or Milk of Magnesia can be taken if needed.
- Anusol or witch hazel pads can help ease hemorrhoid pain.

Heartburn
- Avoid spicy or greasy foods, eat small frequent meals & avoid bedtime snacks.
- Prop up the head of the bed 6 inches
- Tums, all Histamine$_2$-blockers and the proton pump inhibitors (except for omeprazole) are safe in pregnancy. Antacids are considered safe for use after the first trimester.

Nausea and Vomiting
- Eat a package of soda crackers before rising from bed in the morning.
- Eat frequent, small meals and adding ginger may help
- Eat high protein, high carbohydrate, citrus and salty foods
- Avoid greasy, spicy and fatty foods
- Pyridoxine 50 mg PO bid
- Trial of doxylamine (Unisom) 25 mg PO bid (not FDA-approved).
- Metoclopramide 10 mg PO ac and hs
- Ondansetron 4 mg PO q4h prn severe nausea/vomiting
- Acupressure wrist bands or "relief band" may be of benefit to some patients.

Varicose veins
- Compression stockings
- Avoid standing or sitting for prolonged periods of time or crossing legs.
- Elevate legs above the level of the heart while at home and while sleeping.

Backache
- Avoid lifting anything over 10 pounds and lift with the legs.
- Frequent light aerobic exercise
- Pelvic tilt exercises
- Heating pads to the affected area
- Sleep on the side with a pillow between the legs and knees bent.

Headache
- Rule out preeclampsia or excessive eye strain
- Stress reduction and massage techniques
- Acetaminophen as needed for analgesia

Leg cramps
- Often from too little calcium or potassium in diet
  - ➤ Recommend 1,200-1,500 mg elemental calcium daily
- Stretch leg muscles and keep legs warm at night

Nasal Congestion
- Stay well hydrated
- Use warm mist humidifier and saline nasal sprays

Insomnia
- Avoid stimulants at bedtime
- Take warm, relaxing bath before retiring to bed
- Explore patient's worries or concerns
- Investigate for underlying mood disorder or social stressors

Screening for Gestational Diabetes (GDM)
- **One Hour Glucose Tolerance Test** with a 50-gram oral glucose load
  - Perform in all women between 24-28 gestational weeks.
  - Perform at the first prenatal visit for any of the following high-risk groups: Marked obesity (body mass index ≥ 30), personal history of GDM or glucose intolerance, macrosomia, unexplained stillbirth, malformed infant, family history of DM, ≥ 2+ glucosuria or certain ethnic groups
  - With history of GDM, screen with fasting chemsticks from initial prenatal visit
  - 3 hour glucose tolerance test (GTT) for 1 hour glucose levels ≥ 140 mg/dL.
- **3 hour Glucose Test Abnormals (100-gram oral glucose load)**

	Carpenter-Coustan (C-C) Criteria*	NDDG Criteria*
Fasting	≥ 95 mg/dL	≥ 105
1 hour	≥ 180 mg/dL	≥ 190
2 hours	≥ 155 mg/dL	≥ 165
3 hours	≥ 140 mg/dL	≥ 145

Diagnosis of Gestational Diabetes
- Two or more abnormal values on a 3 hr GTT confirms GDM
- Elevated fasting glucose≥ 105 mg/dL‡ may indicate need for insulin initiation.

White Classification of Diabetes in Pregnancy

Class	Age of onset	Duration	Vascular disease	Insulin needed
A₁	Any	Any	No	No (diet only)
A₂	Any	Any	No	Yes
B	> 20 yrs	< 10 yrs	No	Yes
C	10 -19 yrs	10-19 yrs	No	Yes
D	< 10 yrs	> 20 yrs	Nonproliferative retinopathy	Yes
F	Any	Any	Nephropathy	Yes
R	Any	Any	Proliferative retinopathy	Yes
H	Any	Any	Heart disease	Yes

Management of Diabetes During Pregnancy
- **Nutrition:** recommend 35-40% carbohydrate, 25% protein and 30-40% fat
  - 30 kcal/kg/day if pregestational weight is at ideal body weight
  - 25 kcal/kg/day if pregestational weight 20-50% > ideal body weight
  - 20 kcal/kg/day if pregestational weight > 50% above ideal body weight
- **Home Blood Glucose Monitoring:** fasting and 1 hr postprandial chemsticks
  - Desire fasting chemsticks ≤ 95 and 1 hr postprandial chemsticks ≤ 130-140
- **Insulin:** typical regimen includes long-acting and short-acting insulins given as multi-dose injections (e.g., NPH/regular or insulin 70/30).
  - Average insulin needs for pregestational diabetics: 0.7 units/kg/d <14 wks, 0.8 units/kg/d 18-26 wks, 0.9 units/kg/d 26-36 wks & 1.0 units/kg/d > 36 wks
- Oral glyburide 2.5-20 mg/day started after 11 gestational weeks an alternative#

Antepartum Testing and Management Considerations
- Class A₁ GDM does not need antepartum testing until ≥ 40 weeks
- Class A₂ GDM and pregestational diabetics typically begin antepartum testing with twice weekly nonstress tests beginning at 32-34 weeks.
- Consider induction of labor after confirming fetal lung maturity for all insulin-requiring diabetics between 38-39 gestational weeks.

Postpartum Care of Diabetes in Women with Class A GDM
- Screen for DM at 6 weeks postpartum with a 75 gm 2 hr glucose tolerance test.
- Breast feeding and continued diet/exercise can improve glycemic control.

‡ - Elevated whole blood or capillary blood glucose ≥ 105 mg/dL.
# - Not FDA-approved and not recommended by ADA or American College of Obstetrics and Gynecology
* - The two criteria for diagnosing gestational diabetes. ADA and Sweet Success use the C-C criteria.
NDDG = National Diabetes Diagnostic Group. Reference: Diabetes Care, 2003; 26: S103-S105

Adapted from the 2002 recommendations by the Centers for Disease Control and the American College of Obstetricians and Gynecologists for the management of Group B Streptococci in Pregnancy.

Screening of Pregnant Women for Group B Streptococci (GBS)
- Universal screening of all pregnant women for GBS colonization recommended between 35 - 37 gestational weeks.
- This approach has replaced the risk-based strategy for deciding which women should receive intrapartum antibiotic prophylaxis.
- GBS screening cultures should be collected by swabbing the lower vaginal introitus and through the anus.

Intrapartum Antibiotic Prophylaxis (IAP)
- Indicated for all pregnant women in labor or with ruptured membranes in the following circumstances:
  ➢ Positive GBS screening cultures
  ➢ Unknown GBS status with intrapartum risk factors (ruptured membranes ≥18 hours, intrapartum fever, preterm labor or preterm premature rupture of membranes).
  ➢ History of a previous infant with invasive GBS disease.
  ➢ History of GBS bacteriuria this pregnancy
- Not indicated for pregnant women with any of the following:
  ➢ Negative GBS screening cultures
  ➢ Unknown GBS status with no intrapartum risk factors
  ➢ Planned cesarean section without labor or rupture of membranes
- Antibiotic treatment prior to the onset of labor or rupture of membranes to eradicate GBS colonization is **not** indicated.
- Ideal IAP is at least 2 doses of antibiotic prior to delivery.
- Adequate IAP is 1 dose of antibiotic at least 4 hours prior to delivery.
- Inadequate IAP is 1 dose of antibiotic given < 4 hours before delivery.

Antibiotics Used for Intrapartum Antibiotic Prophylaxis
- Penicillin G is the drug of choice
  ➢ 5 million units IV x 1 then 2.5 million units IV q4h until delivery
- Ampicillin is an alternative
  ➢ 2 grams IV x 1 then 1 gram IV q4h until delivery
- Cefazolin 2 grams IV x 1 then 1 gram IV q8h until delivery for penicillin-allergic patients with **no history of anaphylaxis**.
- For penicillin-allergic patients with a **history of anaphylaxis**, vancomycin 1 gm IV q12h unless GBS sensitivities to clindamycin or erythromycin are known.

Suggested Approach to the Management of Newborns born to Mothers with Suspected or Confirmed GBS Colonization
- Newborn with signs of neonatal sepsis
  ➢ Full diagnostic evaluation: including a complete blood count, blood culture, chest x-ray, urine culture, lumbar puncture (LP) +/- C-reactive protein (CRP)
  ➢ Empiric antibiotics with ampicillin and gentamicin (LP-) or cefotaxime (LP+).
- If gestational age < 35 weeks and infant received inadequate IAP
  ➢ Limited evaluation: complete blood count, blood culture +/- CRP
  ➢ Observation in house for at least 48 hours
- If gestational age > 35 weeks and infant received inadequate IAP
  ➢ Observation in house for at least 48 hours (24 hours for reliable parents able to comply with home observation and with close clinic follow-up).

References: MMWR, 2002; 51(RR11): 1-22 and Obstet Gynecol, 2002; 100: 1405.

Adapted from the 2002 American College of Obstetricians and Gynecologists Guidelines

Definitions
- Pregnancy-induced hypertension: Blood pressure ≥ 140/90 mmHg developing during pregnancy in the absence of pathologic edema or proteinuria.
- Chronic hypertension: Hypertension preceding pregnancy or developing prior to 20 gestational weeks.
- Preeclampsia: Blood pressure ≥ 140/90 mmHg measured on 2 separate occasions at least 6 hours apart developing after 20 gestational weeks and associated with proteinuria (≥ 300 mg protein in a 24 hour urine collection).

Risk Factors for Preeclampsia
- Nulliparity
- Family history of preeclampsia
- History of preeclampsia in a previous pregnancy
- Obesity (body mass index > 29 kg/m^2)
- Chronic hypertension
- Chronic renal insufficiency
- Diabetes mellitus
- Multiple gestations
- Low socioeconomic class
- Cigarette smoking

Labs for Preeclampsia
- 24 hour urine for total protein
- Complete blood count, creatinine and liver panel +/- uric acid
- Modified or full biophysical profile to assess fetal well-being
- Obstetric ultrasound to rule out fetal growth restriction or oligohydramnios

Criteria for Severe Preeclampsia ("head-to-toe" approach)
- Systolic blood pressure (SBP) ≥ 160 or diastolic blood pressure (DBP) ≥ 110
- Presence of new severe headache +/- visual disturbances
- CNS irritability or eclampsia (a new grand mal seizure with pre-eclampsia)
- Pulmonary edema
- Severe right upper quadrant abdominal pain and liver transaminitis
- Proteinuria ≥ 5 grams/24 hours
- Acute oliguric renal failure
- HELLP syndrome (hemolysis, elevated liver enzymes and low platelets)

Management of Preeclampsia (generally as inpatients)
- Treatment is delivery and one must justify any decision not to do so.
- Mild preeclampsia remote from term may be managed expectantly with at least weekly modified biophysical profiles and labs as outlined above.
  - ➢ Serial ultrasounds every 3 weeks to rule out fetal growth restriction
- Severe preeclampsia remote from term should be referred.
- Magnesium sulfate (Mg) 4 grams IV load then 2 grams/hour drip initiated during labor (or immediately if preeclampsia severe) and continued for at least 24 hrs postpartum to minimize the chance of an eclamptic seizure; follow Mg levels.

Management of Chronic Hypertension in Pregnancy
- Increased risk of preeclampsia, stroke, myocardial infarction, fetal growth restriction, oligohydramnios, preterm delivery or placental abruption.
- Antihypertensives recommended for DBP > 100 or SBP > 160
  - ➢ Methyldopa, hydralazine, labetalol or calcium channel blockers.
- Antepartum testing with modified biophysical profiles twice weekly starting at 32-34 gestational weeks or earlier if poorly controlled.

References: ACOG Practice Bulletin No. 33 in Obstet. Gynecol., 1/02; and NEJM, 1996; 335 (4): 257-64.

Diagnosis of Oligohydramnios
- Amniotic fluid index ≤ 5 cm on ultrasound examination

Etiologies of Oligohydramnios
- Uteroplacental insufficiency
  - Preeclampsia, chronic hypertension, collagen vascular diseases, chronic renal insufficiency or Type I Diabetes with vascular disease.
- Placental abruption
- Twin-to-twin transfusion syndrome
- Chromosomal anomalies
- Congenital urinary tract anomalies
- Fetal demise
- Postdates pregnancy (at least 42 gestational weeks)
- Ruptured membranes

Management of Oligohydramnios
- Sterile speculum examination to rule out ruptured membranes
- High resolution ultrasound examination to evaluate for fetal anomalies
- Consider amniocentesis for karyotype analysis (if feasible).
- Consider a short course of aggressive PO or IV rehydration with reassessment of amniotic fluid volume in clinically hypovolemic patients
- Consider induction of labor if patient is at term or post-term.
- Patients remote from term with intact membranes should have a high-risk obstetrical consultation.

Diagnosis of Polyhydramnios
- Amniotic fluid index ≥ 25 cm on ultrasound examination

Etiologies of Polyhydramnios
- Congenital anomalies of the intestinal tract or nervous system
- Fetal hydrops
- Maternal diabetes mellitus
- Multiple gestation pregnancy
- Maternal syphilis
- Chromosomal anomalies (e.g., Trisomy 18 or Trisomy 21)
- Idiopathic

Management of Polyhydramnios
- High resolution ultrasound examination to evaluate for fetal anomalies
- Reinvestigate for maternal diabetes or syphilis
- Consider amniocentesis for karyotype analysis
- Can choose to expectantly manage patients with weekly nonstress tests.
- Consider referral for serial amnioreduction if hydramnios is severe and patient having respiratory compromise.
- Consider referral for a trial of indomethacin 25 mg PO qid x 48 hours
  - Indomethacin may cause life threatening fetal ductus arteriosus constriction.

References: J. of Perinatology, 1990; 10: 347, Obstet. Gynecol., 2002; 100: 134, Obstet. Gynecol. Survey, 1991; 46: 325 and Am J. of Obstet. Gynecol, 1994; 170: 1672.

Postpartum Blues/Depression
- "Postpartum blues" occurs in up to 85% of all women
  - Symptoms begin in the first week and may include sadness, fatigue, insomnia, anxiety, headaches, irritability, poor appetite and mood swings.
  - Usually resolves spontaneously during the first 2-4 weeks
- Postpartum depression occurs in 10-20% of all women
  - Onset anytime within the first 6 months postpartum
  - Symptoms may include anhedonia, poor concentration or indecisiveness, fatigue, guilt, anorexia, agitation, anxiety, psychomotor retardation, sleep disturbance, tearfulness and feelings of hopelessness or worthlessness.
  - Mothers often find it difficult to function and to take care of their infant.
  - Adolescent mothers 3 x more likely to abuse drugs or alcohol if depressed
  - Selective serotonin reuptake inhibitors are the antidepressants of choice
    - Sertraline and paroxetine can be used in breast feeding mothers.
  - Depression after Delivery hotline available (1-800-944-4PPD)

Exercise
- Post-cesarean section, women should avoid lifting >10# for at least 6 weeks
  - Avoid sit-ups, jumping jacks or high-impact aerobics for at least 6 weeks
  - Recommend against driving for at least 2 weeks.
- Following a vaginal delivery women may resume light exercise immediately
  - Gradually increase to prepregnancy level of exercise over the first month

Constipation/Hemorrhoids
- Drink 8-10 glasses of water daily and eat high fiber foods
- May benefit from a stool softener such as docusate sodium 100 mg PO bid.
- Anusol cream or witch hazel pads can help soothe hemorrhoid discomfort.

Episiotomy Care
- Sitz baths 3-4x/day for perineal discomfort
- Avoid intercourse until the perineal discomfort has completely resolved

Breast Engorgement
- If breastfeeding, women can either pump the engorged breast(s) or increase the frequency of nursing.
- If bottle feeding, mothers should use a tight-fitting bra or bind breasts with an ace wrap, avoid any nipple stimulation or hot water on the breasts.
  - Ice packs to the affected breast(s) 3x/day

Inadequate Milk Supply
- Increase hydration by drinking 8-10 glasses of water daily
- Can pump breasts between sessions of nursing
- Apply warm compresses to breast to help encourage let down
- Metoclopramide 10 mg PO tid-qid can help stimulate milk production
  - Avoid with depression. Can cause diarrhea, sedation or extrapyramidal symptoms and effects on infants are unknown (although thought to be safe).
- Avoid combined oral contraceptive pills or patches for at least 6 weeks.

Late Endometritis
- Generally presents with low-grade fever, pelvic pain and foul-smelling lochia
- Onset is between 2-6 weeks postpartum
- Treat with doxycyline 100 mg PO bid or clindamycin 300 mg PO qid x 14 days.
- May need to hospitalize if patient appears toxic.

Mastitis
- Presents with fever, breast pain, warmth, redness +/- flu-like symptoms
- Breastfeeding women should continue to nurse
- Treat with warm compresses to affected area 3-4x/day
- Dicloxacillin or cephalexin 250-500 mg PO qid x 10 days.
- Exclude possibility of a breast abscess and hospitalize if pt appears toxic.

Reference: Southern Medical Journal, 2004; 97: 156-61.

Etiologies of Back Pain

Condition	History and risk factors	Exam Findings
Mechanical Low Back Pain (MLBP)	• No "alarm" symptoms • No radiation down legs • Precipitating event common	• Normal neuro exam • Paraspinous muscle tenderness • Negative SLR test
Vertebral compression fracture	• Often worse with sitting • Acute onset • H/O osteoporosis	• Focal bony tenderness • Dorsal kyphosis • Loss of height
Spondylolysis or spondylolisthesis	• Subacute/chronic LBP • Some have sciatica	• Typical findings are same as in MLBP
Degenerative joint disease of the spine	• Chronic LBP • Often osteoarthritis of other joints	• Typical findings are same as in MLBP • Limited spine ROM
Herniated intervertebral disc	• Radicular back pain • Sudden onset • Usually follows a precipitating event • Worse with spine flexion, coughing, straining	• Positive SLR test >30° • May have positive crossed SLR test • See nerve root syndromes below
Spinal stenosis "neurogenic claudication"	• Crampy pain radiating down both legs • Pain improved with spine flexion	• Good peripheral pulses • May have paresthesias, +/- focal neuro deficits if stenosis severe
Pelvic causes • Endometriosis • Fibroids	• Dysmenorrhea • Dyspareunia • Menorrhagia	• Enlarged uterus • Uterosacral ligament nodularity
Abdominal aortic aneurysm	• Abdominal pain • Age > 50 • Multiple risk factors for vascular disease	• Pulsatile abdominal mass • Abdominal bruit • Decreased leg pulses
Osteomyelitis	• Intravenous drug use • Fever, malaise • H/O tuberculosis • Unremitting night pain	• Focal spine tenderness • Neurologic deficits if an epidural abscess
Metastatic cancer or myeloma	• Weight loss • Fever and chronic LBP • Age > 50 years • Unremitting night pain	• Focal spine tenderness • Neurologic deficits or incontinence suggests cord compression
Ankylosing Spondylitis	• Male 20-40 years • Morning back stiffness • Activity improves pain	• ↓ Chest excursion • ↓ Spine flexion
Cauda equina syndrome	• Bowel/bladder incontinence • Bilateral leg weakness	• Saddle anesthesia • ↓ Anal sphincter tone • Neuro deficits in legs

SLR = straight leg raise, LBP=low back pain, ROM=range of motion, h/o=history of

Alarm Symptoms and Red Flags for Low Back Pain

• Unremitting back pain not relieved in supine position or at night	
• Fever	• Known history of cancer
• Unexplained weight loss	• Chronic immunosuppression
• Bowel/bladder incontinence	• Active intravenous drug use
• New back pain in person > 50 years	• Bilateral leg neurologic deficits

Lumbosacral Radiculopathies

Nerve Root	Symptoms	Signs
L4	• Pain/numbness of anteromedial thigh/knee	• Weak quadriceps/iliopsoas • Decreased patellar reflex
L5	• Pain/numbness of posterolateral thigh/calf & dorsomedial foot	• Weak extensor hallucis longus and ankle dorsiflexion • Normal reflexes
S1	• Pain/numbness of posterolateral thigh/calf & lateral foot	• Weakness of toe flexors and ankle plantar flexion • Decreased ankle reflex

Work-up of Acute Back Pain
- If nonradicular and no alarm symptoms, no lab or radiographic testing needed
- Plain spine x-rays indicated for any alarm signs/symptoms, history of trauma, active alcohol or injection drug use or failure of pain to improve after 4-6 weeks.
- Bone scan or MRI can assess for spine fractures, cancer mets or osteomyelitis.
- MRI study of the spine is indicated for a high suspicion of an epidural abscess, vertebral osteomyelitis, cauda equina syndrome, spinal stenosis, herniated intervertebral disc or vertebral metastases.
- Abdominal ultrasound to screen for an abdominal aortic aneurysm or dissection.
- Labs (if malignancy or infection possible): complete blood count, blood cultures, erythrocyte sedimentation rate, alkaline phosphatase +/- prostate specific antigen and serum and urine protein electrophoresis testing.

Medical Treatment of Acute (<4 weeks) and Subacute Back Pain (4-12 weeks)
- Encourage patients to remain active. No role for bed rest.
- Avoid heavy lifting > 10 pounds, prolonged sitting for > 30 minutes at a time, limited twisting/bending and no strenuous exertion until symptoms resolved.
- Consider physical therapy or spinal manipulation if pain persists > 3 weeks. Back exercises essential long-term to minimize recurrent flares of back pain.
- Scheduled NSAIDS for the first 1-2 weeks then taken as needed thereafter.
- Muscle relaxants helpful if component of muscle spasm for the first 1-2 weeks.
- Epidural corticosteroid injections may offer temporary relief of chronic sciatica
- Decompressive surgeries indicated for cord compression from spinal stenosis, metastatic cancer, epidural abscess, spondylolisthesis, cauda equina syndrome and possibly for sciatica refractory to conservative therapy >4-6 weeks.

Medical Treatment of Chronic Back Pain (> 12 weeks)
- Multidisciplinary approach involving cognitive-behavioral therapy, patient education, supervised exercise program, weight loss (if appropriate) and meds.
- Antidepressants or anxiolytics helpful for the 1/3 of patients with mood disorders
- Analgesics: scheduled NSAIDS or acetaminophen for mild-moderate pain
  - Options for moderate-severe pain: nortriptyline or desipramine, paroxetine or citalopram, tramadol or chronic opioid therapy (see chronic pain section for dosing guidelines) are all options individually or in combination.

References: NEJM, 2001; 344: 363-70. Am. J. Physical Medicine & Rehab, 2005; 84S: S29-41. Primary Care Clinics in Office Practice, 2004; 31: 33-51 and NEJM, 2005; 352: 1891-8.

Clinical presentations of gout
- **Acute gouty arthritis**
  - 80% of cases are attacks of monoarticular arthritis and $\male/\female$ ratio= 9:1.
  - Most common joints affected are knees and 1st metatarsophalangeal joints.
  - Elderly patients with gout more likely to present with polyarticular arthritis
  - Typically, swelling, redness & tenderness of the joint, fever & leukocytosis
- **Interval gout**
  - The period between acute gouty attacks usually completely asymptomatic
- **Chronic tophaceous gout**
  - Clinically or radiographically identifiable collections of urate crystals (tophi) in periarticular connective tissue
  - The most common locations are in the hand or feet joints, the helix of the ear, the Achilles tendon and the olecranon bursa
- **Asymptomatic hyperuricemia**
  - Serum uric acid level > 7 mg/dL
  - No indication for standard gout therapy in asymptomatic individuals

Diagnosis of gout
- Polarizing microscopy of joint fluid shows negatively birefringent urate crystals
- Presumptive diagnosis by history of: acute attacks of monoarticular arthritis followed by asymptomatic periods; rapid resolution of inflammation with NSAID or colchicine therapy; involvement of the 1st metatarsophalangeal joint (podagra); +/- hyperuricemia (although gouty attacks occur with normal uric acid levels); and sterile joint fluid from an affected joint
- Histologic exam of tissues with gouty tophi showing urate crystals

Precipitating factors of acute gout
- Trauma, surgery, starvation, alcohol intake, protein overindulgence
- Myeloproliferative or lymphoproliferative disorders with marked leukocytosis
- Medications: chemotherapy, nicotinic acid, warfarin, loop and thiazide diuretics, cyclosporine, ethambutol, pyrazinamide, baby aspirin, didanosine and levodopa
- Chronic renal insufficiency
- Endocrine: hypothyroidism, hyperparathyroidism and obesity
- Miscellaneous: hypertriglyceridemia or psoriasis

Complications of gout
- **Renal stones:** urate or calcium oxalate in 20% of untreated hyperuricemia
- **Chronic urate nephropathy**
  - Uric acid deposition in the renal medullary interstitium leading to fibrosis
  - Typically causes mild proteinuria and isosthenuria

Pretreatment labs when gout is first diagnosed
- Complete blood count, uric acid, glucose, renal panel, liver panel; 24 hour urine for uric acid and creatinine can be checked prior to gout prophylaxis.

Acute treatment of gout
- Nonsteroidal anti-inflammatory drugs (NSAIDs)
  - Treatment of choice for young patients with no comorbid conditions
  - Ibuprofen 600 mg PO q6h x 3 days then bid x 4 days
  - Indomethacin 25-50 mg PO tid x 3 days then bid x 4 days
  - Naproxen 500 mg PO bid x 3 d then 250 mg PO bid x 4 days
  - Sulindac 150-200 mg PO bid x 7-10 days

> Use with caution in elderly patients, a history of gastritis/peptic ulcer disease, renal insufficiency, blood dyscrasia, CHF or severe liver disease
- Colchicine 0.6 mg PO q1-2h x 3 until pain resolved or patient develops diarrhea, nausea or vomiting. Avoid intravenous colchicine for risk of severe neutropenia.
  > Avoid with severe renal failure (CrCl<10 mL/min) or hepatic insufficiency
- Corticosteroids or corticotropin
  > Effective for patients with renal failure, hepatic failure or if neither NSAIDs nor colchicine can be used.
  > Typical regimen is 0.5 mg/kg/day (to 60 mg) PO prednisone x 3 days then decrease 10-15 mg/day every 3 days until off.
  > Intra-articular triamcinolone acetonide or methylprednisolone 20-40 mg (large joints) or 5-20 mg (small joints)
  > 0.6 mg/kg dexamethasone or 60 mg triamcinolone acetonide intramuscular
  > Corticotropin 25 units SQ x 1 (small joints) or 40 units SQ x 1 (large joints)
  > Extreme caution with diabetes, immunosuppression or systemic infection

Prophylaxis of Gout (≥ 3 attacks/year) or Treatment of Tophaceous Gout
- Inhibitors of uric acid
  > Allopurinol initiated at 100 mg PO daily at least 2 weeks after an attack of acute gout and ↑ 100 mg every 2-3 weeks until maximum dose achieved.
  > Indicated when uric acid >10 mg/dL, 24 hour urine uric acid > 700 mg, presence of tophi, nephrolithiasis or serum creatinine > 2.0 mg/dL.
  > Add colchicine 0.6 mg PO qod (CrCl 10-34 mL/min.), daily (CrCl 35-49 mL/min. or age ≥ 70) or bid (CrCl ≥ 50 mL/min.) or low-dose NSAIDS and continue for 3-6 months after serum uric acid level normal (< 6.0 mg/dL)
  > Maximum allopurinol PO dose depends on renal function: 300 mg daily (creatinine clearance ≥ 90 mL/min.), 200 mg daily (60-90 mL/min.), 100 mg daily (30-59 mL/min.) and 50 mg daily (< 30 mL/min.)
- Uricosuric medications
  > Indicated when 24 hour urine uric acid < 700 mg
  > Contraindicated with CrCl < 50 mL/min., history of nephrolithiasis or need for low-dose aspirin therapy. Increases bleed risk for pts on anticoagulation.
  > Probenecid started at 250 mg PO bid and titrated up to maximum 2 gm/day
  > Sulfinpyrazone 50 mg PO bid and titrated up to maximum 200 mg PO bid

Presentation of Pseudogout (calcium pyrophosphate crystal disease)
- Self-limited attacks of acute monoarticular arthritis
  > Same joints involved as in gout, but greater propensity to affect the knee.
  > Commonly affects individuals over the age of 65.
- Asymptomatic chondrocalcinosis (calcium pyrophosphate crystal deposition)
- Polyarticular arthritis that may mimic osteoarthritis or rheumatoid arthritis

Diagnosis of Pseudogout
- Synovial fluid with positively birefringent calcium pyrophosphate crystals
- Identifying calcium pyrophosphate crystals by histologic exam of tissues.
- Chondrocalcinosis identified on x-ray provides a probable diagnosis.

Treatment of Pseudogout
- Can use NSAIDs, steroids or colchicines as in acute gout
- No role for hypouricemic or uricosuric medications

References: J. Rheumatology, 1992; 19: 8, Curr Opin. Rheumatology, 2000; 12: 213. American Family Physician, 1999; 59 (4): 925-36. NEJM, 2003; 349: 1647-55 and Geriatrics, 2004; 59: 25-31

American College of Rheumatology 1990 Diagnostic Criteria for Fibromyalgia
Must meet all 3 criteria (provides 85% sensitivity and specificity for diagnosis)
- Diffuse, chronic musculoskeletal pain
- Absence of myositis or inflammatory arthritis
- Excessive tenderness at ≥ 11 of 18 predefined anatomic sites (see below)

Associated Findings that Support the Diagnosis of Fibromyalgia
- Chronic fatigue ≥ 6 months resulting in ≥ 50% reduction in normal activities
- Unexplained generalized muscle weakness
- Insomnia and nonrestorative sleep
- Cognitive impairment and/or mood disorder
- Headache (either tension-type or migraine-type)
- Abdominal pain relieved by a bowel movement +/- altered bowel habits
- Musculoskeletal pain ↓ by heat or massage and ↑ by sitting or standing
- Female patient between 20-55 years old
- All laboratory tests normal

Eighteen Trigger or Tender Point Areas in Fibromyalgia
- A picture demonstrating the location of these trigger points can be found at:
  www.fibromyalgia-support.org/fibromyalgia/fibromyalgia-tender-points.html
  ➢ Base of the sternocleidomastoid muscle in the low cervical area
  ➢ The second costochondral junction
  ➢ Muscle attachments to the lateral epicondyles
  ➢ Muscle attachments just posterior to the greater trochanter
  ➢ The medial fat pad of the knee proximal to the joint line
  ➢ Insertion of the suboccipital muscles
  ➢ Mid-portion of the trapezius muscle along its upper border
  ➢ Muscle attachments to upper medial border of scapula
  ➢ Upper outer quadrant of the buttocks (gluteal muscles)

Differential Diagnosis
- There is considerable overlap between fibromyalgia (FM), chronic fatigue
  syndrome (CFS), temporomandibular joint disorder (TMJ) or mood disorders
  with multiple psychosomatic complaints.
- Chronic fatigue syndrome patients tend to have a persistent low-grade fever,
  chills and sore throat that fibromyalgia patients lack.
- TMJ patients complain of pain in the jaw +/- inner ear not present in FM patients
- Patients with a mood disorder and multiple psychosomatic complaints usually
  do not meet the strict tender point criteria needed to diagnose fibromyalgia.

Treatment of Fibromyalgia
- Educate patients that fibromyalgia is a chronic illness, but it is not progressive,
  contagious, infectious or life-threatening.
- **Nonpharmacologic interventions**
  ➢ Regular aerobic exercise, strength training & good sleep hygiene essential
  ➢ Cognitive behavioral therapy
  ➢ Acupuncture, hypnotherapy, biofeedback and massage all may benefit pts
  ➢ Trigger point injections and spinal manipulation are of no proven benefit.
- **Medications**
  ➢ Amitriptyline 25-50 mg PO qhs **or** cyclobenzaprine 10-30 mg PO qhs
  ➢ May add fluoxetine 20-80 mg PO qAM **or** venlafaxine PO 75-300 mg/day
  ➢ Consider adding tramadol 200-300 mg/day PO if symptoms refractory
  ➢ No proven efficacy for opioids, NSAIDS, benzodiazepines or steroids.

References: JAMA, 2004; 292: 2388-95. Rheumatic Diseases Clinics N. Amer, 2002; 28: 405-17 and 437-46. Arthritis and Rheum, 1990; 33: 160 and Arch. Int. Med., 2000; 160: 221.

Plantar Fasciitis
- **Clinical Presentation**
  - ➤ Heel pain worst the first few steps after resting and improves with walking.
- **Exam**
  - ➤ Focal tenderness in areas along the plantar fascia or at the calcaneal origin
  - ➤ Often tight heel cord
- **Treatment**
  - ➤ Calf and Achilles tendon stretching and toe curl exercises
  - ➤ Heel pads (silicone heel inserts tend to be the most effective)
  - ➤ Avoid wearing thin sandals, walking barefoot, jumping or running exercises
  - ➤ Wear well-padded athletic shoes with good arch support
  - ➤ Steroid/local anesthetic injections at areas of point tenderness
  - ➤ Surgery for refractory cases

Metatarsalgia
- **Clinical Presentation**
  - ➤ Pain under metatarsal head(s) made worse by walking, standing or jumping.
- **Exam**
  - ➤ Tenderness with plantar palpation of affected metatarsal head
  - ➤ For equivocal cases, a diagnostic injection of local anesthetic into the dorsal aspect of the affected metatarsophalangeal (MTP) joint relieves the pain.
- **Treatment**
  - ➤ Wear well-padded shoes and may need custom orthotics
  - ➤ Taping techniques to keep affected toes in plantar flexed position

Morton's Neuroma
- **Clinical Presentation**
  - ➤ Pain in the ball of the foot that radiates to the 3rd and 4th toes.
  - ➤ Patients feel like there is a fixed small pebble in their shoe.
- **Exam**
  - ➤ Tenderness with any compression of the 3rd intermetatarsal interspace
- **Treatment**
  - ➤ Silicone shoe inserts or custom orthotics
  - ➤ Cortisone injections directly into the 3rd intermetatarsal space
  - ➤ Surgical excision

Bunions (Hallux valgus)
- **Clinical Presentation**
  - ➤ Pain and skin redness along the medial aspect of the 1st MTP joint.
- **Exam**
  - ➤ Lateral deviation of great toe and red, calloused skin along medial 1st MTP
- **Treatment**
  - ➤ Wide-toed shoes, felt or foam pads to protect bunion, semirigid orthosis to place foot in neutral position and devices to separate the 1st and 2nd toes
  - ➤ Surgical correction of Hallux valgus

Hammer Toes
- **Clinical Presentation**
  - ➤ Often foot pain occurs at the affected metatarsophalangeal joints.
- **Exam**
  - ➤ Claw-like deformity of toes usually with a corn on the top of the toe.
- **Treatment**
  - ➤ Mild cases can be treated with foot manipulation and splinting
  - ➤ Severe deformities usually require surgical correction

Condition	History	Exam Findings	Diagnostic tests
Osteoarthritis of the hip	• Insidious onset • Groin/anterior thigh pain • Activity ↑ pain • Stiffness after inactivity	• Restricted IR/ER • Pain with IR/ER • Anterior hip tenderness • Trendelenberg or antalgic gait	• Pelvis or hip x-rays
Trochanteric bursitis	• Lateral hip pain • Activity ↑ pain • ↑ pain lying on affected side	• Tenderness over greater trochanter • Normal hip ROM	• Clinical diagnosis • No imaging studies needed
Hip osteonecrosis	• Atraumatic • Groin/anterior thigh pain • Activity ↑ pain • 2/3 have rest pain • risk factors* exist	• Restricted IR/ER • Pain with IR/ER • Antalgic limp • Anterior hip tenderness	• Pelvis x-rays • MRI to stage osteonecrosis • Bone scan if x-rays normal and no MRI
Septic arthritis	• Atraumatic • Anterior thigh pain • Pain at night	• Same as for osteonecrosis • Fever	• Arthrocentesis • ESR, blood cultures
Femoral neck fracture	• Fall or trauma • Elderly • Osteoporosis • Groin/anterior thigh pain • Activity ↑ pain	• Leg may be shortened and externally rotated • Inability to walk or antalgic gait • Pain with IR/ER	• Pelvis x-rays • MRI or bone scan if x-rays normal looking for occult fracture
Metastatic disease to hips	• Known cancer • Elderly patient • Night pain • Activity ↑ pain	• Antalgic gait • Anterior hip tenderness • Normal hip ROM	• Pelvis x-rays • Bone scan • Bone biopsy if ? diagnosis
Meralgia paresthetica	• Numbness or dysesthesias of anterolateral thigh	• Normal hip ROM • No tenderness • Negative SLR	• Clinical diagnosis
Aortoiliac disease	• Buttock or thigh claudication • Impotence	• Arterial bruits • Diminished peripheral pulses	• Duplex ultrasound • Arteriogram
L4 radiculopathy	• Back pain radiating to thigh • Dermatomal	• Positive SLR • Weak quadriceps • ↓ patellar reflex	• MRI of lumbar spine

IR=internal rotation, ER=external rotation, ROM=range of motion, ESR=erythrocyte sedimentation rate, SLR = straight leg raise,* - alcoholics, oral steroid use, sickle cell disease, divers, pelvic radiation, post-traumatic

Etiologies of Inflammatory Knee Arthritis
- **Rheumatoid arthritis (RA):** see RA section for diagnostic criteria
- **Systemic Lupus Erythematosus (SLE):** SLE section for diagnostic criteria.
- **Crystal-induced arthritis:** diagnostic arthrocentesis will demonstrate crystals
- **Septic arthritis:** diagnostic arthrocentesis for cell count, gram stain and culture
  - ➢ Requires emergent orthopedic referral and intravenous antibiotics

Etiologies of Anterior Knee Pain
- **Patellofemoral pain syndromes**
  - ➢ Age < 45 (♀ than ♂) and pain exacerbated by repetitive knee flexion
  - ➢ Sunrise x-ray view of knee is the best view to examine for patellar disease
  - ➢ **Chondromalacia patellae:** retropatellar crepitus+patellar compression pain
  - ➢ **Patellar subluxation** (laterally)
  - ➢ **Patella alta** (high-lying patella)
- **Prepatellar bursitis** (or "nursemaid's knee")
  - ➢ Frequently occurs in occupations requiring prolonged kneeling
- **Patellar tendonitis** (or "jumper's knee")
  - ➢ Pain localized to the inferior edge of the patella
- **Osgood-Schlatter disease**
  - ➢ Tibial tubercle epiphysitis seen in adolescents
- **Anterior cruciate ligament injury**
  - ➢ Generally occurs after traumatic accident with immediate hemarthrosis
  - ➢ Laxity with Lachman test (87 % sensitive, 93% specific), anterior drawer test (48% sensitive, 87% specific) or pivot test (61% sensitive, 97% specific).

Etiologies of Medial Knee Pain
- **Osteoarthritis** (of medial knee compartment)
  - ➢ Typical findings are morning stiffness < 30 minutes, knee crepitus, absence of warmth or effusion in a patient over 50 years with osteophytes on x-rays.
- **Anserine bursitis**
  - ➢ Medial pain located 3-5 cm below the joint line
  - ➢ Pain occurs with motion and at rest (particularly at night)
- **Medial collateral ligament strain**
  - ➢ Pain increased during valgus stress maneuver
- **Medial meniscal tear**
  - ➢ Knee pain with twisting, squatting or stair use. Knee may lock or give way
  - ➢ Exam: often a knee effusion, medial joint line tenderness (76% sensitivity) and McMurray test is 97% specific and 52% sensitive

Etiologies of Lateral Knee Pain
- **Osteoarthritis** (of lateral knee compartment): clinical & x-ray findings as above
- **Lateral collateral ligament strain**
  - ➢ Pain increased during varus stress maneuver
- **Lateral meniscal tear**
  - ➢ History identical to that of medial meniscal tear
  - ➢ Exam: often a knee effusion and lateral joint line tenderness
- **Iliotibial band syndrome**
  - ➢ Focal aching or burning pain at the lateral femoral condyle

Indications for Knee X-rays in Patients with Knee Trauma (Ottawa Rules)
- Age ≥ 55 years
- Tenderness of the fibular head or isolated tenderness of the patella
- Inability to fully bear weight on leg for 4 steps
- Inability to flex the knee to 90 degrees

Imaging to Assess for Internal Derangement of the Knee
- MRI is the best imaging study to evaluate for damage to the menisci and ligaments of the knee.
- Plain x-rays are not helpful if an internal derangement of the knee suspected.

Reference: Annals of Internal Medicine, 2003; 139: 575-88.

Epidemiology

- Prevalence of 1 case per 133 persons over age 50 years in U.S.
- Polymyalgia rheumatica occurs in 40% of patients who have temporal arteritis.
- 20% of patients with polymyalgia rheumatica develop temporal arteritis.
  - American College of Rheumatology diagnostic criteria for temporal arteritis: Age ≥ 50, new temporal headache, temporal artery tenderness or pulse deficit, erythrocyte sedimentation rate ≥ 50 mm/hour and vasculitis on temporal artery biopsy
  - Presence of ≥ 3 criteria has 93.5% sensitivity and 91.2% specificity
  - 50% of patients have jaw claudication, 20% have visual impairment, mono- or polyneuropathies in 30% and 10-15% have subclavian stenosis.

Clinical Manifestations of Polymyalgia Rheumatica

- Chronic aching and morning stiffness in the neck, shoulders and pelvic girdle
- Pain present for >1 month and worsens with movement of the affected area
- Malaise, fatigue, anorexia, weight loss and low-grade fevers in 1/3 of patients.
- Synovitis of the knees, wrists and the metacarpophalangeal joints in ≤ 50% of patients & even more have subdeltoid and subacromial bursitis by shoulder MRI

Exam

- Decreased active range of motion of shoulders, hips and neck due to pain
- Normal muscle strength
- May detect synovial thickening in affected knees, wrists or metacarpo-phalangeal joints

Diagnosis of Polymyalgia Rheumatica

- Onset after the age of 50 years
- Bilateral aching and morning stiffness >1 hour of at least 2 of the following 3 areas for at least 1 month: neck, shoulders or pelvic girdle
- Erythrocyte sedimentation rate ≥ 40 mm/hour
- Exclusion of other diagnoses that can cause similar symptoms
- Rapid response to prednisone ≤ 20 mg/day within a few days.

Laboratory Findings in Polymyalgia Rheumatica

- Elevated erythrocyte sedimentation rate
  - Normal erythrocyte sedimentation rate can be seen in 7-20% of patients
  - Elevated C-reactive protein or interleukin-6 levels may be more sensitive tests for both diagnosis and for monitoring of disease flares
- Normocytic anemia may be present
- Rheumatoid factor negative
- Imaging studies play no role in the diagnosis or monitoring of this condition
  - For atypical cases, an MRI or ultrasound of the shoulder can identify subacromial or subdeltoid bursitis and help confirm the diagnosis.

Treatment of Polymyalgia Rheumatica

- Prednisone 10-20 mg PO daily x 2-4 weeks
- Decrease prednisone dose approximately 10% every 2 weeks until a minimum effective dose has been reached
- Calcium and Vitamin D supplementation while patient on steroids
- Typically, polymyalgia rheumatica is a self-limited disease that eventually resolves after 1-3 years.

Reference: NEJM, 2002; 347 (4): 261-71 and Cleveland Clinic J of Medicine, 2004; 71: 489-95.

American Rheumatism Association Criteria for Rheumatoid Arthritis:

Must have at least four of the following seven criteria present for ≥ 6 weeks

- Morning stiffness ≥ 1 hour
- Inflammatory arthritis of ≥ 3 joints with soft tissue swelling or effusion:
  - ➤ Typical joints are proximal interphalangeal, metacarpophalangeal, wrist, elbow, knee, ankle and metatarsophalangeal joints
- Arthritis of hand joints
- Symmetric arthritis
- Rheumatoid nodules: over bony prominences or extensor surfaces
- Positive rheumatoid factor (RF) in 80% of rheumatoid arthritis patients
- Joint space narrowing, juxtaarticular osteopenia and bony erosions by x-ray

Other Clinical Features of Rheumatoid Arthritis (RA)

- **Labs:** Anemia of chronic disease (33-60%), leukocytosis and/or thrombocytosis
- **Autoantibodies:** positive antinuclear antibody (ANA) in 30-40%
  - ➤ Positive anti-citrulline antibody highly specific for rheumatoid arthritis
- **Symptoms:** fatigue, tactile fevers, weight loss and depression are common
- **Late exam findings:** ulnar deviation, "swan neck" finger deformities, volar subluxation and radial drift of the carpal bones. Olecranon or retrocalcaneal bursitis both can occur.
- Subluxation of C1 on C2 can lead to spinal cord compression or radicular pain.
- Cricoarytenoid joint arthritis (seen in up to 30%) causes hoarseness or stridor.
- Erythrocyte sedimentation rate or C-reactive protein levels may help to assess disease activity.

Treatment Options for Rheumatoid Arthritis

- **Nonpharmacologic:** range-of-motion exercises, regular aerobic exercise, physical therapy and splinting of fingers/wrists to prevent deformities.
- **Nonsteroidal anti-inflammatory drugs:** these do not alter disease progression.
- Consider prednisone 10 mg PO daily until disease-modifying drugs take effect.

Disease-modifying and biologic antirheumatic drugs

Medication	Dosing	Side effects	Things to follow
methotrexate	7.5–20 mg PO qweek	↓ Folate, hepatitis, bone marrow ↓, diarrhea	LFTs and CBC
hydroxychloroquine	200–400 mg PO daily	Retinopathy, headache, nausea and vomiting	Retinal/visual acuity checks q6-12 mo.
leflunomide*	20 mg PO daily	Hepatitis, anemia, HTN	LFTs, CBC & BP
sulfasalazine	0.5-1 gm PO daily-bid	Hepatitis, marrow ↓, HA, nausea and vomiting	CBC and LFTs
azathioprine	1-2.5 mg/kg/day PO	Nausea and vomiting, bone marrow ↓	CBC and baseline LFTs + renal panel
infliximab	3-10 mg/kg IV at 0, 2 and 6 wks then q8wks	Reactivation Tb, headache, nausea, vomiting and dyspnea	PPD or any active infection
etanercept	25 mg SQ 2x/wk or 50 mg SQ qwk	Reactivation Tb, injection site reaction	PPD or any active infection
adalimumab	40 mg SQ every other week	Reactivation Tb or other infection	PPD or any active infection
anakinra	100 mg SQ daily	Neutropenia, infections	CBC or infection
minocycline	100 mg PO bid	Hyperpigmentation	Skin exam
cyclosporine	2.5 mg/kg PO daily	Renal insufficiency, anemia and HTN	CBC, renal panel and blood pressure
rituximab	1 gm IV q2wks x 2	Serious infections	CBC & infections

LFTs = liver function tests, CBC = complete blood count, Tb = tuberculosis, PPD = purified protein derivative
HA = headache, *-teratogenic; therefore good contraception essential during use by either woman or partner
References: Arthritis Rheum, 1988; 31: 315 and NEJM, 2004; 350: 2167-79, 2572-81 and 2591-602.

Disease	Test	Specificity	Sensitivity	Positive Predictive Value	Diagnosis
Systemic Lupus Erythematosus (SLE)	antinuclear antibodies (ANA)	57%	93%	Moderate	Yes
	anti-double-stranded DNA	97%	57%	95%	Yes
	anti-cardiolipin/Lupus anticoagulant	Yes	No	Low	No
	anti-Smith antibodies	High	25-30%	97%	Yes
Drug-induced Lupus	anti-histone antibodies*	High	95%	High	Yes
Rheumatoid Arthritis	rheumatoid factor	No	50-85%	Moderate	Yes
	anti-citrullinated peptide antibodies	90-95%	50-85%	High	No
Scleroderma (CREST)	antinuclear antibodies (ANA)	54%	85%	High	Yes
	anti-centromere	99.9%	65%	High	Yes
	anti-Scl70	100%	20%	High	Yes
Mixed Connective Tissue Disease	antinuclear antibodies (ANA)	No	93%	High	Yes
	anti-U₁-RNP (ribonucleoprotein)*	High	Moderate	High	Yes
Polymyositis Dermatomyositis	creatinine phosphokinase (CK)	No	High	Low	No
	anti-Jo-1 antibodies	Yes	30-50%	High	Yes
	muscle biopsy	Yes	Moderate	High	Yes
Sjogren's syndrome	antinuclear antibodies (ANA)	52%	48%	Moderate	Yes
	anti-SSA/Ro (Sjogren's syndrome A)‡	87%	8-70%	~40%	Yes
	anti-SSB/La (Sjogren's syndrome B)	94%	16-40%	~40%	Yes
Wegener's granulomatosis	anti-proteinase 3 antibody	High	Moderate	High	Yes
	c-antineutrophil cytoplasmic antibodies	50%	95%	High	Yes

Adapted from Robert Gonzalez, M.D., Rheumatologist at Ventura County Medical Center, Ventura, CA and S. Medical J, 2005; 98: 185. CREST = calcinosis, Raynaud's phenomenon, esophageal dysmotility, sclerodactyly and telangiectasias. *- false positive in cutaneous lupus erythematosus, Dis. = Disease ‡ = false positives from SLE.

Disease	Test	Dis. Activity	Tests for End-Organ Damage and Additional Notes
Systemic Lupus Erythematosus (SLE)	antinuclear antibodies (ANA)	No	Positive anti-SSA (Sjögren's syndrome A) in cutaneous lupus erythematosus. Follow serial renal panel, urinalysis with micro and complete blood count with differential
	anti-double-stranded DNA	Yes	
	anti-cardiolipin/Lupus anticoagulant	Yes	
	anti-Smith antibodies	No	
Drug-induced LE	anti-histone antibodies*	No	Usual meds procainamide, hydralazine or isoniazid
Rheumatoid Arthritis	rheumatoid factor	No	X-rays of affected joints, baseline PPD and pulmonary function tests, Follow complete blood count with differential and liver panel with most therapies
	anti-citrulline antibodies	No	
Scleroderma (CREST)	antinuclear antibodies (ANA)	No	Anti-centromere specific for CREST syndrome. Chest x-ray, screening pulmonary function tests, blood pressure checks, renal panel, urinalysis with micro, baseline barium swallow and esophagogastroduodenoscopy for dysphagia
	anti-centromere	No	
	anti-Scl70	No	
Mixed Connective Tissue Disease	antinuclear antibodies (ANA)	No	Renal panel, complete blood count with differential, creatinine phosphokinase, urinalysis + micro & BP checks
	anti-U1-RNP (ribonucleoprotein)*	No	
Polymyositis Dermatomyositis	creatinine phosphokinase (CK)	Yes	Note: electromyogram can help to diagnose myositis. Consider search for malignancy in adult dermatomyositis. Follow creatinine phosphokinase in response to therapy
	anti-Jo-1 antibodies	No	
	muscle biopsy	No	
Sjögren's syndrome	antinuclear antibodies (ANA)	No	Schirmer test for ↓ tear production. Saxon test for ↓ saliva production. Needs dental care and eye exams.
	anti-SSA/Ro (Sjögren's syndrome A)‡	No	
	anti-SSB/La (Sjögren's syndrome B)	No	
Wegener's granulomatosis	anti-proteinase 3 antibody c-antineutrophil cytoplasmic antibodies	Yes	Diagnosis secured with biopsy of nasopharyngeal lesion. Ear/Nose/Throat exam, chest x-ray, renal panel and urinalysis +/- pulmonary function tests
		Yes	

Acromioclavicular (AC) joint separations
- Clinical presentation: AC joint tenderness and pain with shoulder abduction
- Diagnostic tests: shoulder x-rays will confirm Type II-VI AC joint separations
- Treatment of type I-II and most type III separations: Wear a sling for a few days, then resume daily activities and return to sports in 3-4 weeks.
- Treatment of type IV-VI separations: referral for operative repair.

Burners, stingers or brachial plexus injuries
- Clinical presentation: sharp, burning shoulder pain radiating down the arm after a blow to the shoulder that also pushes the head and neck to the opposite side.
- Diagnosis: history and motor, sensory and reflex exam of extremities
- Treatment: most cases require only rest. Return to play after complete symptom resolution, normal neuro exam and full cervical spine range of motion.

Shoulder instability
- Clinical presentation: patients with anterior subluxation feel the shoulder slipping out of joint with abduction and external rotation.
  - ➤ Acute dislocation presents as pain with any shoulder movement
- Diagnosis: anterior instability diagnosed by a positive apprehension test
  - ➤ Dislocation via exam and anteroposterior and axillary shoulder x-rays
- Treatment: an acute anterior dislocation may be reduced in many ways: the self-reduction, traction-countertraction, external rotation or gravity methods.
  - ➤ Glenohumeral instability usually requires surgical correction.

Impingement syndrome
- Clinical presentation: anterolateral shoulder pain exacerbated by overhead activities, lying on affected side and night pain is common.
- Diagnosis: Usually have positive Neer, Hawkins and supraspinatus tests
- Treatment: NSAIDS and a rotator cuff stretching and strengthening program
  - ➤ Consider a subacromial steroid injection if no improvement in 6 weeks

Rotator cuff tears
- Clinical presentation: same as with impingement syndrome, but atrophy of shoulder muscles seen more frequently.
- Diagnosis: very limited active abduction of shoulder and MRI when necessary
- Treatment: same as for impingement syndrome. Consider surgery for refractory pain and failed physical therapy rehabilitation.

Adhesive capsulitis
- Clinical presentation: progressively decreasing passive and active shoulder range of motion and pain with shoulder activity.
- Treatment: aggressive shoulder stretching program +/- glenohumeral steroid injection. Occasionally, requires range of motion treatment under anesthesia.

Glenohumeral degenerative arthritis
- Clinical presentation: deep shoulder pain with progressively limited range of motion.
- Diagnosis: anteroposterior and axillary shoulder x-rays
- Treatment: NSAIDS and stretching exercises to preserve range of motion

Fractures of the clavicle
- Clinical presentation: localized pain with abduction and clavicle deformity
- Diagnosis: anteroposterior x-ray of the clavicle
- Treatment: arm sling for all mid-clavicular and nondisplaced medial or lateral clavicle fractures, but refer all **displaced** medial or lateral clavicle fractures.

AFP, 2004; 70: 1947-54. Southern Medical J, 2004; 97: 748-54 and Ortho Clin N. Amer, 2002; 33: 479-95.

ACR Criteria for Systemic Lupus Erythematosus Classification
4 or more of the following 11 criteria serially or simultaneously for diagnosis:
- **Malar rash** – fixed erythematous rash over malar eminences.
- **Discoid rash** – erythematous plaques with adherent scale and follicular plugging. Atrophy and scarring can occur in older lesions.
- **Photosensitivity**
- **Oral ulcers** – usually painless
- **Arthritis** – nonerosive, oligoarticular with swelling and tenderness of joints
- **Serositis**
  - ➤ Pleuritis – pleuritic pain, pleural rub or unexplained pleural effusion
  - ➤ Pericarditis – documented by rub, electrocardiogram of pericardial effusion
- **Nephritis**
  - ➤ Overt proteinuria > 500 mg/day or ≥ 3+ protein on dipstick **or**
  - ➤ Active urinary sediment
- **Neuropsychiatric disorder**
  - ➤ Seizures or encephalopathy
  - ➤ Psychosis
- **Hematologic**
  - ➤ Hemolytic anemia
  - ➤ Leukopenia (white blood cells < 4,000/mm^3)
  - ➤ Lymphopenia (lymphocytes < 1,500/ mm^3)
  - ➤ Thrombocytopenia (platelets < 100K/ mm^3)
- **Immunologic**
  - ➤ Anti-double-stranded DNA antibodies
  - ➤ Anti-Sm (Smith) antibodies
  - ➤ Antiphospholipid antibodies (positive lupus anticoagulant or anticardiolipin antibodies or false-positive venereal disease research laboratory test)
- **Antinuclear Antibody (ANA)** – positive

Treatment Guidelines for Systemic Lupus Erythematosus
- **Options for Cutaneous Lupus Erythematosus**
  - ➤ Hydroxychloroquine 200-400 mg PO daily
  - ➤ Chloroquine 100 mg PO tid **or** quinacrine 65 mg PO tid
  - ➤ Pimecrolimus 1% cream under hydrocolloid dressing bid x 3 weeks
  - ➤ Sunscreen
  - ➤ Topical corticosteroids
    - Fluorinated steroids for thick facial plaques x 2 weeks
    - 1% hydrocortisone cream bid for facial patches or thin plaques
    - Lotions are more appropriate for scalp lesions
- **Options for Lupus nephritis**
  - ➤ Prednisone 0.5-1 mg/kg PO daily indicated for all types of lupus nephritis except for mesangial class I or II nephritis that usually requires no specific therapy.
  - ➤ Cyclophosphamide 750 mg/m^2 BSA IV qmonth added for diffuse, proliferative glomerulonephritis (500 mg/m^2 dosing for elderly, obese or CrCl < 40 mL/min.
- **Options for lupus vasculitis or lupus cerebritis**
  - ➤ Prednisone 0.5-1 mg/kg PO daily +/- pulse cyclophosphamide as above
- **Options for lupus oral ulcers**
  - ➤ 0.1% triamcinolone in orabase paste applied daily as needed
- **Options for lupus arthritis or serositis**
  - ➤ Mild arthritis and serositis treated with NSAIDS and acetaminophen
  - ➤ Moderate-severe disease treated with prednisone 0.5-1 mg/kg PO daily

ACR = American College of Rheumatology, BSA = body surface area
References: Arthritis Rheum, 1982; 25: 1271. Arthritis Rheum, 1997; 40: 1725. J Am Acad Dermatology, 2004; 51: 427. Clin. Nephrology, 2002; 57: 95. AFP, 2003; 68: 2179 & Dermatology clinics; 2000; 18: 139.

Name	Orthostatic hypotension	Sedation	Anticholinergic	Anxiety and agitation	GI upset, diarrhea and nausea	Sexual Dysfunction
Selective Serotonin Reuptake Inhibitors						
citalopram	None	Low	Low	Low-moderate	Moderate	Moderate
escitalopram	None	Low	Low	Low-moderate	Moderate	Moderate
fluoxetine	None	None	Very low	Moderate-high	Moderate	Moderate
fluvoxamine	None	Low	None	Low	Moderate	Moderate
paroxetine	None	Low-Moderate	Low	Low	Moderate	High
sertraline	None	Very low	Very low	Low-moderate	Moderate	Moderate
Mixed Noradrenergic/Serotonergic Agonist Antidepressants						
bupropion	None	None	None	Moderate	None	Low
mirtazapine	None	High	None	None	None	None
nefazodone	Low	Low-moderate	Low	None	Low	None
venlafaxine	None	Low	Low	Low-moderate	None	Moderate
Tricyclic antidepressants	Moderate - high	High	Moderate-high	None	Low-moderate	Low-moderate

Name	Other Uses / Miscellaneous comments	Comments
Selective Serotonin Reuptake Inhibitors (SSRIs)		SSRI side effects:
citalopram	Panic attack and neuropathic pain / minimal drug interactions	• Headache, diarrhea, constipation, tremor, nausea and sweating
escitalopram	Generalized anxiety disorder / minimal drug interactions	• Sexual dysfunction
fluoxetine	Obsessive compulsive or premenstrual dysphoric disorder, bulimia and panic disorder / most activating SSRI and longest drug half-life	• Serotonin syndrome from drug interactions consists of following tetrad:
fluvoxamine	Obsessive compulsive disorder / long drug half-life and more nausea	➢ delirium ➢ autonomic instability
paroxetine	Obsessive compulsive, post-traumatic stress, premenstrual dysphoric and generalized anxiety disorders, panic disorder and social phobia	➢ neuromuscular dysfunction ➢ fever
sertraline	Obsessive compulsive disorder, panic attacks, post-traumatic stress disorder, panic disorder and premenstrual dysphoric disorder	• Discontinuation syndrome: flu-like symptoms, vertigo, emesis and migraine headaches
Mixed Noradrenergic/Serotonergic Agonist Antidepressants		
bupropion	Smoking cessation	Avoid if seizures/eating disorder. Anxiety & may cause less conversion to mania
mirtazapine	Generalized anxiety disorder, somatization disorder, panic disorder / useful adjunct for opiate withdrawal (especially antiemetic effects)	Weight gain (less with higher doses), rare tremors, low mania induction, sedation
nefazodone	Generalized anxiety disorder and insomnia / useful for fibromyalgia	Hepatotoxicity, orthostasis. Watch for drug interactions.
venlafaxine	Generalized anxiety disorder, bipolar disorder and panic attacks. Very effective for geriatric depression / minimal drug interactions	Nausea (less with long-acting formulation), headache and hypertension
Tricyclic antidepressants	Neuropathic pain, chronic pain, migraine prophylaxis and clomipramine and imipramine indicated for panic attacks	Severe overdose → cardiac & neuro toxicity, orthostasis, caution in elderly

Name	EPS effects	Sedation	Anticholinergic	Orthostasis	Comments/potential side effects
aripiprazole (A)	Low	Low-moderate	Low	Low	Headache, nausea, vomiting, akathisia and anxiety
chlorpromazine‡	Low	High	Moderate	High	Photosensitivity, rare cytopenias
clozapine (A)	Very low	High	High	High	Agranulocytosis, seizures, weight gain and excessive salivation
fluphenazine	High	Moderate	Very low	Very low	GI upset, headache, edema, leukopenia and akathisia
haloperidol‡	High	Moderate	Very low	Very low	Akathisia, anxiety and lethargy
olanzapine (A)	Low	Moderate	Low-moderate	Low-moderate	Agitation, headache, rhinitis, weight gain, hyperglycemia and hepatitis
perphenazine	Moderate	Low	Low	Low	Anorexia, rare cytopenias, hepatotoxicity
quetiapine (A)	Very low	Moderate	Low	Low-moderate	Agitation, headache and weight gain
risperidone (A)	Low-moderate*	Low-moderate	Very low	Moderate	Nausea, anxiety, tremor, weight gain and hyperglycemia.
thioridazine‡	Very low	Moderate	High	High	Decreased libido, retrograde ejaculation, weight gain and QT prolongation
thiothixene	High	Very low	Very low	Very low	Agitation, photosensitivity, hepatotoxicity
ziprasidone‡ (A)	Low	Moderate	Very low	Low-moderate	QT prolongation, headache, weakness

EPS= extrapyramidal side effects. *-risperidone has low risk of EPS if daily dose < 6 mg and moderate risk if ≥ 6 mg/day. Note: all antipsychotics (especially the typical neuroleptics) can cause parkinsonism and hyperprolactinemia (except for clozaril). All atypical antipsychotics can cause hyperglycemia and diabetes. QT = QT segment of electrocardiogram. Anticholinergic side effects: dry mouth, constipation, urinary retention, blurred vision, confusion, flushing and can worsen narrow-angle glaucoma. ‡ - Drugs that can prolong the QT interval & may cause Torsades de pointes. (A) = atypical antipsychotics and the remainder are the 'typical' antipsychotics.

Name	Therapeutic Uses	Usual Dosage Range	Comments/Side Effects
Benzodiazepines			
alprazolam	Panic disorder and Panic disorder with agoraphobia	0.25 - 1 mg PO tid prn	Benzodiazepine side effects: Sedation, dizziness, anterograde amnesia and physical dependence. Best for short-term use
clonazepam	Post-traumatic stress disorder	0.25 - 1 mg PO tid prn	
diazepam	Social phobia	5 - 10 mg PO q6h prn	Risk of benzodiazepine withdrawal syndrome (including seizures) with abrupt discontinuation
lorazepam	Alcohol withdrawal and akathisia	1 - 2 mg PO tid prn	
Heterocyclic Compounds			
clomipramine	PD, PTSD, OCD, SP and GAD	100 - 200 mg PO qhs	Drowsiness, anticholinergic side effects, tachycardia & nausea. Dangerous in suicidal pts
imipramine	PD, PDA, PTSD, SP and GAD	50 - 200 mg PO qhs	
Selective Serotonin Reuptake Inhibitors			
fluoxetine	OCD and PMDD	20 - 60 mg PO daily	SSRI side effects: headache, diarrhea or constipation, tremor, nausea, vomiting, sweating and sexual dysfunction. Fluoxetine is most activating, paroxetine has anticholinergic effects and fluvoxamine has the most nausea.
fluvoxamine	OCD	50 - 300 mg PO daily	
paroxetine	PD, PDA, PTSD, OCD, SP, GAD & PMDD	10 - 60 mg PO daily	
sertraline	PD, PDA, PTSD, OCD and PMDD	50 - 200 mg PO daily	
Other Anxiolytics			
buspirone	GAD	5 - 20 mg PO tid	Nausea, HA, dizziness, fatigue and restlessness
propranolol	Performance anxiety and essential tremor	20 - 40 mg PO q12h	Fatigue, bronchospasm and sexual dysfunction
venlafaxine	GAD and PMDD	75 - 225 mg XR PO daily	Hypertension, agitation, tremor, nausea, HA, somnolence, dizzy, dry mouth and constipation

PD = Panic disorder, PDA = Panic disorder with agoraphobia, PTSD = Post-traumatic stress disorder, SP = Social phobia, GAD = Generalized anxiety disorder, PMDD = premenstrual dysphoric disorder, OCD = Obsessive compulsive disorder, HA = headache. Anticholinergic side effects: dry mouth, blurry vision, constipation, urinary retention, confusion and flushing

PEDIATRIC DRUGS		*Age*	*2m*	*4m*	*6m*	*9m*	*12m*	*15m*	*2y*	*3y*	*5y*
		Kg	5	6½	8	9	10	11	13	15	19
		Lbs	11	15	17	20	22	24	28	33	42
med	***strength***	***freq***	***teaspoons of liquid per dose*** *(1 tsp= 5 ml)*								
Tylenol (mg)		q4h	80	80	120	120	160	160	200	240	280
Tylenol (tsp)	160/t	q4h	½	½	¾	¾	1	1	1¼	1½	1¾
ibuprofen (mg)		q6h	-	-	75†	75†	100	100	125	150	175
ibuprofen (tsp)	100/t	q6h	-	-	¾†	¾†	1	1	1¼	1½	1¾
amoxicillin or	125/t	bid	1	1¼	1½	1¾	1¾	2	2¼	2¾	3½
Augmentin	200/t	bid	½	¾	1	1	1¼	1¼	1½	1¾	2¼
(not otitis media)	250/t	bid	½	½	¾	¾	1	1	1¼	1¼	1¾
	400/t	bid	¼	½	½	½	¾	¾	¾	1	1
amoxicillin,	200/t	bid	1	1¼	1¾	2	2	2¼	2¾	3	4
(otitis media)‡	250/t	bid	¾	1¼	1½	1½	1¾	1¾	2¼	2½	3¼
	400/t	bid	½	¾	¾	1	1	1¼	1½	1½	2
Augmentin ES‡	600/t	bid	⅜	½	½	¾	¾	¾	1	1¼	1½
azithromycin*§	100/t	daily	¼	½†	½	½	½	½	¾	¾	1
(5-day Rx)	200/t	daily	--	¼†	¼	¼	¼	¼	½	½	½
Bactrim/Septra	---	bid	½	¾	1	1	1	1¼	1½	1½	2
cefaclor*	125/t	bid	1	1	1¼	1½	1½	1¾	2	2½	3
"	250/t	bid	½	½	¾	¾	¾	1	1	1¼	1½
cefadroxil	125/t	bid	½	¾	1	1	1¼	1¼	1½	1¾	2¼
"	250/t	bid	¼	½	½	½	¾	¾	¾	1	1
cefdinir	125/t	daily	--	¾†	1	1	1	1¼	1½	1¾	2
cefixime	100/t	daily	½	½	¾	¾	¾	1	1	1¼	1½
cefprozil*	125/t	bid	--	¾†	1	1	1¼	1½	1½	2	2¼
"	250/t	bid	--	½†	½	½	¾	¾	¾	1	1¼
cefuroxime	125/t	bid	½	¾	¾	1	1	1	1½	1¾	2¼
cephalexin	125/t	qid	¼	½	¾	¾	1	1	1¼	1½	1¾
"	250/t	qid	--	¼	¼	½	½	½	¾	¾	1
clarithromycin	125/t	bid	--	½†	½	½	¾	¾	¾	1	1¼
"	250/t	bid	--	--	--	¼	½	½	½	½	¾
dicloxacillin	62½/t	qid	½	¾	1	1	1¼	1¼	1½	1¾	2
loracarbef*	100/t	bid	--	1†	1¼	1½	1½	1¾	2	2¼	3
nitrofurantoin	25/t	qid	¼	½	½	½	½	¾	¾	¾	1
Pediazole	---	tid	½	½	¾	¾	1	1	1	1¼	1½
penicillin	250/t	bid-tid	--	1	1	1	1	1	1	1	1
cetirizine	5/t	daily	-	-	-	-	-	-	½	½	½
diphenhydramine	12.5/t	q6h	½	½	¾	¾	1	1	1¼	1½	2
prednisolone	15/t	daily	¼	½	½	¾	¾	¾	1	1	1¼
prednisone	5/t	daily	1	1¼	1½	1¾	2	2¼	2½	3	3¾
Robitussin	---	q4h	-	-	¼†	¼†	½	½	¾	¾	1
Rondec	---	q4h	-	-	-	-	¼†	¼†	½	½	1
Triaminic	---	q4h	-	¼	¼	¼	½	½	1	1	1
Tylenol w/ codeine		q4h	-	-	-	-	-	-	-	1	1

* Dose shown is for otitis media only; see dosing in text for alternative indications.

† Dosing at this age/weight not recommended by manufacturer.

‡ AAP now recommends high dose (80-90 mg/kg/d) for all otitis media in children; with Augmentin used as ES only. §Give a double dose of azithromycin the first day. t: teaspoonful = 5 mL.

Reproduced with permission from the Tarascon Pocket Pharmacopoeia, 2006, Tarascon Publishing.

Normal Hematologic Values by Sex and Age

Age (years)	Hgb (gm/dL)		Hematocrit (%)		MCV (fL)		MCH (pg)	
	Mean	Lower limit	Mean	Lower limit	Mean	Lower limit	Mean	Lower limit
0.5-2	12.5	11.0	37	33	77	70	28	24
2-4	12.5	11.0	38	34	79	73	28	24
5-7	13.0	11.5	39	35	81	75	29	25
8-11	13.5	12.0	40	36	83	76	29	25
12-14 - ♀	13.5	12.0	40	36	85	78	29	26
12-14 - ♂	14.0	12.5	42	37	84	77	29	26
15-17 - ♀	14.0	12.0	41	36	87	79	30	27
15-17 - ♂	15.0	13.0	46	38	86	78	30	27

Hgb=hemoglobin, MCV=mean corpuscular volume, MCH=mean corpuscular hemoglobin and pg=picograms

Etiologies of Anemia
- Most common cause of anemia in childhood is iron-deficiency anemia

Microcytic anemias [low mean corpuscular volume in femtoliters (fL)]
> Mentzer index = MCV/RBC: ≥14, iron-deficiency; ≤12, thalassemias

- Iron-deficiency anemia (IDA)#
- Anemia of chronic disease
- Lead toxicity
- Thalassemias (alpha- or beta-)

Normocytic anemias (normal mean corpuscular volume)
- Anemia of chronic disease
- Aplastic anemia
- Myelodysplasia, myelophthisic process or leukemia
- Acute blood loss
- Storage diseases
- Hemolysis

Macrocytic anemias (MCV > 2 standard deviations above the mean)
- Hemolysis
- Folate deficiency* or Vitamin B12 deficiency
- Chronic liver disease
- Hypothyroidism

* - Can occur with chronic use of methotrexate, mercaptopurine, phenytoin or trimethoprim-sulfamethoxazole or with goat's milk diet (decreases vitamin B12 and folate stores). RBC = red blood count (million/µL/mm³).
\# - high-risk group: low-income & immigrant children, ex-preemies, breastfed infants with no supplemental iron, children with chronic inflammatory diseases, menstruating adolescents & ages 6-36 months and puberty

Screening for Anemia
- Screen children with hemoglobin and lead level at 9-15 months of age.
- Screen hemoglobin annually from ages 2-5 years of age.

Work-up of Anemia
- If history and exam suggest IDA, no special work-up of anemia is necessary.
- Recheck newborn screen for presence of hemoglobinopathies & hypothyroidism
- If history or exam suggests another cause of anemia or patient has failed a therapeutic trial of iron, check a complete blood count, reticulocyte count, ferritin
  > Ferritin level ≤ 20 mcg/L suggests and ≤ 10 mcg/L is definitive for iron-deficiency anemia and a level > 50 mcg/L argues against iron deficiency.
  > Reticulocyte count elevated in acute blood loss, hemolysis or thalassemia and low in all other causes of anemia.
  > Consider a bone marrow biopsy for pancytopenia, presence of nucleated or tear drop red blood cells, or any abnormal immature white blood cell forms.

Management of Iron-Deficiency Anemia
- Prevention and treatment of iron-deficiency should start with dietary changes.
  > Encourage intake of iron-fortified solids from 4-6 months of age.
  > Formula-fed infants should use iron-fortified formulas.
  > 2-4 mg/kg/day elemental iron (up to 15 mg/day) for ex-preterm or low birthweight breast-fed infants starting at 12 months of age.
  > No cow's milk until ≥12 months & limit milk intake to <24 ounces/d until 5 yr.
- Interventions initiated once anemia diagnosed.
  > Start with iron-rich foods. Check hemoglobin in 4 wks & desire↑ ≥1 gm/dL.
  > If inadequate rise, start 4-6 mg/kg/d elemental iron. Repeat screen in 4 wks

References: Ped. Clin N. Amer, 2002; 49: 877. Advances in Ped., 2001; 48: 385 & Pediatrics, 2001; 108: 1

The Approach to the Adolescent Patient
- Use every visit as an opportunity for education and risk assessment
- Interview the adolescent patient alone and emphasize confidentiality
- Use an unhurried, non-judgmental approach
- Use open-ended questioning and avoid assumptions
- Remember the BiHEADSS mnemonic
- Key features to these questions are they do not assume anything about the adolescent such as having a family or being heterosexual, etc.
- Always summarize the information and give a follow-up plan

Sample Questions using BiHEADSS
- **Bi - Body Image**
  - ➤ How do you feel about your body and how it has changed recently?
- **H – Home**
  - ➤ Where do you live? Who lives with you?
  - ➤ What happens when people disagree in your house?
- **E – Education/ Employment**
  - ➤ Tell me about your school.
  - ➤ What are you good at? What are you having trouble in?
  - ➤ Where do you go after school?
  - ➤ Do you have a job at the moment?
- **A – Activities/ Accidents/ Ambition**
  - ➤ What do you do for fun?
  - ➤ What do you do with your friends?
  - ➤ Have you ever been injured or injured anyone?
  - ➤ Have you ever been involved in an accident?
  - ➤ What would you like to do later in life?
- **D – Drugs/ Depression**
  - ➤ Many kids your age have experimented with alcohol and drugs. Have you or your friends ever tried any drugs? **or**
  - ➤ When was the first time you tasted alcohol?
    - o **CAGE** questionnaire for affirmative answers
    - o **C** – Have you ever thought about **cutting back** your drug use?
    - o **A** – Do people **annoy** you when they talk about your drug use?
    - o **G** – Do you ever feel **guilty** about your drug use?
    - o **E** – **Eye-opener** - Do you sometimes drink first thing in the morning?
  - ➤ Do you ever feel sad or down?
- **S – Suicidality**
  - ➤ Have you ever thought about hurting yourself?
- **S – Sex**
  - ➤ Have you ever had a sexual relationship with someone else?
  - ➤ How are you protecting yourself from AIDS?

Exam, Lab screening and Health Maintenance
- Check blood pressure to rule out hypertension
- Annual pap smear and chlamydia screening for all sexually active girls
- Assure vaccinations are up to date (including menactra and Tdap)
- Cholesterol screening every 3 years for a family history of heart disease

Adapted from the AMA guidelines for adolescent preventive services. Baltimore: Williams & Wilkins, 1994.
Menactra = meningococcal conjugate vaccine, Tdap = tetanus, diphtheria and pertussis booster vaccine

Diagnosis of Attention Deficit Hyperactivity Disorder (ADHD)
- Must meet the Diagnostic and Statistical Manual of Mental Disorders IV criteria
- The behavioral symptoms are present in ≥ 2 settings (e.g., school and home) and some symptoms started before age 7 years.
- There is significant impairment in social, academic or occupational functioning
- The symptoms are not better accounted for by another psychiatric disorder
- Parents & teachers complete ADHD questionnaires (e.g. Conners or Vanderbilt)
- Assess child for comorbid conditions: conduct or oppositional defiant or mood disorders, hearing or visual impairment, substance abuse or learning disabilities
- No need for any labs, MRI or other imaging studies unless diagnosis equivocal; complete exam, vision and hearing screens must be done.

Diagnostic & Statistical Manual of Mental Disorders IV (DSM-IV) Criteria
Inattentive type: ≥ 6 symptoms of **inattention** that are inappropriate for child's developmental level have persisted for ≥ 6 months
- Does not pay close attention to details and makes careless mistakes
- Has difficulty sustaining attention in tasks or play activities
- Does not seem to listen when spoken to directly
- Does not follow through on instructions and leaves tasks unfinished
- Frequently loses equipment necessary for tasks or activities
- Easily distracted by extraneous stimuli
- Often forgetful in daily activities

Hyperactive/impulsive type: ≥ 6 symptoms of **hyperactivity-impulsivity** have persisted for ≥ 6 months
- Often fidgets with hand or feet or squirms in seat
- Often stands up in situations in which he/she is expected remain seated
- Often runs or climbs in situations when it is inappropriate
- Has difficulty playing or engaging in activities quietly
- Seems to be indefatigable or have tireless energy
- Talks excessively
- Often blurts out answers before questions have been completed
- Has difficulty awaiting his/her turn
- Interrupts or intrudes on other people's conversations or activities

Combined type: meets criteria for both inattentive & hyperactive/impulsive types.

Treatment of Attention Deficit Hyperactivity Disorder in school-aged children
- Provide patient and family with information, anticipatory guidance and ADHD resources (www.chadd.org, www.add.org or www.oneaddplace.com).
- Behavior therapy: structured environment, firm limits/rules & simple instructions.
- Work with the school to develop an individualized education program for child.

Medications used to treat Attention Deficit Hyperactivity Disorder

Oral Medications	Starting Dose	Maximum Daily Dose	Side effects
methylphenidate	2.5-5 mg bid	60 mg	• Motor tics
d-methylphenidate	2.5 mg bid	20 mg	• Insomnia
Concerta	18 mg/day	72 mg	• Weight loss
Metadate CD or ER	10 mg/day	60 mg	• Hypertension
Ritalin SR or LA	20 mg/day	60 mg	• Tachycardia
dextroamphetamine	2.5-5 mg bid*	40 mg	• Nausea/vomiting
Adderall XR	5-10 mg/day*	30 mg	• Anorexia
clonidine¥	0.05 mg/day	0.3 mg	• Sedation, hypotension, dry mouth
guanfacine¥	1 mg/day	3 mg	• Dry mouth, sedation, dizziness
atomoxetine	0.5 mg/kg/d	1.4 mg/kg‡	• Dry mouth, insomnia, nausea
bupropion SR¥	0.7 mg/kg bid	6 mg/kg#	• Tremor, nausea, dry mouth, HA

* -lower dose if 3-5 yrs; higher dose if ≥6 yrs. ‡ -max dose 100 mg/day. # -max dose 400 mg/day. ¥ -alpha-agonists & Wellbutrin not FDA approved for treatment of ADHD in kids, but many studies show effectiveness.
References: Pediatrics, 2001; 108: 1033. Pediatrics, 2000; 105: 1158. NEJM, 2005; 352: 165. HA=headache

Clinical Presentation
- Typically begins between 2-3 weeks of age and resolves by 3-4 months.
- Presents as inconsolable crying often accompanied by drawing up the legs or head and gaseous distension.
- Tends to occur in the late afternoon, ≥ 3 hours/day and ≥ 3 days/week
- Rule out other causes of crying and irritability such as infection, hunger, wet diaper, gastroesophageal reflux disease or desire to be cuddled.

Potential Contributing Factors
- Formula use (conflicting evidence regarding human or cow's milk allergy as a factor in colic)
- Swallowing air during feedings (aerophagia)
- Intake of various foods by nursing mothers such as milk products, cauliflower, broccoli, cabbage, eggs, chocolate, wheat, nuts and caffeinated beverages may affect babies.

Parental Education
- Parents need to take a break to avoid the risk of shaking the baby.
  - ➤ Consider a family member, friend or babysitter to watch baby periodically
- Parents must have someone to call if they feel like they might hurt the baby.
- Colic is not an illness.
- Colic is not contagious.
- Colic does not damage the baby in any way.
- Colic is not caused by bad parenting.
- Colicky babies probably have more gas because of aerophagia.

Management of Colic
- No randomized controlled trials to support any method that decreases colic.
- Burp baby more frequently while he/she is feeding.
- Breastfeeding mothers can try eliminating milk products, eggs, wheat and nuts from their diet.
- If the baby is formula fed, can switch to a hypoallergenic formula, especially for a strong family history of atopy, food allergies or signs of cow's milk protein intolerance (e.g., blood in the stool); no benefit from switching to soy-based formulas. If the infant is breastfed, continue breastfeeding.
- Try carrying the baby in a front sling or carrier.
- Try swaddling the baby.
- Can try a warm water bottle lightly applied to the abdomen.
- Lay the infant belly down on your lap and rub his/her back.
- Take the child for a car or stroller ride
- Try soothing baby with the ambient noise of a vacuum cleaner or running dryer
- Try a child swing.
- Simethicone drops "not proven effective", but are benign and have a possible placebo effect.
- No benefit of infant massage or chiropractic treatments.
- Most folk remedies are not harmful (e.g., chamomile tea or homeopathic tablets); however, caution parents about the lack of standardization of strength and dosage in these supplements and they have no proven benefit.

American Family Physician, 2004; 70: 735-42.

Adapted from the North American Society for Pediatric Gastroenterology and Nutrition Clinical Guidelines for Constipation in Infants and Children

Definitions
- Constipation: hard stools passed ≤ 2 times per week or difficulty defecating causing discomfort to the child for at least 2 weeks.

Evaluation of Constipation in Infants and Young Children
- **History:** duration, diet, toilet training history, pain or bleeding with defecation, withholding behavior, encopresis, delayed passage of meconium (> 24 hours), toileting behavior outside of the home or presence of abdominal pain
- **Family History:** constipation, Hirschsprung's disease, celiac disease, cystic fibrosis, thyroid or parathyroid diseases
- **Exam:** fecal mass on abdominal exam
  ➤ Signs of spina bifida occulta: sacral dimple, tuft of hair or dermal sinus
  ➤ Anal exam: presence of perianal erythema, fissure, fistula or stenosis
  ➤ Rectal exam: presence of fecal mass, anal wink, good rectal tone
  ➤ Complete neurologic exam including cremasteric reflex check
- **Assess for Red Flags:** fever, vomiting, bloody diarrhea or guaiac-positive stools without an anal fissure, failure to thrive, an abnormal neurologic exam or a tight empty rectum or abnormal anal tone on rectal exam
- **Evaluation of Refractory Constipation**
  ➤ Thyroid panel, calcium level, lead level and celiac panel
  ➤ Plain-film abdominal x-ray to assess for fecal mass in colon
  ➤ MRI of the lumbosacral spine if any concern of spinal dysraphism
  ➤ Consider measuring a colonic transport time using radiopaque markers.
  ➤ Evaluation for Hirschsprung's disease: anal manometry, barium enema and rectal biopsy looking for the absence of ganglion cells
  ➤ Sweat chloride test if any concern of cystic fibrosis

Management of Functional Constipation in Infants < 1 Year
- **Fecal disimpaction**
  ➤ Rectal disimpaction once with glycerin suppositories. Avoid enemas.
- **Dietary changes**
  ➤ Increased intake of prune, pear, apple or white grape juice if > 6 months old
- **Medications**
  ➤ Lactulose (10 mg/15 mL) 2.5-10 mL PO daily titrated to effect.

Management of Functional Constipation in Children > 1 Year
- **Fecal disimpaction**
  ➤ Rectal disimpaction with phosphate soda **or** saline enemas (> 2 years old); use with caution in kids that have electrolyte, cardiac or renal disorders.
- **Dietary changes**
  ➤ Increased intake of fluids, whole grains, fresh fruits, vegetables, high sorbitol juices +/- sorbitol gum
- **Exercise and Psychosocial Interventions**
  ➤ Encourage daily aerobic exercise
  ➤ Educate parents to avoid pressuring kids to potty train. Unhurried potty time right after meals. No scolding for soiling. Give bathroom pass at school.
- **Maintenance therapy given as needed**
  ➤ Mineral oil 1 mL/kg (not to exceed 15 mL) PO daily for children > 5 years - Use with caution in younger kids or in those at risk for aspiration
  ➤ Magnesium hydroxide 2.5-5 mL/dose PO daily-qid; titrate to effect.
  ➤ 70% lactulose solution 0.5 mL/kg (up to 15 mL/dose) PO bid-tid
  ➤ Polyethylene glycol powder (Miralax) 0.8 gm/kg (up to 17 gm) mixed in 8 ounces water PO daily.
  ➤ Wean maintenance therapy to minimum effective dose with the aim to control constipation via dietary and lifestyle changes

References: Amer. Fam. Physician, 2002; 65: 2283-90 and J. Pediatric Gastro. Nutrition, 1999; 29: 612-26.

Nocturnal Enuresis

- The involuntary loss of urine that occurs **only at night** in girls older than 5 years and boys older than 6 years.
  - Affects 10-20% of 1st grade boys and 8-17% of 1st grade girls.
- Primary nocturnal enuresis if incontinence have never been continent.
- Secondary nocturnal enuresis if incontinence recurs after ≥ 6 mo. of continence

Evaluation of Nocturnal Enuresis

- Complete history and exam (check for abnormal gait and spinal dysraphism)
- Family history of nocturnal enuresis or Attention Deficit Hyperactivity Disorder
- Check urinalysis and urine culture (rule out diabetes or infection)
- Inquire about encopresis and chronic constipation that can be associated.
- Any diurnal incontinence? (positive answer→ rule out complicated enuresis)
- If complicated enuresis suspected, consider a voiding cystourethrogram to rule out an ectopic ureter in girls or posterior urethral valves in boys.

Management of Nocturnal Enuresis

Family Counseling

- Avoidance of punishment and humiliation
- Improve child's access to toilet.
- Provide good lighting in case fear of the dark a hindrance.
- Avoid fluids for at least two hours prior to bedtime.
- Empty the bladder at bedtime
- Child's participation in morning clean-up
- Encourage parents to keep an enuresis diary.
- Positive reinforcement system for "dry" nights
- Equipment and educational resource for parents at www.pottymd.com

Conditioning Therapy

- Enuresis alarm systems
  - Best rate of permanent cure (70-75%)
  - The alarm sounds when the child begins to void and eventually trains the child to awake when he/she senses a full bladder.
  - Complete a trial of at least 3-4 months prior to discontinuation.

Pharmacologic Agents

- Desmopressin (DDAVP)
  - 0.2 mg PO qhs titrated to 0.6 mg qhs if needed
  - 1-4 sprays (10 mcg/spray) intranasally qhs
  - Very effective but high relapse rate (80-90%) upon discontinuation.
  - Best used intermittently for sleepovers, campouts, etc.
- Imipramine (use with caution and only in consultation with a pediatrician)
  - 25 mg qhs (ages 6-8 yrs), 50 mg qhs (8-12 yrs), 75 mg qhs (>12 yrs)
  - Taper dose over 4 weeks when discontinuing therapy
  - Typically for 3-6 months of therapy
  - Acute overdoses are potentially fatal from cardiovascular collapse.

References: Amer. Fam. Physician, 2003; 67: 1499-506 and Pediatrics & Child Health, 1997; 2(6): 419-21.

General Guidelines and Definitions
- **Definition of fever:** rectal temperature ≥ 38°C (100.4°F)
- **Toxic appearance:** lethargic, inconsolable, pale or cyanotic, extreme irritability, and often manifest tachypnea, tachycardia and/or poor perfusion.
- All toxic-appearing infants should be hospitalized on empiric antibiotics for a complete sepsis work-up (complete blood count, chest radiograph, blood cultures, **catheterized** urine culture and lumbar puncture).
- **Older infants** are those children between 3 months and 3 years of age.
- **Serious bacterial infections:** meningitis, bacteremia, sepsis, pneumonia, pyelonephritis, cellulitis, septic arthritis, osteomyelitis or bacterial gastroenteritis

Guidelines for Evaluation of Nontoxic Older Infant with Fever < 39°C (102.2°F)
- Well-appearing children with herpangina, hand-foot-mouth disease, croup, roseola, Fifth's disease, varicella or primary herpes gingivostomatitis do **not** need a work-up for superimposed bacterial infection.
- Careful history and exam to identify likely sources of bacterial infection
- If no obvious source of bacterial infection found
  ➢ No tests or antibiotics needed
  ➢ Acetaminophen or ibuprofen as needed for fever control.
  ➢ Re-evaluate in 48 hours or sooner if condition deteriorates.
- If a source of infection is found
  ➢ Targeted lab tests based on source of infection
  ➢ Empiric antibiotics to cover likely bacterial pathogens

Guidelines for Evaluation of Nontoxic Older Infant with Fever ≥ 39°C (102.2°F) and No Obvious Source of Infection
- If the child is **up-to-date** with his/her pneumococcal/Hib vaccinations, the chance of occult bacteremia is probably ≤ 0.5%.
  ➢ 0.3% of well-appearing febrile infants 3-36 months old have serious bacterial infections and only 3 in 10,000 have sepsis or meningitis.
- A nontoxic child can be observed **without** any labs if there is: reliable caregiver, close follow-up and an understanding that clinical deterioration may occur.
- If the clinician and family choose to perform labs, consider the following:
  ➢ Consider a complete blood count with differential and a blood culture
  ➢ Consider rapid viral antigen tests for influenza A & B, RSV and parainfluenzae 1, 2 & 3 (winter months) or enteroviral PCR (summer & fall) if clinical suspicion is high since concomitant bacterial infection is very rare.
  ➢ Recommend a **catheterized** urinalysis with microscopy, gram stain of unspun urine and urine culture in all boys < 6 months, uncircumcised boys < 1 year and all girls < 2 years with no other source of infection.
    o Positive nitrite **and** leukocyte esterase on catheterized urine dipstick is 96% specific for a UTI. 20% of pyelonephritis cases have no pyuria.
  ➢ Chest x-ray for cough, tachypnea (>59 breaths/min. 3-6 mo., >52 if 6-11 mo. and >42 if 1-2 yrs), an abnormal pulmonary exam or a WBC >20,000/mm³.
  ➢ Consider a stool culture if there is a history of diarrhea and blood or mucus in stool or >5 white blood cells (WBC) per high-powered field on stool exam
  ➢ Lumbar puncture (LP) if history or exam worrisome for meningitis
- Consider empiric antibiotics for WBC ≥ 20,000 **and** ANC >10,000 per mm³
  ➢ Ceftriaxone 50-75 mg/kg IM daily for fever of unknown source until culture results are known at 48 hours
  ➢ Antibiotics given before an LP may cause false-negative CSF cultures
- Follow-up in 24 hours if fever persists, clinical worsening or 48 hours otherwise

ANC = absolute neutrophil count, CSF = cerebrospinal fluid, UTI = urinary tract infection, RSV = respiratory syncytial virus. References: Ann Emer Med, 2003; 42: 530. Ann Emer Med., 1999; 33: 166. JAMA, 2004; 291: 1203. Pediatrics, 2000; 106: 977. Pediatrics, 2001; 108: 1275 and AFP, 2001; 64: 1219-26.

Definitions and Miscellaneous Facts about Young Infants (< 3 months old)
- **Definition of fever:** rectal temperature ≥ 38°C (100.4°F)
- **Toxic appearance:** lethargic, inconsolable, pale or cyanotic, extreme irritability, and often manifest tachypnea, tachycardia and/or poor perfusion.
- **Serious bacterial infections:** pyelonephritis, bacteremia, meningitis, pneumonia, septic arthritis, cellulitis, bacterial gastroenteritis or osteomyelitis
- **Well-appearing infants 29-90 days old** with obvious varicella, roseola, Fifth's disease, herpangina, hand-foot-mouth disease or herpes gingivostomatitis do **not** need an extensive work-up for concomitant bacterial infections.
  - ➤ Consider checking for viral antigens to include influenza A & B, RSV and parainfluenzae 1, 2 & 3 (winter months) or enterovirus PCR (summer & fall) if clinical suspicion is high since concomitant bacterial infection is very rare.
- Otitis media should **not** be considered the cause of fever in young infants.
- The use of c-reactive protein to identify infants at high risk for serious bacterial infection is under investigation and should not be used as an isolated marker.

Criteria for Febrile Infants at Low Risk for Serious Bacterial Infections

Nontoxic appearance and normal exam	Full term (≥ 37 wks gestation)
No history of unexplained jaundice	No underlying medical illnesses
Age > 28 days	WBC ≥ 5,000 and ≤ 15,000 per mm³
Catheterized (cath) urinalysis with < 5-10 WBC/hpf, a negative nitrite **and** leukocyte esterase tests **and** a negative urine gram stain on unspun urine sample	
Absolute band count < 1,500 per mm³	No history of perinatal antibiotics
No history of intrapartum maternal fever	No inadequate intrapartum antibiotics*

* - adequate intrapartum antibiotics are at least a single dose of antibiotic given ≥ 4 hours prior to delivery

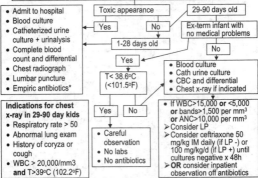

WBC= white blood cells, CBC= complete blood count, ANC = absolute neutrophil count, LP=lumbar puncture (negative if <10 WBC/mm³ if >30 days old), PCR=polymerase chain reaction, RSV=respiratory syncytial virus
* -Empiric antibiotics = ampicillin + gentamicin if no meningitis or ampicillin + cefotaxime if meningitis present
References: Ann. Emer. Med., 2003; 42: 530. Pediatrics, 2001; 98: 311. Pediatrics, 2004; 113: 1662. AFP, 2001; 64: 1219. Pediatrics, 1994; 94: 390 and JAMA, 2004; 291: 1203.

Metatarsus Adductus (MA)

- Congenital deformity characterized by medial deviation of the forefoot and a "c-shaped" curve along the lateral border of the foot.
- 10-15% association with developmental dysplasia of the hip
- 85% resolve spontaneously by 12 months of age

Diagnosis

- A line bisecting the heel and the sole of the foot at the arch should cross either the second or third toe in a normal foot.
- This same line will cross the fourth or fifth toe in a child with MA.

Management

- Teach parents stretching exercises to bring the forefoot to neutral position.
- Rule out club foot deformity and refer for a fixed deformity or for a club foot.
- Consider serial casting beginning ~ 6 months of age and changed every 2 weeks for persistent deformity.
- Consider a metatarsal osteotomy at 12 months of age for deformities refractory to serial casting.

Internal Tibial Torsion

- Caused by medial rotation of the tibia below the knee; often asymmetrical.
- Tibial torsion is the normal position in newborns. If pronounced, it presents with intoeing at 1-2 years of age when the child is weight bearing.

Diagnosis

- With the child in a sitting position and the legs outstretched, rotate the legs such that the patella are both aligned directly upwards.
- If the lateral malleolus is anterior to the medial malleolus, the patient has internal tibial torsion

Management

- Tibial torsion usually resolves spontaneously by 8 years of age.
- Reassure parents that this condition generally resolves spontaneously.
- May resolve faster if child avoids prone sleeping and sitting on their feet.
- Consider supramalleolar osteotomy if the patient has significant ambulation problems at 9-10 years of age.
- Splints and orthotics are of no benefit.

Medial Femoral Anteversion (MFA)

- Caused by excessive internal rotation of the femur
- Tends to present with intoeing at 3 - 6 years of age (girls > boys).
- Classically, children sit in the "W" position with their feet out to each side.
- Spontaneous resolution occurs in about 95% of cases by 10 years of age.
- Rule out cerebral palsy

Diagnosis

- Assess degree of hip rotation with child in prone position and knees flexed.
- Normal hip internal rotation (IR) for children > 2 years is 30-60º.
- Normal hip external rotation (ER) for children > 2 years is 30-40º.
- Medial femoral anteversion if hip IR > 70º and/or hip ER < 20º.

Management

- Encourage children to sit cross-legged.
- Follow hip range of motion ever 6-12 months to document improvement.
- Consider a femoral derotational osteotomy in children older than 10 years with <10º hip ER and gait problems; surgical complications are not uncommon.

References: Amer. Fam. Physician, 2003; 68: 461-8 and Current Opinions in Pediatrics, 1997; 9(1): 77-80.

Differential Diagnosis of a Limp by Age Group		
Toddlers (< 4 years)	Ages 4 – 10 Years	Children > 10 years
DDH	Legg-Calve-Perthes*	SCFE*
Osteomyelitis*	Osteomyelitis*	Osteochondritis dessicans*
Mild cerebral palsy	Toxic synovitis*	Toxic synovitis*
Trauma +/- Abuse*	Discitis*	Osgood-Schlatter disease*
JRA or reactive arthritis*	Leg length discrepancy‡	Tumors of spine or bones*
Septic arthritis*	Septic arthritis*	

DDH = Development dysplasia of hip, SCFE = slipped capital femoral epiphysis, JRA = juvenile rheumatoid arthritis, ‡ = difference > 1 inch may explain limp, * = indicates a painful condition

Developmental Dysplasia of the Hip (DDH)
- Screen all newborns with Ortolani and Barlow maneuvers for hip instability.
- Older kids can present with a Trendelenberg gait and uneven height of knees or with uneven gluteal folds when they are supine with hips and knees flexed.
- Refer to a pediatric orthopedist for an abnormal hip exam, x-ray or ultrasound.

Juvenile Rheumatoid Arthritis (JRA)
- Diagnosis: objective joint inflammation persisting > 6 weeks, onset < 18 yrs (usually age 1-4 yrs), morning stiffness ≥ 1 hour +/- rheumatoid factor +.
- Subtypes include systemic, polyarticular or pauciarticular JRA.

Osteomyelitis/Discitis
- Usually acquired hematogenously and typically child is younger than 5 years.
- Diagnosis: technetium-labeled bone scan or MRI scan will be abnormal.
- Exam: decreased range of motion, painful gait, fever +/- swelling or erythema.
- Labs: leukocytosis, ESR ≥20 mm/Hr in 92% & CRP>1.9 mg/dL in 98% of cases

Legg-Calve-Perthes Disease (LCPD)
- Osteonecrosis of the femoral head between 4-9 years old. Male: Female = 5:1
- Exam: trendelenburg gait, ↓ hip abduction/internal rotation; 10% bilateral
- Diagnosis: hip x-rays identify femoral head necrosis. Refer to orthopedist.

Septic Arthritis
- Presentation: usually <2 years, T>38.5ºC and refusal to walk +/- ill-appearing
- Exam: hip external rotated/flexed, hip effusion, passive hip movement painful
- Four variables: T>100.4ºF; WBC >12K; ESR>40 mm/hr; unable to bear weight. Risk for septic arthritis: 1 variable=3%, 2=40%, 3=93.1% & 4 variables=99.6%.
- Diagnosis: arthrocentesis with joint drainage and blood cultures

Slipped Capital Femoral Epiphysis (SCFE)
- Presentation: Male:Female=2:1; usually an obese child between 8-16 years old
- Exam: trendelenburg gait and hip usually flexed and externally rotated
- Diagnosis: AP and frogleg hip x-rays identify "a slip" affecting the femoral head.

Toxic Synovitis (usually follows a respiratory viral infection)
- Exam: afebrile, non-toxic child, limited hip abduction & external/internal rotation
- Labs: usually mild leukocytosis, normal ESR and CRP<1 mg/dL
- Lacks the four variables typically seen in septic arthritis. Ultrasound not helpful.

Osgood-Schlatter Disease (osteochondritis of the tibial tuberosity)
- Presentation: progressive anterior knee pain in an adolescent ♂ > ♀ involved in jumping sports. Squatting typically worsens the pain.
- Exam: localized tenderness and prominent tibial tuberosity. Clinical diagnosis.

Long Bone Tumors (e.g., femoral osteosarcomas)
- Presentation: adolescent with focal pain and swelling at rest and at night; often recent mild trauma. X-rays show a lytic or blastic lesion with ill-defined borders.

Osteochondritis Dissecans
- Presentation: painful knee from fragmentation of the articular surface of the patella or the femur during the teenage years or the twenties.
- Diagnosis: AP, lateral, sunrise and tunnel X-rays

ESR=erythrocyte sedimentation rate, CRP=C-reactive protein, AP= anteroposterior, WBC= white blood cell count
References: Pediatrics, 2002; 109 (1): 109. AFP, 1999; 60: 177. AFP, 2000; 61 (4): 1011. Current Opin. Pediatrics, 2001; 13 (1): 29. Clinical Ped. Emer. Med, 2002; 3: 129 & J. Bone Joint Surg Am, 1999; 81: 1662

Definition:
- Usually diagnosed in children < 2 yrs whose weight is consistently < 5th % or whose weight crosses & falls below 2 major growth curves within 6 months.

Etiologies of Failure to Thrive (FTT) in Children Two Years or Younger
- **Inadequate caloric intake**
  - Non-organic: poor feeding technique, inappropriate food for age, inadequate quantity of food offered or incorrect preparation of formula.
  - Psychosocial problems: dysfunctional relationship between parents and child, child neglect or abuse or behavior problems affecting eating.
  - Craniofacial: cleft palate, chronic nasal obstruction or adenoidal hypertrophy
  - Neuro: neuromuscular disorders, hypotonia, cerebral palsy or brain tumor
  - Severe developmental delay
  - Gastrointestinal (GI): pyloric stenosis, malrotation, intussusception, duodenal atresia, gastroesophageal reflux or feeding problems
- **Inadequate absorption**
  - GI: inflammatory bowel disease, celiac disease, cystic fibrosis (CF), milk protein allergy, biliary atresia, short-gut syn. or necrotizing enterocolitis.
- **Increased metabolism**
  - Endocrine: thyroid disease or diabetes mellitus
  - Infections: tuberculosis, toxoplasmosis or HIV infection
  - Chronic cardiopulmonary diseases: bronchopulmonary dysplasia, CHF, CF
  - Gastrointestinal: chronic liver disease
  - Renal disease: chronic renal failure or renal tubular acidosis
  - Malignancies
- **Defective utilization**

Inborn errors of metabolism	Lead toxicity
Chromosomal anomalies	Congenital infections

Work-Up of FTT
- Evaluate growth curves appropriate for underlying condition (e.g., Down syn.)
- History: gestational age at birth, birth weight, complications with pregnancy or delivery, any growth restriction, recent acute illness or any chronic illnesses?
- Dietary, feeding & stooling history (including formula preparation); vomiting?
- Developmental assessment; metabolic disease→ developmental regression
- Psychosocial history: living situation, parental employment and economic status, family stressors, spousal abuse, substance abuse, parental physical. mental illnesses (e.g., postpartum depression) or siblings with FTT.
- Observation: parental-child interaction, developmental assessment, observation of feeding for signs of swallowing dysfunction, infant behavior
- Strongly consider public health nurse visit for home evaluation
- Exam for dysmorphic features, signs of cleft palate or neurologic, cardiopulmonary, endocrine or gastrointestinal disorders.
- Labs to consider **if dietary interventions fail** and history and exam suggestive: complete blood count, urinalysis, urine culture, calcium, electrolytes, renal panel, thyroid stimulating hormone, stool studies for ova and parasites and malabsorption, HIV test, tuberculosis skin test and sweat chloride test

Management of FTT
- Diet: increase caloric intake ~50% (130-140 kcal/kg/day) in children <2 years)
  - Limit fruit juices, carbonated drinks and low-calorie foods
  - Food diary to assess actual calorie intake
- Children to avoid meal distractions (e.g., television or video games)
- Referrals to address the psychosocial problems in the household
- Check into food stamps, Women, Infants and Children and community services.
- Follow-up at least monthly until catch-up growth has been documented.
- Hospitalize for child abuse, severe FTT or failure of outpatient management.

References: Pediatric Rev., 1997; 18: 371. Pediatric Rev., 1992; 13: 453 and AFP, 2003; 68: 879.

Adapted from the American Academy of Pediatrics (AAP) Practice Guideline on the Management of Acute Gastroenteritis in Young Children Ages 1 month to 5 years.

Note: The following guidelines apply only to acute diarrheal illnesses lasting < 10 days and no signs of failure to thrive.

Evaluating the Degree of Dehydration

Characteristic	Mild (<5%)	Moderate (6-9%)	Severe (>10%)
Heart rate	Normal	Mild increase	Marked increase
Mucous membranes	Normal	Dry	Very dry
Mental status	Alert	Irritable or listless	Lethargic or obtunded
Urine output	Normal	Diminished	Markedly decreased
Skin turgor	Normal	Decreased	Markedly decreased
Fontanelle	Normal	Slightly sunken	Sunken
Eyes	Normal	Sunken orbits	Deeply sunken orbits
Skin	Pink + warm	Capillary refill > 2 seconds	Cool and mottled

Management of Acute Gastroenteritis with Mild or No Dehydration

- Breastfeeding should be continued in breastfed infants
- Continue age-appropriate diets
  - Rice, wheat, potatoes, breads, cereals, yogurt, fruits and vegetables.
  - Avoid fatty foods, fruit juices, soft drinks, candy and desserts.
- Mild dehydration should be corrected with 50 mL/kg of an oral rehydration solution (ORS) over 4 hours: examples include the World Health Organization rehydration solution, Rapolyte solution or Rehydralyte solution.
  - ORS = ½ teaspoon each of baking soda and table salt + 8 teaspoons sugar (or 1 cup of baby rice cereal) mixed in 1 liter of water
- Lactose-containing formulas/foods can be consumed safely in most children

Management of Acute Gastroenteritis with Moderate Dehydration

- ORS at 100 mL/kg over 4 hours given in frequent, small aliquots then reassess.
- Reassess degree of hydration after four hours and continue ORS until patient is adequately hydrated.
- Resume breastfeeding +/- age-appropriate foods as above once rehydrated.
- For vomiting, ORS can be administered in 5 mL aliquot every 1-2 minutes.
- If diarrhea significant, maintenance fluids can be administered at 10 mL/kg per stool (up to 250 mL) using a maintenance solution: examples include Pedialyte, Naturalyte, NutraMax, Infalyte, Lytren or Gastrolyte.

Management of Acute Gastroenteritis with Severe Dehydration

- Intravenous fluid (IVF) therapy with 20 mL/kg isotonic fluid bolus and repeat isotonic fluid boluses until moderate dehydration or normal mental status then continue ORS or IVF at 1.5-2x maintenance until fluid deficit resolved.

Antidiarrheal and Antiemetic Agents

- The AAP recommends against the use of any antidiarrheal or antiemetic agents including bismuth subsalicylate or adsorbents such as kaolin-pectate and fiber.
  - Promethazine is contraindicated in children < 2 years

Contraindications to Using Oral Rehydration Therapy

- Intractable vomiting, decreased level of consciousness and ileus.

References: Canadian J. of Pediatrics, 1994; 1(5): 160-4 and Pediatrics, 1996; 97(3): 424-35.

Adapted from the 2004 American Academy of Pediatrics (AAP) Practice Guideline on the Management of Hyperbilirubinemia in the Newborn Infant 35 or More Weeks of Gestation

Principles of Hyperbilirubinemia in Newborns
- Jaundice in infants < 24 hours of age is pathologic until proven otherwise.
- Direct bilirubin > 2 mg/dL indicates hepatobiliary dysfunction or sepsis

Common Cause of Newborn Jaundice

Physiologic jaundice	ABO/Rh incompatibility	Congenital hemolytic disorders	Metabolic disorders
Polycythemia	Cephalohematoma	Hypothyroidism	Neonatal sepsis

Risk Factors for Severe Hyperbilirubinemia
- Family history of hemolytic disorder
- Cephalohematoma
- High-risk ethnicity*
- Excessive newborn weight loss
- Gestational age<36 wks

- Prior infant with hyperbilirubinemia
- Breastfeeding
- Neonatal sepsis
- Delayed meconium passage
- Jaundice in 1st 24 hours

- ABO/Rh incompatibility
- Male gender (minor risk)
- Gestational DM
- Polycythemia
- Congenital hepatobiliary disorder

* - Asian or Native American Indian and DM = diabetes mellitus

Labs to Evaluate for Newborn Jaundice
- Total and direct bilirubin and serum albumin
- Direct Coomb's test to evaluate for ABO or Rh incompatibility
- Complete blood count
- Reticulocyte count and peripheral blood smear exam if hemolysis suspected
- If hemolysis confirmed, send labs to check for congenital hemolytic diseases.
- Consider a urine culture for any signs of sepsis or for direct hyperbilirubinemia.

Management of Hyperbilirubinemia in Newborns ≥ 35 Weeks

Age (hrs)	Total serum bilirubin level (mg/dL)			
	Low risk# infant phototherapy level	Medium risk‡ infant phototherapy level	High risk¶ infant phototherapy level	Exchange transfusion levels if intensive phototherapy fails*
12 hrs	9	7.5	6	≥ 18
24 hrs	12	10	8	≥ 19
36 hrs	13.5	12	9.5	≥ 21
48 hrs	15	13	11	≥ 22
72 hrs	18	15	13.5	≥ 24
96 hrs	20	17	14.5	≥ 25

\# - low risk = ≥38 weeks and well, ‡ - medium risk is 35-37 6/7 weeks or ≥38 weeks + risk factors and ¶ - high risk = 35-37 6/7 weeks + risk factors. Risk factors: isoimmune hemolytic disease, glucose-6-phosphate dehydrogenase deficiency, asphyxia, lethargy, temp. instability, sepsis, acidosis or serum albumin<3 gm/dL. Intensive phototherapy is 430-490 nm wavelength light of at least 30 μW/cm² per nm measured at skin.
* - failure of intensive phototherapy if the decline in total serum bilirubin within 6 hours is < 1-2 mg/dL

Goal: prevention of acute or chronic bilirubin encephalopathy (kernicterus)
- Presentation: acute encephalopathy with hypertonia, retrocollis, opisthotonus, fever and high-pitched cry. Chronic form with athetoid cerebral palsy, hearing loss, dental-enamel dysplasia, upward gaze palsy +/- cognitive impairment.

Miscellaneous
- Continue breastfeeding infants at least every 2 hours
- If dehydrated or nursing poorly, consider supplemental formula between nursing
- Can discontinue phototherapy when total serum bilirubin < 13-14 mg/dL.
- All jaundiced newborns discharged <48 hours need recheck within 2 days

References: Pediatrics, 2004; 114: 297-316 and e130-153 and Amer. Fam. Physician, 2002; 65: 599-606.

Adapted from the 2005 Childhood and Adolescent Immunization Schedule approved by the CDC, the AAP and the AAFP. Available at www.cdc.gov/nip/acip

General Immunization Guidelines

- Check immunization status every visit and immunize whenever possible
- Understand contraindications for the various immunizations
- No need to restart any vaccination schedule
- Catch-up vaccinations are given at least 4 weeks from the last dose with the exception of HBV_3, Hib_4 and PCV_4 for which the wait is at least 8 weeks and $DTaP_4$ and $DTaP_5$ for which the wait is at least 6 months.
- High-risk children include those with sickle cell disease, asplenia, HIV-positive, chronic cardiopulmonary diseases, hematologic malignancies, chronic renal failure, nephrotic syndrome, diabetes, transplant patients or any other immunocompromised state.

Recommended Childhood Immunization Schedule

Age	Vaccinations
Birth	• HBV_1
2 months	• $DTaP_1$, Hib_1, PCV_1, IPV_1, HBV_2
4 months	• $DTaP_2$, Hib_2, PCV_2, IPV_2
6 months	• $DTaP_3$, Hib_3, PCV_3, IPV_3[1], HBV_3[1]
12 –15 months	• $DTaP_4$, Hib_4, PCV_4, MMR_1 and Varicella[3]
2 years	• HAV[4] and PPV_1[5], PCV (catch-up)[2]
4 – 6 years	• $DTaP_5$, MMR_2, IPV_4, Tuberculosis skin test in high risk kids[6]
11-12 years	• dT[7], meningococcal conjugate vaccine (MCV-4)[8], Tdap[9]
Yearly	• Influenza[10]

DTaP = Diphtheria + tetanus toxoid and acellular pertussis, Hib = haemophilus influenzae type b, IPV = inactivated poliovirus, PCV = pneumococcal conjugate vaccine, PPV = pneumococcal polysaccharide vaccine, MMR = measles, mumps and rubella, HAV = hepatitis A virus and HBV = hepatitis B virus

1 – IPV_3 or HBV_3 can be given anytime between 6 – 18 months.

2 – For unvaccinated children 24 – 59 months old: 1 dose of PCV if healthy and 2 doses ≥ 2 months apart for high-risk children (see above list).

3 – Can be given at any visit after 12 months of age. 2 doses given 4 weeks apart for children ≥ 13 years

4 – Give to children at high risk for acquiring hepatitis A virus infection:

- Children living in AZ, AK, OR, NM, UT, WA, OK, SD, ID, NV or CA
- If county has ≥ 20 cases of hepatitis A virus infection/100,000 people/year
- If child has a clotting factor disorders or cirrhosis
- Travel to areas with high endemicity.
- 2nd dose of HAV given at least 6 months from 1st dose and after 30 months of age.

5 - 2 doses 5 years apart for sickle cell disease, asplenia, HIV +, or immunocompromised children who have completed the PCV series and only 1 dose for other high-risk children categories listed above.

6 – Indicated for close tuberculosis contacts, abnormal chest x-ray, immigration from or recent travel to Asia, Middle East, Africa or Latin America, residence in a high prevalence area or immunosuppressed patient.

7 – Given at 11 –12 years and every 10 years thereafter.

8 – Recommended for all adolescents age 11-12 yrs (or at least before high school), military recruits, college freshmen, functional asplenia, complement deficiency, HIV-positive or planned travel to endemic areas.

9 – Tetanus, diphtheria & pertussis booster vaccine at 11-12 years or catch-up vaccination up to 18 years.

10 –Vaccinate all children 6 - 23 months and all children with asthma, cardiac disease, sickle cell disease, HIV+, diabetes and household members of adults at high risk. Must give 2 doses separated by at least 4 weeks (intramuscular vaccine) or at least 6 weeks (intranasal vaccine) to children ≤ 8 years receiving the vaccine for the first time. Intranasal live attenuated influenza vaccine is an acceptable alternative for healthy persons 5-49 years of age. Contraindicated with egg allergy.

References: MMWR, 2002; 51 (RR2): 1-36. MMWR, 1999; 48 (RR12): 1-37. MMWR, 2000; 49(RR09): 1-38.

CDC=Centers for Disease Control. AAP=Amer. Acad. of Pediatrics. AAFP=Amer. Acad. of Family Practice

Risk Factors for Neonatal Sepsis
- Intrapartum: prolonged rupture of membranes >18 hours, intrapartum fever >38ºC or >38.5ºC (if epidural anesthesia used), clinical chorioamnionitis, sustained fetal tachycardia and meconium-stained amniotic fluid
- Group B streptococcal (GBS)-positive women with inadequate intrapartum antibiotic prophylaxis (IAP) (1 dose less than 4 hours prior to delivery).
- Prematurity, low birth weight, multiple births, fetal tachycardia or male sex
- History of prior infant with Group B streptococcal sepsis or mother with Group B streptococcal bacteriuria

Neonatal Exam in Neonatal Sepsis
- Temperature instability, respiratory distress, apneas or bradycardias, cyanotic episodes, lethargy, irritability, poor feeding, vomiting, hypoglycemia, unexplained jaundice, abdominal distension, poor perfusion, seizures, poor tone, high-pitched cry, nuchal rigidity or bulging fontanelle.

Laboratory Values Concerning for Neonatal Sepsis
- White blood count
  - < 5,000 or > 30,000 per µL
  - Immature/total neutrophil ratio > 0.2
  - Absolute neutrophil count < 1,000 per µL
- Platelet count < 150,000 per µL
- Chest x-ray with a focal infiltrate
- Positive blood culture
- Lumbar puncture (indicated for symptomatic newborns or if + blood culture)
  - Cerebrospinal fluid white blood cells >20 per mm^3, protein >65 mg/dL and glucose <50 mg/dL are worrisome for bacterial meningitis
- Urine culture (catheterized or suprapubic tap) for late-onset sepsis (> 7 days)

Role of C Reactive Protein (CRP) in the Neonatal Sepsis Work-up
- Serial CRP levels can help to exclude cases of neonatal sepsis
  - Serial CRP levels can be drawn at 12 and 36 hours of life and if both values are ≤ 1 mg/dL the negative predictive value for neonatal sepsis is 99%.
- Can allow early discontinuation of antibiotics if 2 CRP values 24 hours apart are ≤ 1 mg/dL (first level must be ≥ 12 hours of life).

The Asymptomatic Newborn Whose Mother is GBS+ and had Adequate IAP
- Recommend close observation in the hospital for at least 48 hours.
- Sepsis work-up only for worrisome clinical signs or risk factors as above.

Empiric Antibiotic Therapy for Neonatal Sepsis
- Cerebrospinal fluid normal
  - ampicillin 100 mg/kg IV q12h + gentamicin 2.5 mg/kg IV q12h
- Cerebrospinal fluid abnormal or unobtainable
  - ampicillin 150 mg/kg IV q12h + cefotaxime 50 mg/kg IV q12h

References: Pediatrics, 1999; 104: 447. Pediatrics, 2001; 108: 1094. Pediatrics, 2000; 106: 256. Inf. Dis. Clin. North Amer., 1999; 13: 711. Pediatrics, 1998; 102: 41. Pediatric Infectious Dis J, 2000; 19: 531. Pediatrics, 2000; 106: 256. Pediatrics, 2000; 106: 4 and AFP, 2003; 68: 1103-8.

Apgar Scoring

	Sign	0	1	2
A	Muscle tone	Flaccid	Arms & legs flexed	Active motion
P	Pulse (heart rate)	Absent	< 100	> 100
G	Grimace (reflex irritability)	No response	Grimace	Cough, pulls away, sneezes
A	Appearance (color)	Pale or central cyanosis	Peripheral cyanosis (acrocyanosis)	Completely pink
R	Respiratory effort	Absent	Slow, irregular	Good, crying

Newborn Resuscitation

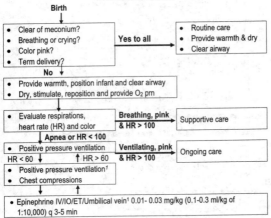

Birth

- Clear of meconium?
- Breathing or crying?
- Color pink?
- Term delivery?

Yes to all →
- Routine care
- Provide warmth & dry
- Clear airway

No ↓

- Provide warmth, position infant and clear airway
- Dry, stimulate, reposition and provide O$_2$ prn

- Evaluate respirations, heart rate (HR) and color

Breathing, pink & HR > 100 → Supportive care

Apnea or HR < 100 ↓

- Positive pressure ventilation

HR < 60 ↓   ↑ HR > 60

Ventilating, pink & HR > 100 → Ongoing care

- Positive pressure ventilation[1]
- Chest compressions

- Epinephrine IV/IO/ET/Umbilical vein[1] 0.01- 0.03 mg/kg (0.1-0.3 ml/kg of 1:10,000) q 3-5 min

[1] consider endotracheal intubation if + pressure ventilation ineffective here

Adapted with permission from Tarascon Pediatric Emergency Pocketbook, 4th Edition, Tarascon Publishing.

Pertinent Maternal History

- Gestational age at the time of delivery and adequacy of prenatal care
  ➤ If born before 34 weeks, did the mother receive 2 doses of steroids?
- Any complications during the pregnancy or intrapartum course?
  ➤ Preeclampsia, diabetes, hypertension, thyroid disease, collagen-vascular disease, isoimmunization, seizure disorder or infections such as HIV.
  ➤ Any evidence of chorioamnionitis?
- Any history of maternal tobacco, alcohol, prescription or illicit drug use?
- Group B streptococcus (GBS) culture status
  ➤ If GBS +, did the child receive adequate intrapartum antibiotic prophylaxis?
- Maternal blood type O or Rh negative?
- Hepatitis B surface antigen (HbsAg), Rubella, HIV and PPD status
- VDRL, chlamydia and gonococcal status
- Meconium staining during delivery?

The Newborn Exam

- General appearance: healthy or ill? term or preterm?
- Small(<10% for gestational age), average or large (>90% for gestational age)
- Normal vitals: axillary temp. 36.7-37.4°, respiratory rate < 60, heart rate 100-160
- Head: check fontanelles and suture lines, any cephalohematoma, molding, caput succedaneum or a "step off" that can represent a depressed skull fracture
- Eyes: check red reflex, corneal light reflex and spacing
- Ears: shape and position (low-set), skin tags or pits
- Nose: patency of nares (choanal atresia), any nasal flaring
- Mouth: color of lips, intact palate (cleft lip and/or palate) and symmetric movement of palate with crying
- Neck: masses, thyroid goiter or torticollis
- Chest: Pectus deformity, auscultation of lungs (grunting, retractions or stridor)
- Cardiac: rate, rhythm, any murmur(s), quality of femoral pulses
- Abdomen: 2 or 3 vessel umbilical cord, any masses or organomegaly
- Male genitalia: testes descended, urethral position, scrotal/groin masses
- Female genitalia: normal external female genitalia
- Anus: Assure patency and normal position
- Extremities: number of digits, Ortolani/Barlow maneuvers (hip stability) and check clavicles for a fracture
- Spine: any sacral dimple, cysts, sinus tracts, skin defects or tufts of hair
- Skin: color, perfusion, nevi, petechiae or other rashes
- Neurologic: Moro, grasp and suck reflexes, tone, symmetry of movement, any excessive jitteriness or irritability
- Dubowitz exam if gestational age unknown or in question

Health Maintenance

- 0.5% erythromycin ointment to both eyes (prevents ophthalmia neonatorum)
- 0.5-1 mg Vitamin K intramuscular injection (prevents hemorrhagic disease of the newborn)
- Check baby blood type and Coombs status if mother is blood type O.
- Newborn metabolic/genetic screen after 24 hours of life and before discharge

- Hepatitis B vaccination should be given within 12 hours of birth.
  > Hepatitis B immunoglobulin if mother HbsAg + (7 day window for Hepatitis B immunoglobulin if mother's HBsAg status is unknown)
- Hearing screen prior to discharge

Nutrition

- Encourage breastfeeding and provide tips to moms having difficulty nursing
- For formula-fed infants, the daily caloric needs for a healthy term infant is about 110 cal/kg/day which is approximately 5 ounces/kg/day.
  > Always hold the newborn for feedings. Do not prop a bottle up for feeds.

Miscellaneous
Prior to discharge the baby should have demonstrated the following:

- Passed a meconium stool
- Voided (often happens during delivery)
- Able to thermoregulate in an open crib
- Able to nurse or bottle feed successfully at least twice
- Stable vital signs for at least 12 hours
- No excessive jaundice
- No significant bleeding from the circumcision site (if done)
- Stable blood sugars (if large for gestational age or mother diabetic)
- No other social or medical concerns

Psychosocial Assessment
- **A public health nurse or social worker should be involved to help assess home safety and assist the family if any of the following risk factors exist:**
  > Have children been taken from their custody in the past?
  > Parental substance abuse
  > Family history of child abuse or neglect or domestic violence
  > Mental illness in a parent or caretaker
  > Unstable parental housing situation
  > Financial or food insecurity
  > Young maternal age < 18 years

Parental Education
- Keep sick visitors away from the baby for at least the first month of life.
- Avoid smoking in presence of baby
- Rear facing car seat secured in the back seat.
- Infants should sleep on their back or side ("Back to Sleep" Campaign).
- Avoid submersing baby in water until the cord has fallen off and always check the water temperature prior to starting any bath
- Soap should not be used on newborns more than every other day.
- Clean cord site with alcohol or water several times daily.
- Wipe female infants from front to back when cleaning the diaper area.
- No medical indication for circumcision of male newborns
- Parents should be instructed in how to properly use a bulb syringe and how to take a rectal temperature and seek medical care for any temperature>100.4ºF.
- Anticipatory guidance to help siblings adjust to new infant

References: Adapted from the American Academy of Pediatrics Practice Guideline for Hospital Stay for Healthy Term Newborns (Pediatrics, 1995; 96 (4): 788-90.)

- **Candidal diaper dermatitis** – bright red with sharp borders, satellite lesions and involves the intertriginous areas.
  - ➤ Antifungal creams
- **Capillary Hemangiomas** – red, elevated nodule comprised of multiple intertwined vessels typically on the face or trunk.
  - ➤ Often will enlarge during the first year and slowly regress in size
  - ➤ 90% spontaneously regress by age 9 years.
- **Cavernous hemangiomas** – large subcutaneous nodules also comprised of vessels that give the skin a bluish hue.
- **Cutis marmorata** – diffuse reticulated bluish-purple mottling of skin
  - ➤ Usually caused by cold exposure
- **Erythema toxicum neonatorum** – intense erythematous patches with a central yellowish papule
  - ➤ Occurs in up to 50% of newborns starting the first 10 days of life
  - ➤ Resolves spontaneously during the first two weeks of life
- **Harlequin color change** – differential coloration of dependent half of body when lying down (red) versus the non-dependent half (pale).
  - ➤ Most common in low birth weight babies
- **Irritant dermatitis** – generally a red, scaling papular rash of the diaper area sparing the intertriginous area without satellite lesions.
  - ➤ Treat with A&D ointment or diaper creams with zinc oxide & keep area dry.
- **Milia** – 1-2 mm whitish-yellow papules on the face from epithelial-lined cysts
  - ➤ Present at birth and resolve spontaneously after several months.
- **Miliaria rubra (or "prickly heat")** – 1-2 mm light red vesicles at intertriginous areas due to obstruction of sweat flow during hot weather.
  - ➤ Minimized with lightweight, loose clothing and avoidance of greasy creams
- **Mongolian spots** – slate grey to blue-black patch located over the lumbosacral area, buttocks and occasionally elsewhere, including the extremities.
  - ➤ Most common in African-american and Asian-american children
  - ➤ Typically fades by age 7 years
- **Neonatal acne** – papules and pustules on face of similar appearance as adolescent acne vulgaris
  - ➤ Usually develops during the first few weeks of life and resolves by 3 months.
- **Nevus Flammeus** (or "stork bite") – a salmon-colored patch at the nape of the neck, the glabella, forehead or upper eyelids. Fades over the first year.
- **Port Wine Stains** – purplish-red flat hemangioma present at birth.
  - ➤ Klippel-Trenaunay-Weber syndrome if associated with hemihypertrophy of an extremity or Sturge-Weber syndrome if the first branch of the trigeminal nerve is involved (risk of glaucoma and/or intracranial hemangiomas).
- **Sebaceous Gland Hyperplasia** – 1-2 mm yellowish papules on the nose and cheeks of newborns.
  - ➤ Spontaneous resolution by 2 months of age
- **Seborrheic dermatitis** (or "cradle cap") – pink patches with greasy yellow scale on face, intertriginous areas and scalp
  - ➤ Use baby oil and a soft brush for scalp lesions
  - ➤ Facial or body areas can be treated with 0.5% hydrocortisone cream daily.
- **Transient Neonatal Pustular Melanosis** – 2-4 mm yellowish pustules most often on the neck, forehead, lower back, abdomen and legs.
  - ➤ Rash presents at birth
  - ➤ Disappears in 1-2 days leaving light pigmented macules with a collarette of scale that eventually fade over the first 3 months.

Respiratory Distress
Signs: nasal flaring, grunting, retractions, tachypnea and/or cyanosis
Transient Tachypnea of the Newborn: most common respiratory disorder of term infants. Tachypnea occurs soon after birth & resolves in the first few hours of life.
- Chest x-ray may show some hyperinflation with fluid in the fissures.

Meconium Aspiration Syndrome (MAS): amniotic fluid usually with thick particulate meconium. Symptoms will begin in the first couple hours after birth and often worsen with time.
- Chest x-ray with hyperinflation, perihilar infiltrates +/- streaky atelectasis
- Babies at risk for pulmonary hypertension
- Careful DeLee suctioning of oropharynx after delivery of the head ↓ risk.
- Intubation and suctioning of the trachea immediately after delivery is indicated for all depressed babies.

Respiratory Distress Syndrome (RDS): occurs almost exclusively in premature infants < 35 weeks gestation.
- Chest x-ray with "ground glass" appearance and air bronchograms
- Often associated with apnea/bradycardia episodes.

Pneumonia: very rare in newborns
- Risk factors: untreated group B streptococcus-positive mother, chorioamniotis or prolonged rupture of membranes > 18 hours.
- Chest x-ray can mimic the appearance of RDS or MAS

Congenital Heart Disease (CHD)
Clinical presentation: may present with respiratory distress, cyanosis, difficulty feeding, sweating with feeds or poor weight gain (failure to thrive).
Acyanotic with Normal Pulmonary Blood Flow on Chest x-ray
- Bicuspid aortic valve, idiopathic hypertrophic subaortic stenosis, coarctation of aorta and pulmonic stenosis

Acyanotic with Increased Pulmonary Blood Flow on Chest x-ray
- Atrial septal defect, patent ductus arteriosus, ventricular septal defect and anomalous pulmonary venous return

Cyanotic with Decreased Pulmonary Blood Flow on Chest x-ray
- Tetralogy of Fallot

Cyanotic with Increased Pulmonary Blood Flow on Chest x-ray
- Truncus arteriosus, single ventricle, transposition of the great arteries and total anomalous pulmonary venous return
- **Atrial Septal Defect:** fixed split S$_2$ and systolic ejection murmur
- **Ventricular Septal Defect:** harsh systolic murmur at left sternal border
- **Patent Ductus Arteriosus:** differential cyanosis and continuous "machinery" murmur
- **Coarctation of the Aorta:** decreased femoral pulses

Ear/Nose/Throat Problems
- **Choanal atresia:** present with respiratory distress or poor feeding. Babies are pink while crying and cyanotic when calm
- **Cleft lip/palate:** presents with incomplete fusion of the lip and/or palate
  ➤ Referral for reconstructive surgery and speech therapist
- **Nasolacrimal duct obstruction:** presents with persistent tearing from eye
  ➤ Manage with nasolacrimal duct massage. Refer for surgery if lasts > 1 year.
- **Neck mass:** fetal goiter, cystic hygroma, thyroglossal duct cyst or sternocleidomastoid hematoma (will resolve spontaneously)
  ➤ Check thyroid studies and refer for surgery if nonthyroidal process.

Gastrointestinal Problems
- **Umbilical cord granuloma:** treat with silver nitrate applications
- **Umbilical hernia:** can refer for surgery if persists past age 4 yrs. Avoid taping.
- **Vomiting:** bilious or non-bilious? Overfeeding, gastroenteritis, reflux, brain lesion or congenital anomaly (e.g., pyloric stenosis, esophageal atresia, duodenal atresia or malrotation)
  - ➤ **Pyloric stenosis:** intractable, projectile vomiting < 2 months of age
    - o Diagnosis is by abdominal ultrasound or upper GI barium study
    - o May feel an "olive"-sized mass in epigastric area on exam
    - o Labs show a hypochloremic metabolic alkalosis
- **Gastroesophageal reflux:** 50-70% of infants have regurgitation. A minority have reflux with feeding refusal, hematemesis, anemia, failure to thrive, apparent life-threatening events (ALTE), recurrent pneumonia or bronchospasm
  - ➤ Interventions: if child doing well, reassure parents, use upright position and burping with feeds, can thicken milk or formula with rice cereal.
  - ➤ Consider an esophageal pH probe test for reflux with: ALTE, recurrent pneumonia, bronchospasm, chronic cough, apnea or chronic irritability
- **Delayed Passage of Meconium > 2 days**
  - ➤ Cystic fibrosis, meconium plug, imperforate anus or Hirschsprung's disease.

Genitourinary Problems
- **Scrotal/groin mass**
  - ➤ Inguinal hernia: usually does not transilluminate and involves canal
  - ➤ Hydrocele: transilluminates and confined to the scrotum
- **Undescended testes:** wait 12 months before surgical intervention
  - ➤ Consider checking a karyotype and refer to a pediatric urologist.

Hematologic Problems
- **Polycythemia:** presents with plethora, acrocyanosis or poor perfusion
  - ➤ Diagnosis: hematocrit (hct)>65% by venous blood draw
  - ➤ Treat with partial exchange transfusion or rehydration; transfusion indicated for hct>70% or if child is symptomatic (lethargic, poor feeding or tachypnea).

Metabolic Problems
- **Hypothermia:** rectal temperature < 36.4°
  - ➤ Usually from environmental losses and inadequate swaddling, but consider sepsis or congenital hypothyroidism in an ill baby.
  - ➤ Treat with rewarming in an incubator.
- **Hypoglycemia:** glucose < 40 mg/dL in a term infant
  - ➤ Signs: listless, hypotonia, jitteriness, seizure or poor feeding
  - ➤ Prematurity, sepsis, diabetic mom, perinatal hypoxia or low birth weight
  - ➤ Treat with frequent feeds or 10% dextrose in water intravenous drip
- **Hypocalcemia:** calcium < 8.0 mg/dL in a term infant
  - ➤ Signs: same as for hypoglycemia and tetany
  - ➤ Prematurity or mother with diabetes or hyperparathyroidism
  - ➤ Treat with 0.5 mL/kg IV/IM 10% calcium gluconate

Neurologic Problems
- **Spinal Dysraphism:** presents as a sacral mass +/- lower extremity weakness (meningocele or meningomyelocele) or as a dimple, dermal sinus or tuft of hair in the sacral area (spina bifida occulta)
  - ➤ An ultrasound of the lumbosacral spine is warranted for clinical suspicion

Ophthalmological Problems
- **Leukocoria:** presents as the absence of a red reflex in an eye
  - ➤ Congenital cataract or retinoblastoma

Adapted from the 2004 Amer. Academy of Pediatrics, Amer. Academy of Family Practice & Amer. Academy of Otolaryngology-Head and Neck surgery Guidelines for Acute Otitis Media & Otitis Media with Effusion

Definitions
- **Acute Otitis Media (AOM):** acute onset of signs and symptoms of an ear infection, fluid in the middle ear and signs of middle ear inflammation
- **Otitis Media with Effusion:** asymptomatic, uninfected fluid in the middle ear

Management of Acute Otitis Media (AOM)
- Observation for 48-72 h is an option for all children ≥ 2 yrs with nonsevere AOM or ≥ 6 months if nonsevere illness, uncertain diagnosis and follow-up ensured.
  ➤ Nonsevere illness is mild otalgia and fever <39°C (<102.2°F)
- Treat pain with acetaminophen and/or ibuprofen +/- topical benzocaine (if >5 yr)
- If symptoms worsening after 48-72 hrs, start antibiotics or change antibiotics.

Suggested Initial Empiric Oral Antibiotic Choices for AOM in Young Children
- Amoxicillin 80-90 mg/kg/d ÷ bid for temp <39ºC (<102.2ºF) & nonsevere otalgia
- Amoxicillin-clavulanate (Augmentin) 90 mg/kg/day of amoxicillin divided bid for temperature ≥39ºC (<102.2ºF) **or** severe otalgia
- Penicillin-allergic patients **without** a history of urticaria or anaphylaxis
  ➤ Cefuroxime axetil 30 mg/kg/day PO divided bid
  ➤ Cefdinir 14 mg/kg PO daily
  ➤ Cefprozil 30 mg/kg/day PO divided bid
  ➤ Cefpodoxime proxetil 10 mg/kg PO daily
- Penicillin-allergic patients **with** a history of an urticarial or anaphylactic reaction
  ➤ Azithromycin 10 mg/kg/day on day 1 then 5 mg/kg/day x 4 days
  ➤ Erythromycin-sulfisoxazole 50 mg/kg/day (based on erythromycin) divided qid
  ➤ Trimethoprim-sulfamethoxazole 6-10 mg/kg/day of trimethoprim divided bid

Suggested Antibiotics for Initial Antibiotic Failures after 48-72 hours
- Amoxicillin-clavulanate 90 mg/kg/d of amoxicillin divided bid
- Ceftriaxone 50 mg/kg IM daily x 3d (for Augmentin failures or penicillin allergies)

Duration of Antibiotic Therapy
- Traditional 10 d course for kids with severe AOM or < 5 yrs; except ceftriaxone
- Low-risk children ≥6 years with nonsevere AOM treated for 5-7 days.

Management of Recurrent AOM (≥ 4 episodes in a year)
- Minimize risk factors: passive smoke exposure, daycare, supine bottle feeding, pacifier use after 6 months of age and allergen exposure in atopic children
- Allergy control with intranasal steroids or antihistamines (if applicable)
- Influenza, pneumococcal and haemophilus influenzae vaccinations
- PO chemoprophylaxis: amoxicillin 20 mg/kg **or** sulfisoxazole 50 mg/kg daily

AOM with Pressure Equalizing Tubes or with Ruptured Tympanic Membrane
- 0.3% ofloxacin otic 5 drops in ear(s) bid (age<12 yrs) and 10 drops bid (>12 yrs)

Management of Otitis Media with Effusion (OME) in Children < 3 years
- Diagnosis by pneumatic otoscopy and tympanometry can confirm diagnosis
- Hearing eval. for OME ≥3 months, learning problems or hearing loss suspected. Test sooner if children at high risk for speech, language or learning problems.
  ➤ Bilateral hearing impairment of 20 decibels or worse is significant
- Language testing conducted for all children with ≥20 dB hearing impairment
- If no hearing impairment in low-risk child, recheck effusion every 3-6 months
- Treatment of OME ≥ 3 months **and** significant hearing impairment
  ➤ Tympanostomy tube insertion
  ➤ Adenoidectomy indicated only for nasal obstruction or chronic adenoiditis
- Treatments with **no proven benefit** for OME
  ➤ Antihistamines, decongestants, steroids, antibiotics or tonsillectomy

References: Pediatrics Infectious Dis. J, 1999; 18: 1. Pediatrics Infectious Dis. J, 1999, 18: 1152. Pediatrics Infectious Dis. J, 2001; 108: 239. Pediatrics, 2004; 113: 1451-65 and Pediatrics, 2004; 113: 1412-29.

Screening History

- History of chest discomfort?
- History of palpitations?
- History of syncope, near syncope or severe exertional lightheadedness?
- History of high blood pressure?
- Have you ever been knocked unconscious or suffered a concussion?
- Have you ever had a seizure?
- Do you ever get out of breath during exercise?
- Do you have any vision problems?
- Have you ever experimented with drugs, alcohol or cigarettes?
- Are you currently seeing a doctor for any reason?
- Are you currently taking any medication including performance-enhancing steroids or supplements?
- Do you have any allergies to medicines or bee stings?
- Is there any family history of sudden death or heart disease?
- Are there any weight requirements for your sport?
- For females: when was your last period and do you have monthly periods?
- Do you have any hearing problems?

Exam

- Blood pressure, height and weight
- Visual acuity
- Cardiovascular: diminished femoral pulses (coarctation of aorta), systolic murmur, irregular heart rhythm, pericardial rub
- Respiratory: wheezing or prolonged expiratory phase
- Abdomen: organomegaly
- Genitourinary: inguinal hernia and undescended testis
- Musculoskeletal: quick exam of joints and back (scoliosis)
- Skin: molluscum contagiosum, herpes simplex, impetigo, tinea corporis or scabies
- Signs of Marfan syndrome: long, thin digits, arm span > height and pectus carinatum/excavatum, hypermobile joints, long, thin face and myopia
- Down Syndrome: rule out atlantoaxial instability

Contraindications to Sports Participation

- Cardiac: active myocarditis or pericarditis, hypertrophic cardiomyopathy, severe uncontrolled hypertension, possible coronary artery disease and uncontrolled ventricular dysrhythmias
- Neurologic: symptoms of postconcussive syndrome (no contact sports), poorly controlled epilepsy (no swimming, weight lifting, sports at height), recurrent neck and upper extremity dysesthesias/paresthesias (no contact sports)
- Splenomegaly or acute infectious mononucleosis within the last 3-4 weeks (avoid contact sports)
- Skin infections as above (no sports with skin-to-skin contact)
- Marfan syndrome (no contact sports)
- Sickle cell disease (no contact or high exertion sports)
- Atlantoaxial instability which is common in Down syndrome and rheumatoid arthritis (no tumbling, diving or contact sports)

References: American Family Physician, 2000; 61: 2683-90.

Adapted from the American Academy of Pediatrics Recommendations for Preventive Pediatric Health Care

Frequency of Well Child Checks
- Daily newborn care in the hospital
- Initial clinic visit: 2-3 days if discharged before 24 hours, any jaundice, exclusively breastfed infants or presence of any other medical/social risk factor.
- Follow-up clinic visits: 2 weeks then at months 2, 4, 6, 9, 12, 15, 18 and 24, then at years 3, 4, 5, 6 and 8 and then annually from year 10 to 21.

Interval History
- Assessed at every visit
- Interval infections since last visit
- Diet including iron and fluoride intake and Vitamin D (in breastfed infants)
- Middle childhood: school performance, hobbies, exercise + family dynamics
- Adolescents: as above and involvement in after school or community activities, use of drugs, tobacco and alcohol and whether they are sexually active

Measurements
- Height and weight at every visit
- Head circumference at every visit until 2 years of age.
- Blood pressure (BP) measurement at every visit beginning at 3 years of age.
  - ➤ BP standards are based on gender, age and height.
  - ➤ BP tables at www.nhlbi.nih.gov/guidelines/hypertension/child_tbl.pdf or in The Fourth Report on the Diagnosis, Evaluation and Treatment of High Blood Pressure in Children and Adolescents (Pediatrics, 2004; 114: 555-76)
- Childhood obesity if > 95% body mass index
  - ➤ Nutritional counseling and referral to weight management program
- Malnourished if < 5% weight-for-height
  - ➤ Dietary counseling, frequent weight checks, consider visiting nurse or public health nurse evaluation of home and social situation
- Short stature if < 5% height for age (unless constitutional based on calculated mid-parental height)
  - ➤ Consider work up for short stature unless constitutional delay is suspected.
- Failure to thrive if chronic poor weight gain causes the child to cross 2 lines on the child's growth curve in a 6 month period.
  - ➤ See Failure to Thrive section (page 183)

Vision Screening
- Red reflexes assessed in newborns to screen for congenital cataracts or retinoblastomas
- Strabismus screening: corneal light reflex test at 12 months and cover/uncover test or photoscreening at 3 years of age or earlier if history or exam suggests strabismus (see section on Strabismus and Amblyopia on page 207)
- **When to refer patients to an ophthalmologist:**
  - ➤ Any infants with white reflex on fundoscopic exam
  - ➤ An abnormal corneal light reflex, cover/uncover or photoscreening test
  - ➤ Visual acuity of 20/40 or poorer (20/30 or poorer if ≥6 years old)
  - ➤ 2 line visual acuity difference on the Snellen chart between the two eyes

Hearing Screening
- Universal screening of all newborns for hearing impairment using either evoked otoacoustic emissions or auditory brainstem response testing.
- Repeat screening audiograms at each visit from age 4 to 10 years.
- Referral to an audiologist for
  - All abnormal newborn hearing screens, speech delay or significant parental concerns over child's ability to hear
  - Hearing impairment if ≥ 25 decibels at one or more frequencies.

Immunizations
- See section on Childhood Immunizations (page 186)

Anemia (see anemia section (page 173 for details on diagnosis and treatment)
- Screen all children with hemoglobin check at 12 months of age.
- Children at high-risk for iron-deficiency anemia (low-income families, Women, Infants and Children (WIC)-eligible children, immigrant children, ex-preemies, breastfed infants with insufficient supplemental iron & children with chronic inflammatory or infectious conditions) should also be screened at 18 months, yearly from age 2-5 years and adolescents during puberty.
- Prevention and treatment of iron-deficiency should start with dietary changes.

Metabolic Screening
- Universal newborn screen tests for hypothyroidism, hemoglobinopathies, galactosemia, phenylketonuria and possibly more depending on the state.

Screening Urinalysis
- Screens for hematuria, proteinuria, glucosuria and asymptomatic bacteriuria
- Initial test at 5 years of age
- Repeat annually in sexually active adolescent males and females

Lead Screening
- Lead level for high-risk infants at 12 & 24 mo.; 36-72 mo. if not previously done.
- Public health nurse home evaluation for all confirmed high levels.

Screening for Tuberculosis (Tb)
- All children should have a tuberculosis skin test placed prior to entering school
- Annual testing for HIV-infected children beginning at 1 year of age.
- Prior bacillus Calmette-Guerin (BCG) vaccination is **not** a contraindication to PPD testing.
- Testing every 2-3 years for children exposed to high-risk adults beginning at 1 year of age (adults with documented Tb, HIV-infected, intravenous drug users, homeless, recently incarcerated adults and the children of migrant workers).

Cholesterol Screening
- Screen children with a family history of premature cardiovascular disease, cerebrovascular disease, peripheral vascular disease, diabetes or hyperlipidemia; also screen if children are obese, have diabetes or smoke.
- Initiate screening by checking a total cholesterol as early as 2 years of age.
- If total cholesterol ≥ 200 mg/dL → check a lipoprotein analysis

- Dietary intervention for LDL-cholesterol ≥ 130 mg/dL
  - Initiate American Heart Association Therapeutic Lifestyle Changes diet
  - Regular aerobic exercise and weight reduction program
  - Recheck lipoprotein analysis in 6 months
  - Consider drug therapy for children >10 years with **either** a worrisome family history and LDL-cholesterol ≥160 mg/dL despite a trial of diet and exercise for 6 months **or** if LDL-cholesterol >190 mg/dL regardless of family history.
  - First choice is a bile acid sequestrant (e.g., cholestyramine or colestipol)
  - Second choice is a statin for children over 6 years old; follow liver panel.

Screening in Sexually-Active Adolescent Women
- Annual pelvic exam and pap smears
- Annual screen for chlamydia (even if asymptomatic) +/- gonorrhea
- Consider screening for other sexually transmitted diseases if clinically indicated

Fluoride Supplementation
- Indicated between 6 months-16 years for children who do not drink fluoridated water or if fluoride content of drinking water is < 0.6 ppm.

Dietary Fluoride Supplementation Schedule

	Concentration of Fluoride in Water in Parts per Million (ppm)		
Age	< 0.3 ppm	0.3-0.6 ppm	> 0.6 ppm
Birth-6 months	0	0	0
6 mo-3 years	0.25 mg	0	0
3-6 years	0.5 mg	0.25 mg	0
6-16 years	1.0 mg	0.5 mg	0

Screening for Scoliosis (see section on Scoliosis, page 204)
- Screen each visit for school age children: examine for curved spine, uneven hip or waist crease, uneven nipple line or uneven shoulders.
  - Scoliosis x-ray series and orthopedic referral for abnormal exam

Injury and Violence Prevention
- Avoid prone sleeping position to prevent (SIDS): "Back to Sleep" initiative
- Advise against spanking as a method of discipline
- Traffic safety: rear-facing car seats until 12 months **and** ≥ 20 pounds, front-facing car seats between 1-4 years **and** ≥ 40 pounds, seat belts and booster seats for kids 4-8 years old until they are > 6 years, ≥ 4'9" **and** ≥ 80 pounds.
- Prevention of falls/accidents: stairway gates, window locks, cabinet latches, outlet guards, fences around pools/spas, poisons and firearms locked away.
- Burn prevention: smoke detectors and water heater set < 130°F
- Safety helmets & protective gear for biking, skateboarding & in-line skating
- Keep Poison Control number (1-800-222-1222) accessible. Avoid ipecac.
- Sunscreen use
- Screen children for depression
- Discuss sex, drugs, alcohol and driving with adolescents.
- Ask adolescents about gang involvement or if they have ever used a weapon.

Dental Health
- Dental referral at 3 years
- Avoid bedtime bottle
- Brush teeth and gums and floss daily by 12 months of age

Anticipatory guidance: the topics outlined for anticipatory guidance during a visit are new areas to be addressed and build off the areas discussed during prior visits.

Growth and Development: the developmental milestones will occur within a certain time interval and the following ages serve as a rough average within this time period. Refer to Denver Developmental screen for more details.

Normal Growth of Infants and Children
- In general, infants/children should grow along their individual growth curves
  - Pediatric growth charts available from the Centers for Disease Control at: www.cdc.gov/nchs/about/major/nhanes/growthcharts/clinical_charts.htm

Average Weight Changes at Different Ages
- Regains birthweight (BW) by 2 weeks, doubles BW by 5-6 months, triples BW by 12 months and quadruples BW by 24 months of age.
- 2 weeks-3 months→ weight increases about 1 ounce daily
- 3-12 months→ weight increases about 1/2 ounce daily or 1 pound/month
- 12-24 months→ weight increases about 1/2 pound/month

Average Height Changes at Different Ages
- Infants double birth length (BL) by 3-4 years and triple BL by 13 years
- 0-12 months→ average height increase is about 10 inches
- 12-24 months→ average height increase is about 5 inches
- 24-36 months→ average height increase is about 3 1/2 inches
- 3 years-puberty→ average height increase is about 2 inches/year

Average Head Circumference at Different Ages
- 0-3 months→ head circumference increases about 2 cm/month
- 4-6 months→ head circumference increases about 1 cm/month
- 6-12 months→ head circumference increases about 1/2 cm/month
- 12-24 months→ head circumference increases about 2 cm

Two Week Check
Anticipatory Guidance
- Diet: breast milk or formula only. Avoid honey until 1 year. Do not use the microwave to warm formula in bottles.
- Behavior: hiccups, sneezing, startle response all normal. Normal stooling patterns can vary from 1-10 bowel movements a day at this age.
- Safety: car seat faces backwards, sleep supine, avoid smoke exposure
- Equipment needs: bulb syringe, thermometer, smoke detector. Seek attention if rectal temperature is ≥100.4∘F.
- Family issues: respite care and support for caretaker(s)

Growth and Development
- Motor: lifts head momentarily when prone, regards face, symmetric movements
- Language: startles to loud sounds
- Vision screening: infants should be able to track to midline by 2 weeks of age.

Two Month Check
Anticipatory Guidance
- Diet: upright feeding position, no solids until at least 4-6 months. Vitamin D 200 IU/day (e.g., Poly-Vi-Sol 0.5-1 mL PO daily) for exclusively breastfed infants until they ingest at least 500 mL/day vitamin-D fortified milk (or formula).
- Behavior: crying is to indicate wants or represents colic
- Safety: crib sides up, sunscreen/hats, bath water temperature
- Stimulation: mobiles, music, reading to baby, talking to baby
- Family issues: father involved. Need time alone for parents

Growth and Development
- Motor: lifts head 45° when prone
- Language: starting to vocalize, responsive smile, attentive to voices
- Vision screening: children should be able to track past midline by 2 months.

Four Month Check
Anticipatory Guidance
- Diet: the American Academy of Pediatrics encourages exclusive breastfeeding until 6 months; however, if parents insist they may start rice cereal. Avoid a bottle in bed, egg whites or fluid milk products.
- Behavior: teething (1st teeth between 4-12 months), drooling
- Safety: falls, choking on small items
- Stimulation: rattles, floor play, encourage vocalizations, sibling play

Growth and Development
- Motor: head steady when upright, follows objects past midline, can bring hands together, grasps rattle, holds bottle
- Language: laughs, squeals, spontaneous smile, coos, orients to voice
- Vision screening: children should be able to track objects 180° by 4 months.

Six Month Check
Anticipatory Guidance
- Diet: pureed food, supplemental fluoride if either breastfed or fluoride is not present in the drinking water, limit juices
- Behavior: stranger anxiety, bedtime schedule, fear of separation
- Safety: gates for stairs, latches on cupboards, no walkers, cover all electrical outlets
- Stimulation: rattles, read board books, talking to baby

Growth and Development
- Motor: rolls over, sits without support, reaches for objects and able to transfer objects between hands
- Language: turns to sound, babbles

Nine Month Check
Anticipatory Guidance
- Diet: introduce infant cup, finger foods, spoon use. Avoid soda pop
- Behavior: bedtime and nap schedules, wear shoes, brush gums/teeth
- Safety: poisons locked away, poison control number (1-800-222-1222), reliable babysitters, climbing hazards, choking danger
- Stimulation: blocks, interactive simple games, reading to baby

Nine Month Growth and Development
- Gross motor: crawls or scoots, pulls to stand and bangs 2 cubes together
- Fine motor: feeds self cracker and pincer grasp
- Language: nonspecific paired consonants (baba, mama, dada) and jabbers
- Social: plays peek-a-boo or pat-a-cake and waves "bye bye"

One Year Check
Anticipatory Guidance
- Diet: whole milk and eggs okay, wean bottle, limit sweets and brush teeth.
- Behavior: set limits, consistency in house rules, shoes, no spanking
- Safety: front-facing car seat if child over 20 pounds

Growth and Development
- Gross motor: cruises, walks holding on and drinks from cup
- Fine motor: good pincer grasp with both hands
- Language: dada, mama specific

Fifteen Month Check
Anticipatory Guidance
- Behavior: temper tantrums, feeds self, understands "no"
- Safety: doors, choking, sunburn, falls
- Stimulation: introduce body parts, play naming games and read books

Growth and Development
- Gross motor: walks well, stoops and recovers and climbs stairs
- Fine motor: scribbles and stacks 2 blocks
- Language: 3 words (excluding dada/mama) & indicates wants without crying

Eighteen Month Check
Anticipatory Guidance
- Diet: avoid junk foods, soda, reinforce dental hygiene
- Behavior: difficulty sharing, independence, sleep fears, self comfort, toilet training readiness (dry naps, can walk and pull pants up/down, can signal when he/she needs to use the bathroom and wants to use a potty chair)
- Safety: street/water safety

Growth and Development
- Gross motor: walks backwards, climbs onto chair and removes a garment
- Fine motor: feeds self with spoon and stacks 3 cubes
- Language: 7-20 words and points to 3 body parts

Two Year Check
Anticipatory Guidance
- Diet: encourage regular meals with family and flossing teeth. Change to 2% milk. May start to brush teeth with a small amount of fluoridated toothpaste.
- Behavior: temper tantrums, defiance
- Safety: knives, electric equipment, constant adult supervision
- Stimulation: peer play, painting, crayons, reading

Growth and Development
- Gross motor: runs well, throws and kicks a ball, puts on clothing and goes up and down steps alone
- Fine motor: stacks 4 cubes, imitates housework and draws a vertical line
- Language: At least 20 words and making 2 word phrases
- Social: begins playing well with others

Three Year Check
Anticipatory Guidance
- Diet: first dental exam, avoid sweets and soda pop
- Behavior: night fears, fantasy play, better with sharing
- Discipline: time out
- Safety: matches, fire safety, firearms must be locked away, bike helmet
- Stimulation: play groups and preschool, limit television (1-2 hours/day)

Three Year Growth and Development
♦ Gross motor: rides tricycle, dresses with help and broad jumps
♦ Fine motor: stacks 6-8 cubes and can wiggle thumbs
♦ Social: can pretend play
♦ Language: 3 words sentences, knows name & age, 75% of speech intelligible.
♦ Objective visual acuity testing at 3 years of age and repeated each visit until 10 years of age and thereafter if the history suggests visual impairment.

Four Year Check
Anticipatory Guidance
• Behavior: imagination, lying, imitates adults, curiousness
• Safety: avoid adult themes on TV, stranger caution, booster chair when they have outgrown their car seat and are ≥40 pounds until they are 8 years old **or** > 6 years and at least 4'9" and 80 pounds. Avoid having a child in the front seat, especially if an airbag is present. Teach pedestrian safety skills.
• Stimulation: TV alternatives, drawing, outdoor activities
Growth and Development
♦ Gross motor: hops, dresses without help, balances on one foot
♦ Fine motor: copies a circle & cross, buttons clothes and draws a 3-part person
♦ Language: 4 word sentences, knows 3-4 colors and speech 100% intelligible

Five Year Check
Anticipatory Guidance
• Diet: importance of breakfast
• Behavior: school readiness, separation anxiety, importance of sleep; praise child for cooperation and positive accomplishments
• Safety: knows home address/phone number, sexual abuse, playground safety
• Stimulation: school activities
Growth and Development
♦ Gross motor: skips and can heel-to-toe walk
♦ Fine motor: draws a person with at least 6 body parts and copies a square
♦ Language: speaks in simple conversations and knows full name

Grade school Years
Anticipatory Guidance
• Behavior: early sex education, chores, manners
• Safety: helmet use, reinforce street/water/fire safety, seat belts
• Stimulation: reading, exercise, after school activities
Growth and Development
♦ Gross motor: rides bicycle, climbs well, bathes self
♦ Fine motor: cuts with scissors, can draw and paste
♦ Social: participates in school and group activities

Middle School Years
Anticipatory Guidance
• Diet: avoid junk foods, address obesity and eating disorders
• Behavior: sex education, sexually transmitted disease education, drug use, smoking and high risk behaviors
• Safety: helmet use, drug use, seat belts, firearms
• Stimulation: encourage goal setting, exercise, after school activities and encourage community involvement.

SIDS = sudden infant death syndrome and LDL = low-density lipoprotein

References: Pediatrics, 2000; 105 (3): 645. Pediatrics, 1994; 94 (4): 566-7. Pediatrics, 1998; 101 (1): 141-7. MMWR, 1998; 47 (RR-3): 1-36. Pediatrics, 1999; 103 (1): 173-81 and Pediatrics, 2004; 114: 555-76.

Croup (or Laryngotracheobronchitis)
- **Clinical Features**
  - Affects children with peak ages 6 months to 3 years in fall-winter.
  - Barky cough, inspiratory stridor, hoarseness, fever and coryza.
  - Causes: parainfluenza 1, 3, respiratory syncytial virus (RSV) or adenovirus
  - Neck x-rays with subglottic narrowing ("steeple sign") and normal epiglottis
- **Management of Croup**
  - Cool mist humidifier
  - Steroids: dexamethasone 0.15-0.6 mg/kg/day orally or intramuscularly **or** budesonide 2 mg nebulized daily for 2-3 days total therapy
  - Racemic epinephrine 0.05 mL/kg/dose (max dose 0.5 mL) in 3 mL normal saline nebulized for moderate-severe croup
  - Antipyretics and encourage oral hydration
  - Clinical improvement and no stridor after 3 hrs of observation for moderate-severe croup can be managed as an outpatient with daily follow-up.
  - Admission criteria include any of the following: stridor at rest, ill-appearing, moderate-severe symptoms despite therapy or significant parental concerns

Bronchiolitis
- **Clinical Features**
  - Fever, coryza, congestion, cough +/- wheezing and feeding difficulties
  - More severe cases can exhibit nasal flaring, grunting, retractions and apnea
  - Exam: fine rales, diffuse wheezing +/- and signs of severity as above
  - Chest x-ray: hyperinflation, patchy infiltrates and/or atelectasis
  - Causes: RSV, parainfluenza, adenovirus, mycoplasma and influenza B.
  - Risk Factors: prematurity, low birth weight, crowded living conditions, day care, passive smoke exposure, bottle fed infants, ill contacts, winter-spring.
  - Rule out foreign body aspiration especially for focal findings on exam/CXR.
- **Prevention of RSV infection**
  - Palivizumab (monoclonal antibody) 15 mg/kg monthly from November to March for high-risk infants: <2 years with chronic lung disease requiring treatment in prior 6 months; ex-preemie ≤28 weeks until 12 months old; ex-preemie 29-32 weeks until 6 months old; exposed kids with severe immunodeficiency syndrome.
- **Management of Bronchiolitis**
  - Hospitalize for respiratory distress, hypoxia, dehydration or high-risk < 6 mo.
  - Nasopharyngeal swab for RSV antigen for isolation purposes if hospitalized.
  - Apnea monitoring indicated for moderate-severe bronchiolitis.
  - Droplet isolation and careful handwashing for all close contacts.
  - Albuterol 0.15 mg/kg/dose benefit equivocal. Can use if clinical response.
  - Racemic epinephrine 0.05-0.1 mL/kg/dose nebulized may be beneficial.
  - No role for steroids in most cases (unclear benefit for the intubated infant).
  - Consider ribavirin for high-risk infants (chronic heart or lung disease, cystic fibrosis, < 6 weeks or immunocompromised) with severe bronchiolitis.
  - Mainstay of therapy is hydration, supplemental oxygen and suction.

Upper Respiratory Tract Infections in Children
- **Clinical Features**
  - Cough, rhinorrhea (frequently mucopurulent) and low-grade fever
  - Exam: non-toxic, no increased work of breathing, unremarkable exam
- **Management**
  - Educate parents that antibiotics are not indicated for the common cold
  - Bulb syringe to suction out nose, may use a humidifier near the bed
  - The use of decongestants and antitussives (codeine or dextromethorphan) for symptomatic relief for infants > 6 months of questionable benefit.

References: J. Pediatrics, 1999; 135(2): 45. Pediatric Clinic North Amer., 1999; 46 (6): 1167. NEJM, 2001; 344 (25): 1917. Ped. Inf. Dis. J., 2002; 21: 873. Pediatrics, 2001; 108(3): 52 & AFP, 2004; 69: 535 and 325.

Definition
- Lateral curvature of the spine as measured by the Cobb angle > 10 degrees usually accompanied by some degree of vertebral spine rotation.

Classification of Scoliosis
Idiopathic Scoliosis
- Infantile form: 2 months - 3 years, left sided thoracic, male predominance
- Juvenile form: onset between 3-10 years of age, high risk of progression.
- Adolescent form: onset after 10 years of age (80% of all scoliosis cases).

Secondary Scoliosis
- Systemic disorders: Ehlers-Danlos or Marfan syndromes or homocystinuria
- Neurologic syndromes: tethered cord, syringomyelia, neurofibromatosis, muscular dystrophy, cerebral palsy, poliomyelitis, Friedreich's ataxia, Riley-Day syndrome or Werdnig-Hoffman disease.

Evaluation of Scoliosis
- Red flags: significant back pain or marked spine stiffness, a left thoracic curve, an abnormal neurologic examination, sudden rapid progression in a previously stable curve and onset before 8 years of age.
  > These patients (and those with infantile or juvenile scoliosis) should be referred to a pediatric orthopedist & have a MRI study of the spine
- Routine scoliosis screening with an Adam's forward bending test should begin by 8 -10 years and end at 16 years. Routine school screening is controversial.
  > The Adam's forward bending test screens for a rotational deformity.
- A scoliometer placed in the midline at the vertebral level of maximum rib prominence measures the angle of thoracic rotation.
  > An angle of thoracic rotation > 5-6 degrees requires a work-up.
- Tanner staging should be determined once scoliosis identified.
- A standing posteroanterior spine radiograph to measure the curve using the Cobb method and to determine the Risser stage for all abnormal exams.

Risk of Spinal Curve Progression

Cobb angle (degrees)	Risser Stage	Risk of progression	Referral/Management
10 - 19	2 - 4	5 – 15%	X-ray every 6 months
10 - 19	0 - 1	15 – 40%	X-ray every 6 months
20 - 29	2 - 4	10 – 30%	Refer if curve > 25°
20 - 29	0 - 1	40 – 70%	Refer if curve > 25°
29 – 40	2 - 4	40 – 70%	Refer
29 – 40	0 - 1	70 – 90%	Refer
> 40	0 - 4	Not applicable	Refer

Management of Scoliosis
- Patients with spinal curves < 25° can be followed with serial scoliosis x-ray series every 6 months.
- Controversy exists about the benefit of bracing children with moderate curves between 25 – 40%.
- General consensus that surgery should be performed for curves > 40°.

References: Amer. Fam. Physician, 2001; 64: 111-6 and Amer. Fam. Physician, 2002; 65: 1817-22.

Febrile Seizures Definition
- Simple febrile seizure: a generalized seizure lasting <15 minutes in a febrile child between 6 months and 5 years old who is neurologically normal and has no evidence of meningitis, metabolic disturbance or recent trauma.
- Complex febrile seizure: duration >15 minutes, focal or recurrent within 24 hrs.

Management of Febrile Seizures
- Airway, Breathing, Circulation
- Benzodiazepines indicated for prolonged seizures (>15 minutes)
  - Lorazepam 0.05-0.1 mg/kg intravenous push x 1 **or**
  - Diazepam 0.5 mg/kg to max of 5 mg per rectum (2-5 yrs); 0.3 mg/kg (6-11 yrs); 0.2 mg/kg (>11 yrs): may repeat x 1 in 5-10 minutes if seizures persist.
- Antipyretics
- Search for underlying source of infection and treat accordingly
- No lumbar puncture needed for **simple** febrile seizures with a normal neurologic exam, hemodynamically stable, no petechiae and no nuchal rigidity.

Long-term treatment of children after a simple febrile seizure
- The American Academy of Pediatrics recommends against either continuous or intermittent anticonvulsant therapy in children with simple febrile seizures.
- Antipyretics may be given to a febrile child to increase their comfort, but these have never been shown to decrease the chance of a recurrent febrile seizure.
- Option to use diazepam 0.5 mg/kg PO (max 5 mg) at onset of a febrile illness.

Evaluation of the Child with a First Nonfebrile Seizure
- Applies to children ages 1 month to 21 years of age
- No history of epilepsy, trauma, signs of meningitis or metabolic disturbance
- Exclusion of breath-holding spells, syncope, gastroesophageal reflux, pseudoseizures, complex migraines, night tremors or micturitional shivering
- Laboratory tests: consider sodium, glucose, calcium +/- urine drug screen
- Lumbar puncture: no role unless patient has a focal neurologic exam, nuchal rigidity, is a child < 6 months or has a prolonged altered mental status.
- Electroencephalogram should be performed >48 hours post-seizure in every child in awake and sleep states and with hyperventilation and photic stimulation.
- Neuroimaging
  - An emergent CT scan for children with a prolonged Todd's paralysis (postepileptic hemiparesis) or prolonged postictal state for several hours.
  - A nonurgent MRI scan for any child with an abnormal neurologic exam, an unexplained cognitive impairment, focal seizures, children ≤ 1 year of age and those with an abnormal electroencephalogram that does **not** show benign partial epilepsy of childhood or primary generalized epilepsy pattern.

Treatment of Children after a Nonfebrile Seizure
- Antiepileptic drugs (AEDs) can ↓ the risk of a seizure recurrence by about 50%.
  - The first-line antiepileptics (phenobarbital, phenytoin, valproic acid and carbamazepine) have unacceptable physical side effects 20-30% of time.
  - Long-term AED use may cause cognitive, behavioral & psychosocial effects.
- Seizure remission is the same whether AEDs are started after the first or second unprovoked seizure; may start AEDs after the 1st or 2nd seizure.
- Antiepileptic treatment does not decrease the risk of developing epilepsy.
- Safety issues: bicycle on sidewalk, use helmet, swim only with a partner, avoid bathtubs, no driving unless seizure free for 2 years, avoid activities where a fall from height is possible.

References: Pediatrics, 1999; 103(6): 1307-9. Neurology, 2000; 55: 616-23 & Neurology, 2003; 60: 166-75.

Definition: definitive urinary tract infection (UTI) based on a positive urine culture.
- Suprapubic aspirate with ≥1,000 colonies (cfu)/mL, catheter urine with ≥10,000 cfu/mL or clean catch urine with ≥100,000 cfu/mL of a single organism.
- Urine cultures from plastic bags or other non-sterile specimens are unreliable.
- Urinalysis for UTI
  ➢ Positive nitrite: 53% sensitivity and 85-98% specificity
  ➢ Positive leukocyte esterase (LE): 83% sensitivity and 78% specificity
  ➢ Positive gram stain of unspun urine: 81% sensitivity and 83% specificity
  ➢ Any positive nitrite or LE or bacteriuria: 99.8% sensitivity & 70% specificity

Bacteriology of childhood urinary tract infections
- > 80% E. coli > klebsiella > proteus or enterococcus or Group B streptococcus

Suggested management of children ≤ 6 years with first urinary tract infection
- Recommend inpatient management if: < 3 months of age, ill-appearing, inability to take oral medications **or** any concern about safe outpatient management.
  ➢ Empiric antibiotics until culture results known: ampicillin and gentamicin
  ➢ Discharge criteria: afebrile > 24h, normal white blood count and eating well
- Outpatient management possible if > 3 months and well-appearing
  ➢ Empiric antibiotics should be guided by local E. coli and klebsiella resistance data until culture results and sensitivities are known.
  ➢ Antibiotic options include: oral trimethoprim-sulfamethoxazole (> 2 months), cefixime, cefpodoxime, cefprozil, loracarbef or cephalexin or ceftriaxone 50 mg/kg IM daily (> 1 month) until culture results and sensitivities known.

Duration of antibiotics for treatment of urinary tract infections
- < 3 months: 14 days of total antibiotics
- < 2 years with pyelonephritis: 14 days of total antibiotics
- < 2 years with uncomplicated UTI: 10 days of total antibiotics
- > 2 years with uncomplicated UTI: 3 days of total antibiotics

Imaging studies for urinary tract infections
- Indicated for all boys regardless of age, all girls < 5 years and for recurrent UTIs
- Continue prophylactic antibiotics until imaging studies are completed.
- Renal and bladder ultrasound: examine for hydroureter, hydronephrosis, bladder trabeculations or diverticula, duplicated collecting system, posterior urethral valves or stones
- Voiding cystourethrogram (VCUG): analyze for vesicoureteral reflux (VUR)
  ➢ Initial study may be performed as soon as the urine is sterile.
  ➢ Repeat VCUG q2 years for grade 1-3 VUR and q3 years for grade 4-5 VUR
- Radionuclide cystography: may be performed instead of a VCUG to follow VUR
  ➢ Radiation exposure 1% that of a conventional VCUG
- ^{99m}Tc dimercaptosuccinic acid (DMSA) scan: can differentiate pyelonephritis from simple cystitis & can detect renal scarring 3-6 months after UTI treatment.
  ➢ Can **not** distinguish pyelonephritis from renal scarring during acute infection

Prophylactic antibiotics
- Indicated for any degree of VUR (until resolved), for recurrent UTIs and consider in children < 2 years with pyelonephritis (especially if DMSA scan reveals renal scarring)
- Best options: trimethoprim-sulfamethoxazole (>2 months) or nitrofurantoin

References: Pediatrics, 1999; 103: 843. Clinics of Family Practice, 2003; 5: 367. Pediatrics, 2005; 115: 426 and 1999 Cincinnati Children's Hospital Clinical Practice Guidelines at www.cincinnatichildrens.org.

Recommended Ages for Attempting Ocular Alignment Screening Tests
- **Age 6-24 months**: Hirschberg corneal light reflex test. The reflection should fall in the same location in the cornea of each eye.
- **3-4 years**: Cover/uncover test
- **5-6 years**: Snellen visual acuity test

Indications for Referral to an Ophthalmologist
- Visual acuity ≤ 20/40 for kids 3-5 years or ≤ 20/30 for kids ≥ 6 years.
- Any eye movement seen on the cover/uncover test suggests strabismus.
- Any child with a white reflex behind the eye (leukocoria).

Strabismus
- **Definition:** constant (tropias) or intermittent (phorias) eye deviation that causes malalignment of the visual axis and dysconjugate gaze.
  - ➤ Deviation lateral (exotropia), medial (esotropia) and vertical (hypertropia)
  - ➤ Intermittent deviations are respectively exophoria, esophoria & hyperphoria.
- **Pathophysiology:** The brain suppresses the visual input from the strabismic eye to allow for a clearer image beginning at ≥ 3 months of age.
- If this preferential suppression of visual input persists beyond age 5-6 years, children develop monocular vision loss (amblyopia).
- Strabismus surgery **before age 6** once the visual acuity goal is reached.

Treatment of Accommodative Strabismus
- Optical correction of astigmatism or hyperopia (farsightedness) with glasses results in ocular convergence and thus corrects accommodative strabismus.

Amblyopia
- **Definition:** visual loss not related to any structural abnormality of the eye or visual pathway.
- **Strabismic Amblyopia** – secondary to strabismus (most common subtype)
  - ➤ **Treatment:** patch the "good eye" for all but 1-2 waking hours every day which forces the strabismic eye to improve its visual acuity.
  - ➤ Treatment of amblyopia is more urgent than treatment of the strabismus (surgical realignment of the visual axis).
- **Anisometropic Amblyopia** – related to farsightedness or astigmatism
  - ➤ **Treatment:** corrective lenses needed for anisometropic amblyopia.
- **Deprivation Amblyopia** – caused by a congenital cataract, ptosis, hyphema, nystagmus or retinoblastoma
  - ➤ **Treatment:** surgical correction of the underlying problem (excision of a congenital cataract, drainage of a hyphema or correction of ptosis).

References: American Optometric Association, 1997. Care of the patient with amblyopia. 2nd ed.: 57. Pediatrics, 1996; 98(1): 153-7 and Amer. Fam. Physician, 2001; 64: 623-8.

Index

Index

Page left blank for notes

Page left blank for notes

Page left blank for notes

Page left blank for notes

Page left blank for notes

Page left blank for notes

Page left blank for notes

Page left blank for notes

Page left blank for notes

Page left blank for notes

Page left blank for notes

Page left blank for notes

Page left blank for notes

Page left blank for notes